ART OF MEDIAEVAL ASSAM

ART OF MEDIAEVAL ASSAM

By

RAJATANANDA. DAS GUPTA

DEPT.OF ART, BANARAS HINDU UNIVERSITY

COSMO PUBLICATIONS

2023 New Delhi

COSMO

ART OF MEDIAEVAL ASSAM

Published by COSMO 2023

Published by
COSMO PUBLICATIONS
for
GENESIS PUBLISHING PVT. LTD.
24-B, Ansari Road, Darya Ganj,
New Delhi-110 002,
INDIA

Printed in India

INTRODUCTION

Dr. Rajatnandan Das Gupta has long been interested in the art of Eastern India and hence it is appropriate that the present publication should be on Assam, an area which has been somewhat neglected by scholars but unjustifiably so.

To understand the art of the peoples of any particular province it is essential, I believe, to have an acquaintance with their history and their religious and social background. Dr. Das Gupta is attuned to this viewpoint and accordingly this monograph on Assam is not merely an account of its architecture, sculpture, painting and other arts but also provides the essential coverage of the land and its people. Assam has a long past and was known to the Mahabharata and Ramayana and to the Chinese pilgrim Yuan Chang. Situated as it is, it inevitably formed a link, cultural and social, between India and South East Asia, a factor of considerable importance in understanding its artistic heritage and achievements. Strangely, Buddhism made no effective inroads into this area and the dominant faith was Hinduism tempered at times with the usual beliefs common to many races in spirits, good and bad, powerful demons and a variety of godlings. As with Sufism in northern India, the activities of certain Muslim divines also attracted to them both Hindus and Muslims. The history of Assam is somewhat complicated with the distribution of centres of power amongst the Chatiyas, the Ahoms, the Jaintias, the Bhuyias and others and then the Muslim domination. But the efflorescence of art in any area usually depends on some great religious upheaval and this also took place in Assam with the advent of a fervent movement or god-love inspired by the creed of absolute devotion to Vishnu in his incarnation of Krishna. No account of Assamese art can afford to ignore the spread of this creed by the gospellor saint Sankaradeva.

A second source of inspiration to artistic activities was the Satra, an illustration both monastic and semi-monastic yet not existing in isolation but penetrating deep into the life of the people. Predominantly concerned with the great Vaishnava movement it left its impress on all forms of art and literature in Assam be they folkish or courtly. One is reminded of how the gospel of Buddha produced a revolution in many parts of India outside Assam in the lives of millions resulting in great artistic achievements.

Much of the early architecture of Assam has disappeared but accounts thereof remain. Nevertheless the existing monuments offer not only variety but also indications of how differing styles came into existence due to influences emanating from other regions as in the case of the Jainteswari temple. As with many other regions so also in Assam we find Islamic buildings with local influences which are discernable even in the austere and standardized plans of these houses of worship. New architectural forms also came into being such as the Sildole temple of Sibsagar evolved from the Dvaikuta class of temples Temples abound in Assam and though of later dates present a variety of inventive architectural devices. There are also brick temples and temples with terracotta panel facings as also with panels and reliefs in stone. So also civil architecture such as the Gorhgaon palace has novel features rising as it does from an architecturally oriented base and not just from a high platform. Even different centres of Assam developed their own styles of architecture. Various influences have crept into Assamese architecture as for instance from Bengal and even Cambodia. This does not occasion surprise. The famous Kamakhya temple, despite restorations, affords a study in how the Assamese integrated constructional and stylistic features taken from different sources into their own distinctive creations.

In the realism of sculpture which, apart from metal images, is mostly an integral embellishment of architecture, the origins were in wood and this wooden tradition asserts itself in the medium of stone and terracotta. Local features and folkish elements are repeatedly to be observed alongside more classical forms. Assam also has its own *maniere* of metal images. The ten-armed Durga from Tinsukia, with her superbly fashioned stylized vehicle, the lion, viciously attacking Mahisha, is conceived most quaintly in a folk tradition but nevertheless exudes the concept of her invincibility through a form of composition not to be seen in other regions of Eastern India.

The art of Assam in many other forms such as snake boundary pillars, curiously shaped metal wares, wood carvings, pottery and terracottas reflects a distinctive civilization which becomes more understandable against the detailed background of history, social life, customs and religious beliefs which the present monograph has rightly laid marked emphasis upon. Art exists not in a vacuum but as a reflection of the life and times of those who created it.

One of the most appealing forms of Assamese art is that of painting. How vivid were the painted Assamese book covers in the recent exhibition at the British Museum, London, in connection with the Festival of India in Britain. This charming aspect of Assamese art is fully dealt with.

The author has rendered a signal service to the art of Assam and the background against which it comes into being and flourished.

KARL KHANDALAVALA

PREFACE

The work Art of Mediaeval Assam is the result of my post doctoral researches. It was financed by the University Grants Commission, New Delhi in 1969 under the Financial Assistance to Teachers schemes.

The history of Assam had attracted very little attention of scholars both Indian and foreign. Her art is still less known. Situated between the cultural borders of India and South East Asia Assam has been left out in studies of Indian art history as well as that of South-East Asia. But my ten-year stay in Assam revealed to me the uniqueness of Assam's culture and art. Assam serves as a bridge between the cultures of South East Asia and India. In the mediaeval times under the rule of the independent Ahom dynasty Assam seemed to have drifted away from the mainstreams of Indian cultural and artistic activities. But due to her independence from Islamic rule (which pervaded over most of India) and resulting isolation of many old styles, motifs and designs (which had undergone a process of metamorphosis and assimilation in the rest of the country) were preserved and coutinued in the arts of Assam till the 19th century.

The entry of the Ahoms, a branch of the great Tai race into Assam in the 13th century and their rule there till the British occupation of Assam in the early part of the 19th century was a turning point in the art history of Assam. Isolation was greater during this period. But a regenerated culture flowered in the valley of the Brahmaputra nurtured by the Ahoms and their contemporary rulers of the Koch, Kachari and the Jaintia dynasties. In this crucible of cultures inhabited by members of the Aryan, Dravidian, Austric and Tibeto-Burman races developed a culture which was as much Indian as it had a personality of its own.

In my present work an attempt has been made in the direction of studying the art of mediaeval Assam as a whole keeping in view the different ethnic elements that went into its making. In spite of Assam's isolation artistic ideas and ideals of the Islamic period of India filtered into Assam. This is noticeable in the new motifs and designs, techniques of production and forms in architecture of mediaeval Assam. Again, the affinity of Assam's art with that of South East Asia has also been indicated at relevant places.

The sphere of art in which Assam excelled in the period under review is that of manuscript painting. Excellent examples of manuscript paintings produced during this period was the result of Vaishnava regeneration under Sri Sankaradeva (1449-1568 A.D). The Ahoms also continued a school of manuscript illustration having a close affinity with those developed in Tai regions outside India.

The work is amply illustrated with black and white and colour plates as well as line drawings. I am thankful to the Archaeological Survey of India, Eastern Circle, the Birla Academy of Art and Culture, Calcutta and the Bharat Kala Bhawan, Varanasi, for the supply of photographs used in this book. My thanks are also due to the authorities of the Assam, State Museum, the Department of Historical and Antiquarion Studies, Handicrafts Museum, the Gauhati University library all at Gauhati for a large extent of help and supply of relevant photographs.

The late Prof. S.K. Saraswaty not only provided me with constant guidance and encouragement but also graciously permitted me to photograph objects from his personal collection. Prof. Nihar Ranjan Ray was another guiding force behind this work and his constant suggestions and constructive criticism were heaped upon me till his last days. Prof. A.L. Basham had also taken an equally keen interest in my work.

I shall fail in my duties if I don't express my gratitude to the University Grants Commission but for whose financial assistance the book would not have seen the light of the day. I also express my thanks to my friends and students in India and abroad who have assisted me in many capacities in the process of producing "The Art of Mediaeval Assam." I am deeply indebted to Mr. Karl J. Khandalavala for writing the foreword of this humble book.

VARANASI.

18.3.1982

Rajatananda Das Gupta
Department of History of Art
Banaras Hindu University
VARANASI-5

LIST OF CONTENTS

LIST OF ILLUSTRATIONS

1

THE LAND AND THE PEOPLE

Extent and limits of Assam

Assam in the Ahom age was different from Assam as it is today. For the purpose of this thesis Assam would cover the entire Brahmaputra Valley including Goalpara, the submountain regions known as the Jaintia Pargana, the Kachari areas in the Dhansiri, the Mahur and Barak Valleys, the Saidya area, now transferred to N.E.F.A. (Arunachal) and the Dimapur area, now given to Nagaland. The cultural sphere of mediaeval Assam extended over all these areas, as also the Koch Bihar kingdom upto the time of Laksminarayana, who had become a vassal of the Mughals and had his kingdom tagged to the Bengal Subah. Also the Hajo and adjoining areas of Kamarupa or Western Assam though ruled by a Mughal Thanedar or Governor for a while remained one of the chief centres of mediaeval Assamese art and culture.

Modern Assam has been known in the various periods of Indian history by different names. The Ramayana and the Mahabharata call it Pragjyotisa.[1] In later times it is known by the name of Kamarupa, which Muslim historians call Kamru Kamrud[2] and Karu-Kamachhya.[3] In further India Brahmaputra Valley was also known as Weisali. People of the Upper Irrawaddy Valley knew Assam as Atsera[4] and these two adjacent regions had political and cultural contacts in the mediaeval times.

The Kalika Purana mentions that the temple of Kamakhya was at the centre of Kamarupa, whose extents were as follows :

"Karatyanadipurvam yavaddikkaravasinim
Trimsadyojanavistirnam yojanaikasatayatam
Trikonam krsnavarnamcha prabhutajalapuritam
Nadisata samayuktam kamarupamprakirtitam."

(51 : 65-66)

1. Vidyalamkara, J., Bharat Bhumi Aur Uske Nivasi p. 29.
2. Raverty, H.G. Tabaquat-i-Nasiri, of Mihaj-ud-din (Trans) London 1881.
3. Gait, E.A., A History of Assam, p. 16.
4. Ibid.

The above geographical description is corroborated by the Yoginitantra, which according to Gait is a later work. It appears to have been either composed, or revised, after the 13th century, since it mentions the entry of the Ahoms into Assam and also the early Koch kings of Kamarupa. It says :

> "Karatoyam samasritya yavaddikkaravasini
> Uttarasyam kunjagiri karatoyattupaschime
> Tirthasrestha Diksunadi purvasyam girikanyake
> Daksine Brahmaputrasya Laksyam sangamavadhi
> Kamarupam iti khyatah sarvasastresu nischitah."

It further says :

> "Trimsadyojana vistirnam dirghena satayojanam
> Kamarupam vijanihi trikonakaramuttamam."
>
> (*11* : *17-21*)

"According to the same work the country was divided into four portions, viz., Kampith, from the Karatoya to the Sankosh, Ratnapith from the Sankosh to the Rupahi, Suvarnapith, from the Rupahi to the Bharali and the Saumarapith, from the Bharali to the Dikrang. Elsewhere, Ratnapith is said to include the tract between Monas and Silghat on the north bank of the Brahmaputra, and Bhadrapith, the corresponding portion of the south bank, while Saumarapith, as before, the most east·rly tract."[1]

Assam always had close social and cultural contacts with the countries of south-east Asia. Many a tribe of Assam has a counterpart in some or the other south-east Asian country. Also, similarity exists between the rural cultures of the Assamese Hindus and the rural peoples of the countries extending from Burma in the west to Indonesia and the Philippines in the east. This is corroborated by the references in the Mahasiddhasara Tantra according to which the Asvakranta group of Tantras are followed in worship by the peoples living between the Karatoya river and Java.[2]

Ratnapith was the region of the Koches. The Ahoms first settled in the Saumarpith. The Ahoms called this land 'Mung-dun-chun-kham' or 'the land of golden gardens.' Two other names 'Munglung and Mungdun' were also used by the Ahoms for Assam.[3] According to Taranatha, the 17th century Tibetan historian, the north-eastern provinces of India, Kamarupa, Tripura and Hasama, were collectively known as Girivarta since they were mountainous.[4]

1. Gait, E.A., A History of Assam, p. 11.
2. Chatterji, B.R. India and Java : Greater India Society Bulletin, No. 5, Pt. I, Calcutta 1933, p. 28.
3. Barua, G.C. Ahom Buranji, p. 4.
4. Dacca University History of Bengal, Vol. I, Dacca 1948, p. 183.

"After the recovery of Western Assam from the Moguls in July 1682, during the reign of Gadadhar Singha, the boundaries of Assam remained unaltered and fixed till the occupation of the country by the British. The Assam of those days was practically the same as the Brahmaputra Valley or Assam Proper of the present day—the district of Goalpara.[1] It was bounded on the north by the Bhutan hills, on the west by the Manaha river and the Habraghat Pargana, on the south by the Naga, Khasi, Mikir and Garo hills and on the east by the Mishmi, Singphou and Khamti ranges."[2]

Dr. John Peter Wade who came to India in 1792 recorded in his 'Geographical Sketch of Assam' an account of Assam between 1796 to 1802 A.D. This is preserved in the India Office Library, London. He writes :

"The kingdom of Assam is seven hundred miles in length and from sixty to eighty in breadth. In a few places, however, of Upper Assam where the mountainous confines recede furthest, the breadth greatly exceeds this proportion ; and it will be within a very moderate calculation to consider the surface as containing about sixty thousand square miles. . . From this computation may be deducted the numerous rivers, which everywhere intersect the country. I shall not offer a vague conjecture on the sum of this deduction ; but it will not be exaggeration to say that the remainder exhibits a highly fertile soil throughout ; for even the great number of hills which are interspersed in every part of Assam are susceptible of cultivation, and increase considerably the superfices of the country fit for culture. From this computation of square miles are excluded all the dependencies and conquered countries in or beyond the mountainous limits which surround Assam in every direction ; as well as several provinces of Eastern Bengal which formerly acknowledged their subjugation to the Assamese Government.'[3]

"Assam is a valley. It extends between the parallels of 25-45 and 27-30 degrees of North Latitude and from 90-95 to between 98 or 99 degrees of East Longitude. This extent to the eastward beyond the capital Garhgaon is of course conjectural; for it was not my fortune to meet with a single native who has travelled to the utmost limit of Assam in that quarter. The kingdom is separated by the great stream of the Brahmaputra into three grand divisions called Uttarkol or Uttarpar, Dakhinkol or Dakinpar and the Majuli or great island. The first denotes the provinces lying on the north side of Brahmaputra, the second those on the south. The Majuli is a large island in the middle. It is also divided into Upper and Lower Assam ; the first includes the country above Kaliabar, where the river

1. Goalpara however remained culturally bound to Assam, though some inevitable changes crept in due to closer political contacts with Bengal Sabah.

Bhuyan, S.K. Tunkhungia Buranji, Introduction, pp. xxvi-xxvii.

Ibid.

diverges into two considerable streams as far as the mountainous confines to the north and south. This division included the whole of Assam at an earlier period ; but the lower provinces to the westward having been afterwards annexed by conquest to the dominion of Swargadeo, became a separate Government under an officer entitled Burra-Phukan with the powers of a Viceroy. The destination of Uttarkol and Dakhinkol were previous to the period in question, applicable only to Upper Assam ; and the more learned among the natives affect to confine those appelations even now to the eastern provinces only."[1]

Routes from Assam to other countries

During the Ahom rule Assam maintained trade, diplomatic and cultural relations with India on one side and with Bhutan, Tibet, Upper Burma, Shan States, Manipur, Tripura and the adjoining countries on the other. In the earlier ages, during the days of King Bhaskara Varman, there was a route to China. The king makes a reference about this to his guest, the great Chinese traveller Yuan Chwang, who had visited Kamarupa, and who recorded this in his writings.

(*a*) *The route to Hindustan.* In ancient times this was also known as the route to Magadha, the heart of Hindustan. The main route from Kamarupa to Bengal, Bihar and Orissa was by the rivers Brahmaputra and the Ganges. In the middle of seventh century, when Bhaskar Varman invited Hiuen Tsiang to Assam, the pilgrim started from Magadha, passed by Champa (modern Bhagalpur), Kajangala (Rajmahal) and Pundravardhana (Rangpur) and so going eastward reached Kamarupa.[2] This must have been the usual route from Magadha. Bhaskar Varman also followed the same route to meet Harsha at Rajmahal.[3] Nalanda also could be reached by the same route in just two days.[4] A messenger from Kongyadha (Ganjam) also reached Kamarupa quite quickly evidently following the same route.[5]

In the mediaeval period practically the same route was followed. Later it developed into two separate routes. "The first one followed the Brahmaputra along its north bank and the eastern extremity of Assam could be reached. Secondly, from Eastern Bengal it was possible to enter by skirting the Garo hills along the south bank of the Brahmaputra. The third route followed upstream the Kapili and the Dhansiri rivers east of the Khasi-Jaintia hills. This route also led into the south bank of the Brahmaputra."[6]

1. Bhuyan S.K., Tungkhungia Buranji, 2nd Ed. 1968, Gauhati, pp. xxvii-xxviii.
2. Beal, S. : (Si-Yu-Ki) Buddhist Records of the Western World, 1-2, London, 1905. Vol. II, p. 195.
3. Beal, S. (tr) : Life of Hiuen Tsiang, London, 1888, 1914, p. 86.
4. Ibid., p. 169.
5. Ibid., p. 169.
6. Vidyalamkara, J. Bharat Bhumi Aur Uske Nivasi, p. 164.

"The two rlver valleys of Assam, those of the Brahmaputra and the Surma are separated by a semi-circle of hill ranges forming the present hill districts of Assam. There is a drop between the Naga and the Jaintia hills through which flow the Kapili and Dhansiri from north to south thus joining the valley of the Lauhitya and the Surma."[1] Beyond Bengal the trade route extended up to farther western part of Aryavarta. "It followed the following route starting from Peshawar and ending in Assam : Peshawar—Saharanpur—Wazirabad—Lahore—Jullundur—Raiwind—Ferozepur—Bhatinda—Delhi—Lucknow—Katihar (Tirhut)—Parbatipur (Eastern Bengal)—Assam. A second route starting from Allahabad, passed through Banaras and Bhagalpur to Calcutta. Three roads thus led towards the Himalayas, connecting eastern India and Nepal. The westernmost one starts from Hajipur (Bihar) towards Raxaul in the Terai, the second from Katihar (Bihar) towards Jogbani and the easternmost one from Gitaldah (Koch Bihar) to Jayanti in the north."[2]

(*b*) *Routes to Bhutan and Beyond.* Bhutan had the closest trade, as also religious and artistic ties with Assam. It also served as a meeting place for Assamese, Tibetan and Chinese traders and craftsmen. Often ambassies were exchanged between the two lands. The last envoys from Bhutan to the Ahom court came in 1801 A.D.[3] Numerous passes and ways, known as Duars, still connect Assam and Tibet through Bhutan. These Duars were wider than mere passes and were governed by the Bhutanese officials whose subjects were Assamese and Kacharis. The important ones mentioned by Pemberton[4] are as follows :

Along Darang—
(a) Booree Gooma dooar
(b) Kulling
Along Kamrup—
(a) Gurkholah dooar
(b) Baksha or Banska dooar
(c) Chappa gooree dooar
(d) Chapakhamar dooar
(e) Bijnee dooar

At the longest, these Duars were about 220 miles from the foothills.[5] The route to Tibet runs through the Himalayan mountains parallel to the course of

1. Vidyalamkara, J. Bharat Bhumi Aur Uske Nivasi, pp. 211-13.
2. Ibid.
3. Bhuyan, S.K., Jaintia Buranji, 2nd ed. 1964, Gauhati, p. 151.
4. Pembertan, R.B., Report on Bhutan : Reprint, Indian Studies Past and Present, 1961, Calcutta. p. 15.
5. Ibid., p. 12.

the Brahmaputra. The Tabaquat-i-Nasiri says that between Kamarupa and Tibet there are thirty-five mountain passes through which horses are brought to Lakhnauti. [Lieutenant Rutherford stated that the Khanpha Bhoateas or Lhasa merchants, just before the Burmese invasion had unreserved commercial intercourse with Assam.] The commercial transaction between the two countries was carried on in the following manner. At a place called Chouna, two months' journey from Lhasa, on the boundary between the two States, a mart was established. On the Assam side, there was a similar mart at Gegunshur, four miles from Chouna. An annual Caravan, consisting of about twenty persons, would carry one lakh rupees worth of silver bullion from Lhasa to Chouna, as also considerable quantity of rock salt for sale to the Assam merchants. The latter brought rice, which was imported into Tibet from Assam in large quantities, as also Assam silk, iron, lac, animal skins, buffalo horns, pearls etc."[1] Even now, during three winter months, large numbers of Bhutia merchants come with their merchandise down to the plains of Assam in Kamrup and Darrang, where they barter or transact with Assamese traders. During their temporary stay in Assam the Bhutanese also visit the temple of Hayagriva—Madhava at Hajo in Kamrup. They claim it originally had a Buddhist shrine, and the position of Hayagriva as a god of Mahayanaism is well known. "Through Bhutan, along the mountains, was also a trade route to Kabul. Tavernier mentions that in his time merchants travelled through Bhutan to Kabul to avoid paying the duty that was levied on merchandise passing through Gorakhpur. From Kabul the Caravans parted for Tartary and Balk."[2] Thus products of Assam passed into Central and Western Asia and thereon to the Mediterranean sea.

(*c*) *Routes to Burma and China.* These routes were of far greater importance since they connected Assam with two highly cultured nations of the east. In the field of art, there was a lot of exchange between these nations. As early as the days of Bhaskar Varman and Yuan Chwang, we come across references about an eastern route from Assam to China via Upper Burma. "To the east of Kamarupa, the country is a series of hills and hillocks, without any principal city, and one can reach the south-west (of China); hence the inhabitants were akin to the Man and the Lao."[3] The pilgrim was also told that the total time needed for this journey was about two months and that the road to Sse-Chaun was hazardous and unhygeinic.

Even as far back as the 2nd century B.C. this route was used, as has been

1. Gait, E.A., A History of Assam,
2. Whiteby, J.L., The Periplus of the Erythrean Sea, Thesis for Ph.D. at London University, 1940, pp. 572 ff.
3. Beal, S., : (Si-Yu-Ki) Buddhist Records of the Western World, 1-2, London, 1905, pp. 198-199.

recorded by Chang Kien, the Chinese ambassador to the Yue-Chi country. The products of China reached Bactria by way of Sse-Chuan and Yunnan and Afghanistan[1]. On the way these passed through India, the first section of the route, from Yunnan and Sse-Chuan, being the Brahmaputra Valley.

The Assam-Burma route from China has been detailed in the 8th century A.D. Chinese work, Kia-tan.[2] "Starting from Tonkin, the southernmost of the commercial centres of China, the route passed by Yunnansen, Yunnan-fou and Ta-li-fou. Going westward, it crossed the Salouen at Young-Chang (Young Changfou), on the west of the river. Further westward it reached the town of Chou-Ko-Leang (to the east of Momeen); between Shiveli and Salouen. The route bifurcated there, the principal one descending by the valley of the Shiveli to join the Irrawady on the South-West, while the other carried on directly to the West. Starting from Chou-Ko-bang, the principal route crossed the frontier of Piao (Burma) near Lo, the frontier town of Nan-Chao, and passing through the country of mountain tribes, it reached Si-li midway between Tagaung and Mandalay. The route then passed by Toumin (Pagan) and reached the capital of Burma Sriksetra (Prome). Leaving Prome it crossed a range of black mountains to the west (the modern Aracan range) and so reached Kamarupa. The second route, starting from Chou-Ko-leang, went right westwards to Teng Chong (Momein); then crossing the Mi mountains, it reached hi-Shousi, on the Irrawady (Bhamo or near about to the north); from thereon, the river Longtsiuan (Magaung), it passed the town of Nagansi, and going westwards crossed the river Min-no (Chindwin) and the mountains between it and reached Kamrupa".[3]

In the sixteenth century, Buddhagupta, an Indian Buddhist monk, mentioned in his biography the route from Gauhati to Pagan in Burma, which he had himself used.[4]

The Ahom conquerors of Assam had used the Patkai pass which gave access to Upper Assam. From Sadiya five passes served as outlets from Upper Assam. These were the Dipong pass, the Mishmi route, the Phungan pass (to China), the route via Manipur to the Irrawady Valley and the Patkai pass.[5] The Patkai pass was also used by the Burmese invaders to Assam in 1816 A.D.

The Patkai pass and the adjoining ranges were originally known as Doikau-

1. Pelliot, Bulletin du lEcole Francaise d'Extreme Orient, '04, pp. 142 ff.
2. Bagchi, P.C., India and China, p. 18 ff.
3. Ibid.
4. Tucci, G., 'The Sea and Land Travels of a Buddhist Sadhu in the sixteenth century', Indian Historical Quaterly Vol. VII, pp. 683-701.
5. Mc. Cosh, J., 'On the various lines of Overland communication between India and China', Proceedings of the Royal Geographical Society, London, Vol. V, pp. 47-54.

rang or Nine United Hills, since at this place nine hills converged. This name was given by Sukapha, the first Ahom ruler of Assam, who entered Assam through the above pass, which runs from Nora or Pong, in 1228 A.D. Later, in 1339-40 A.D., the then Ahom king Chudangpha, and the Nora ruler Surunpha, made a treaty at Nongyang Pani, which specified the Patkai[1] pass as the boundary between their two kingdoms. Then Doikaurang was renamed Patkai, or the 'place where an oath was taken by killing a fowl'. [Pat=cut ; Kai=fowl ; Seng=oath ; Kan=taken] Two figures, of the Ahom and the Nora rulers, were carved on the rock face of the pass.

Races and communities

(*a*) *Hindus.* In the mediaeval period caste Hindus did not play any direct role in politics. They formed the bulk of the intelligentsia, whose descendants are now known as the Assamese or Assamiya in general. But they were the brain in the body politic of Assam and were invariably placed as high officials of State, especially as ambassadors or Katakis, due to their knowledge of Sanskrit. During the last phase of Ahom rule, they also were well versed in Indian languages like Nagari or Hindi, Persian, Bengali and also English. The Hindus also served as the Bej or physicians, priests, teachers. Thus they were engaged in intellectual pursuits.

The Hindu society was divided into castes. The Brahmins were at the top. Next were the Kayasthas. The Kalitas, a caste peculiar to Assam, ranked only next to the Kayasthas. They are said to have descended from ancient Aryan settlers who had adopted Buddhism. Hence they were known as the Kula-hepta (who have lost their caste) and thence to Kalita. Kalitas are known for their predominantly Aryan features and fair skin. The Kalitas are pure agriculturists and hence rank high in village socio-economic set up. Those that are engaged only in agriculture are regarded as Bar Kalitas (higher Kalitas). Those who engage in some craft are, on the other hand, known as Haru Kalitas (lower Kalitas). In Assam the agriculturist ranks higher than an artisan. Kalitas are now more or less Hinduised, though still act as priests for the Doms or sometimes the fisher-folk. At one time they sometimes intermarried. This unorthodox behaviour also hints at the Buddhist origin of the Kalitas.

The Brahmins were divided into groups. There were two inferior sections, the Habungiya and the Bariya. The Habungiyas derive their name from where they live. They are said to be the descendents of the men who were dressed as Brahmins and put in front of the Ahom phalanx by an Ahom king, so that the adversary will hesitate to kill the royal troops in fear of killing Brahmins in the

1. Peal, S.E., 'Note on the Old Burmese route over the Patkai via Non-gyang, J.A.S.B., 1879. Vol. II, p. 75.

process. Since then these impersonators have claimed Brahminhood and formed a community by themselves. The term Baria is derived from Bari or the widow. According to one tradition, the Baria are descendents of either Brahmin widows who remarried or lived a clandestine marital life with men of other castes. As a result, they and their illegitimate children were excommunicated by the orthodox Brahmins. Gait however quotes another tradition according to which the Barias are descendents of mixed Brahmin and non-Brahmin parentage.[1]

Other important castes were the Kaivartas, Kumhars (potters), Tati (weavers), Kamar (blacksmiths), Sonar (goldsmiths), Kabar (bell-metal workers), Mali or Phumali (gardeners or flower sellers), Natis (temple dancers), Dhoba or Dhobi (washerman), Haris and Chandalas.[2]

(*b*) *Muslims*. Muslims, through small in number, were an important community. They excelled in the field of arts and crafts. The Assamese Muslims were quite Hinduised, as has been noted by Mughal chroniclers of Mir Jumla. They were generally referred to as the Garias and the Marias, though the former term eventually became derogatory. The Garias claim Gaur or Bengal as the country of their origin and hence the name.[3] The Marias are expert workers in brass and turn out artistic metal ware and utensils. Maria is derived from the root Mara or to beat[4] i.e., they make their wares by beating brass sheets into shape. They are descendents of Muslim prisoners-of-war taken during the rule of Suhungmurg, the Ahom king. Their general, Hussain Khan, was killed in March 1533. His followers were taken prisoner and settled in various parts of the country. Initially the prisoners were given land for cultivation but when they failed they took to metal working.[5] As already described the Muslim artisans were also organized into professional or local khels and rendered service to the State, as Khanikars and Paiks.

(*c*) *Women*. Women enjoyed more freedom of movement in mediaeval Assam than in any other part of India. This was because Assam was never under Islamic rule. Consequently Muslims there were more native rather than Muslim in their practices. The Ahom women also enjoyed the privilege of both divorce and remarriage on being widowed. The Hindu women, however, were guided by their caste as also regional customs and practices.

Assamese women have been praised for their charm, beauty and intelligence

1. Gait, F.A., A History of Assam, p. 258.
2. Ibid.,
3. Ibid., p. 96.
4. Ibid., p. 97.
5. Ibid., p. 96.

by Mughal and European travellers.[1] "Women were refined and enlightened and active and versatile in their accomplishments. Women acted as dancers in temples. They were attached to the households of nobles and princes and were known as Ligiris."[2]

Some ladies of the Ahom nobility, like Mula-Gabharu,[3] actually fought the Muslim invaders. During the Moamaria rebellion Radha[4] Rukmini was one of the rebel leaders and fell fighting the royal forces. The name of Princess Jayamati[5] is still regarded with devotion, since she was declared a 'santi' or saint after she suffered death at the hands of the executioners of Lora Raja, who tried to find out from the princess the whereabouts of her husband prince Gadapani, one of the aspirants for the throne. During his unlucky period 1714-44, king Siva Singha handed over charge of the Government to his consort Phuleswari or Pramatheswari Devi. After her death the king married her sister Ambika Devi and once again handed over the office of the ruler to her. After the death of the second wife, the office was held by the king's third wife, Sarvesvari Devi, till 1744 A.D.[6]

Although the women did not form khels, nor were regarded as Paiks in their individual capacities, yet they offered their products to the state in the shape of a specified quantity of silk thread and yarn.[7] Women also took an active part in agricultural activities.[8]

(*d*) *The Ahoms.* The Ahoms were not an indigenous community of Assam. They entered Assam in 1238 A.D., after having been driven from their homelands in China and South-East Asia due to political events.

"The Ahoms are Shans belonging to the great Tai family of the human race. This family extends from the Gulf of Siam northwards into Yun-nan and thence westward to Assam. It comprises several divisions, viz., Siamese, Laos, Shans, Tau Mau or Taikhe (Chinese Shans), Khamti and Ahom."[9]

The conquest of Yun-nan by Kublai Khan took place in the year 1253 A.D. but it is possible that the Chinese inroads into Yun-nan began some years previous to the final conquest of the country, and the general disturbances caused some of the Shans to migrate to other countries, as was the case with the Ahoms branch.

1. McCosh, J., Topography of Assam, pp. 22-23.
2. Gait, E.A., A History of Assam, p. 259.
3. Ibid., p. 259.
4. Bhuyan, S.K., (ed.). Asamar Payda Buranji, Gauhati, [illegible], p. 101.
5. Ibid., p. 16.
6. Ibid., pp. 65-69.
7. Gait, E.A., Ibid. p. 271.
8. Ibid., p. 271.
9. Cushing, Shan Grammar, Rangoon, 1871.

Probably, however, the Ahoms required but little encouragement to shift their quarters, for the Shans are restless by nature and are constantly moving from place to place even in times of peace."[1]

"The Ahom legend that the two brothers Khulung and Khunlai, from whom they claim descent, came down from heaven and established themselves at a place called Mung-Ri-Mung-Rang, seems to be identical with the Shan legend mentioned by Dr. Cushing, except that the habitat of the Shans is said to have been Shweli Valley. Mung-Ri-Mung-Rang is thought by Sir George Seolt to have some connection with Mong-Hi-Mong-Ham, a place in the Hsephsawng Panna on the bank of the river Mekong in the Chinese Shan States. Wherever may have been the exact abode of the Ahoms before they entered Assam, it is very probable that they formed one of the tribes included in the Shan kingdom of Mung-Mau, which at that time was probably identical with what was known to the Manipuris as Pong."[2]

The present day name Assam is thought to have been derived from the tribal name Ahom. Prior to that the land was variously known as Pragjyotisha and Kamarupa. In the Buranji's, the local chronicles of the Ahoms, Assam is designated as Asam or Asham.[3] The Mughal chronicles too used the name Asham.[4] "The Ahoms used to call themselves not 'Ahom', but like the Northern Shans', Tai."[5]

Regarding the etimology of the word 'Ahom', Grierson maintains that 'the word is a corruption of Asham. Shan is the Burmese corruption of Sham, which is the true spelling and pronunciation of the name of the well known tribe. Again, according to P.R. Gurdon, the initial A in the name is intriguing. "The Muhammadan historians called the Ahoms, 'Asam'. If this suggestion is correct, 'Ahom' must be comparatively speaking, a modern corruption. In Assamese, 'Sh' become a gutteral h. It is a very probable that this tribe gave the modern name to our Province of Assam, the old name for the country being Saumarpiths".

(*e*) *Divisions in Society*. "The Ahoms are divided into a number of exogamous groups called phoids or Khels, the principal ones being seven in number, the term Satgharia ('belonging to seven houses') which is now-a-days applied to them.

The composition of these seven principal divisions has varied from time to time, but they are said to have originally consisted of the following : The Royal

1. Hastings, J. Encyclopaedia of Religion and Ethics, Vol. 1, Edinburgh and New York, 1908. p. 234.
2. Ibid.,
3. Bhuyan, S.K. (ed.) Asamar Padya Buranji, pp. 78-79.
4. Sahabuddin Talish, Tarikh-i-Asham, Tr. by Pavie T.
5. Hastings, J., Ibid., p. 234.

Family, The Buragohain, The Bargohein, The Chiring, The Deodhai, The Mohan, The Bailungphoids.

The whole of the superior exogamous groups are further divided into two main divisions, called Gohains and Gogois. But there are also some decidedly inferior phoids, such as the Chaodangs, who were the public executioners in the old days, as well as Lickchans Ghaifalias and others, with whom Ahoms of the upper classes will not inter-marry."[1]

The rest of the people, who included plains-tribals and caste Hindus, were initially debarred from high government offices, which were reserved for true born Ahoms. The subjects were also divided into convenient groups for professional and economic convenience. "The adult population of Assam was divided into Khels having to render specific services to the State, such as arrow making, boat building, boat plying, house building, provision supplying, fighting, writing, revenue collecting, road building, catching and training of elephants, superintendence of horses, training of hawks and superintendence of forests. Sometimes Khels were organised on a territorial basis, e.g., the Dimaruguria—Khel consisting of the men of Dimaruguri. Each Khel was like a guild, to which lands were allotted for cultivation by the constituent members, free of rent in return of the services they rendered to the State. The strength of a Khel ranged from 300 to 100. Each Khel was put under a 'Phukan', if it was an important one, a 'Rajkhowa' or a Barua if it was of less importance. The Khanikar Khel was placed under a 'Barua'. A Phukan commanded 6,000 men, and a Rajkhowa or Barua was in charge of 3,000 men. A 'Barua' was generally a departmental or administrative head. An adult male whose name was registered for State services was called a 'Paik' and four 'Paiks' constituted a unit called 'Got'. One man in a 'Got' had to serve the State for three months in a year, at the end of which his place was taken by a second man from the 'Got' and so forth. The remaining three 'Paiks' looked after the cultivation and other domestic concerns of their absent comrade. In cases of emergency two men and sometimes even three men were recruited for State services from each Got, or the Got maximum was reduced from four to three Paiks. The levy of the man from each Got was called 'Mul', of the two 'Dowal' and of the three 'Tewal'. The Ahom Khel system was organised by Momai Tamuli Barbarua in 1609 under the direction of the reigning monarch Swargadeo Pratap Sinha. The Muslims, and in fact all non-Ahoms, did not suffer any disability on account of their religious faiths. Up to the year 1772, the Gohains and the Phukans were all appointed from among the Ahoms ; the highest office to which a non-Ahom could look forward was a Baruaship. A large number of Muslims were appointed in several departments of the State, minting of coins, painting, carpentery etc."[2]

1. Hastings, E. of R & E, Vol. I, p. 235.
2. Bhuyan, S.K., Anglo-Assamese Relations, pp. 10-11.

Both the Paik and the Khel have their counterparts in Thai society known as the Prai and the Lake respectively.[1] Prai was a word which had "probably the same origin as Paik, by which, according to Sir G. Grierson, "the Ahoms of Assam, a branch of Lao-Tai, designated the individuals forming the rank and file of their corvee system, which very closely resembled that of Siam."[2] Lake and Lake Sui were divisions of the people into departments of public service and its members were exempted from personal services to the king in exchange for cash or kind.[3]

In Assam, the most important Khel from the point of view of artistic activities was the Khanikar Khel or guild of artists and artisans. "A Khanikar could be a sculptor, an engraver, a carpenter, a maker of earthen images, a painter, a class of 'Paiks' (labourers under the Ahom kings) whose principal duty was to paint, make images etc.[4] Actually, the Khanikars were a professional rather than a caste group. Muslim artisans and craftsmen were incorporated in the Khanikar-Khel under a Superintendent known as the 'Khanikar Barua'. Muslim ladies have still retained their skill in artistic weaving."[5] One of the greatest Assamese painters of the early 18th century was Muslim Khanikar named Dilbar.[6]

Khanikars of a particular Khel usually lived in the same neighbourhood or formed a village if the number of members was large enough. One of the settlements where the members of the Khanikar-khel lived is even today known as the Khanikar gaon.[7] This village lies to the north of the royal palace of Garhgaon near Sibsagar town.

Among the Hindu members of the guild most belonged to the Kayastha caste and were known for their aptitude in Kayathali Vidya or Kayasthika Vidya, which included knowledge in calligraphy, painting, wood-carving and other fine arts."[8]

Dalbagan, near Garhgaon, was a colony of Muslim Khanikars.[9] Muslim Khanikars received State patronage to the last days of the Ahom rule, as we find from the 'Report on the Province of Assam' by Mill in 1884. One family of Muslim Khanikars was supported by the State even as late as the days of Purnananda Buragohain.[10] As regards the institutions for training in Khanikarship, there were

1. G. Grierson, Siam, Vol. I, p. 235.
2. Ibid., pp. 235-36.
3. Ibid. p. 235.
4. Bhattacharya, B.N. Pronouncing Anglo-Assamese Dictionary.
5. Bhuyan, S.K., Annals of the Delhi Badsahate, Gauhati, 1947. p. 18.
6. Ibid, p. 20.
7. Gogoi, L, Buranjiye Parasha, Nagar,
8. Datta-Barua, H.N., Prachina Kamrupiya Kayastha Samajar Itivritto. Introduction Vi,.
9. Allamah Shah Sayed Mukibul Haque, "The advent of Muslims to Assam", Assam Tribun Magazine, Section 27.3.60.
10. Ibid.

no fixed centres, as in the case of the arts like music and dancing. Eminent teachers taught pupils who gathered round them, usually in their own homes. It was the typical oriental system of education, with the teacher more important than the institution.[1] The trained Khanikars usually settled in their own villages.

"The village Khanikar enjoyed an important position in the cultural life of the people. Without him no 'Bhaona' or theatricals could be imagined. For, he not only painted the scenes and sets but also dressed the actors and designed their costumes and accessories. Masks or "Mukha's were also made by him for super-human roles, for Hanuman, and semi-human beings. He had derived his inspiration and perfected his skill in the arts from an accumulated fund of hereditary knowledge."[2]

(*f*) *Religion.* "Possibly Buddhism had not penetrated so far as the Upper Mekong Valley before the Ahoms left Mung-Ri-Mung-Rang, their ancient site; or Buddhism had become so inextricably mixed with the worship of the gods of earth and sky as to become indiscernible. Apart from the god Chumseng or Chum Deo, whose worship was conducted by the Ahom king, assisted by the Chiring Phukan, the Ahom possessed various gods, amongst whom the following seem to have been more important : Phu-Ra-T-Ra (God the Creator), Lengdon (god of Heaven, the Hindu Indra), Kaokham (god of water, the old Vedic deity Varuna), Lengbin and Lengdin (god and goddess of earth), and Phai (god of fire, the Hindu Agni). Chumseng, who was daily worshipped at the king's house, was not regarded as a god himself. According to Ahom tradition, Chumseng was given to the Ahom progenitors Khunlung and Khuntai by Lengdon, the god of heaven. Chumseng was thus worshipped as a fetish—something supernatural, possessing a power to do good to the king and his people. Chumseng was perhaps an ammonite, something of the nature of the Hindu Salgram or even a precious stone (which the etomology of the name, i.e., Chum='Precious' and Seng='Stone', would certainly suggest). The stone or image, whatever it was, could not have been large, as at the coronation ceremony it was hung around the king's neck."[3] It is believed to be 'a jewel set in a cylinder.'[4] * The worship was conducted in complete secrecy, none but the king being allowed to view Chumseng. The king could see Chumseng only twice a year. The mysticism attached to the Chumseng worship accounts for the doubt as to

1. Bhuyan, S.K., Ahomar Din, p. 61.
2. Barua, B.K., Ankiya Nat, Introduction, pp. xxv-xxvi.
3. Hastings, J., E. of R. & E., p. 236.
4. Bhuyan, S.K., Tungkhungiya Buranji, second impression, 1968, Gauhati, p. 231.

*According to S.K. Bhuyan, Purandar Singha, the last king of Assam, is said to have sold the Chumseng or Chumcheng in Calcutta during his flight to that city.

what Chumseng actually is. "Old people say that Chumseng lies concealed somewhere in Assam at the present day."[1]

"The Ahoms performed ceremonies called Saifa and Umpha for the good of the crops and the State, the latter being on a grander scale than the former and conducted by the king himself. A ceremony called Sarkai, the object of which was scaring away evil spirits from the country, was also performed ; the peculiarity of this ceremony was that a man who had lost several wives by death was offered up as a sacrifice."[2]

The Rikkhvan ceremony was semi-religious and magical. It was an expiation ceremony (lit. rik='call', and Khwan='life') performed at the coronation of a king, in times of danger or after victory. "The king sat in full dress on a platform, and the priests and astrologers poured holy water over his head, whence it ran down his body, and then through a hole in the platform on to the chief bailong or astrologer, who was standing below. The king then changed his clothes, giving those which he had been wearing and all his ornaments to the chief bailong."[3]

Buddhism weilded very little influence on the Ahoms, though Hinduism gradually absorbed and turned them more or less into an Assamese caste. "The religious temper of the period was one of non-interference and tolerance. Not only did the monarchs as a rule tolerate religious sects other than their own but they patronised all persuations in equal measure. The Ahom kings did not altogether abandon their ancestral religion and practices though they adopted Hinduism and the Hindu way of life. Their coronation ceremony was solemnised mostly according to Hindu rites and the Ahom ceremony of Rikkhvan was performed at the end of a victorious triumph or to bring prosperity to the country. Every Hindu king, on ascending the throne, assumed two names, one in Hindu form and the other in Ahom—the Ahom gods and legends also came to be identified with Brahmanical counterparts so that both the Ahoms and the Hindu population were made to feel that after all the pantheon of the two peoples was essentially the same, the only difference being that of language and of emphasis."[4] The Ahoms, it would appear, were also sympathetic towards this kind of synthesis. This made their Hinduisation easier and welcome.[5]

"Hinduism became the predominant religion, pre-eminently since the reign of Sib Singh. Nevertheless, the Ahom priests, the Deodhais and Bailongs, resisted

1. Hastings, J., E. of R. & C., p. 236.
2. Ibid.,
3. Ibid.,
4. Gait, E.A., A History of Assam, Calcutta, 1963, p. 256.
5. Chatterji, S.K., Kirata Jana Kriti, Calcutta, p. 57.

the change and succeeded in continuing the observance of certain ceremonies, such as the worship of the tutilary God, Somdeo."[1] Important Siva temples were built, and older ones renovated, at Sibsagar, Bisnath Dergaon, Neghriting, Parihareswar (Dubi in Kamrup) and Umananda and Sukleswar at Gauhati. Siva, as the consort of Sakti (Durga), the most revered of all Hindu deities, enjoyed a special place in Assam.

Saktism was the most widely accepted sect in Assam. It was patronised in the middle ages by the Koch, Chutiya, Kachari, Jaintiya and the Ahom rulers under different names like Kamakhya, Tamreswari (Kesai-Khati), Rana-Chandi, Jayanteswari and Durga respectively. "The advent of the Tungkhungiya dynasty, with Gadadhar Singh as the first ruler, marked the rescuing of the Sakti influence."[2] His son Rudra Singh, towards the end of his rule, evinced Sakta tendencies."[3] 'The reign of Sib Singh, the son and successor of Rudra Singh, saw the growing influence of the Sakta priests. He became the disciple of Krishnaram Bhattacharya and gave him the management of the Kamakhya temple. When his chief queen Phuleswari became the de facto sovereign, she was even more under the influence of the Brahmanas than her husband, and, in her consuming zeal for the new faith, she committed an act of indiscreet zeal for the new faith, which was destined to have far-reaching and disastrous consequences."[4] This eventually led to the Moamaria Rebellion by Vaisnava subjects. It indirectly brought about the downfall of the Tungkhungiya dynasty and as a consequence Assam lost its independence.

Next to Saktism, Vaishnavism was the dominant sect in Assam. Eventually it claimed more adherents than the former sect. "The Vaisnava religion obtained a strong footing in the counting in the latter part of the 15th century when Sankaradeb (1449-1569), the fountain-head of Bhagavati movement in Assam, appeared on the scene."[5] "Vaisnavism received official recognition when Jayadhraj Singh enrolled himself as a disciple of Niranjan Bapu, whom he established as the first Gosain of the great Auniati Satra."[6] For some time, during Gadadhar Singh's reign, Vaisnavism suffered royal wrath. But Gadadhar's son, Rudra Singh, reinstated the Gossains and aided the Satras or Vaisnava monasteries. "Rudra Singh got made a list of Satras and their Mahants and gave royal recognition to them. . . Rudra Singh appointed a Satriya Barua to look after management of the Satras."[7]

1. Gait, E.A., A History of Assam, p. 287.
2. Ibid., p. 288.
3. Ibid., p. 288.
4. Ibid., p. 288-89.
5. Ibid.
6. Ibid., pp. 289-90.
7. Ibid., p. 290.

Buddhism proper never did take root in Assam, not even in the Ahom period. But Ahom theology and ethics appear to have been touched by Buddhism, either before or after the entry of the Ahoms to Assam. "Dr. S.K. Bhuyan has tried to find out some traces of Buddhist influence in the Ahom scriptures the most significant of which is Phura-Tara-Alam, known also as Phura-Alang and Min-Mang Phura lang . . . . The book expounds the virtue of non-violence in deed and thought, in the form of an exhortation given by the Almighty God Sikia to Lengdan and other deities to rule the earth according to the principle of Ahimsa, non-violence."[1] There are also traces of Crypto-Buddhism in many Hindu shrines. The temples of Hayagriva-Madhava and Asvakranta at Kamarupa and the rock-cut image of Bodh-Janardan at Gauhati betray their Mahayana affiliations. But Buddhism was never really a dominant force in Assam, from the earliest times to the last days of Ahom rule.

The Bodo Group is another dominant racial element in mediaeval Assam. The main branches were the Kacharis and the Koches. Other kindred tribes were the Chutiyas, Borahis and Morans. The Jaintias, who belong to the Mon-Khmer linguistic group, were another important tribe and played a dominant role in the cultural life of mediaval Assam.

The Kacharis were an important group of the Bodo family. They were rivals of the Ahoms in the Brahmaputra Valley. Their more Hinduised counterparts are the Koches who ruled Western Assam and Northern Bengal from Koch Bihar.

"Their physical aspect renders it likely that they came from beyond the mountains to the North-East of Assam Valley. The Morans, the most easterly branch of the race and perhaps the latest settlers in Assam, have indeed a tradition that they came from Main Kaing in the Hukong Valley on the Upper reaches of the Chindwin river. The story goes that there once dwelt three brothers named Moylang, Moran and Moyran. Moylang, the eldest, remained in Upper Burma ; Moyran, the youngest, migrated to Nepal, and was lost there ; whilst Moran, the second brother, is said to have crossed the Patkai pass, the route of many subsequent invasions, and to have settled on the Tiphuk or Diphuk river, where he became the ancestor of the tribe which bears his name.

It is certain, however, that some 2000 years or more ago, Bodo peoples must have covered the whole of the Assam Valley, the greater part of Northern Bengal and Surma Valley. The most significant sign of their presence in this area is the Bodo elements in the names of rivers, such as, Dikho, Diphu, Dibong, etc., also

1. Ibid., p. 291.

traceable in such names as the Tista on Dista, near Darjiling, the Tiphuk in Upper Assam and the Tipai or Dipai in Kachar."[1]

The Bodos, or Kacharis, are known as Boro-ni-fisa or Bodo on the plains and on the north bank of the Brahmaputra up to the Bhutan Hills. In Central Assam, however, they are known as the Dimasa, and occupy the tract between the Khasi-Jaintia Hills and the Naga Hills.[2] The ruling branch of the tribe was known in the Buranjis or Ahom chronicles as the Kachari (pronounced as Kasari). These, when Hinduised, took the name of Haidamba or Hedamba and traced descent from the Pandava hero Bhima and the demoness Hidimba. At the time of Kach invasion on the Kacharis, the Kachari king was styled as "Lord of Hidimba."[3] Explaining this epic connection, Gait remarks that "Dimaur is in reality corruption of Hidimbapur, but it seems more likely that Hidimba was an old name of Cachar, which the Brahmanas afterwards connected with the Kachari dynasty, just as in the Brahmaputra Valley they connected successive dynasties of aboriginal potentates with the mythical Naraka."[4]

"In the thirteenth century it would seem that the Kacharis kingdom extended along the South bank of the Brahmaputra, from the Dikhu to the Kallang, or beyond, and included also the valley of the Dhansiri and the tract which now forms the North Cachar subdivision.[5] The Hindu kingdom of Kamata had a considerable Bodo population. In the 14th century too Dikhu was the boundary between the Ahom and the Kachari dominions. During the next century the two nations clashed with each other. In 1536 the Kacharis were given a crushing defeat by the Ahoms, their capital Dimapur was sacked and the Kacharis shifted their capital to Maibong on the Manur river.[6] Another of their cities was located near Kasomari Pathar on the Dayang river.[7] According to the Darrang Raj Vamsavali, the new capital of the Kacharis was also attacked by Chilanei, the brother and general of Koch king Naranarayan,[8] and Kacharis became vassals of the latter for some time. The Kacharis extended their dominions during the last part of the 16th century over areas which included Nowgong and Cachar.[9]

"The position of the valley of the Surma which is now called Kachar did not

1. Hastings, J., E. of R. & E., Vol. I, p. 759.
2. Ibid. p. 753.
3. Gait, E.A., A History of Assam, p. 303.
4. Ibid., p. 303.
5. Ibid., p. 300.
6. Gait, E.A., A History of Assam, pp. 300-301.
7. Ibid., p. 303.
8. Ibid.
9. Ibid., p. 304.

form part of the dominions of the Kachari Raja till the 17th century, when it was acquired by him as the dowry of a Tipperah princess whom he married."[1]

At the beginning of the 17th century, the Jaintias clashed with the Kacharis over the prince of Dimarua, who owed allegiance to the Kacharis. The Jaintia king was defeated and imprisoned in the Kachari city of Brahmapur or Khaspur.[2] Eventually, the Kacharis clashed with the Ahoms, when the next king of Jaintia, a vassal of the Kacharis, became friendly with the Ahoms. The Ahoms were defeated again, and to celebrate this victory Maibong was renamed as Kirtipur.[3] Also, there had been two Mughal raids on the Kacharis during the Governorships, first of Islam Khan and then of Qusim Khan (1612), of Bengal,[4] Friendly relations with the Ahoms were restored during the rule of Bir Darpa Narayan (1667).[5] The Kachari king Tamradhuraj, defeated by the Ahom king Rudra Singh, in 1706, fled to Khaspur, on the plains of Cachar. Tamsadnanaj was eventually captured by his ally, the Jaintia king, but now the Ahoms sided with the Kacharis.[6]

The rules of the next few kings were important from the point of architectural activities. A rock temple was excavated at Maibong in 1721.[7] Harischandra also had a brick palace built at Khaspur in 1771, at the wishes of the queen-mother Lakshmi-Prara Devi.[8] Harischandra's queen, Lakshmi Devi, had a Siva temple built at Khaspur in 1798 when the former was already dead.[9]

The royal family was getting increasingly Hinduised. This culminated in the formal declaration of their adoption of Hinduism by the king Krishnachandra and his brother Govindachandra. They were also connected to the line of Bhima, the Pandava hero.[10]

The end of the Kachari Rajas was near. Internal dissention and the Manipuri raids soon broke the kingdom into two.[11] Govindachandra sought help of the British, and then of the Burmese, when the former showed reluctance. Eventually, the Burmese were driven out by the British, who feared appropriation of Kachari territory by the Burmese, in the early 19th century.[12]

1. Hastings, J., E. of R. & E. 'Dimasa' by C.J. Lyall Vol. I. p 753,
2. Gait, E.A., A History of Assam, p. 304.
3. Ibid., p. 305.
4. Ibid. p. 305.
5. Ibid., p. 306.
6. Ibid., pp. 307-308.
7. Ibid., p. 308.
8. Datta, D., Kacharer Prastar Lipi, Silchar 1957, p. 10.
9. Ibid., p. 16.
10. Ibid., p. 309.
11. Gait, E.A., A History of Assam, p. 309.
12. Ibid., p. 310.

The Kacharis kept the fundamentals of their tribal religion even while passing through various stages of Hinduisation, during the medieval period.

"All the temples of the Bodo family follow a religion of fear, and are haunted by many gods or spirits, who have to be propitiated by offerings of food etc. Within the historic times the Chutiyas of Upper Assam were wont to offer human sacrifices at their famous copper-rooted temple at Sadiya ; but this habit may have been due to imitation of the Saktist Hindus . . . These are indications of a now decaying belief in tombs and among the Bodos of Northern Assam there are sects, for instance, calling themselves Musa-arisi, sons of the tiger . . . so also there are those who belong to the clan of sacred cactus, the Siju (Eupherbia), and are proud to call themselves Siju-arui . . . . There seems to be no belief in a supreme deity or creator. Among the Western Bodos, gods are freely borrowed from the Hindu pantheon, one of the most popular being Kuvera, the god of wealth."[1]

The so-called 'chess-men' monoliths and the 'Y-shaped' columns of Dimapur evidently have phalic significance and Siju symbolism respectively. These were worshipped as cult objects. Later on, the Kachari Rajas worshipped Ranachandi as their patron deity. According to tradition, it was not an iconic form of Ranachandi that was worshipped, but a sword which King Nirbhayanarayana is said to have received from the goddess.[2] The goddess was mentioned in their inscriptions and in the coins of Govindachandra.[3] At least three, if not more, temples of Ranachandi were built by the kings at Khaspur. Many a tiger-like image in stone has also been recovered from Maibong. These evidently had totemic significance.

The Koches were the most westerly and Hinduised of all the Bodo tribes. They were regarded as a Hindu caste in North-Bengal and Western Assam. "The Koches are frequently referred to as Kuvacha in the Puranas and Tantras.[4] Some of the Koches, specially the leading families, took the honorific title 'Rajbanshi' or the 'royal-clan', to identify themselves with the family of Naranarayana. This gave rise to some anthropological confusion among modern European scholars. Speaking about the Rajbanshis, Gait says that, "It originally referred to an entirely distinct community of Dravidian affinities but was afterwards adopted by the Koches west of the Monas river, who, when they attonned to Hinduism, appropriated the caste name of the most numerous Hinduised community in their neighbourhood."[5]

1. Hastings, J., E. of R. & E., Vol. II, p. 754.
2. Datta, D., Kacharer Prastar Lipi, Silchar 1957, pp. 6-7.
3. Ibid., p. 8.
4. Gait, E.A., A History of Assam, p. 47.
5. Ibid.

Though ethnologists are divided on the identification of the racial stock of the Koches, most of them regarded this group as belonging to the Mongoloid race or having a great percentage of Mongolian blood.[1] "There seems, however, to be no doubt that the true Koches were a Mongoloid race, very closely allied to the Mechas and Garos ; and we find that in Jalpaiguri, Koch Bihar, and Goalpara, the persons now known as Rajbansis are either pure Koches, who, though dark, have a distinctly Mongoloid physionomy, or else a mixed breed in which the Mongoloid element usually preponderates."[2]

"The Koch language is now practically extinct, but the traces of it which remain show that it was almost identical with Garo."[3] After the flight of Nara Singh, the half-brother of Naranarayan, to Bhutan, the Koch dialect of Kamata spread there, as a large number of Nara Singh's followers settled in that country. "The historian of Mir Jumla's invasion in the middle of the seventeenth century says that the people of that country then spoke a dialect allied to that of the Koches."[4]

Religion

Traces of tribal religion were meagre in the royal clan. The people were generally under the influence of Hinduism, and to some extent, Islam and Tantrik Buddhism.

The patron deity of the royal family was Kamateswari. She was also the patron deity of the capital city, Kamatapur (near present Gosanimari). The deity is said to have been installed by the Kamata King, Niladhwaj, towards the middle of the 15th century.[5] The present temple is situated on an elevated plot of land, to the South-East of the fortifications.[6] Destroyed by Hussain Shah of Bengal in 1493, the temple and the idol, along with the Kamakhya temple of Gauhati, were restored by Visva Singha in the 16th century.[7] The present temple of Kamateswari was built by King Prananarayana in 1665.[8] (The kings of Kamata, as well as the Koch Kings, also built a number of famous highways ; the Gohain, which Kamal Ali built during the days of Naranarayan, is the most famous).

Side by side with Saktism, Tantrik Buddhism[9] was also present in the Koch period, before the advent of the Vaisnava preacher Sankaradeva. Some minor

1. Ibid., p. 48.
2. Ibid, p. 48.
3. Ibid.
4. Ibid., p. 51.
5. Ahmad, K.A., Koch Biharer Itihasa, Vol. I, Koch Bihar, 1936, p. 40,
6. Ibid., p. 41.
7. Ibid.,p. 42.
8. Ibid.
9. Ibid., p. 61.

preachers, probably belonging to the Natha-Sahajiya sect, like Sona Rai and Rupa Rai, also flourished in Kamata.[1] Sankaradeva shifted to the Koch court after persecution by the Ahoms.[2] The king and his brother regarded him as their Guru. He weilded considerable moral influence. Madhabadeva, the disciple of Sankaradeva and the founder of the Mahapurushiya sect, was also given protection by King Lakshminarayan.[3] Damodaradeva, the founder of the Bamunia sect of the Eka Sarana Nama Dharma, also took refuge (due to Ahom persecution) in the court of King Parikshit of eastern Kamarupa.[4] The royal family and its minor branch were all very sympathetic towards this neo-Vaisnavite movement of Sankaradeva and majority of them accepted this creed. As a result, for some time, animal sacrifice was stopped in the Kamata kingdom. Some followers of Chaitanyadeva of Bengal also came to preach his brand of neo-Vaisnavism in Kamarupa.[5]

Islamic preachers, known as Pirs, also entered the Kamata kingdom and won over many a follower. They evoked admiration from both Hindus and Muslims. Many Dargahs or Thans were erected at the sites of their exploits, and at their graves. Of these, the following appear prominently in popular beliefs and ballads. Tonsa Pir, Shah Garib Kamal, Ismail Gazi, Ghyasuddin, Shah Sultan, Satya Pir, Ekdil Shan, Gazi Pir, Shah Madar, Khoaz Pir.[6] Some of them, according to local traditions, clashed with local Hindu rulers in course of their preaching and converting missions. Hajo was also a centre of Islamic religious activities in mediaeval Assam.

Shah Garib Kamal preached in Western Assam in the 17th century.[7] Ismail Gazi was a popular Muslim preacher of the 15th century.[8] Ghyasuddin Aulia, the preacher of the 16th century, was buried at Garudachala near Hajo. There, he had earlier founded a Muslim place of worship, which later came to be known as Poa-Mecca or 'quarter-Mecca', i.e., a lesser Mecca. The mosque was enlarged in 1657 by the Mughal Emperor Shah Jahan.[9]

Some Hindu converts to Islam also became preachers. They were successful in bringing the two communities together. One such was Maidalan (Mahidalana), alias Satya Pir.[10] His Hindu followers identified him with Satyanarayana, one of

1. Ibid., p. 60.
2. Ibid., p. 61.
3. Ibid., p. 63.
4. Ibid., pp. 64-65.
5. Ibid., p. 66.
6. Ibid., pp. 67-73.
7. Ibid., pp. 67-68.
8. Ibid., p. 68.
9. Ibid.
10. Ibid., pp. 69-70.

the names of Vishnu. Another preacher, Shah Madar, a native of Medina, reached India when Timur attacked it in 1398 A.D. He next came to Kamarupa and preached on Mondays.[1]

The State of Koch Bihar had increasingly lesser contact with eastern Assam after the former became a Mughal vassal. The Yoginitantra gives a retrospective account of this area, as it does for Saumara or eastern Assam. Muslim and European accounts, as well as the Buranjis of the Ahoms, also throw light on Socio-economic conditions of the area, also known as Ratna Pitha.

Koch Bihar lay on the caravan route from Magadha to China[2] via Assam and Upper Burma. Manya mountain pass gave access to Bhutan and Tibet.[3] The land, according to Muslim chroniclers, was known for its natural products like oranges, pepper, fruits, musk and 'agaru' essence. Cotton and silk were produced, but of poorer quality and on lesser volume in eastern Assam. Ibn Batuta visited Kamarupa in 1346-47 and recorded that the main exports were musk and slaves. People here were also experts in magic and sorcery.[4]

Ralf Fiteh, the English traveller, visited Kamarupa around 1586 and recorded that the "people have ears which be marvelous great, of a span long, which they draw out by devices when they be young[5] . . . There they be all Gentiles, and they will kill nothing. They have hospitals for sheep, goats, dogs, cats, birds and for all living creatures. When they be old and lame they keep them until they die . . . Their small money is almonds, which of ten times they use to eat."[6]

According to Tavernier, guns and gun powder were first discovered in Kamarupa and thence were taken to China via Pegu.[7] The most detailed account of the Ahom dominion is however found in the Tarikh-i-Asham by Shihabuddin Talish, the chronicler who accompanied Mir Jumla during his Assam raids. This will be referred to in the chapter on Cities and City Planning.

"*The Chutiyas* were originally a tribe of the Bodo race. Their kings, being Hinduised, accepted the Tantrik faith. Their goddess was known as Kesai Khati, since human sacrifices were offered to her. The deity was also known as Tamres-wari Mai, since the idol was placed in a building having a roof made of

1. Ahmad, K.A., Koch Biharer Itihasa, p. 72.
2. Ibid., p. 52.
3. Ibid.
4. Ibid., p. 51.
5. Gait, E.A., A History of Assam, p. 48.
6. Ibid., p. 62.
7. Ahmad, K.A., Koch Biharer Itihasa, p. 53.

'copper-sheets'.[1] The Chutiyas occupied the tract on the bank of the Burai river and around Sadiya.[2] It is believed that the Chutiya kingdom was founded towards the end of the thirteenth century when Kamarupa kings lost their hold over the eastern part of the kingdom and the capital was transferred to Kamatapur."[3]

The Chutiya kings assumed the surname Pala, and like their Koch and Ahom counterparts, claimed a divine birth. In the case of the Chutiyas, god Kuvera is said to have graced queen Rupavati, the consort of a Chutiya chief Birpal, alias Birbar, with a son. Birpal was also directed by the god to unearth a sword, a shield and a gold cat which lay hidden under a tree. When the son succeeded the father, he preserved the cat image as a totem, and assumed the name Ratnadhvaja Pala alias Gaurinarayana. This was around 1244 A.D. He was the first king of the Chutiyas.[4]

Ratnadhvaja strengthened his position by subduing neighbouring princes like Bhadrasena and Nayapala. He next threatened to attack Kamata, but was bought back by the offer of a Kamata princess's hand. The capital city Ratnapura was also founded by him. According to the Deodhai Buranji, Ratna Pala also threatened the Bengal Sultan, but eventually they became friends. However, contemporary Muslim accounts do not mention this event. A city was also founded at Sindhu Kshetra, later known as Sadiya.[5]

About the middle of the 14th century the Ahoms and the Chutiyas clashed, but there was a reconciliation in 1376 A.D. However, the Ahom king Sutupha was treacherously murdered by his Chutiya hosts. As a result, the Chutiyas were severely punished by the next Ahom king, Tyas Khamti. In 1513 A.D., the Chutiya king Dhirnarayan sent a naval invasion force on to the Ahom territories which was repulsed. The Chutiyas were finally routed in a battle by the Ahom king Suhungmung in 1523 A.D. As a condition of the treaty with the Chutiyas, the Ahoms demanded the formers' heirloom, the gold cat. On being refused, the Ahoms crushingly defeated the Chutiyas at Mathadang. The royal family perished, except an infant prince. The whole of the Chutia territory was annexed and put under an Ahom governor, the Sadiya Khoa Gohain.[6]

The Jaintias. "The dominions of the Rajas of Jaintia included two entirely distinct tracts of the country, namely, the Jaintia hills, which are inhabited by a

1. Barua, K.L., Early History of Kamarupa, p. 276.
2. Ibid., p. 271.
3. Ibid., p. 270.
4. Ibid., p. 272.
5. Ibid., pp. 274-75.
6. Ibid., pp. 275-76.

Khasi tribe called Synting, and the plains country south of these hills and north of the Barak river, in the Sylhet district, now known as the Jaintia parganas, the inhabitants of which are Bengali Hindus and Muhammadans. The former tract was the original home of the dynasty. The latter was a later annexation, but it was this area which first bore the name of Jaintia, and which is mentioned in Pauranik and Tantrik literature as containing one of the fifty-one famous shrines sacred to Durga."[1]

"The Khasi and Jaintia Hills, situated in Assam, were located between 20°48′ and 26°7′N and 90°45′ and 90°51′E (in pre-partition periods), approximately occupying an area of 6157 sq. miles . . . ."[2] The country is divided into three natural zones, viz., the 'Bhoi' region in the north, sloping down to the Brahmaputra valley, the 'Ri-Lum', an irregular high land with the highest peak at Shillong (6,449 ft.) and the 'War' area, a narrow strip of land in the south, overlooking the plains of the Surma valley.[3]

"There is practically no difference between the inhabitants of the Khasi and the Jaintia Hills. They are both of the same physical type, and they speak the same language Khasi -- which is remarkable as being the only surviving dialect in India, excluding Burma, of the Mon-Khmer family of languages."[4] The speakers of the Mon-Khmer dialects in India, also to be found in Chotanagpur region, like the Khasi-Jaintias, raised megaliths for their dead. Their ancestors are said to have entered India in the remote past.

"The evidence of philology, therefore, suggests the hypothesis that the Khasis and Syntengs are remnants of the first Mongolian overflow into India who established themselves in their present habitat at a very remote period and who, owing to their isolated position maintained their independence, while their congeners in the plains below were submerged in subsequent streams of immigration from the same direction."

The Khasi tradition says that they originally came from the east. According to Gurdon this is quite true, since they must have had entered Assam across the Patkai range, the route which was used in historic times by incoming tribes tike the Ahoms, Khamptis and Singphos.[5] Another cultural trait that connects the Khasi-Jaintias with other races of South-East Asia is matrilinial descent.

1. Gait, E.A., A History of Assam, p. 311.
2. Bareh, H., The History and Culture of the Khasi People, Shillong, 1967, p. 8.
3. Ibid., pp. 8-9.
4. Gait, E.A. Ibid, p. 311.
5. Gurdon, P.R.T., The Khasis, pp. 11-12.

The term Khasi has a particular significance. Kha means born of and Si refers to an ancient mother. Khasi, therefore, means born of the mother. It is relevant to note here that various Khasi clans bear their mother's name. . . . Synteng holds a similar significance. According to tradition, Teng was the ancient mother, and therefore, Synteng means the children of the ancestral mother. . . . Jaintia seems to have been an Aryanization of the original Khasi word Synteng (Zaintein, which developed into Jaintia)."[1]

Like all other Assamese kings and chieftains, the Jaintia kings also claimed a divine origin. This aspect, as also their matrilinial descent, have been explained with a Hinduised background in the tradition of Jayanti Devi, who was the first female ruler. Since then matrilinial descent has been the rule in Khasi royal lines. The Jaintia Buranji (the Assamese chronicle about the Jaintias) explains it through the following story.

In the ancient times, a line of Brahmin rajas ruled the Jaintias, the last of whom was Jayantia Rai. He had a daughter by the grace of goddess Durga and the child was named Jayanti. Since she had no brothers, her father sought to instal her as his successor. She was married to Landhabar, the son of the royal priest Chandibar. She ascended the throne taking the name Rani Singha. Eventually, the marriage fell through when Landhabar forced sexual union with his wife, unclean at that time due to her menstrual period, as believed by the Hindus. Rani Singha turned her husband out. He then gave up the decent, orthodox manners and lived with an old couple belonging to the rude Garo tribe. Later on, Rani Singha was repentant. As directed by Durga in a dream she took a bath in the mountain stream, Sutnga. There a double emerged from her body and remained in the stream. The maiden was named Matsyodari (the one from the fish's belly) since she was swallowed by a large Barali fish. As willed by the goddess, Landhabar caught that very fish and hung it in his house for being used later on. On return home Landhabar used to find all sorts of edibles in his house for him to eat. This continued for a few days, until he caught Matsyodari who used to come out of the Barali fish to work and keep the house for him. After this, they began living together and were happy. A son was born to them. Landhabar was made the local chief. He took the title Sultan after overthrowing a Muslim ruler. After Landhabar his son succeeded to the throne and took the title Bargohain (as an imitation of the Ahom title). Eventually Bargohain clashed with the men of Rani Singha following a deer hunt. He was taken captive, but later recognized by Rani Singha as the son of her husband and her double, whom she regarded as a sister. After a while, Bargohain was made the king of Jaintia and Rani Singha who was a part of Durga, left this world and entered the nether

1. Bareh, H., The History and Culture of the Khasi People, pp. 12-13.

world. Bargohain started digging the place to find Rani Singha, but stopped when directed by the deity in a dream. At that spot he unearthed a piece of metal, out of which he was asked to make an image of Jayanti Devi and worship it as an icon of Durga. The goddess also directed Bargohain to ensure that from then onwards the king's sister's son would be the ruler and that the system would continue for all times to come. The place where Jayanti Devi went to the nether world was known as Muktipura (city of deliverence)."[1] According to another version, Bargohain was given a copper icon of the ten-armed Durga to worship and the capital was named Jayantapur.[2] Apart from Jayantapur, other Khasi States do not figure prominently in the mediaeval Assam politics and culture.

A line of Brahmin kings mentioned in the Jayantia Buranji starts with Kedareswar Rai and ends with Jayanta Rai, the father of Ja anti Devi, alias Rani Singha. A tentative chronology of these kings, as given by Dr. Bareh, follows :[3]

Kedareswar Rai	—	1119-1130 A.D.
Dhaneswar Rai	—	1130-1150 A.D.
Kandarpa Rai	—	1150-1170 A.D.
Manik Rai	—	1170-1190 A.D.
Jayanta Rai	—	1190-1240 A.D.

We are on surer grounds with the next group of rulers, beginning with Parbat Ray. Gait[4] assigns sixteen years for each ruler, on an average. They are :

Parbat Ray	—	1500-1516 A.D.
Majha Gosain	—	1516-1532 A.D.
Burha Parbat Ray	—	1532-1548 A.D.
Bar Gosain	—	1548-1564 A.D.
Bijay Manik	—	1564-1580 A.D.
Pratap Ray	—	1580-1596 A.D.
Dhan Manik	—	1596-1605 A.D.

According to Gait, once again, Parbat Ray (the Lord of the Hills, as his name suggests), first extended the rule of the Jaintias to the plains (Jaintia Parganas), in about 1500 A.D. By this time the Jaintia kings had been greatly Hinduized. All their constructions are associated with Hindu worship. Their tribal religion did not play any part in the artistic activities of the Jaintias. With the growth of

1. Bhuyan, S.K. (edited by), Jaintia Buranji, Gauhati 1964, 2nd Edn., pp. 17.
2. Ibid. p. 10.
3. Bareh, H., A History and Culture of the Khasi People, p. 58.
4. Gait, E.A., A History of Assam, p. 313.

political power and prosperity, Jaintia was drawn into the internal politics of Assam. In the middle of the 16th century Chilarai, the brother of Naranarayan, invaded Jaintia and made it a vassal.[1] As part of the treaty, the Jaintia king was to pay the annual tribute of 10,000 rupees, and horses, and three hundred 'Nakoidao's (a kind of Sabre). Also, from then on the Jaintia coins could not bear the name of the ruling chief, but had to be like the Narayani Mudra or Koch coins. The coins carried the following inscription :

> Obverse side—"Sri Sri Sivacharanakamalamadhukarasya".
> Reverse side—"Sri Sri Jayantapurapurandarasya Sake.[2]"

This agreement continued up to 1750 A. D.[3]

In the beginning of the 17th century, Jaintias and Kacharis clashed during the rule of Dhan Manik. His successor, Jasa Manik (1605-25), as part of his strategy, brought Ahoms into the conflict to punish the Kacharis. One of his daughters was married to the Ahom king. He himself married a Koch princess, brought back an icon of Kali from Koch Bihar and installed it at Jaintapur under the name Jayanteswari Devi.[4]

Ahoms and Jaintias clashed again till finally the former broke off all relations with the latter during Lakshminarayan's reign. This king built a fine palace at Jaintapur. The reading on its dedicatory inscription, according to Gait, is 1680 A. D.[5] The next king, Ram Singh (1697-1708), figures prominently due to his conflict with the Ahoms and the Kacharis. Finally both the chieftains submitted to the Ahom king Rudra Singha. For some time the Jaintias fought with their kinsman, Syiem Khairam. In 1770, king Chatra Singh clashed with the British and in 1774, the British forces occupied the Jaintia territory.[6] The British and the Jaintias eventually became friendly, with the former protecting their ally when threatened by Burmese forces in 1824. The capture of a British subject from Sylhet, for being sacrificed to Jayanteswari estranged relations with the British. This territory was annexed by the British in 1835 during the rule of Rajendra Singh.[7]

1. Gait, E.A., A History of Assam, p. 314.
2. Ahmad, K A., Koch Biharer Itihasa, Vol. I, pp. 110-111.
3. Ibid,, p. 111.
4. Ibid., p. 153.
5. This event has been recorded in a fine miniature painting, in the Assamese manuscript Sankha-chuda Vadha, produced during the rule of Rudra Singha's son Siva Singha.
6. Gait, E.A., Ibid, p 319.
7. Ibid., p, 320.

4. Political Condition of Assam in the Mediaeval Age

The entry of the Ahoms into Assam ushers in the mediaeval age there. And the end of the Ahom rule, in the first quarter of the 19th century, brings about the close of that period in Assam. Sukapha, the Shan or Tai adventurer, left Maulung in 1215 A.D. with a following of about 9,000 members of his tribe, and reached Khamjang in Assam in 1228 A.D.[1] Apart from the Ahoms, the country was then ruled by various Bodo chieftains. The extreme west of Assam, then known as Kamata, was under the hegemony of the later kings of Kamarupa. The ruler of this line was Prithu (1200-'28 A.D.).[2] But due to the advance of the Kacharis, the capital of these kings was removed from North Gauhati to Kamatapur in the west[3] Kamatapur has been identified with Gossamimari, fourteen miles to the southwest of present day Cooch-Behar town.[4] In Upper Assam, the growing Ahom territory was surrounded by the Moran and Barahi principalities. Both these tribes belonged to the Bodo race. In 1253 Sukapha founded the capital at Charaideo, near Sibsagar, Badaneha and Thakumtha, who ruled over the Morans and the Borahis, respectively, were his contemporaries.[5]

The Chutiyas were powerful neighbours of the Morans and the Borahi. They ruled around Sadiya or Vidarbha.[6] The founder of the dynasty was one Bir Pal. Though of Shan and Bodo origin, these people claimed to be Hindus and traced their descent from the legendary king Bhismaka, the father of the epic heroine Rukmini. In the thirteenth century they were ruling from their capital Ratnapara and continuously fought the Ahom infiltrators.[7]

Another important power at that time were the Bhuiyas or Baro-Bhuiyans. The Bhuiyas, who were ruling north of the Brahmaputra and east of the Chutiya kingdom at the time when the Ahoms entered Assam, claimed to be descendants of Samudra, the minister of Arimatta, who, it is said, seized the throne on the expulsion of Arimatta's son Ratna Singh.[8] Eventually the line split into two and the branch that had its seat at Lakshmipur became more powerful, politically. Lakshmipur gave its name to the present district of Lakhimpur, where the Bhuyan or Bhuiya families number greater than the branch which settled at Bardowa in

1. Gait, E.A , A History of Assam, Calcutta, 1963, p. 78.
2. Barua, K L., Early History of Kamarupa, Shillong, 1933 p. 200.
3. Ibid , p. 243.
4. Ahmad, K.A , Koch Biharer Itihasa, Pt. I, p. 30
5. Gait, E.A , Ibid, p. 79.
6. Ibid., p. 42.
7. Ibid., p. 43.
8. Ibid., p. 40.

present Nowgong district. Sankaradeva, the Vaishnava saint of mediaeval Assam, was born in the Bhuiya family of Bardowa.[1]

The last of the Kamata kings was overthrown in 1498 A.D. by internal dissension.[2] Nilambar, the last king of this dynasty known as the Khyan or Khen, was overthrown by Hussain Shah, the Muslim ruler of Bengal, on invitation by his own minister, who had some personal grudges against his master. Hussain Shah occupied the country as far as the Barnadi river. He left his son as the governor of the conquered territories. Soon Muslim power in Western Assam perished. This happened when they clashed with the Ahoms in an attempt to annex the latter's dominions.[3]

Thus the entire area was left without any strong ruler and, for some time, was governed by petty chieftains mostly belonging to the Koch, Mech and other Indo-Mongoloid tribes that were more or less Hinduised. Finally, the Koch chiefs of Chikanagram[4] (the present Goalpara) became supreme and ruled over an area roughly corresponding to the territories of the Kamata kings. Their progenitor was Hariya Mandal. His two sons, Bisu and Sisu, became powerful when Muslim power perished in the conflict with the Ahoms. Of the two brothers, Bisu, the elder, became the ruler of the tract between Karataya, in the West, and Bar Nadi, in the east, and took the Kshatriya name Bisva Singh, about 1515 A.D. He moved his capital from Chikanagram to Koch Bihar where he built a fine city.[5] Though he was friendly with the Ahoms, his sons Nara Narayan and Chilarai clashed with them.[6] They became worthy rivals of the Ahoms and were overlords of the minor principalities of Kacharis, Manipur, Jaintia, Tippera, Sylhet, Khairam and Dimarua. Nara Narayan even clashed with the Padsoh of Gaur, Sulaiman Karrani.[7] To get rid of this powerful foe, Nar Narayan pledged obedience to the Mughal Emperor, Akbar, in 1578.[8]

After Nar Narayan, the Koch line split into two, the major branch ruling at Koch Bihar and the minor at Hajo. This was in 1581 A.D.[9] In 1596 A.D., Lakshminarayana, the son of Nar Narayan, declared himself to be a vassal of the Mughals.[10] Parikshit, who was ruling from Hajo was also defeated by the

1. Gait, E.A., A History of Assam.
2. Ibid., p. 45
3. Ibid, p 46.
4. Ibid., p. 49.
5. Ibid., p. 50.
6. Ibid., pp. 50-51.
7. Ibid., p. 55,
8 Ibid., p. 56.
9. Ibid., p. 57.
10. Ibid., p. 65.

Mughals. In 1616 A.D. Hajo was put under the Mughal governor Mukarram Khan.[1] Eventually, the line of Parikshit was put under Ahom tutelage and protection, when the last independent ruler of the line, Dharma Narayan[2], was defeated and killed by the Mughals. Since then, the Koches have been ruling at Mangaldoi as vassals of the Ahoms. The Western Koches, however, continued to rule as vassals of the Mughals, to the west of the Sankosh river.

Of all the different peoples, it were the Ahoms who played the prominent role in Assam's political life. They ruled the land for six hundred years. With British occupation the mediaeval period comes to a close in Assam.

5. The Neo-Vaisnava Movement

The Neo-Vaisnava movement of the 15th century was the most singular factor in the artistic life of Assam. Though overlooked in the Buranji's, this movement brought about a cultural and artistic renaissance in mediaeval Assam. The movement 'Eka Sarana Nama Dharma,' or single minded devotion to Visnu-Krisna, started by Sri Sankaradeva (1449-1569 A.D.), has been followed by the majority since then. Sankaradeva was not only a religious reformer but also a great litterateur and artist. The greatest impact of his movement was felt in the fields of literature, dance, drama and painting.

While other forms of art were also inspired, arthitecture, being patronised by the ruling clan, was an exception. Initially the Ahom kings were disinterested in this reformist movement, since their religious life was guided by Ahom and Saktist Hindu tenets Sankaradeva started preaching during the days of king Suhungmung in Upper Assam From Jayadhvaj Singh (1649-63) to Ratnadhvaj Singh (1677-81), the Ahom king , with a few exceptions, showed due respect and courtesy to Vaisnava Gosains and accepted initiation. They made grants and endowments for the maintenance of Vaisnava monasteries. The most important Satras of Eastern Assam were set up under their patronage.

Vaisnavism received official recognition when Jayadhvaj Singh enrolled himself as the disciple of Niranjan Bapu, whom he established as the first Gosain of the great Auniati Satra. Hearing of the fame of Banamali Gosain, then living in Koch Bihar, he sent for him and gave him land for setting up Satras at Koliabar and Majuli. Chakradhvaj Singh (1663-70) also showed great reverence to Banamali Gosain. King Udayaditya (1670-72) took initiation from a Vaisnava Mahant of

1. Gait, E.A., A History of Assam, p. 67.
2. Ibid , p. 70.

Ahatguri Satra. Subsequently, however, he was unduly influenced by Paramananda Bairagi, an unknown sanyasi from Brindaban. Ramadhvaj Singh (1672-74) became a disciple of the Vaisnava Mahant, Narowa Thakur Sujinpha (1575-77), and Atan Bunah Gohain was the disciple of Moamora Satra. Sulikpha Lara Raja and Bandar Bar Phukan, Governor at Gauhati, were disciples of Banamali Deva of Dakhinpath Satra. King Rudra Singh also pursued a liberal policy towards the Vaisnava Mahant and his disciples. Immediately after his coronation he helped settle the Vaisnava Mahants, who had been persecuted by his father Gadadhar Singh, at their respective Satras. Rudra Singh drew up a list of the Satras and their Mahants. He gave royal recognition to them. Those included in the royal register were called Etakiya Mahants. Rudra Singh appointed a Satriya Barua to look after the management of the Satras.[1]

The Mahants were graded according to the importance of their respective Satras and were assigned seats at the Bar-Sabah or court, when the king addressed it. They blessed the kings and offered Prasad and Nirmali (Sanskrit Nirmalya) on special occasions.[2]

Sankaradeva : Sankaradeva was the founder of the neo-Vaisnavite movement in mediaeval Assam. By his teachings and through his religious institutions, Sankaradeva changed completely the social and artistic life of Assam. "Sankara was born in a Bhuyan family at Alipukhuri, a place about sixteen miles from the present town of Nowgong, on the south bank of the Brahmaputra in the bright dasami of Asvin in 1371 Saka (1449) . . . . Sankara's family was called Siromani Bhuyan, being the chief among the Bhuyans. His father was Kusumbara. Sankara's mother died within three days of his birth and he was brought up by his grand-mother Khersuti. When Sankara was twelve years old he was sent to a village school maintained by 'Mahendra Kandali, an erudite Sanskrit scholar."[3]

. . . . "His scholarship in Sanskrit and knowledge of the scriptures were well revealed in the number of translations and adaptations he made in Assamese in the later years of his life. He compiled a work on Vaisnavism, in Sanskrit, styled Bhokti Ratnakara, and also composed many Sanskrit verses that were incorporated in his plays."

"Sankara completed his study at the age of twenty-two (1470) and came out a finished scholar. Soon after his return from school, official responsibilities of managing the family estates fell upon his shoulders. Now, he also married

1. Gait, E.A., A History of Assam, pp. 289-90.
2. Sadar Amin, H.K , Asam Buranji,, 2nd Edn., 1962, Gauhati. p, 110
3. Barua, B.K., Sankaradeva, Vaisnava Saint of Assam, Gauhati, 1960, p. 3.

Suryavati, a Kayastha girl. Suryavati died four years after her marriage, leaving behind a girl named Haripriya. During this time Sankara also lost his father. These two bereavements filled his youthful mind with overwhelming sorrow and he even contemplated of renouncing the world. After giving his daughter in marriage to a Kayastha young man Hari and handing over the administrative responsibilities to Jayantadalai and Madhab-dalai, Sankara set out on a long and extensive pilgrimage (1481 A.D.) . . . . He visited most of the sacred places and temples of northern and southern India . . . . At these holy places he came in contact with Vaisnavite teachers of various schools, and entered with them into many learned and theological discussions. The results of these discussions and the influences they exercised over his mind were reflected in the Vaisnavite movement which he subsequently started in Assam. After twelve years of such wandering through many sacred seminaries of Vaisnavite learning, Sankaradeva returned home a much-travelled man, acquiring first-hand knowledge of Vaisnavite theology-texts, made up of worship and management of Institutions."[1]

"Soon after his return Sankara married again. He moved his residence from Alipukhuri to a near-about village Bardowa. Now his mission of life took a definite shape; he started with fresh impetus and vigorous enthusiasm his religious movement for mass conversion. At Bardowa he set up a Satra (monastery) and erected a Namghar (village-hall for daily devotion and place for community singing), where he held religious discourses. Around him, he collected a group of devout disciples and held daily devotional recitation known as Nama Kirtan. The official name of Sankaradeva's Vaisnavism is Ekasarana dharma—the religion of supreme surrender to One; and that One is Vishnu, who in the form of Narayana assumes incarnations from age to age. The most popular incarnation in which Vishnu is worshipped is that of Krishna. The surrender to One is very rigorously enjoined. For an Ekasaraniya, the worship of other gods and goddesses is strictly prohibited.[2]

Sankaradeva enjoins :
"Anya devideva nakariba seva
nakhaiba prasada tara
murtiko nacaiba giho naposiba
bhakti haiba vyabhichara"[3]

According to Dr. Banikanta Kakati, "the Ekasarana system is not a religion of bargain and barter between God and men or of sacrifice and easy recompense;

1. Barua, B.K., Sankaradeva, Vaisnava Saint of Assam, pp, 3-4.
2. Ibid, pp. 4-5.
3. Ibid., p. 127.

it is one with exclusive emphasis on slow spiritual outlook by laying flesh and spirit in the hands of the Lord."

During the early period of his missionary activities, Sankaradeva received a complete text of the Bhagavata Purana from Puri, through Jagadish Misra, a pundit of Tirhut in Bihar. After a year Sankara set upon translating it into simple metrical Assamese and also started on other poetical creations based on the same Purana.[1] In 1516 Sankaradeva had to leave Bardowa due to the hostility of the Kacharis.[2] He moved to Gangmase and finally to Dhuwahata, in the Majuli island, which lay within Ahom territory. During his fourteen years stay at Dhuwahata, Sankara won over Madhavadeva, a Sakta pundit, who later became his chief disciple. He also ran a religious discourse, arranged by the orthodox priestly class, who were against the democratic creed of Ekasarana dharma.

Sankara once again left Ahom territory due to a sad and unfortunate incident. Following an unsuccessful Keddah operation, Sankara's men earned the Ahom king's displeasure. The king, who had given Sankara the charge of the elephant catching operation, beheaded his son-in-law, Hari. Madhabdeb, however, was released, since he was a Sanyasi.

Sankara's next centre of religious activity was Patbausi, near Barpeta, which was within the dominion of the Koch King Nara Narayana. He established a Satra and Namghar at Patbausi in about 1546 A.D.[3] The major part of his religious and literary activities took place at Barpeta where he also converted eminent Brahmin scholars like Damodaradesa, Harideva and Ananta Kandali. Eventually, on Sankaradeva's death, three sub-sects of this creed were headed by the three Brahmin disciples.

About 1550 A.D. Sankaradeva set out for a second pilgrimage and during it, he met Chaitanyadeva of Bengal and the grand-daughter of Kabir, the two eminent Vaishnava preachers of the age.[4]

On return from the second pilgrimage, Sankaradeva started once again his religious and missionary activities. But this caused dissent among the Brahmins in the Koch court. The Koch king Nara Narayan arranged for a religious debate between Sankaradeva and eminent Brahmins. Again Sankara emerged

1. Barua, B.K., Sankaradeva, Vaishnava Saint of Assam, p. 6.
2. Ibid., p. 6.
3. Ibid., p. 7.
4. Ibid., p. 8.

victorious. The king was so impressed by the profundity of the saint that he also expressed the desire to become his disciple.[1] But Sankaradeva refused to accept a king as a disciple, since it was not possible for such high placed persons to follow the democratic practices of the Ekasarana dharma.

The king's brother, Chilarai, built for Sankaradeva a Satra at Bheladanga, which was in the vicinity of the Koch capital. Sankaradeva nominated Madhavadeva for the apostolic seat. From then on the creed came to be known as the Mahapurushiya sect, since the disciples of Madhava regarded him as a Mahapurusha. It was in Koch Bihar that Sankara breathed his last in the year 1569 A.D.[2]

The Satra institution and its role in mediaeval art and life : The Satra is a unique institution, not only of mediaeval Assam, but of the entire mediaeval India. "It may be monastic or semi-monastic in form. The former type resembles, to a certain extent, the Buddhist monasteries of ancient times and the mathas of the mediaeval age. But the importance of this institution lies in the fact that it is intimately connected with the Assamese society and it has become a part and parcel of Assamese life. Contributions of this institution towards the spread of Vaisnavism, in particular, and the cultural development of Assam, in general, are indeed great. The high percentage of people professing Vaisnavism in Assam is accountable to the activities of this institution during the last four centuries of the Christian era. It is because of the evangelical activities of this institution that many non-Aryan tribes today profess Vaisnavism in Assam."[3]

A Satra includes the following members :

(i) Adhikar and Deka-Adhikar

(ii) Bhakat

(iii) Sisya

"The head of a Satra is popularly known as Adhikar or Satriya . . . . He is the religious head and spiritual guide of the flock under his care. The formal initiation ceremony, Sarana, and the confirmatory bhajana are conducted under his direct supervision. Next to the Adhikar in power and prestige is the Deka-Adhikar who usually becomes the head after the death of Adhikar. When the Adhikar is absent or goes out on a tour, the Deka-Adhikar performs the duties of the head."[4]

1. Barua, B.K., Sankaradeva Vaishnava Saint of Assam.
2 Ibid, pp. 8-9.
3. Sarma, S.N., The Neo-Vaisnavite Movement and the Satra Institution of Assam, Gauhati, 1966, Intro., p. xii.
4. Ibid.. p. 102.

"Though the term bhakat (Sk. Bhakta) means any devotee, yet it is popularly applied to mean those devotees who either hold ecclesiastical office of the Satra or lead the life of a celibate within the Satra campus . . . . such unmarried devotees are called Kevaliya-bhakati . . . . Celibate devotees are recruited in their early years. Under guidance and supervision of the elder celibates they remain as apprentices for a few years. When they are sufficiently acquainted with the religious tenets and practices, they are formally initiated to the religious order. These apprentices are to wait upon their superiors and receive religious lessons from them."[1]

"Lay devotees or disciples of a Satra are called Sisyas . . . . Every Vaisnava householder in Assam, belonging to the Assamese community, is invariably affiliated to one or the other of the Satras. Customarily, every Assamese youngman of the Vaisnava families must have his initiation before he gets himself married."

The Satras also patronised and encouraged arts and crafts, like dance, drama, music, book-illustration and making of decorative objects for the beautification of the Satra interiors.

For the Bhaona or dramas, mukhas or masks of various kinds were produced to represent many-headed characters of gods as well as mythical beings like Garuda, Naga and Gandharvas. Models and props (chos) for the stage like chariots, vimanas, thrones, trees, etc., were also produced within the Satra.[2] The Satras too had their own khanikars who carved icons of wood. Karala Barhai was a favourite of Sankaradeva and carved an icon of Vishnu for installation by the saints.[3] Other objects made were also ritual in nature, like the altar (Simhasana), cabinets (Karanis) for keeping objects and raised trays (sarai) for temple services.

Paintings and painted wood-work embellished with mica (balichanda) and tinsel (rangpata) decorated important Satras like Barpeta, Kheitiapota, etc. Even the beams and rafters were painted with designs and figures.[4] "While book-illustration was popular even in the 16th century, it assumed prolific proportions between the 17th and the 18th centuries."[5] This art was not only patronised by the Satras, the royalty and the nobility took an equal interest in it. That Assamese painting, whether cultivated in the court or in Satras, is basically of

1. Sarma, S.N., The Neo-Vaishnavite Movement and the Satra Institution of Assam, p. [illegible]
2. Ibid., p. 172.
3. Thakur, Daityari, Sankaradeva Madhavadevar Charita, pp. 85-89.
4. Goswami, C., Anirudhadevar Charita, p. 35 ff.
5. Sarma. S. N., Ibid., p. 176.

the same category and technique, cannot be doubted; the only difference lies in degrees of perfection . . . the Satra institution has also played a considerable part in its growth, preservation and popularity.[1]

"In short, the cultural history of Assam in respect of fine arts and crafts, of education and learning, and of literature and fine arts since the beginning of the sixteenth century till the advent of the British developed centering around the Vaisnava movement which in turn found expressions through the Satra institution."

1. Sarma. S.N., Neo-Vaishnava Movement and the Satra Institution, p. 179.

2

ARCHITECTURE

1. Cities and City Planning

The earliest reference to a capital city during Ahom rule is to Charaideo in Upper Assam. Sukapha founded the first Ahom capital at this place in 1174 Saka[1] (1252 A.D). The city lies by a hillock, of the same name, where the Ahoms worshipped their tribal gods (deo) by sacrificing cocks to them. According to tradition, Charaideo is composed of two Assamese words—charai (bird) and deo (god)—and the compound word is associated with Vishnu riding on Garuda, the divine bird. The Sanskritised form of Charaideo is Vihagadri, or the "hill of the bird." It was also the capital of the Barahi (Bodo), the rulers of Assam before the Ahoms. The Barahis, being devotees of Vishnu, named their city after Garuda.

Charaideo, about 10 to 12 sq. miles in area, was very close to the Naga hills. Two minor towns, Rungkham and Chungkham,[2] meaning in Ahom the "city of golden paddy" and the "city of golden gardens" respectively, were situated between Charaideo and the Naga hills. Rungrung and Govindapur were two other towns in the same chain of habitations.

The capital was later shifted to Garhgaon, near modern Sibsagar, after the accession to the throne of the patricide Suklungmung[3] in 1539 A.D. In the Buranjis we find the Sanskritised form of the name of the capital as Garhgrama. The new capital was surrounded by a huge rampart at the wishes of the queen of Suklungmung,[4] who was known as Chaoching by the Ahoms and as Nangtyap Kham in her native Nara principality beyond the Patkai hills. The ramparts or Garh gave the name to the new city. The city was on the bank of the Dikhou, on a site known as Hemena-bari or the "garden of Hemena."[5] Hemena was only a common citizen. While making the circular ramparts, the king clashed with Hemena, on whose garden part of the rampart was to be built. Since he

1. Gogoi, L., Buranjie Parasha Nagar p. 36.
2. Ibid., p. 37.
3. Gait, E.A., A History of Assam, ed. II, p. 99.
4. Gogoi, L., Ibid, pp. 18-19.
5. Ibid., p. 18.

would not give up his land, the king had to wait until his death before completing the ramparts[1].

Garhgaon remained the de facto capital and cultural centre for about four centuries. Even after the capital was shifted to Rangpur and then again to Jorhat it aroused national pride and drew admiration, both from foreign visitors and enemies. The best description of Garhgaon at its height of glory is found in the Mughal work in Persian, Fatiyah-i-Ibriyah or Tarikh-e-Asham (accounts of Assam), by Sihabuddin Talish, the historian who accompanied Mir Jumla on his campaigns in the east.

The account of Talish : "The city of Garhgaon has four gates* of stone set in mud, from each of which to the Rajas palace, for a distance of three Kos, an extremely strong, high and wide embankment (al) has been constructed for the passage of men. Around the city, in place of a wall, there is an encompassing bamboo plantation running continuously, two Kos or more in width. But in the city the habitations are not regularly laid out. The houses of the inhabitants have been built in a scattered fashion within the bamboo groves, close to the al, and every man's orchard and plough-land are situated in front of his house, one end of the field touching the al and the other the house. Near the Raja's palace, on both banks of the Dikhu river, the houses are numerous and there is a narrow bazar-road. The only traders who sit in the bazar are betel-leaf sellers. It is not their practice to buy and sell articles of food in the market-place. The inhabitants store in their houses one year's supply of food of all kinds and are under no necessity to buy or sell any article."[2]

The eastern section of the rampart was Rajgarh, the royal rampart; the western, Banhgarh, the bamboo rampart; the southern, Ladoigarh and the northern, Pathaligarh, the wide rampart.[3] The actual palace was surrounded by an earthen rampart encompassing an area of one sq. mile. The capital itself was 12 miles long and 10 miles wide.

"In short the city of Garhgaon appeared to us to be circular, wide and an aggregation of villages. Round the Raja's house an embankment has been made and strong bamboos have been planted on it close together to serve as a wall. Round it a moat has been dug, deeper than a man's height in most places and

1. Gogoi, L., Buranjie Parasha Nagar, p 19.

* The four gates were : the Nangalamara (northern) or Salakhamara Duar, the two Simhaduars or lion-gates (western) and the Rajgarh duar (eastern) or the gate of the royal rampart.

2. Gait, E.A., A History of Assam ed. II, p. 153.

3. Gogoi, L., Ibid., p. 19.

always full of water. The enclosure is one Kos and fourteen chains in circumference. Inside it high and spacious thatched houses have been built."[1] Outside the palace enclosure and around it were the houses of the nobles, including that of the Bar Phukan. These houses were large and built of wood; with spacious gardens and sweet tanks.[2] But the beautiful city was ransacked by the Mughal army under Mir Jumla. Temporarily, the capital was shifted to Bakata.[3] The city, being the capital, was successively destroyed by the Moamarias and the Burmese. The Moamarias destroyed by fire important buildings like the Barchara and the Dolakakharia Chara.[4]

Gradually masonry buildings were built at Garhgaon, the chief among them being the Kareng (palace) built in 1752 A.D. The stone gates were added to it by Pramatta Simha, as also the Silsakos (masonry bridges) over the Darika river and the Garakhia Dol (temple of Langkuri or Siva of the Ahoms).[5]

The descriptions of Garhgaon during the 19th century show that in spite of the shifting of the royal offices during the reign of Rudra Singha, the city remained the metropolis of Assam. "Garhgaon, the seat of Government, was of immense extent and was built of bricks and stone . . . . Garhgaon figured in the imagination of the multitudes as the premier city of Ahom supremacy."[6] Garhgaon could boast of paved roads, which became slippery during rains since they were paved with smooth bricks and stone slabs, and this point was remembered in an Assamese proverb (Garhgaon roads are slippery. Young and old have to use walking sticks).

With the rise of the House of Tung-Khung the capital was shifted to Rangpur near the present Sibsagar. The new capital was basically different, most of its buildings being in masonry and stone. The era of wooden architecture was gone. This was symbolic of the gradual Indianisation and Hinduisation of the Ahom royal family. The new capital was also the seat of the Sakta cult which had fallen on evil days during the Vaisnava renaissance under Sankaradeva. The movement thus started by Rudra Singh was continued by his sons and successors, right on to the end of Ahom rule.

1. Gait, E.A., A History of Assam p. 153.
2. Ibid., p, 154.
3. Gogoi, L., Buranjie Parasha Nagar. p, 20.
4. Ibid., p. 21.
5. Ibid., pp. 28-29.
6. Gait, E.A., Ibid,, II, ed., p. 269.

In 1698 A.D. Rudra Singh founded the city of Rangpur.[1] Since masonry buildings were a novelty in Assam he engaged an architect from Koch Bihar, Ghanashyam, who was later converted to Islam. Ghanashyam has been described in the Buranjis as being a Bangal or a foreigner. But we are unable to say with certainty whether he was really a Bengali by birth, or from some other part of India, since Bangal applied to all non-Assamese peoples, including Europeans. Ghanashyam built both at Rangpur and at Charaideo.

"When Ghanashyam had finished his work, and was on the point of departing, richly rewarded by the king, it was accidentally discovered that he had in his possession a document containing a full account of the country and its inhabitants. It was assumed that his object was to betray the Ahoms to the Muhammadans, and he was arrested and put to death."[2]

During the rule of Sib Singh (1714-44) extensions were made to the capital. A census (Piyal) survey was taken of the country around Kamrup and Bakata. The survey register was known as the Pera Kagaz. Garhgaon's fame had spread far beyond Assam's frontiers and "in 1739 four Europeans, whose names appear to have been Bill, Godwin, Lister and Mill, visited Sibsing at Rangpur.[3] The illustrated manuscript, Samkhachudauadha, records the event. It contains the portraits of the four Europeans, along with those of the king, queen and nobles.*

The city of Rangpur was bounded breadthwise by the rivers Dikhau and Nawhang, and lengthwise by the Singh Duar and the Machhkhowa Garh. Within the city walls was the royal city, encircled by a masonry embankment 18 cubits high. Outside it were the houses of the nobles. The area of the royal city was 423 Puras, 3 Bigha, 2 Kottas and 8 Lochas. Three gates led to the royal city ; the Barduar (the Big Gate) in the south, the Paniduar (the Water Gate) in the East and the Na'duar (the New Gate) in the west. The outer embankment was known as the Baj Garh and it contained the Palace as well as the Bhitar Garh (inner embankment) and other buildings. The Bhitar Garh also had three gates, of which the Darika Duar in the south was the main entrance. The other two gates were known as the Chaudang Duar and were in the charge of Chaudangs. Of these, one was the Kalugayan Duar (Ligiri Duar or Mati Gharar Duar) and the other was the Kamalabaria Duar (Gossaingharia Duar or the Chapel Gate). Between the Baj Garh and the Bhitar Garh was the Barchara (main hall). At the

1. Gogoi, L., Buranjie Parasha Nagar, p. 2.
2. Gait, E A., A History of Assam, p. 176.
3. Ibid, p. 190.

* The above manuscript is deposited in the Department of Historical and Antiquarian Studies, Government of Assam, Gauhati.

head of the Barchara was the Batchara (Gate-House). The Kaluganyan Duar was used by the wives and daughters of high officials for going to the Princess's school (Kuanri Tol). The abbots used the Gossaingharia Duar for going to the king to offer him the Prasad or sacrament from the temples. The Barchara was used for the Bar Mel or general assembly, like the Diwan-i-Am of the Mughals. The Barchara was 120 cubits long and 40 cubits wide along the dais. The Ahom counterpart of the Diwan-i-Khas was the Bhitaria Mel. It was held in the Baghar.

The chief buildings of the capital were the Talatal Ghar Palace (1765), the Kharghar Arsenal (1704), the Isanisvara Devalaya (1773), the Ranganath Dol (1704), the Haragauri Dol (West of Ranganath), the Phakua Dol (1704), the Ranghar (Sports Pavilion of Rudra Singh), the masonry Ranghar (1746), Rajeswar Singha's smaller Ranghar, the Natigosain Dol, etc. Many bridges spanned the ditches and rivers around the capital. On these the Namdang Silsako (1703) was the biggest. The royal roads were the Dubariani Ali (Northern), the Paniduariya Ali and the Khari Katiya Ali. Other detached buildings were the Barpalsa Dal and the Bagidal.[1] The temple complexes and tanks at Jaysagar and Gaurisagar were also satellite settlements to the capital city of Rangpur. The temples will be described under the heading Architecture. The Japagar complex has 5 temples while 3 main temples stand at Gaurisagar. In Rangpur the building associated with the Muslims was the shrine built by King Pratap Singh[2] for Shah Milan or Azan Pir. Shah Milan preached Islam in Assam and was respected by the king.

The generally unstable conditions of Gaurinath Singh's reign were responsible for the decline of Rangpur. Yet the accounts of Welsh show that the capital maintained its former glory. He says that Rangpur "was a large and thickly populated town, twenty miles in extent. In the centre was an enclosure, similar to that found at Gauhati. The surrounding country had been very highly cultivated. The nobles held large tracts of land, which were tilled by their slaves".[3]

Gauhati was another important city of the Ahom, though in the initial stages it changed hands between the Mughals and the Ahoms. Although Gauhati ceased to be the national capital during the Ahom period, it still was the biggest town in Lower Assam. It was also the gateway to Assam, in the true sense of the term, though the actual frontier was about 100 miles to the west.

During the Koch period Gauhati became important. Parikshit shifted his capital to North Gauhati and built a palace near the Asvakranta hill.[4] It

1. Gogoi, L., Buranjie Parasha Nagar, pp. 4, 6, 7, 8, 9, 10, 12, 13, 14.
2. Handiqui, B., Guide to Sibsagar, 3rd ed. 1960, Jaysagar, p. 11.
3. Gait, E.A., A History of Assam.
4. Ibid., p 65.

eventually became the seat of the Mughal Thanadar Mir Nurullah.[1] But it was recaptured under the command of Lachit Barphukan and was made the seat of Bar Phukan.[2]

Gauhati, being a place of pilgrimage—it had the famous Kamakhya temple and a number of other temples—was primarily a city of temples. It was also a trading post. A detailed account of its condition in the late 18th century is found in the writings of Capt. Welsh. "At that time Gauhati was an extensive and populous town. It was situated on both banks of the Brahmaputra and extended to the neighbouring hills Along a portion of the river bank there was a rampart, on which were mounted one hundred and thirteen guns of different calibre, including three of European manufacture. The only other fortification of any kind was a large oblong enclosure, a hundred yards from the river, surrounded by a brick wall six feet in height, with a narrow wet ditch inside and out, and containing a thatched building, so large that the whole of the detachment found accommodation in it."[3]

Dimapur was the most important of the tribal capitals, the others being Maibong and Khaspur for the Kacharis, and Jayantapur, for the Syntengs. By the first quarter of the 16th century Dimapur was at the peak of her glory and beauty. But the town collapsed and was abandoned by the rulers after their crushing defeats at the hands of the Ahoms in 1536.

"The ruins of Dimapur, which are still in existence, show that, at that period the Kacharis had attained a state of civilization considerably in advance of that of the Ahoms. . . . Dimapur, on the other hand, was surrounded on three sides by a brick wall of the aggregate length of nearly two miles, while the fourth or southern side was bounded by the Dhansiri river."[4] But Gait also mentions local sources, according to which there was also a wall on the southern side of the city.[5] On the eastern side was a solid brick gateway with a pointed arch, its stones pierced to receive the hinges of heavy double doors. It was flanked by octagonal turrets of solid brick, the intervening distance to the central archway being relieved by false windows of ornamental moulded brick-work.

The curved battlement of the gateway, as well as the pointed arch over the entrance, point directly to the Bengali style of Muhammadan architecture. . . . The excellence of the mortar is shown by the fact that, although the building has evidently been shaken on various occasions by earthquakes, it is still in a ground

1. Gait, E.A., A History of Assam. p. 120.
2. Ibid., p. 158.
3. Ibid, p. 222.
4. Ibid., pp. 301-302.
5. Bloch, T., Archaeological Survey of India, Annual Report 1902-03. p. 302.

state of preservation. Inside the enclosure are some ruins of a temple or perhaps a market-place, the most notable feature of which is a double row of carved pillars of sandstone, averaging about 12 feet in height and 5 feet in circumference."[1]

Some of these huge pillars are curiously shaped cylinders, with a narrow neck topped by a smooth bulbous top. These definitely represent huge lingams as their shapes show. These are somewhat like the Mukhalingam, of the Sunga period, at Gudimallam in the Krishna river valley. The Kacharis also regard the cylindrical thorny cactus which grows in Assam as Siva, the primordial progenitor who is associated with the cult of the phallus. Similarly, they worship as Sakti another variety of cactus which has flat eliptical branches, because its shape resembles the Yonimandala of the Sivalingam. Thus the phallic significance of the cylindrical pillars appears certain.

There are some stylised stone pillars in the Dimapur group which are flat and imitate plant shapes similar to the cactus. There are also some curious V-shaped pillars which are apparently memorial stones. The nearest point at which the sandstone for these pillars could have been quarried is at least ten miles distant. It seems probable that rough blocks of sandstone were brought, set up and then carved on site ; otherwise, they would definitely have been damaged during transportation and erection.

"No two are precisely alike in ornamentation. But all are of one general form, having large semi-circular tops, with concentric foliated carving on the shafts. There are representations of the elephant, deer, dog, duck and peacock, but nowhere is there a human form or head. The inference seems that at that time the Kacharis were free from all Hindu influences."[2] But this contention of Gait does not seem correct, because the Kacharis had been well-nigh Hinduised even before the entry of the Ahoms into Assam in the 13th century. At that period the Kacharis were already known as the Varahis, betraying their Vishnuite leanings. The Charaideo hill was also known as the Vihagadri, claiming association with the bird-god Garuda. Even their tribal deities were but adaptations of Siva and Sakti from the Hindu pantheon. The Kachari kings called themselves Hedombesvara, or the Lord of the Hidimba country. They claimed descent from Ghatotkacha, the son of Hidimba and Bhima, the second Pandava. This association with Hidimba gave the name to their capital, which is but a shorter form of Hidimbapura, or the city of Hidimba. Also, the Kacharis are culturally the most Hinduised of all Assam tribals. They have adopted the Assamese language as the medium of education and correspondence, among themselves and with those outside their fold.

1. Gait, E.A., A History of Assam, pp. 301-302.
2. Ibid., p. 302.

"There are several fine tanks at Dimapur, two of which are nearly 300 yards square."[1] The accounts of Granga, who visited Dimapur in 1839, say that local tradition ascribes the founding of the city to "Chakradhvaj, the fourth Kachari king." Gait's chronology of Kachari kings does not mention the above king at all and the fourth king is Satrudaman,[2] alias Pratap Narayan (1606-10 A.D.). The Kacharis ascribed the destruction of Dimapur "to Kala Pahar, but admitted that they were defeated by the Ahoms about the same time."[3]

After the sacking of Dimapur, "the Kachari kings established themselves at Maibong, a place on the bank of the Mahur river, surrounded by a wall, inside of which the remains of several temples are still visible."[4] The most interesting monument at Maibong, an unfinished rock-hewn temple, was excavated in the Sak year 1633 (1721 A.D.) during the reign of Harish Chandra Narayan described as 'Lord of Hidimba'.[5] But the name of Maibong had by then been changed to Kirtipura [6] by Satrudaman, alias (1606 A.D.) Pratap Narayan. The rock cut inscription at the above temple, dedicated to goddess Ranachandi, gives the precise date as the 5th of Margasira saka 1643 (1721 A.D.).[7] The temple is perched on a huge boulder out of which the structure has been hewn. Externally it resembles a typical Bengali hut[8] (Dochala type). It measures 21′ x 11′. But temple was evidently not completed, since it had not been hollowed out when work was stopped.[9] Another stone inscription at Maibong refers to the building of a stone gateway by a king, Meghanarayana.[10]

The last seat of government was Khaspur, which has about seven important buildings, all built before 1754 A.D.[11] An inscription at Khaspur, dated 1771 A.D., refers to the building of a palace there by King Harishchandra Narayan[12]. It was a brick-city. Though the buildings were not very large they had delicacy of form and line. Terracotta decorations enhanced the beauty of these buildings. The chief among the structures are the Snan Mandir, on the bank of the Madhura river, the main Ranachandi temple, the Singh Darwaza and the Baradwari.

1. Gait, E.A., A History of Assam p. 302.
2. Ibid., p. 419.
3. Ibid., p. 303.
4. Ibid., p. 303.
5. Ibid., p. 308.
6. Ibid., p. 308.
7. Archaelogical Survey of India Annual Report, ; 1905-'07, p. 19.
8. Archaeological Survey of India, Annual Report, Eastern circle, 1913-14, part II, ch. I, p. 29.
9. Bloch, T. R., Archaeological Survey of India, Annual Report Bengal Circle, April 1903, p. 22.
10. Archaeological Survey of India, Annual Report, circle, 1913-14, part II, Ch. I, p. 29.
11. Ibid., p. 29.
12. Gait, E.A., A History of Assam. p, 308.

The Jaintia capital, on the western slopes of the Khasi-Jaintiaa Hills, was called Jayantapur, or Nizpat Jayantapur. Apart from the palace, the grand temple of Jainteswari, the patron deity, was the important building which gave its name to the capital. The temple housed the icon of the goddess brought by Jasa Manik (1605-25) from Koch Bihar.[1]

Another king "Lakshmi Narayan (1669-97 A.D), built a palace at Jaintiapur.[2]. . . . There is an inscription on the gateway in which its erection by Lakshmi Narayan is set forth. It bears an indistinct date which has been read as 1632 Sak, equivalent to 1710 A.D. But since Ram Singh was ruling in 1707, there must be some mistake. The correct reading is perhaps 1602 sak or 1680 A.D.

The Jainteswari temple is unique because of the striking similarity of the bas-reliefs on its outer walls to those on the outer walls of the Bayon temple, Angkor Thom, in Cambodia. The most remarkable scene is one showing the cultivation of land by huge, almost life-size elephants. The elephants, driven by mahouts, are drawing enormous ploughs. Perhaps this was actually practised at Jayantapur, since the city, being at the foot of a hill, has a rocky soil difficult to be tilled by oxen or buffalos. The Khasi-Jayantiyas were linguistically of the same stock as the Mon-Khmer people of Cambodia. Some unrecorded links might have existed between the two sections of the same linguistic groups. Thus we can try to explain the similarity between the Jayantia and Khmer relief sculptures.

No account of the cities and towns of the Ahoms would be complete without mentioning the necropolis at Charaideo, which contained hundreds of graves of royal personages, princes, nobles and other dignitaries. Though the graves, or the Maidams, were built at other places like Jorhat, Gauhati and Goalpara also, according to the exigencies of the times, yet Charaideo occupies a position easily comparable to the cities of the dead in ancient Egypt and Shang China, though on a smaller scale. As will be elaborated in the section on architecture, the graves contained funeral chambers filled with articles for the use of the dead person, including his slaves and attendants. These Maidams became rich stores of gold and jewellery. As a result, the invaders' eyes fell on the sacred graves. Many of these were desecrated and plundered by the Mughals and the Burmese.

The Ahom royal circles, before their conversion to Hinduism, buried their dead. Afterwards, they burnt the dead and then raised a Maidam over the

1. Gait, E.A., A History of Assam, p. 315.
2. Ibid., p. 316.

ashes. Maidams of the latter type were raised over the remains of kings Rajeswar Singha, Lakshmi Singha and Purandar Singha. The ashes were either taken to Charaideo, the ancestral cemetry, or were entombed at the place of cremation itself.

The area between Bibubar and Mathurapur, in the Charaideo region, has hundreds of Maidams built in regular rows and groups. Some royal graves lie at Sargua also. The Maidams of the nobility are to be found at Kunduguri, Bakata, Sekerapar, Khatpathar, and Charing.[1] Like other public and royal buildings, the Maidams were also under the supervision of the Changrung Phukan, his Maidams Phukan and the Maidamia Paiks.[2]

2. Architecture : Wooden

Wood and bamboo structures were made both for religious and lay purposes by common folk as well as by the royalty till the Tungkhungiya period. Even in the Tungkhungiya period no commoner was allowed to build in stone and masonry or to make houses with domes.[3] These were privileges of the royalty. The huge Satras like the Kamalabari were almost wholly built in wood and embellished lavishly with carvings and paintings.

In domestic architecture there was a general plan, though individual variations were often seen. In a land lashed for half the year by torrential rain every thought was given to this phenomenon of nature in house building. Thus in many ways house plans corresponded rather to those of China and Japan than to those of the rest of India. Non-Hindu or half-Hindu tribes like the Miris and the fisherfolk or Doms often built pile dwellings near swamps and river sides to protect the house from rains. These were generally known as the Chang-ghar or houses raised on platforms. But Brahmins and orthodox Hindus of the upper castes always shunned such houses, even though geographical reasons demanded their use, because they were mainly associated with non-Aryan tribes.

Even then everybody raised the plinths as much as possible in proportion to the house. This was done to protect from clogged rain water and dampness. The plinth was often reinforced with bamboo mats and frames. Usually the rural houses were plain and planned with utilitarian motives. The absence of a strict caste system in Assam due to the prevalence of the Eka Sarana Nama Dharma led to the decline of caste-ordained occupational groups as in other parts of Assam. Almost everybody preferred to be a owner-cultivator of his lands. The puritanical attitude of the neo-Vaishnavites was also the case of the general simplicity of the Assamese people At least this is the case now.

1. Gogoi, L., Buranjie Parasha Nagar, pp. 48-49.
2. Handiqui, B.C., (ed) Changhung Phukanar Burani, pp. 5. Part I, Jaysagar, 1959.
3. Barua, B.K., Asamar Loka Sanskriti, p. 129.

The commonest materials after earth were wood, bamboo, ikra (reeds) and straw for roofing. In the plains too where the land was low people raised Bharal Ghars or grain-stores and silos on the principle of the Chang-ghars of the tribals. In the hills tribals built their Chang-ghar on very tall poles so that wild animals would pass under them and leave the houses alone. There wood was easily available and hence people built mostly in wood.[1]

In the premises of the house the following separate units were raised :

1. *Chara Ghar*, or Alahi Ghar. This was the guest room. It had two sloping roofs and was at right angles with the rest of the house. It was connected with the rest of the house by means of a corridor known as the Naora or the Dighali Bat. A separate door opened to the outer courtyard.

Bar Ghar	—	the main room.
Saru Ghar	—	the lesser room.
Maral Ghar	—	the store room.
Sowani Ghar	—	the bed room.
Bulani Ghar	—	the living room or the lounge.
Randhani Ghar or Pak-Ghar	—	Kitchen.
Dhekisal	—	The husking shed.
Tantsal	—	The loom-shed.
Gohali Ghar	—	the cow-pen.
Bharal Ghar	—	the grain store.
Batchara	—	the gate house.
Nam-ghar or Gossain-ghar or Kirtan ghar	—	The private chapel, with or without the image of Vishnu or Krisna. A Bhagavata is kept instead.

All the rooms had two doors, one at the front and one at the back. Normally there were no windows. But due attention was paid to ventilation. Open passages were left between the roofs and the top of the side walls. But in some houses a bamboo lattice was fixed here and these were known as the Dhapalika or Sialtati. Usually all the Ghars were divided by partitions to increase the number of rooms. But the Chara-Ghar was not so divided and was reserved for receiving guests and accommodating them. In winter members of the family gathered in the evening around the fireplace there. The kitchen was on the last row and was

1. Barua, B.K., Asamar Loka Sanskriti, p. 129.

a little detached from the rest of the house for reasons of cleanliness. Nobody was allowed to enter the kitchen without taking a bath and changing his dress also, for the same reason. The cow-pen was further back but it normally had no side walls.

Before building a house people consulted astrologers and the older folk of the locality about the selection of the site, facing the house in the right direction and breaking ground at the proper and suspicious moment. The aphorisms of Dak and Khana, the great woman astrologer, were also followed carefully. For example, an aphorism of Dak lays the following conditions for choosing the site of a house. "It should face the east and should have its back to the west. To the east should be planted cane and to the west a bamboo grove. To the north should be the areca nut palms and the cultivable lands to the south."[1] These sayings were based on actual experience of the climatic and geographical peculiarities of the reign. A similar saying ascribed to Khana is also prevalent in rural Bengal. It says, "there should be pond with ducks in the east and bamboo groves in the west, while the north shall be covered and protected and the south should be laid open. "In both the cases the east is left half closed only, to catch the rays of the rising sun, while the west is chattered by the bamboo groves to protect the house from the scorching rays of the afternoon sun in a tropical setting. The south was left open to receive the cool breeze of the sea.

In the process of building the first step was raising the plinth after enclosing the plinth area with bamboo matting about a couple of feet high. This enclosure was filled with earth, which was usually brought from some good field. Before filling the plinth area was dug over and searched for skeletal or other remains of men or beasts, as these were regarded as inauspicious. The section of the plinth which was outside the actual matting walls was the Pirali or Kanthi. The next stage was planting the central post. It was called Ghai Khuta, Bar Khuta, or the Mula Khuta, all meaning the chief pole. In Assam and Cooch Bihar people tied a piece of red cloth around the top of the Bar-Khuta for auspicious reasons. Other poles were known as Mudhar Khuta, Kumar Khuta, Panir Khuta or Parir Khuta.

Sometimes the bottom ends of the poles were burnt a little to check the attacks of insects, and before planting sand was put into the holes instead of earth for the same purpose. When the holes went too deep for the hands to reach them bamboo contraptions with one split end were inserted to catch the loose earth in order to remove it These were called Thokar ot Khonkauri.

1. Barua, B.K., Asamar Loka Sanskriti, p. 131

Common Varieties of Wood Used

Sal, Salakh, Sonaru, Nahar, Padma, Maj, Amari, Nagatenga, Bansoum, Teli Ui, Thekera, Jamu (Plum), Nim (Margosa), Gamari, Silikha (Haritaki), Karoi, Gandha saroi, Kanhir, Ajar, Panja, Sam, and Pama. Bhaluka bamboo was used for other structures while the Makal bamboo was specially used for the cow-pen poles. Sometimes the trunks of Tal, (Palmyra) and Tambula or Tamal (areca nut palm), and Chowa were used as readymade poles.

For fixing the central pole of the roof and the triangular sections of the gable various types of slot were made on the respective poles. These were of three types, al, kan, and kukur. The gable triangle was the Chati. The simpler type was the Bharahua Chati while the elaborate type, with a king-post and two queen-posts, as in Chinese architecture, was the Phul Chati or the Saru-chati. There were thus three chatis in a building—one in the middle and two at the ends. The two long poles running lengthwise along the bottoms of the chatis were known as Panipotar Marali. The Maralis are either 3 or 5 in number. To prevent sagging of the roof bamboos of the breadth of the roof were laid across joining the central and side Maralis. These were the Jali Banh. The wooden chatis were often decorated with carvings of lotuses etc.

The roofs were usually sloping with only two slanting members. This type is known as the Duchalia. The lattice-like framework of the roof was covered with various kinds of thatch. Thicker varieties of bamboo like the Bhaluka and Jati were split to make the Kami, Rurva or Jethi, the strips of the frame. The thinner bamboos like Mutukia were used whole for this purpose. To prevent the Kamis from decomposition due to rains and insects, these were immersed in water for a few days for seasoning. The horizontal strips were known as Kamis while the vertical ones, which were split and interlaced with the Kamis were the Ruwas or Jethis.

Roofs were of two kinds depending on the technique of binding the frame, Hendali Chal : Sitali Chal : for this type the Kamis pressed down the Jethis and all were tied severely. Various kinds of vines and vegetable fibres were used for binding the different members of the roof as well as other members of the structure. The commonest were thin scrapings from bamboos, called the Tamal, cane and the Dhekia vine. The knots were also very varied, Mata, Rupahi, Tapa, Thopa, Randhani, and Hatisangora. The roof was fixed in two separate pieces, which were never joined first and then raised up to the framework. It was said that people who live under such a roof have endless quarrels. While fixing the roof tying was done from the Mudh pole to the Kum pole and the Panipota pole.

For thatching straw of the Ulu, Saran, Barota was used. Old Buruli straw was also used for a lower stratum on which the new straw was laid, tightly bound between the Kamis and then tied with Tamals of two different kinds, Nalia and Patia or Pithia. Other materials for thatching were the leaves of the Takau and Jengu. While laying the bundles of straw they were first arranged at the Panipota and then gradually laid towards the top or Mudhach. These were sumed by tying and this was known as Madaliwa. The protecting straw from the Panipota was the Aola and these were to be trimmed only on an auspicious day. When complete the house was sprinkled with a little water.

Roofs were also of other types, Tini Chalia, Chauchalia, and Tup-dia or domical. The donis were of two types, e g., Golmuria and Kokaria. The general process of roofing is the same. The shed which was sometimes attached to the Mudh was called the Chali. When a house had a low Mudh such a house was called the Chandapara type. The plinth and the floor area were trampled hard by tying cattle there for some days. This was also considered auspicious.

Naoras were inserted to protect the space between two rooms from rain water. These were made from the carved trunk of the Chowa tree, cut in half lengthwise. The Dhapalika fixed at the Tup was known as the Chhoi. The Dhapalika when used for the Namghar was called the Dhekeri Chali.

The Bharal was made in a little different manner. The raised platform for keeping paddy was given four posts called Dhum or Thum made of trunks of trees or stone. On these were laid lengthwise planks of wood or Dham. This was called the Gadhoi or the Gadhari. On it was fixed a bamboo matting wall or Chonghala. The upright sticks were known as Litikai. The two ends of the Choudhola were joined by means of a splintered bamboo called Pota. The inner walls of the Bharal and those of the Mer and the Duli or the paddy silo were all plastered with cowdung only.

Goats needed a raised platform or Chang of bamboo for resting. Sometimes a separate shed was constructed with a Chang for goats or a chang was made in a section of the Gohali itself. Pigeons were kept in the Tangi-ghar which was a small box-like structure on the top of a long pole. Otherwise old broken earthen pitchers were hung from the roof with the mouth parallel to the ground for the birds to enter. Ordinarily a bamboo was hung horizontally from the roof to serve as a roost for pigeons, which were often domesticated. The manuscript of the Lanka Kanda of the Ramayana from the Gauhati University Library shows the various contraptions for keeping pigeons. Ducks, chickens and pigs were kept in round shelters covered on the top and having a small semi-circular entrance. These Garals were of woven bamboo matting fixed to poles in the ground.

Particulars were either of bamboo matting fixed to frames and poles or were made from Ikra reeds and bamboo splinters and scrapings. The bottom of the partition was protected from direct contact with the clay floor by inserting it into a long bamboo pole split lengthwise and cleaned inside. This bamboo pole was the Barta or the Garila. It was raised on a low bamboo leg or Kukur-cut in a special way. At the corners where the two walls meet the Pola bond already described was used. It as well as the walls were plastered with cowdung and clay. To this mixture rice-husk and crushed oil seed cakes were also added. Coloured earth or earth of ant hills was sometimes added in the plaster to colour the walls. In some places earth from crab holes was also used for the same purpose.

Doors and windows were usually of wood and are made by the village Barhoi or carpenter. But simpler and cheaper houses use bamboo and leaves for these. Such doors and window panes were made from leaves of bamboo, Takou and Topar trees. Doors were of the Dang-die, Salakhalagowa and Chochani types. Doors with the Dang or bamboo bolt for closing night be closed from within or without. The door step was fixed with a bamboo pole or Garali or Duar-dali serving as the chaukath. A bamboo lattice was attached at the top of the door in the manner of the Pan—light of Western architecture. The earliest example of this Dhapalika (lattice) is seen in the Lomasha Rishi cave, Gaya. The door was made to revolve on a bamboo hinge or Ghur-Ghuri. Inside a room bamboo mezzanine floors or Atal were sometimes fixed for keeping things not in use at a time. The floor was usually stretched from one Choli to another.

The front and back yards were as important in Assamese domestic architecture as any of the Ghars of other units. Here people relax, do their household work, arrange for New Year dances and hold Nam Kirtans or community prayer meetings. People celebrate on occupying a new house (Ghar-loa-Sabah) and the bride also has to undergo rituals in her new home regarding the house. It is believed that the divinities Ghar-Jeuti (Griha Jyoti) or Laksmi and Isvara reside at the door step and so nobody sits there or kicks at a door. In the front yard people plant cactus and medicinal plants like Akan (Akanda) and Bahak (Vasaka). But some trees like Khakan and tamarind are avoided. In the back yard Tamol (Tambula) or arecanut palms are planted in a row along the compound wall or fence. No construction work is done in the months of Bhadra, Kartika, Pausha, Magha and Chaitra. It is also avoided on Amavasya (new moon) day and during the period of Agnisara. On the day of the New Year or 1st of Baisakh a mantra propitiating Agni is written in a special ink on the leaves of the Nahar (Nageswara) tree and these are tucked into the thatched roof. The ink is prepared by mixing Gorachana and Kumkuma. New Year messages and sayings were hung in Chinese houses also

House building was always a cooperative venture in Assam. People helped each other in every job including procuring raw materials like wood, bamboo and straw from the forests in the month of Phagun or Falguna. The house was not only a place to live in, but also an institution in itself, in a society where the joint family system prevailed. Each family depended on the other for the construction, maintenance and repair of their houses.

The Nam Ghar

Every village or community has its prayer hall or Namghar. In the Satras, however, the Namghar is called the Kirtan Ghar. Some people also call it Gossain Ghar. The adult population divides itself into groups and they work voluntarily for the construction of the Namghar. Such voluntary labour is known as Haj.

The Namghar complex consists of three or four rooms and structures. They usually consist of the Batchara, Chon-ghar and the Manikuta. The Batchara is simple and has only a Duchalia form. Sometimes it is further simplified into the Dhekeri Chali.

The Namghar faces the east. At the western end of the building is the Tup or the tope or dome. The Tup is formed by means of curved kamis which are wrapped with jute or cane. Where the Tup begins a round piece of wood with a handle is inserted into the poles of the Mudhach. The door towards the Tup, being the main door, is called the Mukh-duar. The jambs and the lintel are carved with various designs and this kind of carving is called Meharaji. Doors with carvings of lions are known as Simha-duar and those with floral scrolls are the phul-tetelikata duar. Open faced lotus flowers were also common motifs.

A Namghar consists of three, five or seven chambers. In the last room leaving the area under the Tup is kept the Daba or the drum, either at the northern or the southern end. The Daba is kept on a platform with three legs. The doors are fitted with bolts for closing from within and are fitted with Kalasa shaped handles on the outer side. The doors on both sides of the length of the building are called the Petduar. The wood of the chati is carved with lotus designs. The date of construction is cut into the Bar chati or the main chati which is held by the Lai-khuta or the main pole. An Atal is made, joining the chatis on which are kept the chons and the Mukhas, the masks and other accessories for the Bhaonas or dramatic performances based on the epics and the Puranas.

In a Namghar the first chamber from the east is reserved for the Asana or the Simhasana containing the Bhagavata Book X. Of the next pair of poles the one to the north is the Lai Khuta. To the south, near the Asana, the Brahmanas and women sit to the north of the room. Westwards from the Lai-Khuta sit other devotees. In this arrangement people who are directly connected with the Namghar like the Udasinas and the Bhakats get the front rows. But people of lower classes and tribals occupy the back rows. Although Ekasarana Nama Dharma denounces caste distinction it persists even in the religious life of Assamese Vaisnavism.

In the chamber containing the Asana are placed wooden sculptures of Garuda, Hanuman and Larua-Gopal or Gopala holding a ball of butter. To the left of Asana is kept the Gacha or the main lamp either of wood or of metal such as iron or brass. The elaborate ones have many branches and some even contain a hundred lamps. Such Gachas are known as the Saikiya Gacha. To the south of the Asana is kept the Thaga or the Thagi, the wooden stand for keeping the Bhagavata while the prayer goes on. In a Namghar with no Manikuta arrangements for the Prasada etc. and the utensils and ritual objects are also kept here in the first chamber. In the section to the west of the Laikhuta sits the main reciter or the Nam-lagowa and to his right sit the group of repeaters. During a Bhaona, the Gayan-Bayan, or the choral and orchestral group sit in the section ahead of the one under the Tup. The centre is left free for the dramatis perseonae or the Bhaorias to act. The Manikuta is to the east of the Namghar across the main structure. The Manikuta has a Duchalia roof. This chamber is like the Garbhagriha in a Hindu temple. In this chamber is an Asana, Gacha, Thaga, Tal or brass cymbals for use at special services for the members of the inner circle, such as the Udasinas and others. Women are not allowed in this sanctum sanctorum. In more elaborate structures there is a special chamber for depositing the Padasila and the Kharam or woodened sandals. A separate Chonghar or green room is attached sometimes in greater and richer satras and their Namghars.

3. Masonry Architecture (13th-19th C.)

At first the Ahoms preferred wood to stone and brick though the Koches and the Kacharis had been using the latter even in the early 16th century. Even after the changeover to more solid media the wooden prototype was copied in stone and brick. Even bamboo structures influenced the Sikharas of many Ahom temples. The scope of the new medium of architecture was varied, and it was used for palaces, temples, amphitheatres, pavilions, bridges, city walls, gates and fortifications. Large tanks and royal highways were also paved and secured with bricks and stones. Although there is but little difference in style between the buildings of the Ahoms and the Koches and Kacharis yet their centres can be conveniently marked. The Ahoms built at Rangpur, Jaysagar, Gaurisagar, Neghreting, Jorhat, Gauhati, Dubi and Goalpara, the Koches at Gauhati and Hajo, while the Kacharis centred their activities at Dimapur, Maibong and Khaspur. At Rangamati in Goalpara is the solitary example of brick-built Muslim architecture in the shape of a mosque. Of the many highways mention may be made of the Gohain Kamal Ali and the numerous ones constructed by the Ahoms. The bridges were almost exclusively to the credit of the Ahoms as were the big tanks in Upper Assam. Great schemes of river transport were undertaken by diverting the river Brahmaputra during the early part of Koch rule in West Assam which included considerable portions of northern and some parts of eastern Bengal. Under the Ahoms the Superintendant of Public Works was the Changrung Phukan. He and his department looked after buildings, roads, bridge construction and excavation of tanks and canals for irrigation. The influence of tribal art in the art and architecture of the period is seen in the Chessmen monoliths and V-shaped pillars of the Kacharis from Dimapur. These still remain a mystery. A serpent entwained pillar of stone with inscriptions also falls in this group.

The earliest standing masonry building of the Ahoms is the temple of Umananda on the Peacock Island in the Brahmaputra near Gauhati which was built in the year 1964 by the order of King Gadadhar Singh.[1]

The new fashion of masonry construction gained momentum during the reign of his son and successor Rudra Simha alias Lechai. He assumed the Ahom name Sukrangpha after coronation. His first activity was to construct fortifications at Teji (Namrup). The next move was the building of the new capital Rangpur at the site of the village of Meteka near modern Sibsagar town. It was named Rangpur or the "City of Joy" as the king immensely enjoyed the falconry arranged there by the Bar Phukan for which he was also rewarded by the king. At the site where Jayamati, the king's mother, was tortured to death by the usurper known as the Lora Raja (Boy-King), was excavated the Jayasagar tank. On its bank was constructed the Devi-Dol or the temple of Devi. Next was the Ranganath temple and its tank was also excavated. Then was constructed the Fakua-Dol. Bridges were termed Silsakos or stone-bridges. Two such were constructed at Dimau and one at Namdang. Three highways were constructed at Meteka, Kharikatia and Dubariyani.

The next ruler Siva Singh's reign is marked by architectural schemes far grander than those of rulers before him or of those that followed. The Sildole (1734) was constructed by his second wife Ambika Devi and was originally called the Muktinath temple dedicated to Muktinatha Siva. "Situated on the bank of Sibsagar tank, the great Sildole temple occupies an area of 4½ acres with the height of 83½ cubits. This temple belongs to the Dvaikuta class, containing two walls, a Garbhgriha and a mandapa Over the Garbhgriha rises the Sikhara with fluted vertical lines. The main sikhara is surrounded by its replicas called Uramanjaris". The Sikharas of this type are locally known as the Kardoi-Siria or ribbed like the Kardoi fruit. The other two temples of this group are the Vishnu dol and the Devidol. They are 40 cubits high and have areas of 3 and 2½ acres respectively.

The Devi-dole on the bank of the Gaurisagar near Rangpur belongs architecturally to the Sibsagar group of temples. But it is conspicuous for its finials. In place of the usual amalakas there is a tier of gold-plated kalasas in tapering sizes placed on a solid circular base made of bricks. The outer walls

1. Neog. M., Pavitra Asam, P. 199.

of the temple are all full of bas-relief panels and each episode or figure is framed by a cusped arched niche familiar in mediaeval Assamese figure composition, whether in reliefs or in painting. Technically these panels are related to the wood carving of the earlier epoch of Assamese art.

The temple of Ugratara in Gauhati, those of Kamesvara and Siddhesvara on the Kamakhya hill and the two temples of Janardana at Asvakranta on the opposite bank of Gauhati were all built during the rule of Siva Singha (1714-44 A.D.).

The temples of Suklesvara and Sudesvara were built at the site where Rudra Singha died at Gauhati, by his second son Pramatta Singha (1744-51 A.D.) who had succeeded his elder brother Siva Singha. The Suklesvara temple houses one of the largest Lingams in India.

At Dergaon and Bisnath Siva temples were built by Pratap Singha. During the rule of Rajesvara Singha the largest number of temples were built at different places. Among them the Navagraha and Vasistha are in Gaubati while Manikarnikesvara is on the opposite bank and Dirghesvari is at Goalpara. In the Navagraha temple the nine phallic emblems of Siva covered with cloths of different colours sacred to the nine planetary gods are worshipped. In 1753 a tank was excavated near the hill; this tank still bears the name Silpukhuri or the stone bound tank. A temple to Durga and a group to Siva, Devi, Vishnu, Surya and Ganesa were constructed at Kamakhya and Negheriting respectively. But the king died before the completion the Negheriting temples.

The last great work of temple building was undertaken by Kamalesvara Singha at the Chhatrakara, Gauhati.

The Ahom monarchs did not lag behind in the sphere of secular architecture. Their buildings were mostly of very fine bricks and were often faced with elaborate terracotta panels which were quite distinct in style from traditional Assamese and Indian idioms. But the brick built temples of the period were faced with stone panels with bas-reliefs. Their inspiration is to be sought in prototypes from Cambodia, especially of the Angkor Wat period.

In Garhgaon was situated the famous faced storied place called the Kareng-Ghar—Kareng in Ahom meaning a palace. The palace was surrounded by a brick wall about two miles in circumference. The most interesting structure of the period is the Rang-Ghar at Rangpur opposite the Talatali Ghar palace The Rang-Ghar as the name suggests was a "house of enjoyment", and in fact it was a pavilion in the royal amphitheatre where orts, parades and folk dances were held on joyous occasions like Rangali Bihu or New Year's Day (13th-14th April) and the like. It was a two storied bricks structure, originally decorated with terracotta panels. A flight of high steps led directly to the first floor where the king alighted from the back of his elephant. Like many contemporary structures it was also derived from "Post and Plank" architecture in wood. It has a double apsidal roof of thatched houses. Even the overhanging ends of straw and thatch are maintained in brick and mortar. A brick built khel-nau or amusement boat decorates the ridge of the roof. The two ends of the boat have heads of Magars or Makaras. During the rule of Rajesvara Singha, a new seven storeyed palace was built at Rangpur, of which two storeys are underground. Both the Rang Ghar and the Talatali Ghar are about three miles west of modern Sibsagar.

The great dearth of remains of masonry structures in Assam is explained by the fact that the highly aristocratic nature of Ahom society restricted the privilege of building in brick and stone to only a few. Only the king could build a house of brick and mortar. He alone could build a house with two round ends. The nobles built houses with one ronnd end. The houses of the Deodhais were built on piles of about 5 to 6 ft. from the ground and the houses of the common men were set up on the earthen plinth or flush with the ground. Similar houses on stilts are still made by tribals of Assam and are known by the generic name Chang-ghar.

The peculiar funeral rites of the Ahoms necessitated the building of elaborate graves or Maidams for the kings and the aristocracy. Like the ancient Egyptians and Shang period China the Ahoms too equipped their dead with belongings, food and even live attendants for their journey in the nether world. The practice of cremating the dead body dates back to Rajesvara Singha when the Ahoms had been thoroughly Hinduised. In the graves the bodies of the rich were laid in boxes ; a water-pot, cup, da, jhapi (bamboo hat), and a pira (wooden stool) were put inside the box with the corpse (E.R.E. Gait : 264). In the meantime a lofty vault had been erected to house the remains of the sovereign. After keeping the coffin cults, its goods and attendants and "the door would then be shut and earth piled upon the wooden roof of the funeral chamber. They covered the head of the dead very strongly with stout poles.

Architecture of the Kacharis

The centres of the Kacharis were Dimapur on the Dhansiri 45 miles south of Golaghat. After its sack in 1536 by the Ahoms, the capital was deserted by the Kacharis and a new capital was established at Maibong, frther south "The ruins of Dimapur which are still in existence, show, that, at that period, the Kacharis had attained a state of civilization considerably in advance of that of the Ahoms. Though the Ahoms were still tied down to timber construction, "Dimapur, on the other hand, was surrounded on three sides by a brick wall of the aggregate length of nearly two miles while the fourth or the southern side was bounded by the

Dhansiri river. On the eastern side was a fine solid brick gateway, with a pointed arch and stones pierced to receive the hinges of double heavy doors. It was flanked by octagonal turrets of solid brick, and the intervening distance to the central archway was relieved by false windows of ornamental moulded brick-work. The curved battlement of the gateway, as well as the pointed arch over the entrance, point distinctly to the Bengali style of Muhammadan architecture." (Gait. 302) "The excellence of the mortar is shown by the fact that, although the building has evidently been shaken on various occasions by earthquakes, it is still in a good state of preservation. Inside the enclosure . . . . are some ruins of a temple, or perhaps a market place, the most noble feature of which is a double row of carved pillars of sandstone averaging about 12 feet in height and 5 feet in circumference. There are also some curious V-shaped pillars which are apparently memorial stones." The stones were brought from a distance of 10 miles at the nearest and they might have been brought as roughly cut blocks which were sculpted in situ. The essentially phallic shape of the pillars point to their affinity with dolmens and menhirs. In the V-shaped pillars there is the representation of Siju plants, a variety of cactus sacred to the Kacharis. There can hardly be any doubt about the motive and ritual nature of these curious pillars often described as the Chess-men monoliths. "No two are precisely alike in the ornamentation, but all are of one general form, having large semi-circular tops, with concentric foliated carving below on the shaft. There are representation of the elephant, deer, dog, duck and peacock, but nowhere is there a human form or head. The inference seems to be that, at this time, the Kacharis were free from all Hindu influences."[1] In scheme and designs the diagrams on the pillars are akin to those on Kachari textiles even today. Dimapur can boast of a number of huge tanks excavated by the kings. The foundation of Dimapur is ascribed traditionally to "Chakradvaja, the fourth Kachari king." The same tradition says that the city owes its destruction to the invasions of the Ahoms and Kala Pahar. The old city at Kasomani Pathar on the Dayang river was also built by the Kacharis.[2]

The new seat of Kachari power was at Maibong on the Mahur river in Cachar district. But it was also invaded in the middle of the 16th century by the Koches under Chilarai, the brother of Naranarayan. In the beginning of the 17th century the Kacharis subjugated the Jaintias and detained the heir-apparent Jas-Manik at Brahmapur which was later on renamed Khaspur, perhaps due to its association with the Khasi-Jayantia prince. Soon after Jas-Manik was released to succeed to the Jayantia throne. Now he conspired with the Ahoms

1. Gait, E.A., A History of Assam, p. 302.
2. Ibid., p. 303.

for a reprisal against the Kacharis. There was a clash between the Ahoms and the Kacharis as hoped by Jas-Manik. But the Ahoms were defeated by the Kacharis at Raha and to commemorate this victory the Kachari King renamed his capital from Maibong to Kirtipur. The name of the king was also changed from Satrudaman to Pratap Singha.

The next important architectural activity was undertaken in 1721 A.D. The inscription on the rock-cut temple mentions that it was excavated at Maibong by orders of king Harish Chandra Narayan, the "Lord of Hidimba". Another king of the line also bearing the name Harish Chandra Narayan titled Bhupati (1771-90 A.D.) is also mentioned in an inscription at Khaspur having erected a palace there in 1771 A.D.[1] In 1790 king Krishna Chandra and his brother Govind Chandra formally accepted Hinduism and accepted Ranachandi[2] as their titulery deity who was amalgamated with the goddess Kali. A temple was built to Ranachandi at Khaspur. It is a structure in brick with a 'Bengali' thatched roof and has a high base. On the three sides are three false doors separated by pilasters while the other side has the entrance. The roof is of the "Eka Sirsa Chauchal" type.[3] Near this temple are two interesting structures, viz., the Baraduari and the Snana-Mandira on the bank of the Madhura or Mahur river. The Baraduari was a tower or a pavilion built on the pattern of the Ranachandi temple. But it has a base as high as one storey. The ground floor appears to have been false, added only with the view to accentuate the height of the edifice. It is called Baraduari as there are twelve doors, three on each side. The Snana Mandir has an elegant dome with projecting Chajjas below it. The dome is a variety of the 'onion' type but greatly flattened. It tops a single celled pavilion. This structure is connected with bathing, but some ascribe it to the goddess while others to the queens and princesses of the Kacharis.

Architecture under the Koches

The Koches of Western Assam were united under Bisu, the son of Haria Mandal of Chiknajhar in the Kuntaghat Pargana of Goalpara district. By 1515 A.D. he subjugated a large section of the ancient kingdom of Kamarupa between the Karatoya in the west and the Barnadi in the east. After his formal entry into the Kshatriya fold he started to reorganize orthodox Hinduism which was in jeopardy in this part of Kamarupa due to crypto-Buddhism and the rise of the

1. Gait, E.A., A History of Assam, p. 308.
2. Gosh, D. & Mitra, p., Itihaser Khaspur (Bengali), Amrita (Magazine). Baisakha 1371 B.E.
3. Ibid.

Naths and Sahajiyas. "He revived the worship of Kamakhya, rebuilt her temple on the Nilachala hill at Gauhati. . . ."[1] He moved his capital from Chikanagram to Koch Bihar where he built a fine city.[2] He then adopted the name Bisva Singha to denote his Kshtriya origin. Bisva Singha died about 1540 and was succeeded by his son Nara Narayana[3] (Malla Deb) after a Brief war of succession. He soon clashed with the Ahom power in Eastern Assam. To reach the Ahoms in their own home he had a 350 km long highway built which was completed in 1547 A.D.[4] under the supervision of the king's brother Gohain Kamol and thus it is still known as Gohain Kamal Ali or Gohain Kamal's road. It reached from Koch Bihar to Narayanpur in the N. Lakhimpur subdivision. They also built a fort at Narayanpur.

The renovated temple of goddess Kamakhya was destroyed by Kala Pahar, the general of the Nawab of Gaur in 1553 A.D. while the Koch king was busy fighting the Ahoms.[5] "But the work of reconstruction of the desecreted temple was immediately taken up by the devout king. The work of reconstruction was entrusted first to one Mahat Ram Vaisya, but he was soon removed for misappropriation of funds and Megha Makdum took over charge. A stone inscription in Kamakhya temple records that in "Sake Turanga Gaja Veda Sasanka Samkhye, i.e., 1487 Saka or 1665 A.D. the temple was finished and dedicated with much enthusiasm."[6] A reconstruction on the Sikhara of the temple was attempted. The lower portion which belongs to the 9th-10th et. period was left as it had been. This spire has a characteristic of its own, met with only in the mediaeval temples of Assam and Bengal. "The Sikhara is halfway in between a real dome and a true spire."[7] This type of dome has been termed as the Lahara Sikhara by Prof. S.K. Saraswati. Since the Sikhara is formed of over-hanging rings formed of stone pieces arranged in that way. As a result the outer side of the roof gave the appearance of a rather wavy outline rather than a smooth spire. The term is derived from Lahara or waves of the sea. Examples of this type of dome are restricted to Kamrup district, Bakreswar in Bengal and Ramgarh on the Damodar river in Hazaribagh district. Rajmohan Nath calls this type of domes the 'Nilachala type' due to their preponderance on the Nilachala Hill, Gauhati and other parts of Kamrup district.

1. Gait, E.A., A History of Assam, p. 50.
2. Ibid.
3. Ibid, p. 52.
4. Ibid., p. 53.
5. Ahmad, K.C.A., Koch Beharer Itihasa, p. 103.
6. Das Gupta, R., An Architectural Survey of the Kamakhya Temple, p. 2.
7. Ibid., p. 11.

The Sikhara of the Kamakhya temple

As a dome it is not full-fledged like those from the late mediaeval temples of Gujarat and Rajputana, whereas it cannot be called a true curvilinear sikhara of the Nagara type. The base of the Mulamanjari is sixteen-sided and the sides rise up almost vertically with very little tendency towards converging to the centre in giving it shape of a dome. This process continues up to the middle of the Mulamanjari, after attaining which there is a sudden tendency towards converging and attaining height till the Sikhara is complete. The Sikhara is essentially a dome rather than a pure Nagara type Sikhara. . . .Another distinguishing feature of the dome is that about twenty projecting horizontal bands decorate the Mulamanjari from the base up to the Skandha of the Sikhara. This reminds one of the wooden spire of the Rathas of Lord Jagannatha and possibly of wooden architecture of one epoch gone by. On the whole the Mulamanjari appears to be a structural prototype of a wooden dome formed of a number of horizontal and vertical batons of wood having a wide and gradual curve. The blanks left in the framework of the dome and filled in as it were with separate and rectangular boards of wood. The horizontal baton like members on the Mulamanjari have small round medallions attached to them at regular intervals for decorative purpose."[1] Similar imitation of wooden and bamboo structures is seen in the Kesavaraya temple of Visnu from Jaysagar in Sibsagar. But here the Sikhara is truer in form and the copy is of a bamboo framework covered with matting and decorated with memerous rosette shaped medallions.

Again turning to the topmost section of the Kamakhya temple we find that it also has a distinct character. "The topmost members or the Padmakosha containing the Amalaka and the Kalasas rise abruptly from the top of the Sikhara, there being no conspicuous Skandha intervening in between. There are three Amalmaka-like members one on the top of another each being smaller in size than the one below. They are not true Amalakas, but are formed of fullbloomed lotuses placed face to face, one top of another. There are no vertical ribs as in the Amalakas of Orissa, but the petals of the lotuses serve the purpose. On the top of these there are three globular members forming the finial and the base for the Kuta which in this case is a Trisula, the symbol of Devi.[2]

That the original sikhara of the temple before its rediscovery by Visva Singha or reconstruction by Nara Narayana was of the true Nagara form is gleaned from the following facts. Firstly, near the temple with its 16th et. Sikhara is a rock-cut depiction of a true Nagara style "temple with an impressive Sikhara".

1. Das Gupta, R., An Architectural Survey of the Kamakhya Temple, pp. 11-12.
2. Ibid , p. 13.

From the very depiction of a temple of the above order in a relief that appears contemporary to the original temple, can we not say that the model the sculptor had before him was the temple of Kamakhya nearby ?"[1] Secondly, we have outside the western gateway a huge stone Kalasa approximately five feet high with a hole in the centre."[2] It is the Kalasa of the original Sikhara. If the Kalasa at present is about a foot high and the earlier one 5 feet in height we can well imagine the height of the original sikhara through a comparison with present sections. It was a ponderous sikhara, tall and elegant like the Orissan and the Chandella prototypes and exactly like the one depicted in the relief nearby The large number of original sculptures and reliefs there also point to the 9th-10th ct. A.D. period for the original temple.

Other acts of renovations were undertaken at Hajo where the ancient and dilapidated temple of Hayagriva-Madhava was rebuilt and repaired[3] by Nara Narayana. The temple was further renovated by Raghudeva in 1583 A.D.[4] Naranarayana is also said to have installed the Banesvara Siva.

After the death of Raghudeb in 1603 A.D. his son Parikshit ascended the throne of the Eastern Koch kingdom. He built a palace at his new capital Asvaklanta near North Gauhati.[5]

4. The Royal Graves or Maidams

The graves of the Ahom royal house were divided into many a section. The bottommost part was the Garbhagriha or the Garbha. At the top was a small furenary shrine with a Ghata finial. Normally these shrines were brick built and had four overhanging caves known as the Charichalia type. Sometimes a Maidam had three storeys also. A brick-built staircase ran up to the top of the grave. The entire Maidam was surrounded by a masonry wall of tall proportions. The funerary shrine too was similarly surrounded and had Toranas piercing the wall.

The construction of the masonry Garbhagriha was preceded by covering it entirely with earth except the small funerary temple. Thus in course of time when tropical vegetation covered the Maidam entirely it looked like a natural mound topped by a small temple.

The Maidams of Charaideo

There are hundreds of Maidams in rows stretching for about 5 or 6 miles from the Pond of Lengibar to Nimanagarh in the Charaideo region. These

1. Das Gupta, R., An Architectural Survey of the Kamakhya Temple, p. 13,
2. Ibid., p. 14.
3. Journal of the Asiatic Society of Bengal, 1855, p. 10.
4. Ahmad, K.C.A., Koch Biharer Itihasa, p. 125.
5. Gait, E.A., History of Assam, p. 65.

belonged only to the kings and members of the royal family. Others were not allowed to build Maidams on these spots. Wherever the king died his body or relic ashes were brought here for entombment. The graves of ladies were to the west of the Deosal of Dol-Bagan while those of the men were to the east.

The graves of the few last kings were not built at Charaideo due to political disturbances. They were as following :

Gauhati——King Chandra Kanta Singh Charing Raja ;

Jorhat——King Purandar Singha Charing Raja ;

Goalpara——Yogeshwar Singha.

The details of burial procedure

The body of the king was taken to Charaideo along the highway Sha-'Nia Ali which is identified with the present Gomotha Ali. After death the body of the king was kept embalmed for a long time with full honour. It was kept in a small necropolis identifiable with present Gomotha. The ponds were named after their use as the corpse-washing pond (sha-'Dhoa Pukhuri), or the spade-washing pond (Kor-dhoa Pukhuri).[1]

The Maidams were looked after by a department under the Maidam Phukan. Under him were the Maidamia Paiks. They looked after the upkeep, rapairs etc. They also looked after the guests and visitors as well as kept in order the approaches and highways. Another officer, the Mochai Phukan, looked after the ceremonial cleaning of the Maidams, offering of lamps and insences to the graves and also the flower gardens around which supplied flowers for funerary rites.

1. The Maidam of Siva Simha

Saka 1666 : **Garbha Griha** —L—12 cubits.

76 : B—10 ,,

———————

A.D. 1642 : H (inner) 14"

H (outer) 19"

Bar Dath—9 (width of walls)

Latha Sil—stone pieces——26000 pieces

Bricks (up to the Tak) ——570000 ,,

Palsil (stone slabs) —— 900 pieces

Gur (blocks) ——

Mah—322 Dnol.

2. From the top of the Tak to the middle of
for
the edifice — a section clay was used as cement
and for
another Surkhi or brick and lime mortar (Karhal)

L—13 cubits) Bricks—87360 pieces.

B—10 „) Gur (blocks)—310

H—13 „) Mah—310 Dhol

Hemp fibre—— 31 seer

Snail lime—— 340 Dhols

Stone lime—— 1060 „

3. **The room on the top**—L (inner) 6 cubits

B „ 4 „

H „ 7 „

Bar Dath Mudhe —2½ cubits.

„ at the back—2 „

L — 11 cubits.

B — 8 „

The Changrung Phukan—Architecture

In the Ahom period public works and building activities were under the Changrung Phukan. A set of three manuscripts on masonry construction during the days of Siva Singha were found in the possession of the late Bhakat Charan Phukan, a direct descendent of the then Changrung Phukan.[1] These deal with the construction of tombs, palaces, temples, bridges, pavilions and aqueducts and also with the ceremonial planting of the Au-Bars or sacred trees of the "ficus" natural order. Over and above the construction methods detailed descriptions and quantities of materials have also been given in these manuscripts.

1. Handiqui, B.C., Changrung Phukanar Buranji.

The Maidams or royal graves

Before the formal conversion to Hinduism the Ahoms buried their dead and the richer section and the royalty built elaborate earthen pyramids over the graves and these pyramids were often topped by small funerary temples. The actual grave was known as the Gahbhara (cave) or the Garbhagriha. On it was the actual mound topped by a masonry shrine complete with Ghatas and Chulas or finials. These temples were generally of Charichalia type. Some of the Maidams also had an intermediary storey and stone or brick stair ways (Jakhala) ran up the top. Around the Maidam were heavy, wide and high walls. A wall pierced by a Torana or gate surrounded the funerary temple at the top. The domical structure of the Maidam was built in several storeys (possibly stepped) in stone, brick, and mortar and was then covered completely with earth and finally it resembled a mound of huge dimensions.

The royal graves are concentrated at Charaideo (in the Sibsagar Subdivision), the ancient capital of the Ahoms. In this region hundreds of graves of various sizes line up for 5 or 6 miles from the Lengibar Tank to the Nimanagarh. This area was specially restricted for persons of the royal family only. Wheresoever the king might die the body or at best his ashes were buried at Charaideo. To the east of the Deo-sal or Ahom shrine the males are buried while the graves of females occupy the western section. But last of the kings were however not buried at Charaideo. Some of the earlier kings who ruled from Dihing are buried elsewhere. Chandrakanta Singha and the kings of the line of Charing are buried at Gauhati. Purandar Singha and the Charing Raja were buried at Jorhat and Jogeswar Singha at Goalpara.

The body of the king was taken to Charaideo by a special road known as the Sa'Nia Ali (the corpse carrying highway). Some identify it with the Gomotha Ali still to be seen. After the death the body was laid in state for quite some time protected by ointments, balms and spices. There was a separate necropolis for keeping the corpses in state. Some again identify it with present Gomotha. In a similar manner we may identify many tanks from their names with those associated with mortuary rites and bathing the corpses as well as washing the spades after finishing the Maidam. The officer in charge of graves was the Maidam Phukan under whom were a number of subordinate officers and the workers known as the Maidamia Paiks. These people looked after the graves, cleared the tropical vegetation, looking after visitors and guests to the Maidams. The Mochai Phukan cleaned the Maidams and had them plastered regularly and offered lamps, flowers and other necessary objects. He also looked after the flower garden at the Maidam.

The Maidam of Siva Singha—1666 Saka or 1744 A.D.

Garbhagriha — $12^c \times 10^c \times 14^c$ inner. The outer height is 19^c.
L. B. H.

Funerary temple — $6^c \times 4^c \times 7^c$
L. B. H.

The base of the grave — 27 Beo

circumference 81 Beo

Height 33^c

The wall — foundation 2^c, 3^c width, about 94 Beo

Measurement of the section — between the roof the Garbhagriha and the base of the funerary temple—$13^c \times 10^c \times 13^c$. The section was built with clay,
L B H

mortar and another with usual mortar. I

(I p. 1.)

The Maidam of Bar Raja 1663 Saka or 1741 A.D. (Phuleswari Devi) or Amvika Devi ?

The queen expired on the 14th of Asvina. In the last week of the month the first spade was struck. After two days stones were put in the foundations. On the fourth of Kartika on a Thursday bricks were laid for the Garbhagriha. On 11th Kartika the funerary temple was completed.

The temple measures within

: Actual height $17\frac{1}{2}^c$

10^c	$7\frac{1}{2}^c$	10^c	:
L	B	H	:

Area of the Maidam

Height 30^c

Circumference $47\frac{1}{2}^c$

The queen's body was laid in the grave on Saturday the 27th Kartika at 9 A.M.

The Maidam of the Dowager Mother (Raj Mao) :

The Raj Mao expired on 15th Aghon in 1959 Saka (1737 A.D.). Workers were sent to Charaideo hill the same day at 3 in the night. On Sunday, the 19th Aghon the first spade was struck. On the last day of the month (Samkranti) which was Thursday, the foundation was laid with stones and on 2nd of Pausa bricks were laid for construction. On the 8th day the Garbhagriha was completed and on the 10th day the body was laid at 9 A.M. The temple measures—

$9^c \times 9^c$) within. Height. $14\frac{1}{2}^c$.
L. H.)

Maidam of Rajesvar Singha

Expired on 20th Jaistha 1769 A.D. The first spade was struck on 19th Asadha, the Friday. On the 21st day 5 stones were laid in the foundation. On the 31st day (Tuesday) bricks were laid at the Dima (Is it the vernacular form of the Anda or the mispherical dome of the stupa. Maidams when covered with earth resembled stupas) The Gahvhara (Garbhagriha) within the Dima (Anda) measures

(10^c/B. (North-South) L.

8^c—B.

13^c—H.

9th. Sravana the door lintel was placed on the grave chambers. 19th of Sravana the Dima was covered fully. On the 31st day the king was buried (Saturday).

Maidam—

27^c Height

circumference 33 Beo.

Area

11 Beo

Men of 16 Faids (clans) engaged in building

,, ,, 2 ,, (,,) : royal litter bearers.

V. Bridges—Ahom

Silsako

Masonry bridges were a speciality of the Tungkhungiya period. Normally bridges are known as Dalangs in Assamese but masonry and stone bridges are famous as Silsako. The tradition of such bridges goes back to the pre-Ahom period. A magnificent stone bridge was built over a channel of the Bar-nadi and "is situated about 8 miles N.W. of North Gauhati on the high alley."[1] This bridge is 140' long and was possibly used by the first invading Turkish army in 1205-06 A.D. It was made by the "later Kamarupa kings" but was destroyed in the earthquake of 1897.

In the first half of Ahom rule, however, like all constructions bridges too

1. Hannay, Journal of the Asiatic Society of Bengal, 1851.

were made of wood and bamboo. But the earliest extant bridge of this age is the one at Garhgaon, over the Darika river. It was built in the early part of the 17th ct. during Pratapa Singha.[1] It joined the two segments of the Dhodar Ali highway cut by the above river. Another Silsako was at Hanhchara over the Garhgaon Ali. This bridge is reached just after leaving the Singha-Duar or the city gate of Sibsagar towards Garhgaon.[2] Its $16' \times 8'$ cubits and the four corners are decorated with four stone female figures gathered from some 10th century shrine or edifice.

The new capital Rangpur had a larger number of Silsakos of which the one at Na-Duar was built in 1703 by Rudra Singha. It measures $202' \times 21\frac{1}{2}'' \times 5\frac{1}{2}''$. It was started on 10th Pausha and was finished in the month of Phalguna.[3] This is still in use. Other minor bridges are in various conditions of decay. They are two at Meteka near Jaysagar over the river Geladimou. Other two were on the Khari-Katiya-Ali and at the Bar-Ali[4] and one over the Dijoi at Charaideo.[6] The last one was built by Gadadhar Singha. It was also named the Rahboi Silsako after a lady named Rahdoi. A minor bridge spanned the Namsai river.

1. Gogoi, L., Buranjie Parasha Nagar, pp. 29-30.
2. Ibid., p 4.
3. Handiqui, B.C., Changrung Phukanar Buranji, p. 4.
4. Gogoi, L., Ibid pp. 12-13,
5. Ibid., p. 44.

3

SCULPTURE

Sculpture of the Ahom period is definitely influenced by the national tradition of wood work. Mostly in reliefs, the sculptural examples whether in stone or in wood itself follow the same tradition. Large panels in terracotta and plaster also follow in the major type, i.e. reliefs. Sculptures in the round are mainly in metal and consist mainly of icons. Like in most regions of the orient art is a hand-maid of religion in Assam and sculpture actually is the embellishment of architectural undertakings. Clay images for the annual worship of Hindu deities like Durga were also made which according to custom were either immersed in the rivers or left to be decayed. In spite of the typical Assamese style we find minor variations in the creations of Western Assam under Koch hegemony and those of Eastern Assam under the Ahoms. Some rock cut sculptures were also attempted during the period though the number is insignificant. The main centres of sculptural activities were at Kamakhya, Hajo, Gosanimari, Garhgaon, Rangpur, Jaysagar, Kalugaon and Sibsagar. Sadiya, Dimapur and Khaspur and Jaintapur are also rich in reliefs and sculptures though they do not fall in the major stylistic group.

Wooden sculptures

The only extant examples of wooden sculptures are to be found in the Satras of Upper Assam and that of Barpeta. Puranigudam in Nowgong district is famous for its wooden image of Dasabhuja in wood with detachable portions which are taken apart and packed every year after the worship in autumn. In the Satras the wooden posts, frames and the screen-walls are all richly carved and brightly painted. The carvings depicting Puranic scenes on the walls of the Barpeta satra are the latest examples of this art. The Assam State Museum, Gauhati, has a typical carved panel from the Kamalabari satra depicting Ganesa sitting on the mouse under a ciuquefoil niche as is customary with mediaeval Assamese art. Here as elsewhere a single figure and sometimes even a group is always placed under one or more foiled arches according to the number of figures they frame. This same arrangement applies to wood carvings, stone panels, terracotta plaques and even miniature painting. The above figure from Kamalabari has a certain naivete which equates it with folk art. The face is in profile though the body is in front conforming to mediaeval Assamess tradition. The figure occupies the narrow vertical panel and its four outstretched arms serve to connect the figure with the frame. The back is cut away like in fret work figures. The elongated arch is elegant and well proportioned. A narrow handle-like projection from the apex of the arch served to join this panel with the wooden wall surface. The same tradition and technique is transmitted to undertakings in stone as we find in the Ahom period panel showing Agni from Tezpur from the Assam State Museum, Gauhati.

Since we find a great similarity in style and details in the terracotta panels, wooden panels, the bas reliefs and the miniature paintings in the Satriya idiom the earlier sculptures and panels in wood of the beginning of Ahom rule perhaps have had affinities with true Ahom book illustrations as found in the Phung Chin manuscript. But the absence of the earlier Ahom wooden buildings containing relief panels deprives us of the opportunity to say anything definitely about the style of relief panels of the age in question. Yet we can guess that the same affinity might have had existed in the early Ahom period. The Fatiyah-i-Ibriyah is full of praise for the Ahom places of Garhgaon fully carved with figures. The wooden phase of Assamese architecture and sculpture suddenly comes to a halt with the introduction of masonry buildings since the days of the Tungkhungiyas. But the Silakutis or hereditary sculptors continued to follow the wooden tradition by embellishing the new buildings with bas-relief panels. Terracotta panels were also freely used now as we see in the Ghanashyam Deul (Nati Gosain Dol) at Jaysagar.

The sculptures of the mediaeval period can be divided into the following schools each patronised by a different authority :

(1) Koch sculptures —Patronised by the Koch rulers of Lower Assam and Koch Bihar.

(2) Ahom sculptures —Patronised by the Ahom rulers of Upper Assam.

(3) Satriya sculptures —Patronised by the Satras all over Assam and Koch Bihar.

There was a definite style followed in the Satras irrespective of their location either in the Upper or the Lower Brahmaputra valley.

The tribal chiefs patronised sculptures and sculptors who belonged to either of the first two schools mentioned above. The preference was mainly determined by the proximity to a particular cultural sphere. But there are some stray images of the early Ahom period of pure Hindu Art tradition found in Upper Assam. Those were probably produced under the patronage of the Bhuyan chieftains of Upper Assam. Those images, like the bronze Durga from Lakhimpur in the Assam State Museum, Gauhati, served as prototypes for most of the metal images of the succeeding ages.

Koch sculptures

In the west, the site of Kamatapur (Gosanimari) in present Cooch Behar has an abundance of sculptures probably of the 15th century. These are mostly carved on blocks of stone lying scattered within the foot. Those blocks belonged to edifices either religious or lay.[1] The sculptures in high relief are isolated figures or are in relevant groups showing epic scenes. These were seen by Buchanan Hamilton in 1808 A.D. and have been recorded by him.[2] Two of these sculptures have been reproduced in the history of Koch Bihar in Bengali by A. Ahmad.

One group shows a pair of Naginis with folded hands in Namaskara mudra and they are richly decked in crowns and jewellery in the upper torso. Below the waist is the serpent body coiled in a graceful circular loop. Though in relief there is great deal of plasticity and volume in the figures as is charateristic with Koch sculptures. The body is in front view and a single serpent-hood tops the crown of the Nagini. This is in the same manner as in the similar figures showing the wives of Kaliya Naga in the Bhagavata, Book X (1539 A.D.) from Nowgong. The ornaments include a many stringed girdle secured with a large flower shaped clasp in the front, a number of bangles of increasing circumference at the wrists, Anantas with a diamond-shaped member on the forearms, beaded necklaces and large wheel-shaped Kundalas. The five-pointed crown is derived from the Pala-Sena sculptures. The entire effect is pleasing and the softness and volume of the female figure is aptly brought about in the heavy globular busts and the full face. That the inspiration is derived from the earlier Kamarupa sculptures is evident when compared to the Janus-like female figures (11th century) from the Kamakhya temple, Gauhati. As is usual in Kamarupa figure composition the figures are placed under arches separately or jointly. Another group placed under a cinquefoiled arch is described by Ahmad as Bala Krishna. Here the child Krisna is hanging between two standing Gopis with his arms around their necks. The agitation of the child-god is depicted by means of placing his prancing legs in two different directions and there is a suggestion of a mischievous smile on his face, reflected at his lips and both of his eyes. The plump body of the child-god adds to volume and depth in the composition and is in contrast to the tall and slim bodies of the young Gopis. Their bodies are gracefully broken in Dvi-bhanga pose around the axis of their figures and they add charm and grace to the otherwise simple composition. With their inner hands the Gopis hold aloft a large bowl, possibly full of butter to reach which the child-god seems to climb up by hanging by their necks. The Gopis are dressed in long skirt-like garments with wide front pleats as in the Mekhela or the Sarong-like garment of Koch and Assamese women. The ornaments are as inthe

1. Ahmad, A., Koch Biharer Itihasa, p. 32.
2. Ibid,, p. 30.

Nagini figures already described. In their outer hands they hold two Chamaras indicating their submission to and veneration for Krisna. The child-god is proportionately larger than the Gopis due to heiratic sealing followed in this religious scene. The faces of the Gopis are as in the terracotta plaques from the Assam valley.

Another important site rich in sculptures of the Koch period is the Nilachala hill at Gauhati housing the Kamakhya temple. The temple in its original form belonged to c. 9 th. ct. A.D.[1] though successive renovations were undertaken, and the final shape was given in 1565 A.D.[2], under the patronage of King Naranarayana. During this renovation a masonry boundary wall was thrown around the temple precincts which was pierced with two buffsandstone gateways. A number of fine reliefs were affixed on the western gateway and on the pillars of the Salas or open halls which run parallel to the left side of the main temple. From the inner side the western gateway has a 'mother and child' scene to the left and a 'woman pouring water to a tired man' to the right of the entrance opening. Within the gate are again two fine sculptures representing a pair of male musicians playing on the conch and the flute respectively. The other interesting sculpture of this group is a 'woman carrying pitcher full of water'. This panel has been affixed to the masonry pillar of the Sala mentioned above. They are carved in bold relief with a suggestion of plasticity and volume specially in the female figures. Single figures are in a single block while the larger groups as in the 'woman and the tired man' scene two separate blocks have been carved and placed side by side to complete the composition. T.N. Ramchandran, writing in 1936-37 says about these sculptures that "interesting carvings revealing exceptional sculptural skill such as is not usually met with in the locality."[3] He says about the excellence of the musician figures in the following words : "Two of them are found in niches facing each other on the sides of the entrance. One shows a conch-blower in profile with an ushnisha on head and a conch held in his mouth, the cheeks bulging out as in the act of blowing the conch."[4]

The flutist has been designated by him as Krisna's Venugopala aspect though the presence of a Krisna figure in a Saktist temple does not seem convincing. In all probability he is simply a temple musician. Ramchandran says about the flutist : "a product of sculptural excellence represents Krisna playing on the flute (Venugopala)." The head dress which is in the shape of flames is a conical cap. A single necklace of "manis" and an undergarment with central and lateral tassels recall the

1. Das Gupta, R., An Architectural Survey or the Kamakhya Temple, 1960. p. 3,
2. Ibid., p, 2.
3. Ramchandran, T.N., Explorations in Assam, Archaeological Survey of India, Annual Report, 1936-37, p. 60.
4. Ibid.

features of the Gupta and Pallava periods in North and South India respectively. The figure is a rare specimen of anatomical perfection."[1]

The right hand panel is another fine specimen of this group. These Ramchandran describes as the "domestic scenes such as a householder doing his daily worship, while his wife is engaged in suckling her child ; a woman worshipper kneeling and pouring water from a spouted vessel into the mouth of an animal whose features are too indistinct to admit any correct identification."[2] Actually the scenes mentioned above need careful reobservation and identification. The scene of the worshipper is separate from the "mother and child" panel. It is a distinct composition full of intense human element as recorded in stone. The mother sits on the ground cradling the child in her arms and it is kicking its legs as the doting mother looks down at the face of the child. The "woman worshipper" panel was perhaps not fully visible when Ramchandran visited Nilachala. Now one can easily see the full panel showing the woman pouring down water from a spouted vessel to the left while the right half shows a tired man sitting listlessly on the ground with his head tilted to the left in fatigue. He holds a rectangular fan with a long handle in his limp right hand. Now it is clear that the woman is pouring the water to the man and not to any "animal" whose identification is difficult. The pillar figure of a woman carrying a pitcher full of water from the Sala near the main temple is a fine study of the female form though the face is badly damaged. The position of the feet and that of the body and the turn of the face all point towards the figure moving towards to the right. The hips jut out to carry the pitcher and she lifts her Mekhela a little with her right hand to save it from getting wet near the bank of the river or pond. The coiffeur is like a topknot like those of Shan, Burmese and Nayar women of Kerala. This type of coiffeur is however not common in Lower Assam. There are some rude sculptures in the antechamber of the Kamakhya temple when the images of Durga, Naranarayana and Sukladhwaja are noticeable.[3] According to tradition the royal brothers were turned into stone when they secretly watched goddess Kamakhya dance in the sanctum in spite of repeated warnings from the priest Kendukalai.*

The sculptures on the walls above the plinth of the Hayagriva-Madhava temple at Hajo also are works of the Koch period and are results of Koch patronage. As the plinth mouldings of elephants show the original temple must have

1. Ramchandran, T.N , Exploration in Assam, Archaeological Survey of India, Annual Report, 1936-37 ; pp. 60-61.
2. Ibid., p. 61.
3. Archaeological Survey of India, Annual Report, 1917-18.

* These portrait sculptures are rare specimens of their type. They have been mentioned by T.G. Aravamuthan in his book Portrait Sculpture In South India.

been a work of the 10th-11th century A.D. But the original temple was restored by Raghu Deb in 1589 A.D. after it had been destroyed by Kala-Pahar.[1] The upper section of the Adhisthana as well as the walls of the Mandapa have a number of relief panels in the usual Assamese manner, i.e., shallow relief figures composed under an arch or a series of arches and following the scheme of the miniature paintings of the Satriya school. One scene on the outer face of the left wall shows a warrior and an attendant riding a low plank-like chariot with a Makara face and a flag post carrying a triangular banner and a yak-tail tassel hanging down from the top of the pole. The indistinct attendant figure at the back of the vigorous warrior reminds one of the painting of Devaki, Vasudeva and Kamsa on the chariot in the Bhagavata Book X (1539 A.D.) from Nowgong. The many wheels of the chariot have smaller figures of prancing horses within their outline pointing towards its being an image of Surya with an attendant or a female companion. A series of arches outline the top of the panel. Other panels either have figures of deities singly or in groups, each placed under its individual arch. One such detached panel now standing near the main entrance shows a deity sitting cross-legged on an aquatic (?) animal in front view, and holding a snake in the left hand. Other interesting type of figures are the corner figures where the two walls meet. These are standing male figures with widely flung mane-like hair. The hair resembles the striped head-kerchiefs of ancient Egyptians. The two wide sections of the mane serve to join the two walls meeting from two sides and the joining line passes through the centre-parting of the hair as it were. The treatment of hair is as in Nepalese and Tibetan sculptures. This is a unique way of hiding the joints of the walls and it serves to preserve the continuity of the figured band on the walls of the Adhisthana. The association of the Bhutanese with this temple might have been responsible for the introduction of such figures here. Like these figures, the Bhortal cymbals and Ban Bati bowls might have entered Assamese material culture through the Bhutanese and Tibetan pilgrims who visit Hajo every winter.

Numaligarh

Numaligarh also abounds in ruins and sculptured blocks of stone which belonged to some important edifice, possibly the Siva temple at the foot of the hill. One of them is a sedant lion figure conventionalized like the Simha-Vyala mentioned in the important Silpa texts like the Samaranganasutradhara, the Aparajitaprichha and the Rupmala.[2] The lion is in front view, is goggle-eyed like the Kirtimukha and its long tongue hangs down. The treatment is purely conventional and the statement of K.L. Barua that the "conventional representation of the lion

1. Neog, M., Pavitra Asam, p. 205.
2. Dhaki, M.A., The Vyala Figures on The Mediaeval Temples of India, Varanasi, 1966, p. 16.

shows that the inhabitants of the Assam valley were not very familiar with the king of beasts"[1] is apt. The lion figure belongs to the 13th-14th et. A.D. as is proved by a four or five lettered inscription in Nagari character of the period[2]. Another important piece from the same site is a vertical panel depicting a cluster of lotus stocks issuing from the depths of water. The sinuous stalks surging upwards carry a large full-blown lotus and three lotus buds surrounding the main blossom. This pillar-like member has the same motif on two faces and was probably used as a corner stone for joining walls as in the Hayagriva-madhava temple at Hajo. The treatment of lotus stocks, buds and leaves remind of similar motifs in sculptures of the Singasri period of Eastern Java.

Ahom sculptures

The earliest stone sculptures of the Ahoms are the rockcut figures. These are reached from Salaguri by going upstream along the Dihing to the south where there is a hill. It represents an Ahom princely figure which the local people regard as the figure representing king Gadadhar Singha. But the Buranjis mention that these sculptures were cut in 1401 A.D., when the emmissaries of the Ahom and the Nara kings during the rule of Swargadeo Sudangpha met at the spot and promised to regard the hill as their common boundary.[3]

An interesting specimen of early Ahom sculpture is the "Snake Pillar" from Sadiya now in the State Museum Gauhati. "The pillar has a square base and a hexagonal shaft tapering towards the top and crowned by a vase. Over it appears the hood of a cobra with its body entwained round the shaft in bold relief. The inscription is incised vertically on the shaft of the pillar including the tail of the cobra and consists of three parts—the main document containing an agreement between the Dihingia Bar-Gohain, the local plenipotentiary of the Ahom king and the Mishmis, a long one-line strip containing a post-script prohibiting the future rulers from breaking the agreement and another short strip in mixed characters."[4]

The pillar was found in about 1920-21 by M. O'Callaghan, Political Officer, Sadiya, a few miles north-east of Sadiya in the Deopani river. It was then broken in two.

"The date of the inscription is not known but it must be later than the first quarter of the sixteenth century, when the country around Sadiya first came under

1. Barua, K.L., Early History of Kamarupa, Shillong, 1936, p. 173.
2. Ramchandran, T.N., Explorations in Assam, Archaeological Survey of India, Annu Report, 1936-37, p. 57.
3. Gogoi, L., Buranjie Parasha Nagar, p 84.
4. Dikshit, K.N., A Note on An Ahom Stone Pillar Inscription ; Archaeological Survey of India, Annual Report.

the occupation of the Ahom kings under Suhung-mung (circa 1524 A.D.). The inscription is the only known lithic record in Ahom language and the pillar on which it occurs is a very interesting momento of the Ahom period of Assamese history.[1]"

The gradual inclination of the Ahom rulers towards Hinduism resulted in the building of the Nagasankara temple (1480 A.D.) at Tezpur by Susenpha.[2] The next group of temples resplendant with reliefs depicting scenes from the Puranas as well as from daily life are unique also as records of contemporary life and manners were founded at Jaysagar (1698), Gaurisagar (1734), Sibsagar (1734), Kalugaon and Rudrasagar (1773) in Upper Assam. In Lower Assam, especially at Gauhati, sculptural activities at this period could not flourish since the Ahom rulers used sculptures belonging to the 10th-11th ct. period for the embellishment of their temples. Terracotta decorations were also a speciality of the 'Bhati' area though they are also to be seen at the Ghanasyama Dol at Jaysagar (1751-1769).

Out of the five temples built around 1698 A.D. the Jay Dol or the Kesavarai Vishnu temple is the most important from the point of view of sculptures as well as architecture. Among all the Puranic and genre scenes there are two equistrian figures of Rudra Singha Maharaja. Another important panel shows Rama, Sita and Laksmana. The real Ahom characteristics emerge from this group of temple reliefs.

The Ahom temple reliefs are framed in rectangular panels with foiled arches for the top. The arches multiply when the number of figures is more than one or two. Actually, the arched margin follows the arrangement of the human or animal figures in the composition. But compared to the Koch reliefs the Ahom reliefs are shallower and there is lesser variation of planes. The technique is definitely reminiscent of wood carving. The flat figures are cut at right angles from the background. The quality of the stone which is porous and shale-like in character, has caused much damage to the panels due to atmospheric actions and the heavy tropical rains of Assam. In most cases the stone has flaked in neat layers and in extreme cases they have been smoothed clean due to actions of rain, water and strong winds, over a course of about three centuries. The human figures have the feet in side view, the body in front view and the faces usually in profile. Sometimes front faces are also met with. The faces are large, a local ethnic characteristic feature as we also see in the Khmer reliefs from Angkor in Cambodia. The profile faces are sometimes remarkably similar to similar faces from Angkor. The front faces also have similar lips and heavy jaw lines and wide foreheads. Such similarity raises the question of some real artistic connection between the

1. Dikshit, K.N., A Note on An Ahom Stone Pillar Inscription ; Archaeological Survey of India, Annual Report of 1924-25, p. 158.

2. Gogoi, L., Ahom Jati Aru Sanskriti., p. 131.

stone carver's technique and ideals for figures between Assam and Angkorian Cambodia. But history is silent about any such connections. The only difference in the human figures is their dress. The Ahom figures are Indian in dress and jewellery. Princely figures wear Chajjedar Pagris as in the miniatures of the period or crowns if they be divine ones. Females are in richly embroidered and patterned Mekhelas. They are with or without blouses and throw a Riha or breast band across the shoulders or in the transverse manner. The hair is either done in a heavy and large topknots or looped-hair knots. The jewellery consists of Gamkharus, Anantas, Galpatas, many strings of beady necklaces and other typical ornaments like the Lukapar, Jangphai-Keru, and Long-Kerus. The front view of the torso was thus intentional, so that the artist had ample space for decorating with motifs from textiles and jewellery. Treatment of trees and animals are conventional and non-realistic but extremely appealing as compositions and design. The face was kept in profile for two reasons. Firstly, a profile is much easier to tackle for the artist. Secondly, in a frontal face the tip of the nose would be the highest plane and was most liable to damage from concussions. Though the second point applies to terracotta panels yet the Silakutis clung to that earlier tradition even when there was a change over to stone as the sculpting medium. The memory of terracotta and wooden panel carving was too strong to be ignored by the stone carvers of the 18th century.

The Debighar situated at the north-west corner of the Jaysagar tank was the site where the annual Durga Puja was celebrated during Rudra Singha[1] and is shaped like a common Do-chala hut though of considerable length. The walls afford ample space for stone panels set in the masonry wall. The figures are mostly of the Devi or other deities with full iconographic details including their respective mounts. There are 11 panels on the longer sides and 9 panels on the broader sides of the temple walls.

The Gaurisagar group of temples, three in number, are dedicated to Devi, Siva and Vishnu. "The main temple in this group is dedicated to the goddess Devidole just as the main temple at Sibsagar is dedicated to Siva and that of Jaysagar to Vishnu. The panels on the walls of these temples represent a bewildering variety of images of gods and goddesses, in which the new-found zeal of the Ahom princes of the eighteenth century, then fully converted to the Hindu faith, found expression. In the main temple of Gaurisagar most of the sculptural panels represent images of goddess[2].

1. Neog, M., Pavitra Asam, p. 34.
2. Archaeological Survey of India, Annual Report, 1929-30, p. 46.

Sibsagar group

Here also the main temple dedicated in 1734 A.D. had two accompanying temples to Devi and Vishnu. But the zeal for figure carving seems to have been extinguished here and we find geometrical, floral and bird motifs prominent in decoration scheme. The entire wall surface of the Muktinath (1734) temple is covered with continuous decorations and it appears as if the temple is wrapped completely in a huge tapestry with woven designs. On the plinths the decorations are in bands of rosettes and sometimes there are bands of peacocks with outspread wings. At the corners where two walls join the peacocks are placed in two halves and the continuity of the peacock band is maintained.

Kalugaon group

Kalugaon has two temples dedicated to Siva and Jagadhattri respectively.[1] Both are commonly known as the Barpatra Dol since they were constructed by Harinath, the brother of queen Phulesvari, and he was raised to the position of the Barpatra. These belong to the reign of Siva Singha and the stone panels of reliefs are in very good condition though the temples themselves are in bad state of preservation. The Jagadhatri temple has a fine gold image of the goddess which will be dealt with in the section on metal sculptures.

The stone reliefs in gray sandstone are still very crisp and fresh and some of the panels showing the different aspects of Durga are full of vitality and movement. The Siva temple is in a worse state of preservation and some of the panels are detached and lying about in the compound of the houses of the priests. One of the finest panels shows Arjuna shooting at the fish-shaped target to win the hand of Draupadi. The right hand corner of the panel is occupied by the muscular and towering figure of Arjuna. Arjuna turns away his face and looks down in the water to see the reflection of the target hung above. There is great tension in the body of Arjuna as he stretches his hand to release the arrow. He raises his left leg a little to get the momentum. At the other end of the panel is the expectant figure of Draupadi standing with a garland and followed by a row of three 'sakhis'. The problem of depth has been eliminated by placing all the women in a single file one behind the other. The composition is framed by a multi-foiled arch.

Of the panels of the Jagadhatri temple mentions may be made of Durga fighting the Mahisasura, Jagadhatri sitting on her lion mount, Bhadra Kali, Laksmi and Saraswati.

The Durga figure is full of vigour and it harks back to the metal image of

1. Neog, M., Pavitra Asam, p. 37.

Durga of the 13th century from Tinsukia (now in the State Museum, Gauhati.). This type seems to have been the proto-type for the future images too as we see from the terracotta plaque of Durga from the Nati Gosain Dol, Jaysagar, built during the days of Rajeswarsingha (1751-69 A.D.). The Jagadhatri image is interesting and far better in workmanship than the gold image of the deity which was worshipped in the temple. Here the Devi sits in Vajrasana on the Ahom type lion with a pronounced snout and the lean body like that of a hound. Bhadrakali is a lone figure standing against the plain background under the usual arch. She is a young woman tastefully dressed and holding a naked sword in the right and a severed human head is displayed in her outstretched left hand. This hand is flatly placed against the background and stretches out of the body and is parallel to the ground. Lakshmi sits on a full blown lotus and is placed at the centre of the panel. She holds her attributes in her four hands and is flanked by two devotees. The Saraswati figure is a fine study of the graceful female form sitting on a full blown lotus supported on a long stalk. The treatment of the lotus is unique as all the petals droop or spread out from the pericarp on which the deity sits with her left leg folded up. The lotus looks like a Bata or the usual 'dish-on-stand' of Assam. The flat face is serene and has a faint and benevolent smile on the lips. The flatness and the smile remind us of the Angkorian figures of Apsaras.

Two isolated figures very badly broken are in the collection of Sri B.C. Handiqui of Jaysagar. One is a fragment of the head of Durga in bluish-green 'serpentine' stone. The stone has a very high gloss like glass or marble. Only the top portion of the head down to the eyebrows remains. The crown is as seen in the miniatures of the Satriya school, i.e., has a high crown and a series of triangles at the front forming a tiara. This piece was found in a deserted temple near Sibsagar which was dedicated to Durga. The life size image of the Devi to which the head belonged was found shattered in the temple. The other is gray sandstone image of Venugopala. Though the torso is headless and broken at the shins yet it is a fine study of the human body though conventionalised. The left leg is straight and the right one is set across the other. The voluminous planes overlap and each section is well developed and rounded. The positions of the broken hands show that they held a flute to the right. Another panel showing the same theme but accompanied by Radha and the Gopis and Gopas and their cattle is in a shrine within the compound of the Mangala-chandika temple, Gauhati. The stele is eliptical at the top. Krisna stands in Tribhanga pose playing on his flute while Radha stands to his right in a graceful pose with a lotus bud in her right hand. The pair is flanked by cowherds and Gopis and there is a number of cattle at the bottom of the composition. An undulating section below Krisna's feet represents the hills. The hair do of Radha which is a looped-top knot is truly native but the very conception of Radha and Krisna is uncommon in Assam Vaisnavism where Radha alone has no place either in literature, art or iconography. Her place is taken in Assamese conception by the multitude of Gopis. The pose of Krisna however is uncommon. He turns left instead of right which is seen in the metal image Venugopala standing in front of the stele in the same chapel.

Asvakranta Temple—(1720 A.D.)—icon

Narayana Sesasayi: The stele is iconographically important as this is regarded as the only Ananta Sayin image in Assam. There are also the ten Avataras depicted in steles on the outer walls of the temple. The vertical panel shows Narayana lying on the serpent Ananta accompanied by Laksmi, the Asvins, Brahma and Durga, all depicted in the firmament. A number of smaller figures of women accompany the proportionately diminutive figure of Laksmi shampooing the feet of her Lord. The lying posture of Narayana is rather stiff as though a standing figure has been uncomfortable thrust down in a concave plane. The hoods of Ananta are transformed into a fern like leaf form, which grow in great variety in Assam. There is a definitely local Mongoloid touch in the face of Narayana, Durga, the Asvins while the figures of Laksmi and her attendants are far superior in anatomical details and their sitting postures are not stiffened. The unique features of the panel are the members on which Ananta itself rests. Just below the serpent body is a low three-tiered stool or "sal-pira", then a tortoise and then a frog. This kind of stands composed of multiple animals, one above the other is a typical features of Assamese art. A stylised double-petalled lotus issues from the right of the animal pyramid. The top of the stele is a cusped multi-foiled arch with a floral band.

A 17th century stone panel of Agni from Tezpur is another interesting specimen of the period. It also was a panel affixed to some temple at Tezpur. Here the god sits astride a bull and holds the Sruk and the Srura, the sacrificial laddles for pouring libations of ghee. The face and the torso are in front view while the body beneath the waist in side view. Heiratic proportions have been responsible for the proportionately large figure of Agni. It is framed on the top by the usual foliated arch. The dress is dhoti, uttariyas, a crown, and the usual Assamese jewellery seen at the Jaysagar group of reliefs.*

Portion of a stele of fine workmanship with a foliated arch showing the Islamic Mihrabi design is lying in the precincts of the Umananda temple Gauhati. The temple itself was construted in 1694 A.D. by the Gargayan Sadikoi Barphukan at the behest of king Gadhadhar Singha.[1] The piece in question is a fine piece

* Three more steles depicting Brahma, Katrikeya and Parasurama also from Tezpur and in the similar style are also deposited in the Assam State Museum, Gauhati.

1. Neog, M., Pavitra Asam, p. 199

of carving still in very good state of preservation, and can rank among the finest creations of the Ahom carvers. It appears to be a fragment of some inscription stele.

Metal images

Metal images were normally of deities and were installed in the various temples and Thans (Sthana or shrine) as Vigrahas or icons. Brass and bronze were the most popular medium for casting images though there are many examples in gold, silver and Astadhatu (Octoallay), an amalgam, the composition of which often varied by altering the proportions of the different metals. Since the icons in the major temples were in gold many of them have been lost during the Burmese invasions of Assam. In some of the icons however jewels have been used for the eyes and the crown-jewels. Most of the images discussed here are in worship and fall within the 'Chalanta' type of images of the deities actually installed in the temples. But the Vaisnava Satras also house metal images of Visnu in his various aspects, specially Krisna, Venu-Gopala and the type known as the Larua-Gopala, i.e., child Krisna, crawling on the ground with a Laru or sweetmeat-ball (Modaka) in his upraised hand.

Chronologically speaking the oldest extant image is of Durga in her Mahisa-suramardini aspect at the Assam State Museum, Gauhati. The image is datable to c. 13th century and was found at Tinsukia in the Lakshimpur district. The metal is very fine brass and the height is 1′ 7½″. Like most examples from Assam Devi here is not attended or accompanied by her children Lakshmi, Saraswati, Kartikeya and Ganesa as is the case with the Dasabhuja images from Bengal. "The goddess has three eyes, ten hands, high breasts, thin waist and three bends in her body. Weapons in her hands are lost. The right leg of the goddess is on the back of the lion, the vehicle of the 'Devi,' the left is touching the back of the Mahisasura. Below her feet lies the head of a buffalo. The lower part of the 'Devi' is draped in clothing almost touching the ankles. The lion is mauling the demon, who is depicted as having terrific look with knitted eye-brows and grinding teeth."[1] The icon is interesting from many angles. Firstly, it is a fine piece of sculpture in metal and the otherwise war-like aspect of the Devi has the grace of a dancing figure. The figure is nimble footed and the arms spread out behind her head in the manner of a halo. The form of the Devi is revealed from beneath her thin Mekhela clinging to her body. The rampant lion is forceful and is in the typical Assamese manner, across between the lion and the 'dragon'. The Asura though cruel in looks is also poised gracefully and his pose reminds of the poses in Thai dancing. He wears a finely pleated kilt-like dress and a peculiar turban. His shoes are having turned up

1. Chowdhury, P D. and Das, M.C., Ancient Treasures of Assam. Through the Assam State Museum, Gauhati, 1959, p 35.

points. The Asura is completely human and the severed head of a buffalo is his only identity with Mahisa or the buffalo demon. The entire composition is fixed to an oblong base.

The lion in Assamese sculpture is conventional. It is slender, long bodied and is either rampant or couchant in position. The beast has some traits of the stag in the shape of its legs and the curved up tail ends up in a stylized tuft of hair sembling the pointed fig or 'chenar' leaf. There are normally two small wings at the shoulders and the long neck curves up like that of a stallion. The snout is snappy like a dragon's but is pointed and wide open revealing a set of fangs and a flickering tongue. The eyes are almond-shaped and the tip of the nose is represented by a nodule. Lions everywhere are depicted in the above manner with minor variations of details. In spite of the fact that the Ahom lion is a mixture of Chinese and Indian elements yet it falls within the Simha Vyala variety[1] of figure mentioned in the Samarangana sutradhar, the Aparajitaprichha and the Rupamala texts. The earliest and the fully evolved figure of this type is the one from Chaukhandi, near Sarnath and belongs to the 5th et. A.D. of the Classical school. The closest counterpart of the Ahom-lion is the Nepalese lion but the latter is heavier in volume and rather static in pose as we see from the images at the Durga temple, Varanasi. A more energetic type of such figures is used as 'tunal' or wooden brackets in Nepalese architecture.[2] The crest of the Ahom kings was also a lion with an upraised paw framed in a 'mihrabi' panel. The lion there is more like those on the flags of Ceylon and Iran, but the former is devoid of the sword, which is seen in examples from the latter countries. The winged lion has the same position in Assam art and in her crafts as the Garuda in Indonesia. Where the Ahom-lion is more stylized it resembles the griffins from Susa[3] (8th-7th et., B.C.) in the Louvres, Paris, from Rhodes[4] (7th-6th et., B.C.) in the British Museum, London, and the stag's head from Pazgryk[5] (4th-3rd et. B.C.) in the Hermitage Museum.

The Bishnupur Satra, Goalpara has a brass image of Madanamohana which was installed in the Satra by the founder who was the grandson (1539-1600 A.D.) of Sankara Deva. Raghudeb (1581-1600) installed the famed brass Madanmohana at Ganak Kuchi in Kamrup. A 12″ high Vasudeva image in brass was dedicated by Lora Raja (1679-81) to the Vasudeva Dol at Kalapani in the Gahpur Mauza in Tezpur. Two sets of brass images of Radha-Krisna are to be seen at the Dhendai Dol, in Gahpur Mauza of Tezpur (1679-83). King Gadadhar Singha donated the Visvanath image in 1685 to the Bisnath temple in Tezpur.

1. Dhaki, M.A., The Vyala Figures on the Mediaeval Temples of India, F. tsps.
2. Thapa, R.J., Nepalese Art : Catalogue of Art Objects Exhibited in Paris, 1966, p. 29.
3. Ghrishman, R., Persia from the Origins to Alexander the Great, 1964, pl. 428.
4. Ibid., Pl. 427.
5. Idid., Pl. 474.

The Chalanta image of Kamakhya at Nilachal, Gauhati, is a fine specimen showing the goddess riding a dragonlike lion with a greatly elongated body. The Astadhatu image of Abhaya Devi is another important Devi icon installed at Abhayapuri in Bijni in the Goalpara District.

Next follows an era when we come across a number of datable images dedicated chiefly by the Ahom kings and queens. On his accession, King Rudra Singha constructed the Phakua Dol at Rangpur in 1703-04 and installed there a gold image of his mother princess Jaymati who had been declared a Santi or saint due to her myrterdom to save the life of her husband, the fugitive prince Gadadhar Simha. In 1708 the Mahisasuramardini image worshipped by the Jaintia kings was brought by the conquering Ahom forces and installed at Rangpur. When the capital was shifted to Jorhat during the Burmese incursions, the icon was reinstalled at the Burhigosai Dol, Jorhat. King Rudra Singha installed the silver 'chalanta' image of Umananda, at the Umananda temple on the Peacock island, Gauhati. The image shows Siva with five faces and ten arms and riding on his bull mount.

Though a Siva temple, queen Phulesvari dedicated a brass image of Durga to the Pariharesvara temple at Dubi in Kamrup district in the year 1740. The brass icon of Mangala-Chandi at the temple on Chattrakara hill, Gauhati, is dated 1795. It is an exquisite work though only about 6″ high. The Jagadhatri image in gold from the Barpatra-Dol at Kalugaon, Sibsagar, belongs to the early 18th century. It was installed by Harinath, the brother of queen Phulesvari, who had been raised to the post of the Barpatra. The four-armed Devi sits on a rampant Ahom-lion. The three eyes of the deity are pieces of sapphire of the undated icons. Three Visnu images from Dihing Nemali Satra are also important.

Conclusion

In concluding our study of Assamese sculptures of the Ahom period we cannot overlook the close affinity that exists between the sculptures of Assam and the regions of South East Asia, particularly with those of Khmer pieces from Angkor. Firstly, the sculptures in both cases are essentially flat and are truly speaking reliefs of varying elevations from the background. Thus they are high reliefs and not sculptures in the round. The flatness of the figures may also be due to the dependence on the wooden phase which definitely preceded that of stone carving in the Ahom period. The figures are made at right angles with the background and thus they give the impression of being figures sawed down the middly vertically and attached to the flat surface of the background.

Secondly, the background is plain and unadorned in Ahom relief panels. Each figure stands free and bold on the clean surface. It is normally not seen in

Indian reliefs, though we are reminded of the plain background in the frieze of Apsaras from Angkor.

There is identity in the facial features of the Ahom-Koch human figures and those from the regions mentioned above. This is neither accidental nor is it due to similarity of technique of carving. This ethnic affinity is explained by the presence of strong Tai (Ahom) Khmer (Khasi) and Tibeto-Burman (Bodo) strains in Assamese population. The artists and models of the Ahom period belonged to the above stocks and their various admixtures. Fergusson says that the different racial elements were more pronounced in ancient and mediaeval India than they are now in the composite Indian population. The wide flat faces with almond-eyes, short noses with flared nostrils, and heavy sensuous lips 'curved upwards in smile'; or the sedate expressionless faces of the Ahom reliefs instantaneously remind us of the Apsaras and genre scene figures from Angkor.

In matters of poses too we find that the Ahom figures are like those from Cambodia and Siam. Firstly, the human figures are rigid and mostly standing. But those in action are depicted in a dramatic manner, that is, the poses seem affected and not spontaneous as in Khmer classic ballet, the prevalence of which is to be seen also in Siam. The archer, the cavalier, the deities and the Asura fighting Durga all appear like characters posed for dance-dramas. Best examples of such delicate yet unreal poses are to be seen in the figures of the Mahisasura fighting Durga of the 13th century from Tinsukia, now in the Assam State Museum, Gauhati, and those of the charioteer and attendant from the Hayagriva Madhava temple, Hajo. But to all intents and purposes they make fine pictures.

The influence of contemporary Burmese sculptures of Hindu deities of c. 11th century are to be seen in the relief panels from Janardana and Suklesvara temples, Gauhati. This source of inscription remains active as we see in the seated deity from Hayagriva Madhava temple Hajo. The Yogasana pose, the narrow waist and the wide shoulders and a tapering crown like the Buddha's usnisa, met within the above figure are of definite Burmese inspiration.

Animal figures are generally conventional and stylized. Though the Assamese artist was more successful with the figures of elephants and ducks, they were quite unfamiliar with those of exotic animals like the lion and the camel. Horse figures are light and spirited and are evidently of Islamic-Persian derivation, but was successfully grafted in totem art of Assam. But the impact of Bhutan and Tibet is to be seen in the metal images and the image of Mangala Chandi from the Chattrakara temple, Gauhati, illustrates the point best.

4

POTTERY AND TERRACOTTA

During the Ahom period the art of pottery and terracotta developed under royal and popular support. The art of figured tile-making received great impetus during the Tungkhungiya period when large masonry buildings were decorated with beautiful and intricate terracotta panels. The best example of this type is the building known as the House of Ghanasyama, the royal architect. These twin arts were in the hands of the potters (Kumhar). A section of them known as the Hiras followed a technique which did not necessitate the potter's wheel for the production of earthen ware. With a glorious past dating back to the Mauryan period, the Ahom examples show the continuity of the potter's art in Assam. Recent excavations at Ambari[1] and the University campus at Gauhati have revealed a large variety of pottery and pottery boats in full size, the latter evidently being ritual in nature. A group of terracotta figurines representing dancers are identical with those of the Mauryan period from Patna.[2] A large variety of pots and pans were made for storing water, oil, 'gur' and other liquid or semi-liquid substance, grains and even clothes and valuables. Their shapes and designs were determined by their nature of use.[3] Cooking was preferably done in earthen vessels and this practice was followed even in the royal kitchen or the Sangmai-sal.[4] Exquisite tiered lamps decorated appliques and figures of the goddess Suvachani were produced in Goalpara region. Sir Edward Gait has left a detailed list of the various types of pottery traditionally used in Assam.[5] The account below follows Gait's classifications.

1. Adkalah : a small pitcher.
2. Akasabanti : lamps used in marriages and in Diwali.

1. Bhattacharya, B K. : Kya Gauhati Kabhi Bharat-Rome Vyapar Ka Pramukh Bandargah Tha ? Dharmayuga, 17.8. 69, pp. 30-1.
2. Sankalia, H D. : Kamrup ki Ghati men Pragaitihasik Avasesa (2) Dharmayuga. 26.4.1970, Pp. 24-26.
3. Handique, B C. : Purani Asamar Silpa, p 36.
4. Ibid, p. 38.
5. Gait. E.A. : Manufacture of Pottery in Assam : Journal of Indian Art ; vol. IV, No. 54, p. 7. January, 1896

3. Akathia : a vessel for cooking rice and curry. The bigger variety is known as the Dukathia.

4. Barmala : a bowl with a rim in which curds and sugar are kept. The smaller variety is known as the Mala.

5. Bhuriki : a bin for storing grains. The larger variety is known as Mathia.

6. Chakali : a flattish and shallow vessel for cooking curry. The deeper type is known as the Paticharu.

7. Chaki : an earthen ware lamp lit with mustard oil and a wick.

8. Charakdan : a hollow 20″ high cylinder used as a lamp stand.

9. Chilim : an earthen ware funnel for smoking tobacco or hemp. The larger variety or the Dhapat-Khowa is for tobacco smoking while the smaller one known as the Bhang-Khowa is used for smoking Bhang or hemp.

10. Charu : a vessel for cooking rice among the poorer classes. The larger variety is known as the Thali.

11. Dama or Daba : earthen ware vessels for making into drums by stretching hide over the mouth.

12. Daskathia : a vessel for cooking rice for three or four persons.

13. Gacha : a lamp stand shaped on the wheel and often decorated with applique ornaments and figures of animals, birds and human shapes.

14. Handi or Hari : a wide mouthed vessel for cooking rice mainly by the Kacharis. It is also used by them for brewing 'Mad' or rice bear.

15. Jang : a longish 'handi' usually made for storing 'Mad' or water by the Kacharis.

16. Jui-dhara : a fire stove or baked clay.

17. Kalah : a dicanter-shaped vessel for storing liquid or semi-liquid substance like 'gur', oil, milk and also water. Its usual capacity is four to five gallons.

18. Khampti-haria : a special kind of vessel with a perforated bottom for steaming rice. The vessel is kept over a pot of water in which water is boiling. Though these are made by Assamese potter their customers are the Khampti people of the Lohit Frontier area of the present Arunachal Pradesh.

19. Mala : a similar sized Charu for religious and ritualistic uses.

20. Mala-Charu : a small tray-like vessel for distributing eatables oı 'prasada' during festivals.

21. Mathia : a large oval-shaped vessel with a narrow mouth and is used for storing grains and clothes. When cloth is stored for a considerable period the mouth is shut tight with a lid pasted over the mouth.

22. Mridanga : it is also known as the 'khol'. It is a long drum, the shape being longer than that of the Dama. Both the ends are stretched with hide for beating.

23. Nad-pat : these are terracotta well-rings. Such rings were inserted one upon another into the well to seal off seepage of sub-oil water into the well. As a result wells were narrower in diameter than those dug in Bihar.

24. Nadia : it is basin used for storing sweetmeats. Though shaped like a Charu it is stronger and has a rim.

25. Nagara : it is a small sized drum.

26. Piala : it is also known as Beria or Deg. It is a shallow Khola with a wider mouth. But the neck is smaller than that of a Khola's. Usually, 'gur', curds and salt are kept in it.

27. Satar : similar to the Akathia and the Daskathia, but it holds food for one person only.

28. Sarai : it is a raised tray for offering food to the idols or to respectable persons.*

29. Tekeli : it is also known as the Bhetua and like the Kalah is used for storing water. Its capacity is between two to four quarts which is much less than that of a Kalah.**

30. Thali : it is a huge vessel which is used for cooking during feasts or for boiling sugar-can juice for preparing 'gur'. Water is also stored in it.†

*Similar ones are also made in metal. But the wheel turned ones seem to have served as models for imitations in wood and metals. But eventually the terracotta ones became less popular due to their fragility. The tall stand at the bottom was responsible for easy breakage. The Ceylonese counterpart of the Sarai is the Bulatbattiya or the Paddikkam which are used for offering betel or 'pan'. Saraı is derived from the Sanskrit Saravam, i.e., a bowl.

**The Tekeli has a special use in marriages where it is used for bathing the bride and the groom at their respective dwellings.

†The word Thali in Assamese is derived from the Sanskrit Sthali or a cooking pot, usually for cooking rice, e.g. Sthali Pulak Nyaya.

The above list by Gait is fairly accurate. But the Tekeli has a minor variation in the Enwa Tekeli which has a long neck and is shaped like a flask. The Nadia with a rim is used in Upper Assam while the one used in Lower Assam is without one. Special types of Tekelis were manufactured for being used as moulds for solidifying gur. While hot and still syrupy the 'gur' was poured into such Tekelis and on cooling the gur was available in roughly shaped lumps. Dergaon in Upper Assam was famous for such long-necked Tekeli moulds (Dergaonr gurar tekeli). The Dunari is a large perforated pot with a handle and has use in marriages. Often the outer side of the Dunari is decorated with applique decorations.

Assam pottery still has a very fine texture and is of pale pink or buff colour. The neck of the Tekeli is given a band of red slip. The Nadia used in Lower Assam is decorated with mat-like designs impressed on the outer side while still damp. The impression is actually given with a piece of plaited bamboo matting.

The pottery industry was scattered all over the land yet places like Dharamtul and Dergaon were famous for the Charu and the Tekeli respectively. These places still occur in proverbs in Assamese associated with their past excellence in pottery production. Other famous centres were Jorhat, Golaghat and Salmara in Majuli island. Other important centres of this industry had been Dharamtul[1] (Nowgong district), Bisnath[2] (Darrang district), Gauripur and Rupsi[3] (Goalpara district), Teok and Golaghat[1] (Sibsagar district) and Hirapara-Palasbari, Rani and Beltola[5] (Kamrup district), Madarkhat and Tinsukia (Lakhimpur district).[6]

All pottery was wheel turned except those which were very large bins or well-rings. Handmade objects were produced by the members of the Hira caste only. The potter's wheel is known as the 'chak' and is about three feet in diameter. "In the centre is a solid disc of tamarind or some other hard wood, sometimes 13 inches in diameter to which the outer rim is joined by four wooden spokes each of which is about 6 inches in length. The outer rim which is 6 inches broad is made of split bamboos bound with cane and covered with a thick plaster of clay mixed with fibres of the Sago palm (Chaur) ; the object of this rim is to increase the weight of the wheel and thereby to add to its momentum. An upright piece of Nageswar wood (Mesua ferrea) or Khair (Acacia Catechu) about 6 inches in length supports the wheel ; it is fixed firmly in the ground and is pointed at the upper end, so as to enable the wheel to revolve freely ; a hollowed out stone is let into the

1 Assam District Gazetteer : Nowgong, Ch. VI, p 147

2. Assam District Gazetteer : Darrang, Ch. V. Pp 157-8.

3. Assam District Gazetteer : Goalpara.

4 Assam District Gazetteer : Sibsagar, Ch VII. p. 162.

5. Assam District Gazetteer : Kamrup.

6. Assam District Gazetteer : Lakhimpur, Ch. VIII.

centre of the disc, where it rests on the point so as to reduce the friction to a minimum . . . the wheel is worked by hand and revolves horizontally . . . . The earth under the wheel is generally scooped away, so that the upper surface of the wheel may be on a level with the ground, on which the operator sits.

2. The rolling board is a flat board or an earthenware tray on which the pottery is shaped by hand when the wheel is not needed. It is locally known as the Aphari.
3. The mould (Athali) is a hollow earthenware basin.
4. The mallet (Baliya Piteni) is 6″ to 12″ in length and is used for beating the soft clay at the time of kneading.
5. The polisher (Chaki) is used to polish the pot while still soft.
6. The kiln (Paghali) is used by the Kumars. But the Hiras burn their ware in the open. In both cases vessels are stacked carefully with layers of straw in between them. Firewood and dry cowdung cakes are used as fuel for the kiln underneath. The stack of earthenware ready for firing is called a Thupa (Sanskrit Stupa—stack or mound).

Normally Kumar women only take part in the final shaping and polishing of the finished clay vessels. But the Hira women help their menfolk at all stages of the process.[1] The potters in Assam are divided into two major groups, viz., the Kumars and the Hiras. The Kumars are real potters and they use the potter's wheel for turning the pottery. The Hiras are also bracketed with the Chandals or Charals.[2] They are similar to the Doms[3] and their organisation and social status. Pointing at the individuality of Hiras, Gait says that "of all functional sub-castes they approach most nearly to the position of a separate caste.[4] The Hiras and the Chandals observe connubium and condominium among themselves and the same Pati or group of Brahmins who are of a lower rank than the actual Brahmins, act as their priests. The Hiras also sell fish like their Dom and Chandal brethren.[5]

The Kumars like other professional castes in Assam are more of a professional group than a real caste group. The name Kumar is derived from the Sanskrit Kumbhakara or the potter. Their community includes also members from the Kalita, Kewat and Koch castes. Thus anybody working in clay is grouped under the Kumar caste. But this large group is also sub-divided into Kumar-Kalitas, Kumar-Kewats and the Kumar Koches. These workers

1. Gait, E.A. : The Manufacture of Pottery in Assam ; Journal of Indian Art, Vol. VI, No. 54, pp. 6-7. Jan. 1896.
2. Gait, E.A., Ibid p. 5.
3. Rai Coonabhiram Barooah Bahadur : Asam Buranji, p. 239.
4. Gait, E.A. : Ibid p. 5.
5. Ibid, p. 5.

in clay however retain their original caste affiliations in matters of social and ritual activities. In Goalpara, however, the Kumars form a separate caste.[1] In the social heirarchy the Kumars are ranked along with the blacksmith (Kamar) and the bell-metal workers (Kanhars). But the Kumars have a position lower than that of the pure agriculturists. The distinctions are not so rigid in Western Assam. A Kumar-Kalita, for example, from the Western districts can easily marry a woman of the Bar-Kalita caste who are pure agriculturists and their next generation can rank as a pure agriculturist Bar-Kalita. But in Upper Assam such an easy entry into the higher caste is not so easy. Some Doms in Tezpur also make rough and large bins for boiling Gur but to them also pottery-making is a secondary occupation.[2]

Potters use a particular variety of fine glutinous clay of a dark blue colour known as Kumar-mati or potters' earth. This is available on banks of particular streams and often settlements of potters (Kumar gaons) grow near such sources of clay. The Hiras likewise used a special variety of earth which was still rarer, and was known as Hira-mati. Molong and Agiathuli in Kamrup were two important places for Hira-mati. This clay is grey in colour and very stiff and is good for hand-modelling. But for wheel-turned pottery this earth is not suitable and hence is not used by the Kumars. Sometimes it is used with Kumar-mati and is used by the Kumars for shaping well-rings in forms or moulds. Such rings were not only used for wells but for pit-latrines also which were so common in the past.[3] When two different earths were mixed together, care was taken to mix them thoroughly after the routine removal of all impurities from them. A quantity of coarse sand was mixed with the clay when it was too stiff for working. It also prevented the wares from cracking during firing in the kiln. Sometimes powdered pieces of old pottery, ashes, paddy husks and fibrous objects are chopped and mixed into clay. In all cases the clay is thoroughly mixed and worked up by means of the feet of the workers or with the help of a mallet.[4]

All utensils except well-rings and flat saucer-like objects are made on the wheel. Next, the objects are somewhat sun-dried and then put into the mould and beaten with mallet for shaping. A little sand is sprinkled in the mould to prevent the vessel from sticking to the mould. Then the vessel is sun-dried again and polished with a piece of smooth stone or a piece of strong rag folded and moistened with water. A coat of red dust or cattle urine is then applied to the vessels and they are ready for putting into the kiln. Saucers are not made on the wheels but are moulded by hand on a flat board.

1. Gait, E.A. : The Manufacture of Pottery in Assam, Journal of Indian Art, Vol. VI, No. 54, Jan. 1896, p, 5.
2. Gait, E.A. : Ibid.
3. Handique, B.C. : Purani Asamar Silpa, p. 36
4. Gait, Ibid p. 5.

2. TERRACOTTAS

Very little is known outside about the terracottas of Assam. The long isolation of Assam during the Islamic rule in India was greatly responsible for this state of affairs. The problem has been further complicated by three factors, viz., an aggressive tropical climate and vegetation always trying to engulf the architectural ventures of man, frequent earthquakes resulting in their destruction and finally the apathy of the Department of Archaeology at the Centre as well as at the provincial level. Yet much of Assamese art has been preserved thanks to the consciousness of the people and their almost fanatical love for the culture of the pre-British days when Assam was ruled by independent native dynasties.

Terracottas though less durable than stone have survived in the shape of ornamental bricks (Ita), facing plaques (Phalakas), a large variety of vessels, lanterns and lamps, incense-burners, royal seals, dolls and toys (Putala) and figurines of a votive nature. "Terracottas (Baked clay) are the vernacular medium of figural sculptures in all early cultures in world art". In India the regional terracottas have "their own characteristic features and the particular trend is distinctively prominent everywhere". During the Ahom rule in Assam (13th – 19th centuries A.D.) the art of terracottas was further developed for making the fine pinkish tile-like bricks (Senduri-Ita) for building as well as for paving the royal roads (Ali), for drainage pipes, refuse bins, soak-pits and rings for Pucca-wells (Nad).

During the present age as in the past the art of pottery-making and terracottas was not confined to any particular region of Assam yet places like Dergaon and Engera were famous for pottery whereas Sadiya, Sibsagar, Gauhati and Goalpara were famous for their terracotta architectural embellishments. Pottery was manufactured by Kumars who made them on the potter's wheel and also by the Hiras who made hand-moulded pottery according to the dictates of their caste. These two castes were grouped together with the Charals (Chandalas) and were collectively known as Doms. Some of the Naga tribes also follow this hand-moulded technique which is similar to that of basket weaving. The potters used to settle in particular localities where the clay was suitable for their trade and such settlements were known as Kumar-gaons. Epigraphic records also testify to the prevalence of brick-making and pottery in the pre-Ahom period. The Sualkuchi Grant of Ratnapala refers to brick-making and the Nidhanpur Grant mentions the potters' pit (Kumbhakara-garta).

Pottery from Dah-Parvatiya (Tezpur) and Sadiya have been stylistically assigned to the 5th-6th century A.D. period. Ancient pottery with light gold paint has also been found at Gauhati. Bana-bhatta mentions among the presents of Bhaskaravarman to Harsha "drinking vessels embossed by skilful artists, mollasses in earthen pots and cups of Ullaka", which were produced in Assam. "The clay seals of Bhaskara also point to the fact that the art of clay modelling was developed." It is datable to 643 A.D. These were found by Spooner during the excavations at Nalanda in 1917-18 along with seals of Harsha. The geneology of the dynasty of Bhaskara was established by R.D. Banerji (J.B.O.R.S. Vol. VI, P 1511920). Compared to all-India standard the seals deserve a high place. A similar object in the shape of a votive tablet with the image of the Buddha in Bhumisparsa mudra was found at Gauhati. "Below the figure is inscribed the well-known Mahayana creed in characters of the eleventh century". During the clearance of the ruins of Dah-Parvatiya were found two terracotta plaques showing a male figure in Yoga-pose in each case. "According to Mr. Banerji the moulding of the torso and the general technique proves beyond doubt that these plaques cannot be later in date than the sixth century A.D." Excavations at Gauhati had yielded some interesting specimens of pottery of many shapes and sizes. In the opinion of K.N. Dikshit "these are older than specimens of ancient pottery so far discovered in other parts of India."

The Dah Parvatiya plaques are some of the best specimens of pre-Ahom terracottas. The terracotta plaques from the area show a close similarity with the art of Bengal. They resemble those from Birhat, Raypur and Paharpur in Rajshahi district. The best one shows a human figure in each case "The moulding of the torso and the general technique proves beyond doubt that these plaques are contemporary with, if not older than, those discovered at Paharpur and cannot be later than sixth century A.D. One fragment shows that human figures reveal the existence of a modified form of acanthus motif in this distant corner of Assam. This device has been noticed in the Gupta temples at Bhumra, Nachna-Kuthara and Deogarh." Dalton noticed from the ruins at Tezpur some urns on black pottery ornamented with flowers. Specimen of earthenwares were discovered from the ruins of the Sadiya region, which according to Hanner, bear close affinity to those found in the Gangetic valley. Sadiya has yielded the finest specimen of Assamese terracottas belonging to circa 10th - 11th century. The composition consisting of three feminine forms in graceful poses resembles the contemporary East Indian style and affinities with Pala-Sena sculptures are only too apparent.

During the Ahom age the pottery industry flourished as these were in great demand as cooking and eating vessels for all classes of people. Those were even used by the royal household for hygienic and ceremonial reasons. Eric T.D. Lambert says the bricks of this period were similiar to those used in Siam in the Ayuthia period. The variety of mediaval bricks and other architectural members in terracotta is astonishing. Bricks were square, rectangular, triangular, round, perforated and fluted. The best examples of edifices decorated with terracotta plaques are the

Ghanasyam Do' l (1751-69 A.D.) at Jaysagar, Sibsagar and the dilapidated temple known as the Na' Math (New Shrine) near the temple of Kamakhya, Gauhati. Baghapara in Goalpara district produced some of the finest terracotta plaques of the 17th century of which the row of geese and the dancing group are the best. "The dancing and the hunting scenes and also the lively figure of the fighting bull stand out most prominently." During the Tungkhungiya period building in brick became popular at Rangpur (present Sibsagar), the capital and other important cities. The beautiful plaques of this period show a variety of subjects from Nature as well as from daily life of the people. In this respect they were identical in style and content with the sculptures and paintings of the period. The Ghanasyam Do'l is the finest of all structures so decorated. The plaque showing Durga is not only similar to the contemporary stone reliefs from the Jagadhatri temple at Kalugaon but also to the image of Mahisasuramardini from Lakhimpur belonging to the 13th century. These examples clearly show that the tradition of terracottas was not isolated from those of contemporary sculpture and painting. So much so each seemed to influence the other. For example two plaques from the Janardana temple, Gauhati (1744-51) depicting a horse and an elephant have their prototypes in the Lava-Kusha Yuddha ms. datable between 1694-1714, and in the Lanka-Kanda ms. They are identical in form, conception and the execution of details. In both cases the figures are framed by multi-foiled arches which is typical of mediaeval Assamese narrative art. The relief panels from Jaysagar and Kalugaon appear identical with terracotta panels of the period, both technically and stylistically. The figures in all these different mediums are ultimately derived from the 16th century miniatures of the Satriya school of painting, which was a product of the neo-vaisnava movement of Sankara Deva.

But the Na' Math near the Kamakhya temple, Gauhati has exquisite full size pillars and pilasters of terracotta in perforated designs. The corners of the building have fin-like projections and are entirely made of figures of acrobats arranged in a vertical row. The facades of these buildings were made to look like wooden structures of Assam by means of terracotta embellishments representing wooden posts, pilasters and carved panels. Though the Ghanasyam Do'l is intact the Na' Math is crumbling. But the terracottas of the latter are far better preserved and have preserved their brilliant burnt earth colour.

The identity with contemporary miniatures is further emphasised in the plaques and slabs of Jaysagar showing hunting and eqestrian scenes. The ever popular Ahom-lion also makes its appearance in the plaques. Some slabs of this group also show beautiful scroll and floral designs of Indo-Persian origin. Many of them are to be met with in the Moghul paintings. Similar motifs were also used on the stone slabs of the Umananda temple (1694 A.D.) at Gauhati.

Dolls and toys were also made in terracottas and grouped under the general term Putala or Puteli. These were sometimes specially made for semi-religious folk ceremonies like Doll's Wedding (Puteli-Bia) in Kamrup by childless women wishing for offsprings. Apart from these the potters or the Khanikars also made Chakras and Mandalas of terracotta for Saiva and Sakta religious practices of the Abhicharika nature. Such objects were discarded or destroyed after the worship which was precisely for obtaining a particular objective. Fairs and festivals were the main occasions for making and selling of toys. Badati Ghat was traditionally famous for its terracotta dolls and toys. In recent times Mazbat is producing terracotta objects to suit modern tastes and contemporary use. In toy making the most popular items were elephants, boats and dolls clad in the native two-piece female costume of Mekhela (Sarong) and Chadar (Odhni). Some older designs are to be seen in the collection of toys by Sri Bhuvan Chandra Handiqui of Jaysagar. There is a Mama-doll less than 6" high carrying a child at the waist. It is clad in a Methani (Sarong) which is hitched up to the breasts in the manner of the women of Bali. The face is pronouncedly Mongoloid betraying the local racial type. Some very interesting dolls are made in the village of Nahira, about 17 miles to the west of Gauhati. Such dolls are cylindrical with one end flattened to form the base and the other end is so pinched that it shows the rudiments of a face with a prominent nose. Two longish pellets attached horizontally to the torso form the outstretched arms. On the chest is the crossed scarf indicated by white lines. This style is reminiscent of the mother goddess figurines popular from the Indus valley period to the Mauryan Age. The crossed scarf or the Channavira became the symbol of the mother goddess and then of fertility. The Nohira dolls thus have preserved some of the most ancient traits of Indian terracotta figurines.

A more evolved form of the Nahira dolls is found in the Goalpara district but these are votive in nature. These female dolls are always shown with little babies on their laps. The face is pinched and bird-like though the body is human. The head dress is fan-shaped and elaborate resembling the Opasa of the Vedic period. Similar head dresses have also been seen in some Harappa figurines. These dolls stand for goddess Suvachani also known as the "Duck-Mother". To emphasise the bird aspect she is actually shown carrying a baby duck in her lap in some cases. Such dolls are also to be met with in the adjoining districts of Mymensingh, Rangpur and Dinajpur in Eastern Bengal.

The gradual decline of the ruling house of Tungkhung, the repeated Burmese invasions in the early years of the 19th century and the final British occupation of Assam by the middle of the same century were shocks too strong for the foundations of the Assamese society and her arts and industries. And the art of terracottas was not an exception.

5

PAINTING

Assamese paintings of the Ahom period are mostly in the shape of manuscript illustration though this technique was sometimes adopted to paint on wooden surfaces of architectural members or pieces of furniture and sundry other objects. These miniatures are executed on the oblong format of Assamese Vaishnava manuscripts and only rarely on technical, historical and Buddhist treatises and also on those belonging to other sects of Hinduism. The preponderence of wooden architecture in Assam restricted the development of mural painting. This kind of architecture divided the wall surfaces even of huge buildings into inconvenient rectangles and no continuous subject could be painted with ease. Yet cloth paintings specially on Muga silk were produced though their number was very small. The extremely humid climate of Assam was also responsible for the unpopularity of mural painting. From the end of the 17th century large masonry buildings became popular. In such edifices stucco and terracotta panels took the place of mural painting. The glorious tradition of fine wood carving in palaces and religious buildings was followed till the end of Ahom rule and hence the Assamese artist did not feel the need for mural decorations as such. Moreover, the wood carving was often embellished with bright colours and hence the want of wall paintings was never much felt. Laquering was also practised to cover paintings on wooden surfaces with a fine transparent film with a slight golden glint. Painting, like most arts, was greatly patronised by the royalty and the church and painters were grouped under the 'Khanikar Khel'[1] or guild of painters under a superintendent known as the Khanikar Barua. The painter like many other artists was also known as the Khanikar. Like other Khels, the Khanikar Khel was an occupational group and it included Hindus as well as Mohammadans, both native and of foreign extraction. As in the case of other aspects of Assamese art, painting also incorporated elements from Mughal, Burmese and Chinese painting style. Paintings

1. Das Gupta, R., Eastern Indian Manuscript Painting, p. 72, 1972.

were generally termed as 'Pratima',[1] 'Chitra' and 'Chabi', and the act of painting was known as 'Lekha'[2] or writing, thus bringing out the essentially linear character of Assamese miniatures and its close relation with the art of calligraphy. Painting was an essential part of the 'Kayasthika Vidya'[3] or 'Kaitheli Vidya', i.e., the training for Kayasthas who as in India proper were initially scribes by profession. There had been great names in painting of the period and even the saint Sankaradeva was a painter of note.

A historical survey :—The earliest reference to painting in Assam (Pragjyotisa) is to be found in the Harivamsa and the Dwarka-lila, both ultimately derived from the Mahabharata. There is reference to Chitralekha, the great master in portrait painting who according to Assamese tradition is connected with Sonitapura which is the present town of Tezpur in Assam. Sonita (blood) and Tez in Assamese are synonymous and hence the modern name of the historic city.* "The princess Usha dreamt that a beautiful youth appeared to her, and was her companion in her walks abroad. She confides this to one of her maids-of-honour, Chitralekha, who had the natural gift of being able to draw a likeness. The maid offered to relieve the anxiety of her mistress by sketching the portraits of all the great men of the time, so that the person in the dream might be identified. As soon as Usha saw the picture of Aniruddha, the grandson of Krsna, the youth of her vision was revealed to her. This artistic incident subsequently led to their nuptials. . . ."[4]

In the Mahabharata Chitralekha is mentioned as a portrait painter of note. "In view of the position that women have occupied in India generally, it is a notable fact that the first Indian painter mentioned by name was a woman. Chitralekha, a word which literally means picture, was the heroine of an incident in the Dwarka Lila, a work of the Epic Age, and probably dating from many centuries before the Christian era."[5] The Harivamsa praises her aptitude in painting in the following lines,

1. "Yar samipat Sanga Devir sadrisyakaya divya alamkaramandita Sri Amvika Devi prakasa Karicha .....adesak sirogata Kari Vadha Ligiraye' pratima sahite likhaila......Saka 1959." Bhagavata Book VI ; colophone page, 1734 A.D. Department of Historical and Antiquarian Studies, Assam, Gauhati.

2. Ibid, Colophone page.

3. Datta-Barua, H N., Prachina Kamarupiya Kayastha Samajar Itivritta, p. [illegible].

*That Sonitapura, the capital of Banasura, was a centre of great artistic activities, is seen from the exquisite door-frame of the 5th century A.D. from Dah-Parbatiya, a suburb of Tezpur and numerous other relics of temples and stone sculpture to be met with in and around the town.

4. Brown, P., Indian Painting, pp. 19-20. 1960, Calcutta.

5. Ibid, p. 11, 1960.

"Vanasuramantrinah Kumbhandasya Kanyayam
Tasya cha chitra lekhanadaksata.[1]

Her memory is carried over till the 16th century when the Assamese poet Pitambara Dvija composed his long narrative work "Usha Parinaya" (1533 A.D.) in verse. Their Chitralekha is said to have learnt the art of painting, specially, the scroll painting from Siva, the Lord of Dance, and of all arts, that emanate from the primordial art form—dance.

"Chitralekha bole Devadeva Mahesvara
Avadhana Kara gosain mango eka vara.
Svarga mancha patale yateka ache prani
Hena vara deha chitralekhibakajani.
....
Hena hauk bulila tridasera adhipati.[2]

References to painting are again found in the Nidhanpur Copper Plate Grant of king Bhaskara Varman, an ally of king Harsa of Kanauj. There are references to portraits hung on the walls of houses in this grant,

"Vasya vihatamatanubhi
Stejobhirlaksmanripatibhavanesu
ud
patresviva bhurisu vilokyate bhaskarasyeva."[3]

References to Chitrasalas are to be found in the Nowgong Grant of Valavarman,

"Yenatulapi satula jagati visalapi bhurikritasala
Pangktih prasadanam
Krita vichitra pi sachhitra.[4]

The Tezpur Grant of Fanamala refers to the well-decorated temple of Hataka Sulin.[5] Actual examples of the linear tradition are found in the Guakuchi Copper Plate Grant of Indrapala (1051 A.D.). At the end of the grant are inscribed Graduda trampling on a serpent, a lotus, a Samkha and a Chakra, all associated

1. *Harivamsa*, 176.
2. Neog, M., (ed.) "Usha Parinaya", p. 51.
3. Vidyavinod, P.N., Kamarupasasanavali, V. 24, p. 31, 1938, Rangpur.
4. Ibid, V. 14, p. 75.
5. Ibid, p. 62.

with Vaisnavism. Just below the drawings is written : "Pusta siri Astahenta.".[1] According to Vidyavinod this line in Prakrit gives some hints regarding the inscriber of the figures in the copper plates. His reading in Sanskrit would be Pustam Sri Astakena or the pictures by Sri Astaka. The Nidhanpur Grant of Bhaskara Varman also mentions the Sekyakara (engraver) as Kaliya.[2] In the above grant Astaka is the name of the engraver and his name has been recorded as Astaka in Kamarupi Prakrit.

The Harsacharita has direct references to the popularity of painting in 7th century Assam as the presents from Bhaskaravarman to Harsa of Kanauj included many an accessory to painting. The presents included "carved boxes of panels for painting with brushes and gourds," and gold painted cages.[3] "Other objects were the fine tinted manuscripts. Volumes of fine writing with leaves made from aloe bark and of the hue of the ripe pink cucumber."[4] It was in the direction of manuscript painting that Assam excelled in the Ahom period. "Portrait painting is found in the border painting of some old Assamese manuscripts before and after the 14th century A.D. Harivara Vipra (14th et A.D.), for instance in his 'Babhnuvahana Parva' refers to paintings on walls.[5]

In the Ahom period we find three distinct schools of painting prevailing in Assam. From the early stage, however, we have only examples in the Tai-Ahom style. In the next phase beginning from the early 16th century the Satriya school inspired by the Vaisnava movement of Sri Sankaradeva takes root and continues with full vigour till the early 18th century when the Gargaon school becomes popular in the court circles. But the Satriya school was followed for illustrating religious texts and epic subjects till the days of king Kamaleswar Singha (1795-1811). But throughout the Ahom period book illustration was the exclusive mode of painting. Murals and scroll paintings did not find favour either in the court circles or in the Vaisnava monasteries of the land. The volume of production of illustrated manuscripts was great but very little exists today in public view. While good examples are preserved mostly in the Satras and homes of the old aristocracy, a large volume had been destroyed due to climatic ravages and the devastating raids of the Burmese during the last phase of Ahom rule. The only places where examples of Assamese book-illustration are to be found outside Assam are the British Museum, London, and the City Palace Museum, Jaipur. In Assam the

1. Vidyavinod, P.N., Kamarupasasanavali, V. 24, p. 140, 1938, Rangpur.
2. Ibid, p. 26, V. 136.
3. Cowell & Thomas, Bana's Harsha-Carita, Ch. VII, 217.
4. Ibid, 212 ff.
5. Chowdhury, P.C., The History of Civilisation of the People of Assam, p. 475, Gauhati, 1966.

State Museum, the Department of Historical and Antiquarian Studies of the Government of Assam, and the Gauhati University Library, all three institutions at Gauhati possess a fair number of illustrated Assamese manuscripts.

I. The Ahom School of Painting

The Ahoms were great patrons of book illustration like their Thai cousins. "The Ahoms brought their manuscripts dealing both with religious and with secular matters."[1] All the Thai tribes between Upper Assam and Upper Burma were designated as the Naras by the people of Assam.[2] Painting was popular among these tribes. They were linked by marriages and paintings often were prized as dowry among these tribes.[3] Thus even after settling down in Assam, the Shan style of painting was continued due to constant contracts with the native land and the kinfolk across the borders of the Patkai. The style in Assam has been designated as the Tai-Ahom style. Being primarily a religious art it remained conservative and maintained many of the earlier traits.

The earliest extant examples of manuscript illustration in Assam are from the Phung Chin manuscript, dated 1473 A.D. in the Ahom language and script. It is a treatise on the Ahom conception of heavens and hells as modified by animism as well as Hinayana Buddhism. The style of painting which is individualistic will be termed, 'Tai-Ahom' in connection with the language in which the work is written. The style of illustration is as different from the Satriya school of painting in Assam as is Ahom, a Tai language, is different from Assamese, an Indo-Aryan tongue. One style is as much Assamese as the other for in Assam the Indo-Aryan and Tibeto-Burman peoples and cultures met to give birth to one composite Assamese way of life.

The Phung Chin and the Suk-tanta Kyempong manuscripts represent the earliest phase of Assamese manuscript illustration. These are written on folios of "tulapat" or locally made paper, folded and stitched together.

The Phung Chin[4] gives a description of the sixteen heavens and an equal number of hells according to the Pheravada as well as Ahom conception. Of these the four, Newasinnyakkasaneya satananwa, Akingchingtana, Wingyana-mingehe-tapan, and Akasamisgchasattanan, are the highest, whereto no female soul can be

1. Bhuyan, S.K., The Administrative System of the Ahoms ; p. 94 ; Aspects of the Heritage of Assam ; Indian History Congress, 22nd Session, Gauhati 1959.
2. Hamilton, F., An Account of Assam, pp. 78-79.
3. Purani Asam Buranji, pp. 19-20.
4. Manuscript No. 25, Gauhati, Department of Historical and Antiquarian Studies,

promoted ; they can only reside in the heaven called Akasanikttaka, Sikkiya, i.e. Sakara or India, lives in the heaven named Chalapehuthamma and rides on his five-headed elephant Ailavana, i.e. Airavata. The Ahom conception of the transmigration of the soul has been described in this manuscript and each concept has been illustrated.

The illustrations, which are presently discussed, are manuscript miniatures in the royal sense. But they can hardly be called painting as such. They are fine drawings outlined in black. Some of them are filled in with colours, restricted to black, brown, red, green, blue and yellow. They are not universally used, but only for particular portions of the illustrations. Gold paint or "Kham" also been used far more sparingly ; the only occasions are to indicate the heart of the Buddha in the mahaparinirvana scene and to show Bodh Gaya in a sort of conventional Mandala showing the Buddhist holy places, the centre of which is occupied by the former.

The name of the scribe, who evidently was the illustrator, too, is given as Chao Kyang Shen, belonging to Kingson Maolung, a principality between the Shan states and southern provinces of China. The date of the manuscript is given in Tai Lakni or Tai era, which when converted to the Christian calendar comes to 1478 A.D. This date, given in the manuscript itself, has given rise to some controversies. Dr. Moti Chandra does not accept it, and thinks that the manuscript is decidedly of a much later date, though he does not assign it to any particular century. Miss Ingrid Aal of Norway, an authority on south-east Asian painting, places the illustrations to a period as late as 1650 A.D. She, however, says that only some of the illustrations of the manuscript can be assigned to that period, while the rest are to be considered much later in date on stylistic ground. Of those that have been assigned to c. 1650 A.D. are the illustrations of the Pillar of Dharma and that of Parinirvana.

The contentions of the scholars are, however, not acceptable. Firstly, they have not been able to give any specific reasons in favour of their views. Before contradicting their views, general traits of the style can be discussed.

The subjects are directly placed on the blank surface of the folio. No landscape serves as background. The majority of the illustrations are of human or of semi-divine beings all depicted in anthropomorphic forms. The human figures are all in front view though the faces are drawn in the three-quarter profile. The depiction is similar as in the frescoes of Ananda Monastery of Pagan.[1]

1. Thaw Ka, The Early Art of Burma, Perspective of Burma, p. 35, An Atlantic monthly supplement.

These frescoes from the Upali Thein ordination hall and a monastery near the Ananda temple belong to the 17th century. But they definitely contain in them elements from a much earlier school. But this school though different from the Mon frescoes from Kyanzittha's temple like the Nagayon, (11th century) and are decidedly the result of Shan domination of Burma, for paintings in a similar style are produced by the Shan people of Upper Burma for ritualistic purposes as well as for decorating processional cars. Pyres for the cremation of Phongyis or Bhikkhus are embellished with similar paintings by the people of Akyab.[1]

After a comparative study of the Pagan (frescoes c. 11th century) and the later Shan influenced style of Burma we can say that the Phung Chin and the Suktanta-Kyempong are examples of Shan colonial art of Indian soil. For, the Ahoms entered Assam almost at the Pagan after its fall at the hands of the Tartars of Kublai Khan in 1287 A.D. In both the countries the Shans began a new dynasty and introduced a new culture, though very soon they were submerged by the superior cultures of the conquered countries.

But the Ahom paintings contain in them some traits of the pre-Shan Pagan style of Nagayon. They had possibly infiltrated into the Ahom circle after Shan painting had itself absorbed Pagan elements in Burma and then transmitted them to the sister kingdom of "Mung-dun-chun-kham", or Assam, under the Ahoms. Intercourse between Upper Assam and Upper Burma had always remained, although the intensity varied from time to time. The chief ambassadors of this cultural exchange had been Buddhist monks who were often appointed abbots in the "bapuchangs" or viharas of the Tai-phake people in Sibsagar and Lakhimpur districts of Assam. The following characteristics of pre-Shan Pagan painting are also presented in those of the Phung Chin manuscript : "Contours and flat fabrics are defined by heavy black lines ; figures are stylized and majestic. Those representing persons of greater importance are large in proportion to the others. . . . There is no linear nor atmospheric perspective, no modelling in light and shade. . . . faces are impressive symbols rather than actual portraits."[2] All these apply to Ahom paintings also. They are all puppet-like and are gracefully posed. Their heads are generally tilted to a side and the expressions are serene and sombre. The dancing scene from the heaven of Sikiya is full of animation, while the Buddha's parinirvana scene shows how successful the simple style had been in expressing the sorrow of the disciples with the greatest economy.

The lines are generally of uniform thickness and are flowing. The curves of the elbows are smooth and not angular and sharp as in the early western Indian

1. Thaw Ka, The Early Art of Burma, Perspective of Burma, p, 16. An Atlantic monthly supplement.
2. Ibid., p. 38, pl. 44.

and Pagan paintings. The fingers are exceptionally long and tapering, full of expression and though they do not form any 'mudras' as such they are equally successful in their mission. One thing that is common to all these illustrations is that they are thoroughly imbibed with the spirit of the text. The men and women are full of humility and devotion as expressed in their poses and have serene and compassionate looks in their eyes. They successfully represent the teachings of the Buddha for the laity.

The two of Buddha figures in the "bhumisparsamudra" are important since they betray their mixed origin. They are all similar and are arranged in a row, each under a cinque-foil cusped arch. Such a representation evidently suggests that they represent icons from some place of Buddhist worship, just as most of the Pala paintings of Buddhist deities did. Moreover, their being placed each under an arch is, according to Basil Gray, another Pala element.[1]

Another manuscript in the same style, the Suktanta-Kyempong[2] comes from Namphakial in the Lakhimpur district. It is a treatise on Lokadharma of Theravada Buddhism. The language is Tai-phake and the script Ahom. The writer is one Prince Noja of Kingwi, a Shan principality and he is also a cousin of Chao Kyang Shen, the scribe of the Phung Chin manuscript. The present copy of the Suktanta-Kyempong was made by one Aichu of the Namphakial vihara, during the abbotship of U. Kandama. The date of the present copy is, however, not known. The original copy, as tradition says, was done about fifty years later than that of the Phung Chin and hence can be placed about 1523 A.D. But since the original one is contemporareous with the Phung Chin manuscript, the present copy preserves in its two illustrations the traits of 15th century paintings.

The Buddha is an illustrated prototype of an icon in a niche as in a Pala painting. The niche is rather unusual, in the shape of a truncated pyramid. The figure has a cold and static expression like the Buddha images from Burma. Like the Phung Chin illustrations it is also a painted drawing. Colours used include blue, yellow, red, brown, black and gold.

According to Basil Gray, "They clearly look to the Buddhist manuscripts of the Pala period, which are organised in the same way with figures in architectural niches."[3] The other sides of the influence is equally apparent. They are all in

1. Basil Gray, 'The Development of Painting in India in the 16th century :' Marg. Vol. VI, No. 3, 1953, p. 20.

2. Manuscript No. 1197, Gauhati. Development of Historical and Antiqarian Studies.

3. Basil Gray, 'The Development of Painting in India in the 16th Century' Marg. Vol. VI. No. 3, p. 20 1953.

"bhumisparsamudra" and the "sanghati" leaves the right shoulder bare. The "usnisa" is tapering and the ears elongated and almost elephantine,—all being attributes of a Mahapurusa. These elements betray their affinity to Siamese Buddha images, from Wat Mahadhatu, Lopburi Thai land.[1]

The illustrations of the Pillar of Dharma and the "parinirvana have been described as naive and have been placed around 1950 A.D. by Miss Ingrid Aal. One thing that can be said in connection with these illustrations is that being examples of religious art they are conservation and hence have remained unchanged for centuries. They show in the later dates the characteristics of the days of their origin among the Tai people in their original homeland.

The Shan style of painting is being continued still by the Buddhist population of the Lohit Frontier Division of the Arunachal Pradesh. The Khampti Buddhist priests or "bapus" in the "bapuchangs" are adept in this art. A number of paintings depicting the punishments in hell and Sujata's offering of milk to the Buddha from the "bapuchang" of Nigru near Namsai are in the collection of late Dr. Verrier Elwin of Shillong. Dr. Elwin suggested to me the title "Hinayana Buddhist painting" for these. But when we take into account those from Ahom manuscripts it is more reasonable to call them Tai-Ahom. Stylistically, and in technique, they are identical with the paintings in the Ahom manuscripts from Namphakial. Over and above style, in respect to composition, architectural details, and costume types also similarities are apparent. The importance of this school is that it represents the only surviving school of the Assamese people, and maintains the continuity of a pictorial style for six centuries. Manuscripts were also produced in this style for mainly in the Lohit Frontier Division.

Though the style of manuscript miniatures of the Tai-Ahoms had usually been line drawings, occasionally filled in with paints, a painted version has also been found. It is a Bhagavata, Book III, on "Sanchipat", dated 1782 A.D., and belongs to the Kamarupa Anusandhana Samiti, now housed in the Assam State Museum, Gauhati. It contains all the traits of Tai-Ahom painting except that the figures are painted and the costume type is more Indianised, being the "dhoti", "uttariya", "pag", and the "tangali" round the waist. But being a late copy it had absorbed some characteristics of the later Darrang school, specially in the treatment of animals.

The original Tai-Ahom characteristics are preserved in the blank background and spacing of figures is in an unconnected manner, though they ultimately succeed in making the whole picture. The faces are in three-quarter profile though in a

1. Benjamin Rowland, 'The Art and Architecture of India : Buddhist Hindu and Jaina,' pl. 166.

few cases as that of Sukadeva and Krsna and Balarama profiles with impersonal faces as in Darrang paintings are to be met with. The fingers are again tapering and the "kadas" at the wrists are in the Tai fashion. The treatment of the feet as well as the faces with staring large eyes is also in the same tradition. Assamese traits are noticed in the Salpira or low stool, the Sarai or a tray on a stand and the Arowan or the royal sunshade held by a Ligira or page.

Nature is not given much importance in a painting intented to eulogise Lord Krsna. Vegetation is at its minimum, and only traces are a few large flower bearing plants or meandering foliage against the monochrome red background.

The treatment of the serpent, Kaliya, being quelled by Krsna is also interesting. There is so much of a dragon in its wreathing body and scaly skin. It is different from the fish holding the Earth in the Phung Chin. The eyes, however, in Tai paintings are not beady but staring and angry and the jaws are prominent, as in this Bhagavata III (1782 A.D.) MS from the Assam State Museum, Gauhati.

Intimate connections remained among the Buddhist of Upper Assam and Upper Burma. It introduced, along with Burmese monks deputed to viharas of Assam, the Burmese style of manuscript writing and illustrations. Burmese "Kambawas", or palm-leaf manuscripts, were also copied. The technique of gilding the letters and of laquering the folios and embellishing them with gold letters were also taught to the "bapus" and the novices. The vihara at Barpathar in the Sibsagar district has a beautiful "kambawa" made during the abbotship of U Kandama in the 19th century.

Objections might be made to include the Tai-Ahom illustrations among paintings, for they are primarily line drawings. Firstly, they have been included in this category as they serve the same purpose as pure painting in as far as they are book-illustrations. Secondly, Indian and Oriental art as such makes not much distinction between the two modes of illustration. William Blake says, "The distinction that is made in modern times between a painting and a drawing proceeds from the ignorance of art. The merit of a picture is the same as the merit of a drawing. The dauber baubs his drawings ; he who draw his drawings, draws his picture." The same foundamentals of Oriental art are expressed by Coomaraswamy when he says that the "identity of draughtsmanship and painting is characteristic of the greater part of Oriental art."[1] The lines of the Tai-Ahom painting thus remain purely calligraphic. What he says about the lines in the frescoes of Ajanta and Sigiriya can also apply to Tai-Ahom line drawings. "The long flowing line and the sense of rhythmic movements are noteworthy. There is a freedom of

1. A. K. Coomaraswamy, Indian Drawings.

drawings and grace of line." An element of sensuous delight prevails the 'ekasarana namadharma', propounded by Sankaradeva, which was one of the many schools of neo-Vaisnavism that originated in mediaeval India.

Information regarding the technique of painting the manuscripts and book covers and also about the carriers and implements are no less ample. But most of them are gathered from floating tradition and by a study of the technique followed by present day miniaturist. The most common carrier for manuscripts in Assam was made from the bark of the Agar tree (Acquilaria Agallocha) and is known as "Sanchipat".

Another material on which writings and paintings were done is "tulapat", which had ginned cotton as its ingredient.[1] "Tulapat", as the name implies, is a sheet made from cotton by felting it. "Tulapat" leaves were made by pressing cotton. This practice of making paper out of felted cotton is a direct inheritence of Assam from pre-Christian times.

The use of "tulapat" was as wide as that of Sanchipat not only for writing but also for miniature painting. The oldest painted manuscript on "tulapat" are the Phung Chin (1473 A.D.) and the Suktanta-Kyempong. Although Dr. Maheswar Neog in his *The Art of Painting in Assam* calls "tulapat", felted cotton, a description of its manufacture, which follows, shows that "tulapat" was not made from cotton at all. It is not yet known if at some centres paper was made from cotton, ginned and felted. The finished "tulapat" looks and feels more like fine lint than like paper as we understand it today. During the Ahom rule, Assam's foreign trade was strictly controlled by the state, and paper does not seem to have been imported from Mughal, and later on British India. The two important sources on Assamese trade with India, viz. Hamilton's *An Account of Assam* (1807-14) and Dr. S.K. Bhuyan's *Early British Relations with Assam* nowhere refer to any kind of paper being imported into during the Tunkhungiya period when manuscript painting reached its zenith. The process of making "tulapat" was indigenous to Assam and possibly was a contribution of the various Tai or Shan peoples, who entered Assam beginning with the Ahoms in the 13th century till the Khamptis in the 18th century.

This process of making "tulapat" has been gathered from Sri Chaikhong-let Gohain, an Ahom pundit of the Namphakial village. "Tulapat" is essentially a paper made from wood pulp. Three kinds of trees were usually selected for the purpose. White "tulapat" was made from the "maihai" tree, the dark brown

1. Maheswar Neog, The Art of Painting in Assam, p. 4.

variety from the "Yamon" and the red variety from a tree the name of which has not been found. The "Yamon" tree has been identified with the "hsa"[1] of the Shan people and "nuni" or paper mulberry in Assamese (Bronsanettia Papyrifera). "The barks of the above mentioned trees were cut up in convenient sizes and then beaten thoroughly. This broke the fibres and separated and loosened them. Then these were boiled till they melted and formed into a fine pulp and became cleared of all impurities. The pulp was next poured over water kept in rectangular ditches of required sizes and it floated on the water's surface. It was then evenly spread all over with a scraper to the shape of the watery surface. Then it was left to cool. When cool, the film of pulp lying on the surface of the water gave a sheet of strong and tough paper. Usually, a "tulapat" folio was made by stitching two single sheets together or by folding a longer sheet in two and then stitching the same. This was done to give strength to the folios. The technique described above is identical to the one described in the Shans at Home which shows that this technique was of extra-Indian origin. Important centres of making "tulapat" were located at Namphkial, Munglong and Narayanpur in the district of Lakhimpur in Assam. The people who made it were mostly Ahoms and other peoples of Shan extraction. The Monpa Buddhists of the Kameng Frontier Division of Arunachal Pradesh also make paper in a similar way from the bark of the "paper-tree" locally known as Sukso.[2]

Palm leaves or "talpat" though common in Burma and Bengal were rarely used in Assam for the 'tala" does not grow in Assam. But palm leaves manuscripts were produced, painted and laquered in the Vihara of Disangpani in the Sibsagar district. That is an area populated by the descendants of the Naras, another Shan tribe related to the Ahoms by marriage and blood. They are all Theravada Buddhists and the abbot of the said vihara was one venerable U Kandamna, a Burmese. The palm leaves were produced mostly during his days in the last century and were copies from heavily laquered kambawa of Burma. They are also gilded and are real works of calligraphy and penmanship. The bamboo strip folios as well as the palm leaves were produced mainly by the Buddhist of Upper Assam, who belong to the Ahom, Khampti, Tai-Phake or Phakial, Nara, Aitonia, Turung and Khamjangiya.[3] Manuscripts and scrolls on silk ("pa" and "muga") cloth were stitched along the top to form a pad. A non-Hindu, Ahom manuscript of "muga" silk with beautiful illustrations is deposited at the Buddhist shrine of Kharghariya Daba, sixteen miles from Sibsagar.

1. Milne, Mrs. L., Shans at Home, pp. 175-76.
2. Verrier Elwin, The Art of the North-East Frontier of India, p. 70.
3. Lila Gogoi, 'Ahom Lipir Puthi', Purbakas, July, 1960, pp. 119 f.

Gold paint was also used but mainly for the more important manuscript illustration and royal letter papers were often docorated with gold-painted "lata" or meanders. The Buddhists of Assam used gold paint to illustrate Theravada manuscripts the oldest specimen of which, Phung-Chin, is dated 1473 A.D. To the Buddhists who are mostly of Tai extraction gold as well as gold paint is known as "kham" where as the Assamese called the art of gilding "Sonarpani-Charowa."[1] Gold was applied both as a paint and as a leaf.

The gold required for the "kham" was usually collected from the sands of the Subansiri, the Burhidihing and the rivers of upper Assam. A class of people known as the Sonowals were employed in the task of gold-washing. The gold in dust form facilitated and quickened the process of making "kham". A piece of papei was smeared with "yang" or the vegetable gum obtained from the "yang-pow" or "Bhot-era" tree. Then it was placed atop a quantity of gold-dust spread on an even and smooth surface and as a result the dust clung to the paper. Then it was left to dry and later cut into convenient sizes. The reverse process was followed to apply "kham" to a selected surface. The surface was smeared with the right quantity of glue made from buffalo hide and the gold leaf was applied to it. The gold now clung to the gummed surface and the paper was left blank. Gold dust was also used when it was mixed with some size of binding material. This process of gold leaf transfer is similar to one of the Mughal ways and has been mentioned in the Silparatna (16th century). Though the Visnudharmottara mentions gold-leaf but the process of transfer was not followed according to it. Dr. Moti Chandra is of the opinion that gold-painting came to Western Indian painting from Central Asia.[2] Namphakial in Upper Assam was a centre of "kham" making. Silver paint was rarely used.

The palette of the Tai artists was very limited—to blue, red, black and gold. They used a thick size for their colours which gave their manuscript a laquered look. The Suktanta-Kyempong manuscript, contemporary of the Phung Chin manuscript, is a good example of the use of the thick size. It was made from buffalo hide and in this way is related to the Vajralepa mentioned in the Visnudharmottara. A quantity of hide was burnt and the ash reduced to a fine powder. To it was added the necessary blue or red colours extracted from the different kind of berries. Sometimes this size was also used to apply "kham" instead of using the "yang" gum. The hide-paste when further diluted served as ink. To it was sometimes added fish's bile to make it perfect. The above techniques have been collected from Sri Chaikhong-let Gohain of Namphakial.

1. Harakanta Barua Sadar-amin, Assam Buranji, p. 123.
2. Moti Chandra, Jaina Miniature Painting From Western India, p. 88.

II The Satriya School

The next group of paintings are the products of the Vaishnava movement of Sri Sankaradeva and being practised as a religious art illustrating the various books of the Bhagavatapurana, shall be termed as the Satriya School of painting. The earliest extant example of an illustrated manuscript of this school is the Bhagavata Book X dated 1539 A.D. from the Bali Sattra in Nowgong district. The style initiated in the early 16th century has marked similarity with the various north Indian schools of miniatures. Of them the Maha Purana manuscript dated 1540 A.D. from Palam near Delhi and the Mrigavati belonging to the mid-16th century at the Bharat Kala Bhawan of Banaras, are stylistically closest to the above manuscript, and those that followed in its wake. The Satriya school prevailed from Koch Bihar in the west to the extremity north east of Assam, an area that came under the cultural influence of the Eka Sarana Nama Dharma. "The inheritors of the mediaeval Pala tradition were in Nepal and Assam, as is indicated anew by the recently published series of miniatures to an Assam manuscript of the Bhagavata Purana dated 1539 A.D. . . . They clearly look back to the Buddhist manuscripts of the Pala period, which are organised in the same way with figures in architectural niches. . . . "[1] The question of the further eye being used in the Nowgong, Bhagavata does not arise for the two following reasons : Firstly, the figures have their faces always in the strict profile whatever the position of the body might be. The further eye cannot be profitably shown unless the faces are in three quarter profile. Secondly, these being descended from the Pala school, the further eye is absent. For, even in the late examples of Pala painting like the Prajnaparamita (No. 4794) of the Bharat Kala Bhawan, Banaras, the further eye is absent though some specifically mediaeval trends like angularity and staccato lines are clearly discernible. Hence to assign a date later than 1539 to this Bhagavata manuscript is arbitrary and cannot be accepted. When compared to the Maha Purana manuscript dated 1540 A.D. from Palam (near Delhi) the identity of style is but apparent. The Mrigavati of the Bharat Kala Bhavan (mid-16th century A.D.) too shows the prevalence of the Jaina or Western Indian style of miniature painting all over the country that flourished in the wake of Neo-Vaishnavism. On the one hand the Satriya school preserved the Pala tradition showing the following traits. These show the figures in silhoutte, the faces always in profile, against a strong red background, and beneath carved arches." "They show that there may have been scattered about in remote areas of Northern India, local styles having in common

1. Gray, B : The Development of Painting In India In The 16th Century ; Marg Vol. VI, No. 3, 1953, p. 20.

the solid red ground and architectural framework as a continuation of the classical and mediaeval schools of painting."

Secondly, mediaeval traits had also made their appearance in the Satriya miniatures. "The technique and finish of the work exhibit strong all-India affiliations, although here and there local conventions are naturally to be expected.[1] A style that prevailed up to Assam in the east can never be bounded by the term Western Indian at a time when research has revealed the actual extent of the school. According to Rai Krishnadas, again, the Apabhramsa school of painting had a history contemporaneous with that of the Apabhramsa languages that prevailed in early mediaeval India. Even Rajsekhara in his Kavya-mimansa placed painters and poets writing in the Apabhramsa dialect in the same group of people, intended with finer sentiments.[2] This Apabhramsa style of painting penetrated Assam along with the Apabhramsa dialect, along with the Neo-Vashnava and Sufi thought from Bihar. The language in which Sankar Deva wrote as did his successors was much influenced by the then Lingua-franca of Northern India and was termed in Assam as Vrajawali or Brajabuli in Bengal. Its connection with the Vraja Bhumi or Vrindaban-Mathura region made it more popular among the Vaishnava preachers who took up the cause of vernaculars for the first time. "In fact the very style of these works both in prose and poetry which is replete with 'tatsam' words set in a highly ornate design, points to a well developed and considerably standardised literary language, which was commonly used in the whole area between Gujarat in the west and Assam in the east and served the cultural and literary need of this extensive region.[3]

The Jaina or the Apabhramsa school of book illustration however had influenced the Rajasthani style of painting.[4] So it did to the Assamese school of miniatures of the early 16th century.

"The confident and versatile style of the Satriya school emerged as an independent mode of expression out of glorious and mixed precedence. Miniatures produced in this style have a state of epic character about them."[5] The following features of western India miniatures are common to those of the Satriya school. "In the human forms, the angularity of the features, the pointed noses . . . the

1. Neog, Dr. M , The Vaishnava Renaissance in Assam : pp 47-48. Aspects of the Heritage of Assam ; Ind. Hist. Cong. Souvenir, 1959.
2. Rai Krishnadas, Bharat ki Chitrakala : pp. 47-48.
3. Bihar Through the Ages : Ch, XIV—Religion, Society and Culture (1206-1526 A.D.) p. 447.
4. Indian Art : Iyar, K, Bharatha, p. 71.
5. Chatterji, S.K., The place of Assam in the History and Civilization of India ; p. 57.

broad chests and thin waist with ultra stylised landscapes and trees and the peculiar methods of depicting rivers and clouds have all a decorative, perhaps, originally symbolic rather than a realistic character. The relative proportions of nature are not regarded and the architecture is often summarily treated. The paintings are unquestionably vigorous. . . . ."[1] Like the Jaina miniatures their Satriya counterparts were also examples of "bourgeoise art" as Mr. N.C. Mehta terms it. They were not products of folk art and it was not until the late 17th century and early 18th century that it was adopted as court art also, under the Tungkhungiyas.

The Nowgong Bhagavata has preserved all the common traits but its identity is hardly to be overlooked in spite of the above elements. Although sceptical about its original date, Dr. Moti Chandra however discerns the following distinctive features in the said manuscript. Their "lyrical draughtsmanship, simple composition, dramatic narration and splendid colour give the Bhagavata illustrations a charm which distinguishes them from similar Bhagavata paintings from Udaipur and elsewhere."[2]

This manuscript carries a date 1461 Saka, at the end though some doubts have been raised by certain scholars regarding its authenticity. There is, however, no apparent reason why that particular date should be written in the manuscript unless it is in some way connected with the manuscript. Secondly, the date falls within the lifetime of Sankaradeva and as there was a great movement of painting started by him it can be safely said that the manuscript is a product of that era. Critics might go far enough to say that the manuscript in question is a later copy of some original one painted in 1539 A D. and that in the later copy the date of the original one was also copied down. Even then we are sure of the existence of a vigorous school of manuscript, miniatures in vogue as early as 1539 A.D. The copy, if it at all is one, however, contains all the traits of the earliest period of the Satriya school of painting. Hence its importance as an example of the painting of early 16th century is as great. When compared to the Palam Mahapurana (1540 A.D.) the identity of style and feeling between the two is irrefutable, and its date thus remains established.

The general composition and layout of the paintings are always horizontal as opposed to the vertical way of contemporary Persia, and Europe. This appears to be due to two different factors. Firstly, the carrier for the manuscript paintings had generally been long folios of Sanchipat (bark of the Agaru tree) where lines

1. Wilkinson, J.V.S., Indian Painting : Indian Art, p 117, Faber and Faber Ltd
2. Neog, M. The Vaishnava Renaissance in Assam : pp. 47-48, Aspects of the Heritage of of Assam 1959.

were written and space (Alekhya Sthana) left for miniatures to be executed. As a result the plan had to be rectangular and stretched to the sides instead of going upwards due to the shape of the folio. Secondly, eastern India including Assam had a long tradition of scroll painting as we know from contemporary literature like Usha-Parinaya (1533 A.D.) of Pitambar Dvija which was an Assamese rendering of the Usha-Anuradha episode from the Vishnupurana.[1] The long shape of the paintings seem to suggest their being inspired by the prevalent form of painting. The process of depicting scene after scene from an episode also place the above conjecture on more solid grounds.

Each painting is divided into two major sections. The background proper is always monochrome red free of any details. The rest of the Alekhya Sthana is painted in flat green on which the actual painting appears superimposed. The most characteristic feature of these miniatures is that each human, animal or any other figure is framed by trifoil arches or "architectural niches" as Basil Gray calls them. As a result the top portion of the background is always of irregular shape, following the contour of the arch or series of arches if the panel is a longer one (L.No. 29A and 15A Chitra Bhagavat). The entire area is never broken into foreground, background or horizon, either by changes in their respective colours or by the introduction of symbolic and significant motifs like grass, plants or clouds. The entire composition appears to be in eye level view, all other perspective being absent here. In this way they conform to the style of the Pats or scroll painting of Nepal as has been indicated by Nandalal Bose.[2]

Representations of pouring rain water, rivers and lakes are of a conventional and unrealistic type. Mountains look like cross sections of them as in a geological diagram. Chariots (ratha) are not happy in that they look like low flat stool with wheels at the bottom and a flag post at the front.[3]

The lack of expression in the faces of human figures are simply compensated by their poses and mudras which are greatly effective. They all are in Abhanga, a few in Tribhanga and almost none in Atibhanga poses.

In depicting an episode parts of it are represented on the succeeding folios. But the technique of continued narration is also followed at times. No attempt to depict the sky in realistic way is perceptible. For, no particular sky-area is left. Where figures are inserted the background is invariably red but the area between the red background and the rest of the Alekhya Sthana is usually painted in equally flat monochrome green. If we take it to be the sky area then of course that

1. M. Neog. (ed) Usha-Parinaya : Dvija Pitambara,
2. Neog, M., The Art of Painting in Assam, p. 9.
3. Ibid.

is the way the sky is depicted. But when there is a scene of pouring rains as in the Govardhana Dharana episode the background is painted bluish green and the heavy tropical downpour of Assam is indicated by means of numerous fine white lines in a slanting way. Clouds are not represented but in L.No. 67 B of the printed edition of the Bhagavata Book X they have been depicted in human form where conversing with Indra. Fire is always indicated like a tuft of multi-coloured (red, yellow and orange) blades of grass or straw as in L.No. 64 A and 48 A of the Chitra Bhagavat. Smoke never accompanies fire.

Vegetation though stylised is varied and the Kadamba, the banana and other willowy trees with flowers are the most common types represented. The usual practice is to fill the crown area in some kind of green and then the leaves and flowers are picked out in minute details. Sometimes (L. No. 47A Chitra Bhagavat) large trees are indicated only by giving larger leaves to the otherwise similar trees. The groves on the banks of the Yamuna are alive with numerous living beings as with the frolic of the Gopas and the Gopis. Here the trees are generally slender with graceful branches and sparce foliage (L.No. 44A Chitra Bhagavat); cuckoos (L.No 30 B Chitra Bhagavat) and other harmless birds and beasts inhabit the trees. The birds are however far from being realistic. They have very slender bodies, some with large claws and heavy legs and being diminutive, look like insects. In the case of insects like bees and beatles the picture is happier. These are very close to nature and being depicted in their original sizes have more details though being oversized look rather out of place (L.No. 44A Chitra Bhagavat). The Tala or the palmyra trees in the episode of the Dhenukasura (L.No. 32 B Chitra Bhagavat) comes closer to the datepalm and this is evidently due to the Assamese painter's unfamiliarity with that variety of palms. Speaking about the great variety of animals we find that Professor K.K. Handiqui has drawn special attention to the maneless Indian lion so common in old Assamese painting and architecture, and the Methon (Assamese bison). The animals and birds are done in the picture in a clear and sympathetic manner . . . . There is some amount of convention and stylisation which of course count for a limitation on the art.[1]

Human figures and superhuman beings in anthropomorphic forms are all characteristic of the school. Human figures in the Gita Govinda manuscript (1696-1714 A.D.) as a rule look taller since they are slenderer when compared to those in the Nowgong Bhagavata. Angularity diminished to a great deal. The postures are not so calculated and jerky as in customary with early Satriya miniatures. The male profiles of the Gita Govinda have great similarity with those in the Nimat Namah manuscript (c. 1500 A.D. of the India Office Library, London).[2]

1. Dutta Barua, B.N. (ed). Chitra Bhagavata, Introduction
2. In Praise of Mandu: Skelton, Robert: Marg, Vol. XII, No. 3, June 1959, pls, 4,7,9.

The only difference is in the costume types in the two manuscripts. The nude is avoided and the only example where it has been shown is in a conventional way and the angle of the body is such as decorum and decency would demand of the female form. Apsaras, Vidyadharas, Devanaris, and Siddhamunis are in no way different from their human counterparts. Only Garuda and the Naginis have been shown in synchretic forms. The Naginis are all human except that they have serpenthood emerging from their coiffeure. This is quite an ingeneous way of depiction of Naginis not to be met with anywhere else. Garuda has a human body but the claws, wings and the beaklike nose give him the superhuman look. Demons are depicted in two ways—either in human form (e.g. Chakravata, Pralambha, Putana, etc.) or in the form of beasts and birds which they had assumed to destroy Krsna. When depicted in human form specially in the case of Chakravata the face is purposefully made hideous and has bristly beards and cropped hair. The serpent Kaliya who was vanquished by Krsna is a wonder compared to the other animal studies of the manuscript. Though stylised, the lithe and powerful body with a multitude ot outstretched hoods and lashing tail, Kaliya makes a wonderful study of animal life. But when Kaliya is vanquished and he salutes Krsna the two hands have been added to his otherwise serpentive body and in Anjali mudra he makes obeisance (L. No. 39B Chitra Bhagavat).

In the case of human figures natural proportions are adhered to. But when in particular episodes Krsna's personality had to be magnified he is shown far larger in size than his companions as in the case of Govardhana Dharana scene (L. No. 69A Chitra Bhagavat).

Sukadeva is shown in the typical pose of Vyakhyana mudra (L. No. 1), while Kamsa's queen is shown in the Vitarka mudra while dissuading her husband from his evil designs (L. No. 10 Chitra Bhagavat). As far as the various poses struck during movement are all calculated and not spontaneous as they are stylised. The various poses of figures look like those in the Sutradhari or religious dance style of Assam that flourished in the Satras. In both the cases the persons always stand with their feet a little outstretched and légs a little bent at the knees as in Kathakali dance style.

The illustrated copy of the Assamese rendering of the Gita Govinda by Ananta Acharya Dvija is an advancement on the style of the Nowgong Bhagavata. It was produced during the reign of Rudra Singha (1696-1714 A.D.) as we find from the following lines in the manuscript :

> "Jar ajnyachakrar bhayat prajagana
> Chaki Chaki Karye 'thake' edi ana mana
> Bhane Kavi Dvijavare bola Hari Hari."[1]

1. Gita Govinda manuscript, Folio No. 17 (obv.) Kamarupa Amsandhana Samiti, Gauhati.

The general characteristic and motifs are present and the colour scheme also remains the same. The most remarkable feature of this manuscript is that the only examples of Raga Mala paintings are contained in it. Their depiction is however incidental and only some of the Ragas and Raginis have been portrayed whenever a change in the Raga in the poem is indicated. Only some of them have been portrayed here. Another important feature is the folio containing the Dasavatara in a panel and the four Vedas, who were rescued by Narayana during the Deluge. An illustration, captioned Jayadeva, the writer of the original Sanskrit text, has been inserted. But he is like any Vaishnava or Brahmin from Assam and does not deserve any special mention.

For the first time in an example of the Satriya school we come across the division of the painted surface into the foreground, background and even of the sky area in case of the above Ms. The foreground though devoid of any vegetation, however, is monochrome green though the rest of the panel is the usual red (F. I. of Gita Govinda Ms.) The treatment of the atmosphere at dusk is a popular theme in Vaishnava literature and is known as the Godhuli-bela. As a subject of painting too it is common to Pahari painting as to this manuscript of Gita Govinda (F. 14 Rev. Gita Govinda). The limited scope of the Satriya school bound by conventionality could also produce which can be called the masterpiece from the above manuscript. The desired effect of dull luminosity of the Godhuli sky just after sun down, is cleverly brought out. The trees and flowering plants stand out contrasted in half silhouttes and successfully emphasise the atmosphere at the 'hour of the cowdust'.

A flight of fancy prompted the artist to depict the piled up clouds in an interesting way (F. 30 Rev. Gita Govinda). The label at the bottom says Meghamurti or shapes formed by clouds. They look two domoniae creatures of ponderous proportions with ape like faces and projecting fangs. Otherwise the treatment of clouds is happy though many improbable colours have been used for them. Though the technique remains the same realism wins over flights of fancy in the Ramayana Lanka Kanda manuscripts where clouds have been depicted.

Here in the scene of Radha's Viraha we find such an example of symbolism. Viraha, or the pangs of separation from the lover has always been compared in Indian literature with flames. As flames burn the outside of a person so burns Viraha the soul of man. Radha is seen surrounded by blazing flames though the season is spring and it clearly brings out her inner feelings (F. 32 Rev. Gita Govinda).

The very passionate nature of the poem full of references to physical union and carnal desires by the lovers has offered the painter of the Gita Govinda to depict Radha and Krsna in a number of poses showing the various states of physical union. Sometimes they are in tender embraces, at others in the state of Viraha while at others in violent passion (F. 32 Rev.) Those form the various dramatic situations from this romantic work. Radha enjoys and flatters herself realising that the actual beloved of Krsna is none but she herself. She hides behind a tree and watches Krsna beating his head in lament since he has come to know of Radha's displeasure due to his alliance with other Gopis. The look of impish delight of a love-lorn damsel and the helplessness of a separated lover is really a situation worth recording in painting (F. 18 obv. Gita Govinda).

Continued narration is a technique which has been often followed to depict the intriguing situations in which circumstances have placed the lovers and their associate Sarasvati, one of the Sakhis of Radha. Here the Sakhi is going to tell Radha how really tender the feelings of Krsna are for her and thus effect a reunion of the lovers. This is done in two halves, but the parts are not separated either by any border or a tree etc. The right half shows Sarasvati running with Krsna's errand to Radha and Krsna waves her godspeed. In the right half she stops in front of Radha and with gesticulations gives her the message. To denote the change in the place of action the landscape at the back is differently depicted. But in order to preserve the uniformity of time, the costume and coiffeure of Sarasvati remain the same.

One of the most well-preserved of the illustrations is of Krsna awaiting Radha. The perfect colour scheme and the way each colour balances the other of the restricted pallette is remarkable. The Syama complexioned body of Krsna stands out from the dark green background. His yellow costume shines flame-like in the forest gloom. The figure of Krsna itself is adorable and the akimbo arms and longing eyes all reflect his impatience. All things concerned this piece can easily be called the 'gem' of the Gita Govinda miniatures

The series of Ragmala painting from this manuscript is however not complete. They being single illustrations are very limited in scope.

The Satriya school continued to be a living one till the last days of the Tungkhungiyas though in the meantime the superior and more versatile style of Garhgaon had developed. The association of the Satriya style with the religious atmosphere of the Satras was perhaps responsible for its popularity as a medium specially when religious texts had to be illustrated. This is seen in the preference of royal patrons for this style when they commissioned artists to illustrate religious texts like the Gita Govinda, the Ananda Lahari or the Ramayana (Lanka Kanda) in the said style. The following are a few of the important illustrated manuscripts executed in this style ;

1. Vanamali Devar Charita of Ramakanta Dvija
2. Sri Bhagavata Matsya Charita of Nityananda Kayastha (1644-50 A.D.)
3. Gita Govinda translated by Kaviraj Chakravarti (1696-1714 A.D.)
4. Lava Kusar Yuddha of Harivar Bipra (1714-1744 A.D.)
5. Ananda Lahari of Ananta Acharya Dvija (1714-44 A.D.) (Sakta text)
6. Ramayana : Sundara Kanda—1715 A.D.
7. Sankara Charita—date unknown
8. Ramayana : Lanka Kanda : C. 1791-1806

The carriers for these manuscripts had been both Tulapat and Sanchipat though the use of the former was very rare. The only remarkable example is the Ramayana Lanka Kanda painted during the days of Swargadeo Kamaleswar Singha (1791-1807 A.D.). Lavishness in decoration, mastery of execution and expansion of the palette with mixed colours are some of the characteristics of the later day paintings when the lavishness and sophistication of the Tungkhungiya court indirectly influenced miniature painting. But certain conventionalities, viz., the 'architectural niche,' basket pattern for water, the use of Mudras and stylised and effected poses of human figures, to name only a few, continue to be used.

The manuscript copy of Lava-Kusar Yuddha, an epic poem by Haribar Vipra (1533 A.D.) in the possession of the Kamarupa Anusandhana Samiti was prepared during the days either of Rudra Singha or Siva Singha (1714-1743.)[1] The present copy along with another of the same were in the possession of Rani Mahendri Devi, wife of Yuvaraj Keshavakanta, the grandson of Swargadeo Chandra Kanta Singha, the last Ahom king. All the characteristic motifs of the Satriya school are present but it is decidedly of a higher standard of execution. We find that these illustrations deserve to be particularly valued as bearing signs of an attempt, at times successful even, at individualization and stylization, which are general traits of old Assamese painting. The flat treatment of the Mughal type of head gear, the decorative, rather than real trees representing a forest, the low-seated chariot, these are some of the characteristics,[2] to be met with in this manuscript. Though contemporary to this, the Ananda Lahari, a Sakta text translated and illustrated by the orders of Siva Singha and Phuleswari[3] again reverts to the old groove.

Human figures here combine both angularity and curveness. In a way the Lava-Kusar Yuddha is a bridge between the stiff angularity of the Gita Govinda

1. Neog, M., Lava-Kushar Yuddha : Introduction, p. 14.
2. Neog, M, Ibid.
3. Goswami, H.C., Descriptive Catalogue of Assamese Manuscript, p. 5.

manuscript miniatures and the graceful curve and realism in the Hastividyarnava. Again, the little angularity that exists is confined to the male figures, but the faces of attendants and priests have well rounded chins, lips and tips of noses. The eyes and eyebrows are still angular in the case of males. But the muscles of the arms and the calf are again well curved though the treatment of the feet are rather careless and disproportionate as in the Nowgong Bhagavata. The curves of fleshy parts of body have been indicated by a succession of thin and thick lines. Male figures are tall, heavily built and muscular. The chin of one of the princes is strangely protruding like those of the western Indian miniatures, though no such example has been found in other manuscripts. The body colour of all except that of Rama is pinkish white conforming to the traditional Champaka Gaura type.

Female figures are very different and their profile faces come very close to the early Pahari school. The forehead is rounded and the chin well curved. The nose loses angularity completely. A great change takes place in the shape of the eyes which when in full view are shaped like a lotus-petal with a long projecting cyllirium line. The pupils are rather small and placed in the centre of the eye the ends of which are however not touched with red. The treatment of hair improves and even the loose strands of hair parted in the middle and hanging at the sides have been deftly brought out with fine strokes.

Another distinguishing feature of this group of painting is that action, violent movements and dynamism are attempted at and successfully also. In the battle scene of Folio 25 Rev. the lithe figure of Lava shooting at the army of Rama is a remarkable study in arrested motion. He is tall and slim and bends forward with his legs set far apart. The bow is bent very much and the tautness of bow string reflects the tense moment before releasing an arrow. The figure of Laksmana shooting at Lava is also interesting as he is seen kneeling down to gather momentum. A combat scene is shown as an explosion (F. 24 Rev.). Chariots in fragments and dismembered bodies of soldiers, elephants pin-cushioned with arrows and horses with drooping bodies and limp legs and tails present a ghastly, though over-emphasised impression of the battle-field. The agony of the animals has been shown in their agape mouths and bulging eyes.

Animal study is still primarily conventional. Thickening of the outline helps bring out the volume of the elephants body (Folio 34 obv.). Modelling is linear and confined to the legs, trunk and throat of the elephant. Horses have large, fine bodies. They are portrayed in a variety of movements though trotting is the usual type. The breakneck speed of a running horse is presented by making his feet thrown parallel to the ground and the body in mid-air. The neck too is outstretched and the manes sweeping back and the mouth wide open under the strain in Folio 25 Rev. In general the horses' breasts and necks are gracefully curved which is counteracted by the stern angularity of the knee joints. The 'Ahom lion' is introduced as one of the many beasts in the forest.

Trees are conventionalised and stylised. They, however, are more colourful and draughtsmanship is confident and fine. Drops of thick white paint applied in various patterns represent the flowers and the leaves are in many bright colours. Shading has been attained at the curves of the tree-trunk by their criss-cross patterns in F. 25 Rev. Flowers like poppies and others of Persian origin have become a common motif from now on the Assamese miniatures.

The Ananda Lahari composed by Ananta Acharya Dvija during the days of Siva Singha and Pramathesvari Devi (1714-44 A.D.)[1] is an interesting specimen of the Satriya school though late in date. All the features of the school are present here. The treatment of the Yogis with drooping moustaches and highly arched thick eyebrows remind us of the motif of Mandarins in Chinese art. Siva and Gauri are seen in a forceful pose of physical union. Conventionality remains in the human figures.

The Sankara Charita[2] though following the Satriya idiom is a great leap forward in portrait painting. The figures are larger, and the faces are as usual in the profile. The four profiles are highly individualistic though the rest of the body is conventionally treated. Angularity and straight lines have been done away with in the human figures. The absence of shading for modelling has been compensated by revealing the body curves at the calf, waist, and arms. The most remarkable are the eyes and the eyebrows the latter indicated in the thinnest lines and sensuous curves But conventionality again reveals itself in the treatment of the frontal face of human figures, background and architectural niches.

The last days of the Satriya style however are remarkable for minuteness of details, lavishness of ornamentation and gorgeousness of colours. All these are to be met with in the Ramayana, Lanka Kanda, manuscript painted during the reign of Swargadeo Kamalesvar Singha (1791-1806 A.D.). The subject matter of the text which deals mainly with a description of the magnificent city of Lanka and the household of the Raksasa king, Ravana, also enabled the artist to make his creation as decorative as possible.

The conventional motifs remain but are made more elaborate and are often stylised and altered. The "stepped pyramid" and the "cusped arch" remain as frames for human figures. But they are not frequent, and entire pictures are

1. Goswami, H.C., Descriptive Catalogue of Assamese Manuscripts, p. 8.
2. Manuscript No. 1, University of Gauhati, Manuscript Section.

framed by bands following the outline of the composition. The palette becomes more extensive due to mixing of the primary colours, which are blended with 'Dhal' or chalk. Gold paint is not used its place being taken by a very bright yellow.

For the day time the sky is painted in a shade of blue coming close to ultramarine while the night sky is of deep blue (Nila). The sun in the sky is a large yellow circle with a darker centre in red and numerous fine lines radiating from the outer circle represent the sun's rays. The night sky is filled with stars and the moon, crescent or full, represented by pale yellow circles of varying sizes. Figures of flying birds are painted on the sky surface, both within and outside the margin. A sort of third dimension is attained this way and the practice is inherited from the Garhgaon paintings (F. 12 Rev).

The depiction of the sea is characterised by novelty and duality. Two different motifs, the basket pattern and also the more realistic series of wavy lines have been followed in Folio 4. Tanks with 'Ghats' on four sides resemble stepped wells and are filled in with lotus flowers. The birds' eye view is the commonest angle of vision. Buildings, forts, and battlements are of heavy masonry and the numerous magnificent edifices and temples of Rangpur constructed during the Tungkhungiya period seemed to have served as model. The battlements are surrounded with rows of 'Bartop' or canons. Successive rows of curves of different shades of blue placed one behind the other represent the clouds.

Human figures retain all the characteristics of the school as seen in F. 162, as seen in those of Ravana and Mandodari. Hanumana and the monkeys are very human except for the furs and the tails. They have angular eyebrows and millstone eyes. Similar is the depiction of Suresa, the demoness (Folio 6). She too is half human and half beast.

III. The Darrang School

Another school of miniature painting saw its birth in the court of the Koch principality known as the Darrang Raj of Mangaldai in the district of Darrang. Closely similar to the Satriya school, from which originated, it soon developed its own characteristics. The number of manuscripts in this style are not many. "It is thus seen that Assam Vaishnavism developed a school of painting of its own and this art was later patronised by the Ahom monarchs and Koch chiefs of the 17th and 18th centuries." Resources and scope of the Rajas of Darrang were naturally limited but even then the zeal of the patron family made the origin of a new school possible Since they were vassals of the Ahom Swargadeos, the influence of Ahom court naturally infiltrated the provincial society of Mohanpur, the seat of Darrang Rajas. The highly sophisticated Garhgaon school of miniature painting also influenced that of Darrang. It was a complete breach from the past traditions in as far as the style is concerned as in the case of Garhgaon itself. The most important example of the later Darrang manuscript miniatures is the Samudra Narayanar Vamsavali (1791 A.D.) otherwise known as the Darrang Raj Vamsavali. But it is proper to deal it under the Garhgaon school though its provanence is different.

The most important manuscripts of the Darrang school are the Tirtha Kaumudi (1686 A.D.) and the Anadi Patan the date of which is not available. But stylistically they are identical. The Tirtha Kaumudi manuscript is deposited in the Department of Historical and Antiquarian Studies, Gauhati, (Ms. No. 1232). Another manuscript with paintings in the borders is a copy of the Sahapari Upakhyan by Dvija Ram dated 1793 A.D. It was found in the Rangmahal village of North Gauhati and is deposited in the Kamarupa Anusandhan Samiti, Gauhati. The scribe who was possibly the artist was one Jinnath. It is an Assamese romance based on Kutuban's Mrigavati (1512 A.D.) in the Avadhi dialect of Hindi. In addition to the Vaishnava literature and political literature of romance, Assamese had works which were "in fairy fiction dressed."[1]

Firstly, the miniatures are always assigned a particular portion of the Sanchi-pat folios which are numbered and the word 'Sri' preceding each number which is a trait inherited from the Satriya School. The miniatures are thus strictly confined to the Alekhyasthana which are often framed with outlines. Though stylistically the miniatures belong to the Satriya school they are far inferior in execution.

2. The primary colours of Dhal, Hengul, Nila, Herital, Kajal or Mahi have been used. Gold paint is not used anywhere. The colours are opaque and done in tempra evidently mixed with Dhal.

3. Human figures are generally short and heavy. Limbs are well developed but short and the heads are large, all these being characteristic of Koch physiognomy. But a more refined type of male figure with tall and slender limbs and a chiselled face has been depicted in the Tirtha Kaumudi.

4. Female figures are also heavy and short like their male counterparts. They are buxon and gracefully curved. The faces are plump and large. The eyes are large, lozenge-shaped or eliptical under a highly arched eyebrow. The chins are not prominent. The eyes are intense and have a savage fury in them. The profusion of hair is bound either in top-knots or in buns at the nape of the neck.

5. Men have small but sharp noses and round staring eyes. The moustache is scorpion-tailed and is well cared for.

1. Bhuyan, S.K., 1936, Studies in the Literature of Assam 1936, p. 14.

6. Treatment of hands and feet are not fine. Hands are claw like with tempering fingers and the feet are broad and flat.

7. The costumes depicted are as in the Satriya school in the case of males. Females are clad in coloured Mekhelas and in many cases the upper torso is bare. But usually a 'chadar' coming from behind the neck hangs with two ends on the chest. In one case the "Riha" is wrapped round the breasts leaving the shoulders bare.

8. Landscape is reduced to the minimum. The background is usually monochrome. Sometime a few plants and flowers dot the ground. The elements of nature, like the watery surface, rocks etc. are conventionally treated.

9. Architecture is "summarily treated" and are mere outlines encasing human figures.

10. The human figures and animals are all in forceful poses and are "puppet-like" or like animated cartoons, modern cinematography.

11. The lack of expression in the faces is compensated by the great use of 'Mudras'. In this respect they antedate the Nepalese banner painting of the 18th century. Both Darrang and Nepal differ from Rajasthani paintings in this respect.

The Tirtha Kaumudi is a guide to Hindu places of pilgrimage within Assam and India as well. Apart from the stylistic considerations its importance as a contemporary encyclopaedia of geography and Hindu traditions is great. It begins with the description of the Sakta place of pilgrimage in the Jayntia hills, describes Kamakhya, the greatest centre of Saktism in India and its description also includes far off places like Kuruksetra and others.

The folio No. 1 shows two male figures captioned kings of Jayantia and Kamarupa. The depiction of the two together helps us assert the date given in the manuscript for Jayantia had close connection with Kamarupa during that period. Jayantiya was subjugated by Sukladhwaj alias Chilarai, the younger brother of Naranarayana who ruled over Kamarupa.[1] The state of vassalage to Koch power continued up to 1730 A.D. as established from numismatic evidences. The Saktipitha at Faljor is one of the fifty-one scattered all over the Indian subcontinent and the above one is supposed to indicate the place where the disected left thigh of Sati had fallen.

1. Khan Chowdhury, A., Koch Biharer Itihasa, Ch. IX, p. 100.

Everything in nature or man-made is conventionally and symbolically represented. The various "Kundas" or springs associated with ritual ablutions are shown as circles filled in with the basket pattern to denote the watery surface. Temples or "Dauls" are shown like four-poster beds with canopies and the presiding deities are depicted within them. The mountains are like "cross-sections of them as in a geological diagram".[1] The various strata of the mountains inside are painted in different colours. Trees are shown like flower plants with small and slender stocks supporting disproportionately large leaves and flowers.

There are scenes of swimming and bathing in the rivers and even of the Vastraharana, but the nude is never depicted below the waist at the most. The lower torso is cleverly hidden in the depth of the water. The bathing scene of Radha and Krsna is the best specimen in this manuscript though not in the nude

Human figures are always shown in the characteristic profile. But in a few places like that of goddess Kamakhya and in two other unidentified deities, the front view of the face has been shown. The faces in this view are surprisingly crude and expressionless as in the earlier Satriya school of painting. The Nowgong Bhagavata (1539 A.D.) for the first time shows this trait which is continued as late as the days of the Tungkhungiyas when the Gita Govinda and the Ananda Lahari also have the same crudity in the frontal view of the face. It is really surprising that Assamese artists, who had such great mastery over the profile and three quarter profile were so incapable of handling the front view of the face. Even no distinction can be made between a male and a female face when shown in front view. The figure of Visnu on the manuscript box of Stuti Govinda (1454 A.D.) manuscript also suffers from the same defect. It seems they too had realised their weakness and so had limited to the minimum the showing of faces in the front view. The front view of torso of goddess Kamakhya is equally unattractive. From above the waist it is a flat triangle and from its side the arms of the goddess radiate like tentacles. The legs which are folded in the Padmasana pose are represented as cylinders projecting from beneath the triangular torso.

In short, with the plain monochrome background, angular figures and their jerky poses, with fish-shaped eyes and disproportionate hands and feet, with thick outlines, conventional rocks and basket pattern watery surface, the Tirtha Kaumudi has a primitive look and almost verges on folk art.

In spite of all these shortcomings the Tirtha Kaumudi is important as it has the proved privileges to represent a style which is the product of the Provincial Satriya school of painting.

1. Neog, M., The Art of Painting in Assam, p. 7.

The other important manuscript in the Darrang style is the Anadipatana. The subject matter is the theory of creation as given in the Bhagavata Purana Book III and Vamana Purana [1] The author of this work is Sankara Deva himself but the date of the present copy is unknown, but it can be sefely placed in the late 17th century. The similarity of style and the inherent crudity of the two manuscripts makes it clear that they are not far removed in date. It belongs to the Kamarupa Anusandhan Samiti, Gauhati.

As has been already said, miniatures from this manuscript are important more as book-illustration and source of information about Hindu mythology than as fine specimens of miniatures. But they are successful inasmuch as they faithfully represent the contents of the folios they accompany. These miniatures like examples of modern art are non-figurative and they convey the message that they are supposed and so the importance of the medium and style is minimised.

In spite of its being a product of the late mediaeval period certain Pala traits still continue. As Basil Gray had suggested in the case of the Nowgong Bhagavata (1539 A.D.) the figures of deities are placed under arches as in the case of the Dasavataras in folio 12 (obv.), and folio 18 (Rev.) for example.

There are some good examples of conventional and most abstract examples of painting in this manuscript. Firstly, the signs of the zodiac have been depicted in a very interesting way. They have all been personified as Lagna or "time". "Lagna" has been represented as a four armed dark male figure surrounded by twelve panels each containing a sign of the zodiac in human or synchretic forms.

The drawing is stylized and very conventional without the least degree of naturalism in the case of the Mount Meru. It has to be so since the painters in the valley of the Brahmaputra could possibly not visualise the dreadfully beautiful scenery of the snow capped ranges of the inner Himalayas. All figures had been reduced to linear and geometrical forms

Meru has been represented as a funnel standing on its narrower mouth and topped by another with its broader mouth showing. The funnels are painted yellow and the broader mouth has tiny eleptical designs all over, representing boulders in a mountain. The lesser mountains are depicted while the top portion of the composition is a multi-foiled arch.

The firmament is a warm red background with the Meru and the four lesser mountains, standing against it. The sun is a seven-petalled yellow flower

1 Goswami, H.C., Descriptive Catalogue of Assamese Manuscripts, 1930, p. 4.

with a blue centre, shining in the sky. Rahu, the demon with only the head rushes after the sun. The profile of Rahu is of a much higher standard in comparison to that of the other male figures in this manuscript. It comes closer to those in the Lava-Kushar manuscript (early 18th century) from the Assam State Museum, Gauhati.

Another queer way of depicting mountains is seen in folio 3 obv. But for the labels, it would have been impossible to identify the mountains. They are shown like flying pieces of torn matting in the scene of destruction of the world by the god Rudra. Perhaps the idea was to emphasise the might of the god of destruction to whom even imposing mountains are as flimsy as mats which can be torn asunder with ease.

The depiction of the various Heavens and Hells are equally stylised and no attempt has been made to recreate Nature. The various zones are indicated only by dividing them with margins or by changing their respective colours. But, for the Ananta Sagara or the Primordial Ocean the basket pattern has been adopted and executed in white on the blue background.

The various regions of the nether world, viz., Atala, Vitala, Sutala and Talatala are depicted in an equally conventional manner (Folio 10 obv.). In Sutala an interesting specimen of architecture is shown. It is diminutive and looks like a chessman. But the most controversial point is from where did the artist come across conception of onion-shaped domes as in Byzantine and Russian architecture ?

Intricate composition and spacing of figures are absent in this manuscript. But it has been attempted at in some places as in Folio 18 (Rev.). In the case of the figures of the daughters of Daksa Prajapati, the figures have been placed one behind the other in a line, and further by dividing the panel into two to depict another section of the group. A faint attempt towards motion has been made in folio 21 (obv.). The horses in the state of flying with the chariot of the sun god have their manes swept backwards by the wind.

The treatment of human figures is no more developed than in the Tirtha Kaumudi but certain distinctive traits make their appearance. The depiction of the face is always in the profile which is a legacy from the Satriya school. And whenever human face is depicted in the front view it is crude as usual as in the Visnu figure from Folio 3 (Rev.). The torso is equally crude in this as well in that of Rudra from the obverse side of the same folio. Heiratic scaling has been followed here and the body is shaped like a "Damaru" of drum of Siva. Moreover, the effect is far from being attractive. The limbs are like stumps coming out of the various regions of the torso. A little modelling has been attempted to round the throat. The terrible aspect of the deity is emphasised as he kicks mountains asunder, devours human thighs, strikes the Dikgajas and flings human beings with his numerous hands.

The human figures are better though very much full of curves, unseemly in the case of males. They are all in profile and movement is indicated by the feet apart and swinging arms. But the torso from the waist to the neck are in the front view thus giving an effect of straint on the figures. The most typical male figures are from Folio 3 (Rev.). They are the denizins of the Bitala region and include Padma, Mayadanava, to mention a few and also Priyavarata from Prithvi. These too are crude and resemble terracotta folk toys painted with gaudy colours. The limbs are disproportionate and cylindrical and attached to the torso as in clay dolls. The noses are long and angular while the chin well curved. The most distinguishing feature is the treatment of the hands. They are expressive being either in Anjali or Vyakhyana mudra as the case may be. Angularity almost vanishes from the figure of Visnu (Folio 9 Rev.), who is described as Purna-brahma. The figure is in profile the portion above waist being far superior to other figures. But there is carelessness in the depiction of hips and thighs which are utterly cylindrical. The profile is softened by curving the chin, lips and the shoulders. The effect is as that of Sarnath Buddha images where the Mahapurusa seems to be filled up with the Rasa of Karuna.

A typical example of the female figure is Devi from folio 3 (Rev.). She is stunted and ill-shaped like a crude clay doll with uneven curves. The chest is left bare and is shown in somewhat front view. The breasts are conical and both project towards the centre of the chest. They all sit in Vajrasana pose and their fingers are all tapering and sensitive and form some 'mudra' or other to express the mood. The minute finger nails are painted white in the true tradition of the Satriya school. Faces of females too are in the strict profile with small but sharp noses and a rounded and not too prominent chin. The eyes are ovoid with black dots for pupils and the corners are touched with red. Eyebrows, however, are not so much curved as in the case of males, though, long. The seventeen daughters of Daksa Prajapati (Folio 18 Rev.) are also identically depicted.

A very interesting figure reminiscent of the flying Gandharvas of Sondani and the painting from Ajanta depicting Indra and the Apsaras in the piece famous as the "descent from the Tushita Heaven". It is the figure of a male fan bearer apparently hovering behind the figure of Visnu in Vaikuntha (Folio 9 obv.). The position of his legs is a little bent at the knees points to this direction. The same folio depicts Krityamuni, one of the residents of Yamalloka as a full blown white lotus placed on a raised 'sarai'. Symbolism has been used to the last degree in this example. The traditional divisions of Aryavarta with their respective masters have been depicted in the same stylised way. Hayagriva has been depicted as a fair complexioned male with four arms like Visnu, but has the face and neck of a horse as the name suggests. The other Avataras are all shown in a long panel, each under a separate niche.

The mythical animals are fai removed from their living counterparts. The artist painted them as they should be and not as they are. The Sesanaga that rests on the Kachhapa is depicted in an unusual manner. The elongated coiled body looks like a cucumber from under which the tail comes out. Mahalloka is presided over by he Godhika or the primordial iguana.

The palette is restricted to the five primary colours. White has been used a great deal and also yellow. The religious nature of the work prompted the artist to use yellow more than other colours. "Dhal" has been freely used as a priming as well as a binding media. The colours are thus opaque.

Another important manuscript in this group is the Sahapari Upakhyan dated 1790 A.D. It is a Lata-Kata puthi" and hence not much can be expected of this manuscript. All the few figures are painted on the borders. They however are all disjointed and each illustration is a separate picture. The background of the borders are always monochrome with no landscape or architectural representation. They are few varieties of "Latas" or meanders as borders also. The most common motif is rosettes in meanders and creepers with large leaves. Conditions that were unfavourable seem to have restricted the embellishment on these illustrations. The human figures follow the Darrang tradition but lines always melt in curves. Every angle of the human figure is softened. The "puppet-like" figures, all in profile have large expressive eyes. The chins and the foreheads are sloping. Contemporary life is well depicted in this short hand method. The Ahom lions topping the roof of buildings have gracefully curved bodies and appear to be flying with their tiny fin-like wings. Architectural details are just like frame works containing human figures. Even the interior is left as the same colour as the background, thus giving an impression of open air life. Water is depicted with a multitude of short parallel or S-shaped lines on the background colour. Fishes are exactly in the same way as in the Tirtha Kaumudi bathing scene.

IV. The Garhgaon School

The next group of paintings that shall be discussed here are the products of the Ahom royal court It was a real court art, for it developed and flourished during the Golden Age of Ahom history under the House of Tunkhung. Its very nature and background sounded a break with the existing Satriya school due to the former's concern with contemporary and temporal aspect of the life in 18th century Assam. A new and secular school of the art of painting thus seems to have been established in eastern Assam under the Ahoms.[1]

This new school of painting which we propose to name as the Garhgaon school of painting* was an example of Court Art as contrasted with the earlier Satriya school which was a Bourgeoise Art. The name itself, which is derived from the traditional Ahom capital near present Sibsagar, shows that the school had enough characteristic of the Court Art to be so classified.

Describing the characteristics of Court Art Stella Kramrisch says, "works of Court Art and thus being dependent largely on the will of one person, are freed from the necessity of creative forms, as peculiar to national geneous. For in this case it is not too subconscious and therefore inevitable intuition of the artist who is brought up in the tradition of his country which is at work but the artist has become a tool in the hands of the potentate who imposes his will on his employee. And it also may be that he calls foreign artists into his country to work according to his wish.[2]

The similar was the case of Assam where Rudra Singha started the movement of court painting by ordering for the illustration of the Gita Govinda (1696-1714 A.D.). His son and successor Siva Singha—to be particular the latter's successive consorts Pramathesvari Devi and Amvikadevi (1741 A.D.)—had all the finest examples of manuscript painting executed by their orders. The new style was limited to the court circle only, though the Bareghar Satra near Garhgaon also had a copy of the Kumara Harana illustrated in the same style. The colophones of the manuscript that would follow show that the paintings were exclusively commissioned by the orders of the royal consorts and it was a matter of great honour for the artists to acknowledge their being selected for the purpose. The colophone of the Gita Govinda manuscript has already been quoted in the preceding pages :

Sankhachuda Vadha

"Hena nripatir mahisiro ajnya pai
Kaviraj Vipre Brahmavaivartak chai
Padabandhe Virachila Purana Pravandha
Sankhachuda name Raja jito satya sandha"

1. Neog., M., The Art of Painting in Assam, p. 10.

*The author has for the first time given the name to the early 18th century Ahom Court painting in his book Eastern Indian Manuscript Painting, 1972

2. On Indian Art -Kramrisch, Stella—Characteristics of Court Art.

Dharmapurana of Kavichandra Dwija

"Hena Siva Singha Raja Ugrasingha Sisukaya
Amvika Janani Jagmao
Tinio Janar Vani Sirogata kari mani
Vadha name sobhana svabhava
Rajar sevaka bara pada Dharmapuranara
Karai lekhailanta manohara."

Bhagavata Book VI

"Yar samipat Sangyadevir sadrisakaya divya
alankar mandita sri Amvika Devi prakasa
Karicha . . . . adesak sirogata kari Vadha
Ligirae pratima sahite likhaila, saka 1659.

Hastividyaranava

. . . . Srijut Srimanta Sivasingha name ji Maharaja
aru tane mahisi sri sri Amvika name

Mahadevi sei dui janar ajnya ratnamalak
Sirat dhari Sukumar Barkathe aei
Hastividyarnava sara sangrahak rachile
Saka 1656 ate chitra karibalai ajnya karile
Dilbar Doshai dui likhakak."

The Darrang Raj Vansavali (1791 A.D.) was similarly written by Suryakhari Daivajna : Colophone –

"Rai Rajesvara Nripavara Payan Sunaya jito nara
Tahar bibhuti sampatti sukha milaya
Krisnar charan Sire dhari Bhanila lechari Suryakhari
Bola Ram Ram papar hauk pralaya."

Thus we see all the hitherto known examples of this school were produced only for the royal courts. Hence there is hardly any reason for not calling the Garhgaon school as court art when compared to the other schools of India. "These schools (Moghul, Pahari and Rajput) for ever remained a court art in the sense that they were created by court patronage and their production was absorbed almost exclusively by court circles."[1]

1 Khandalvala, Karl. Pahari Miniature Painting, p. 18.

The school was grafted into the highly sophisticated body of metropolitan culture of Garhgaon and actually the native genious remained untouched by this new form of art. Just as "the common man was never privileged to see either the Mughal miniature or the Pahari miniature,"[1] the similar was the case with Garhgaon miniatures. The indigeneous Satriya school was as vigorously practised during this period as during pre-Rudrasingha days, so that much so even royal and aristocratic patrons sometimes favoured illustrations of manuscripts in the said style. Manuscripts like the Gita Govinda, Lava Kusar Yuddha, the Ananda Lahari were produced during the period when commissioning paintings in the Garhgaon school remained fashionable. Even as late as the days of Swargadeo Kamalesvar Singha the Lanka Kanda of the Ramayana was produced in the purest Satriya idiom. The following observations about Mughal paintings also hold good for that of the Garhgaon and the Satriya school. "But whereas the former was a vehicle for the portrayal of an aristocratic court life of which the painter was only a spectator the subject matter of Pahari miniature was for the most part in tune with the painter's innermost feelings and religious beliefs and love of epic lore."[2] "Pahari painting is the product of small ateliers maintained by Hill Rajas and nobles." Likewise Garhgaon painting was patronised by the Ahom kings and their vassals the Rajas of Darrang with their seat at Howli Mohanpur near Mangaldoi in Darrang district. "Able miniaturists could find adequate remuneration for their skill only in royal courts. Moreover, the idea of displaying royal art treasures in public museums was foreign to the Rajput princes or even to their Moghul over-lords. Thus in a sense Pahari painting is an aristocratic and court art."[3] In a like manner Garhgaon painting remained unfamiliar to the great masses of Assam.

Particular school of painting is, specially in the case of court art, named either after the seat of government or after the dynasty under whose patronage it flourishes. In the case of Indian art in particular, where the artists and masters usually fight shy of their identity out of an oriental sense of modesty, schools of paintings or other branches of art are not named after those that create them. So, from the very beginning of Indian art history we have had Mauryan or Gupta art on the one hand or the schools of Mathura and Gandhara on the other. Schools of painting have not been named after masters like Bitpalo on Dhiman but after the centres and dynasties that ruled at the period, like the Madhyadesa school or the Pala school of painting. In more recent times Indian painting was named after Akbar or Jahangir period and not after Hunhar or Mansur though their names were known. Rajput painting was classified to the centres of activity

1. Khandalvala, Karl, Pahari Miniature Painting, p. 16,
2. Ibid, p 16
3. Ibid, p. 17

in the various principalities within Rajasthan or in the Punjab Hill states. After the dissolution of the Moghul school with the accession of Aurangzeb, provincialised Moghul schools developed at the various viceregal courts like Awadh, Murshidabad and the Deccan. Since no great royal patron remained worth the name, the schools were named after the places where they flourished.

One such provincialised school developed at far off Garhgaon. Like Tanjore, Garhgaon was also outside the pale of Moghul empire. Yet stylistically the new school patronised by the Ahom court was really Moghul in technique though Assamese in spirit.

We could have termed it the Tungkhungiya school in the manner of Moghul school. But the period of activity was not spread over the entire period of Tungkhungiya rule. It did not grow during this period either. In the second decade of the early 18th century, the school emerges as a mature idiom. Confined as it was mainly during the rule of Siva Singha (1714-44 A.D.) it could not be named after the dynasty to which he belonged. It could have been termed as 'Assamese painting of the Siva Singha period' after the schools of Akbar period or Jahangir period, for example. We could not do it either. For the school in question has no precedence nor any successor, it does not come under the head of native Assamese painting, the privilege which the Satriya school could claim. Thus the only term left for us to use is the one after the capital of Assam.

The first Ahom conqueror king Sukapha had stayed away from time to time at Saloguri, Habung and Simaluguri, after which he shifted his capital to Charaideo in 1238 A.D. The patricide, king Suklengmung eventually transferred the capital to Garhgaon in 1539, and encircled it with a ring of ramparts or walls, which gave the name to the new city Garhgaon or the 'city of ramparts' . . . . Gadadhar Singha, son of Rudra Singha, founded the city of Rangpur, near the site where his mother Jayamati had been tortured to death. The importance of Garhgaon was not to be dimmed by the ascendancy of Rangpur ; it continued to be the capital, and the king and his court frequently visited that hoary city associated with the best days of the Ahoms. . . .Notwithstanding these two rivals of later growth Kapaukhat and Jorhat, Garhgaon figured in the imagination of the people and in their unsophisticated parlance as the premier city in the good old days of Ahom supremacy."[1]

The above reasons we advance in favour of naming Assamese court painting as Garhgaon school, even though perhaps except for the Gita Govinda no other

1. Bhuyan, S.K., Tungkhungiya Buranji, (ed.) Shifting of Capitals.

manuscript was commissioned for when Garhgaon was the capital of Assam. Further, the use of Rangpur, the then capital, for naming the school would lead to confusion with the Rangpur of north Bengal.

But there had been at work many other forces to hasten the downfall of the school at Delhi and they were equally important than Aurangzeb's bigotry, if not more. Manucci, the Italian traveller, says, "Though the Emperor disliked pictorial art, this form of art continued. . . . The Emperor's uncompromising attitude may have been the loss of all values even among the noblemen who patronised the art secretly."[1] The uninspiring conditions of life of the painters at the imperial centre was enough for those that led them, to leave for other centres though it was beset with uncertainty and risks. Burnier's (1658-1668 A.D.) account of the plight of master artists and craftsmen of the day makes the point clear.

The Moghul court soon began to lose its brilliance and the artist began to desert the decaying capital for other centres. "The independent court established by Ashaf Shah at Lucknow emerged with a local style related to the Imperial court the Deccani Qualam flourished. Similarly, there developed a few schools in the Kangra valley, in Jammu, Garhwal and Kulu, as well as in Patna and Calcutta."[2]

Thus the itenerant artists dispersing to foreign capitals "diffused Moghul principles so that local schools already touched with the central current, tended to a greater conformity. A kind of general mixed style accordingly arose, and though a number of local variations have been classified, divergingly distinctive qualities of their own more or less widely from the norm, many 18th century schools are basically close together . . . ."[3] These artists penetrated as far south as Tanjore and Mysore, where a local school flourished up to the middle of the 19th century and to the Maratha country in the west. In a like manner "Moghul principles" penetrated Assam also in early 18th century, and gave rise to a provincialised Moghul school.

Though politically independent of Mughal India, Assam being a Hindu kingdom never lost ties with the parent-country, even during the Moghul rule. Islam had undergone a sea change in Assam much to the dismay of the Mussalmans of Hindustan. The native Muslims of Assam had identified themselves completely with the rest of the population and this has been recorded by Sahabuddin Talish, the chronicler who accompanied Mirjumla during his unsuccessful raids on Assam (1662-63 A.D.). This prompted the great Savant of Islam to launch missionary

1. M. Marg Ashraf, Later Mughal Art, Vol. XI, No. 4, 1958, p. 57.
2. Ibid, p. 58.
3. Wilkinson, J.V.S. Indian Art, Indian Painting, Faber and Faber Ltd., pp. 139-140.

expeditions to that land. "Then after his arrival at Delhi, Mirjumla sent Saleh Pir's family . . . and a good number of highly qualified and respectable Mûslims including Khanikars with their families to Assam. On their arrival at Garhgaon, they were alloted a separate colony to reside in near Dalbagan, seven miles away from Garhgaon."[1] Thus life became richer with the introduction of new elements of luxury, fine arts and music and dancing. The accommodative spirit of the Assamese people who had always welcomed those that had come to settle in their "golden garden", absorbed the immigrants and in no time the latter were assimilated with the original population. The secular section of the Assamese Muslims were mainly employed in the professions in which they possessed special skill, e.g. embroidery, engraving, woodcarving, canon-casting, sword-making and similar fine works. Muslim artisans and craftsmen were incorporated in the Khanikar Khel or the guild of artisans under a superintendent known as the Khanikar Barua. . . . The greatest landmark in the age long contact between Assam and the Islamic world is however the gorgeously illustrated Assamese Manuscript, Hastividyarnava, compiled by Sukumar Barkaith in 1734 A.D. under the orders of the king, Siva Singha, and his chief queen, Maharani Amvika Devi.[2]

Another important step towards the introduction of the Moghul artists was the intense desire of Rudra Singha for a richer and more sophisticated court life. He was impressed by the life of the princes and nobles in the great cities of Hindusthan and tried to emulate them by introducing new and varied customs in Assam that would add to the life of Garhgaon. For this he created two posts, those of the Khaunua and Bairagis. These people were sent to the various cities of north India where they moved among all sorts of people and noted down details about manners and customs, ways of living, court ettiquettes, costumes and jewellery of the places they visited. "On their return home they informed the Swargadeo about their experiences and those that were found beneficial were introduced in Assam. The Moghul court dress consisting of Pagri, Jama and Izar, Hindusthani musicians, dancers and artists and people following many other vocations were adopted to make the life of a few richer and more enjoyable. The Khaund was usually a Brahmin while the Bairagi was sent out in the guise of a wandering mendioant to avoid identifications." It was through these that the Moghul school was introduced.

Though limited in number our study of the new provincialised Moghul style of painting would be concentrated on the following manuscripts. They have illustrations on all the folios, both sides painted. Thus the number of paintings in

1. Allamah Shah Syed Muhibul Haq, Advent of Muslims in Assam, The Assam Tribune, 27.3.60.
2. Bhuyan, S.K., Annals of the Delhi Badshate, Assam's contact with the Muslim World, p. 18.

the Garhgaon style comes to about more than five hundred pictures—numerous enough to be counted as a school of itself.

1. The Dharma Purana of Kavichandra Dvija.
2. Sankhachuda Vadha of Kaviraj Chakravarti, 1726 A.D.
3. Hastividyarnava of Sukumar Barkaith, 1734 A.D.
4. The Kumara Harana—of uncertain date.
5. The Darrang Raj Vamsavali, 1791 A.D.

The Garhgaon school had family resemblance with the other schools originating from the Moghul idiom. Even the great difference of landscape, setting, costumes and manners and customs of the people could not eface the common traits from the provincialised Moghul schools. Over and above the parent school of Delhi, Garhgaon school had much similarity with those of Deccan, Pahari, and with the set of Rasik Priya paintings from the Museum of Fine Arts, Boston, and the Jaipur Razm Namah paintings. Local conditions are too great a force not to make their appearance in the prevalent idiom of art. Pointing to this Dr. S.K. Chatterji says, "it is to be seen to what extent the style of Hindu and Moghul (i.e. Indo-Persian with European influences) painting was modified by Mongoloid, Bodo and Ahom influences."[1] Pictures produced in this style have hence been classified as belonging to the Garhgaon school. "These pictures form separate styles of late mediaeval Indian painting which have their place of honour besides the better known Moghul, Rajasthani, Kangra and other styles."[2]

In the first place the paintings were executed on oblong folios of manuscripts, bound in "pothi fashion" as is typical of Assam. The painting occupies an exclusive area and does not intrude into the script area. The broad margin around the script area as well as the Alekhya-sthana is separated by a narrow carmine border. Sometimes the band is sprayed with carmine (Hastividyarnava) and very rarely with gold paint as in the case of the Assamese Bhagavata manuscripts from the City Palace Museum of Jaipur. The Central punch hole is camouflaged and made one with the lanscape by painting around it a dainty open-face flower of Persian derivation supported by a tender stalk. But the monotony of scheme was sometimes broken, perhaps, intentionally as by Persian painters. "For symmetry in composition the Persian painters often show contempt. They despise the limits of the rectangular borders of their pictures, which intrude freely into the margins or the texts."[3] A

1. S.K. Chatterji, The Place of Assam in the History & Civilization of India, p. 56.
2. Ibid, p. 57.
3. Distinctive Features of Persian Painting, p. 123.

similar tendency is observed in the products of the Garhgaon school also. M. Stchoukine was perhaps the first to observe that Persian painters sometimes devise in one composition three or four separate centres to which the eye is drawn in turn uncertain to rest. The episode of Vedavati's penance from the Sankhachuda Vadha offers us such examples belonging to the Garhgaon school.

Another group of paintings that compare with Garhgaon paintings is the Rasik Priya paintings from the Ross-Coomaraswamy collection, and Ross Collection of the Museum of Fine Arts, Boston. The miniatures are in the Moghul style of the earliest 17th century (school of Akbar). . . . As in Garhgaon here too "the illustrations are placed on the page in the Indian not in the Persian fashion."[1] Now what is the Indian fashion ? They are laid horizontally in the folios and not vertically as in true Persian and also in Moghul manuscript paintings. In Garhgaon as in other schools of Assam, illustrations are always laid horizontally and thus it is the Indian fashion for, the 'pothi-fashion' and shape of the folios of Indian manuscripts from the very beginning demanded that kind of arrangement. Secondly, like the Sankhachuda Vadha, the Kumara Harana and the Bhagavata Book VI, of Garhgaon, "the Rasik Priya affords a unique example of a purely Hindu work—lavishy illustrated by a Mughal artist."[2] A Moghul artist, however, may not mean that he has to be a Muslim or a native of Delhi. All those who worked in that idiom belonged to that class. The Garhgaon artists, Dilbar,[3] Dosa[4] and Vadh Ligira[5] were as much Moghul as the artists of Delhi or any other provincial centre. Other points of similarity between the schools are found in the "soft colouring, treatment of the drapery as well as the general tendency to indicate modelling show the same character. . . . The maitre however and the manners are purely Hindu ; . . . .[6] They all breath a Hindu atmosphere of the aristocratic Hindu household of northern India.

The following miniatures from the Museum of Fine Arts, Boston, are also similar to those from Garhgaon : (cfr. Catalogue No. VI).

1. Coomaraswamy, A.K. Catalogue of the Indian Collections in the Museum of Fine Arts, Boston; Part VI : Moghul Painting, p. 21.
2. Coomaraswamy, A.K., Ibid.
3. Hastividyarnava manuscript folio.
4. Ibid.
5. Bhagavata Book VI and Sankhachuda Vadha manuscript folio.
6. Coomasawamy, A.K., Ibid.

CLXIII

*06.2405 A party of travellers, perhaps a wedding procession, travels in a hilly landscape. A large banyan tree in the centre. Colour chiefly green, pink and purple. Early 18th century. Dimensions 268m × 167m. Ross Collection.

CLXXIV

*07.287. Marraqqua page, with floral borders on both sides. Obverse, an elephant fight, in landscape and with a prince and troops looking on. 18th century. Dimensions 265m × 388m. Gift of Edward W. Forbes.

LXXXVIII

*17.2654. Elephant, a finely shaded drawing with some delicate colour. 17th century. Dimensions 305m × 24m Ross-Coomaraswamy Collection (Mola Ram Series) P. 1. XLIII.

XXXIX

*17.75. Scene from the Mahabharata about 1600 A.D. Dimension 161m × 272m. Pl. XX. Harriet O. Cruft Fund.

Garhgaon school's similarities with the parent Moghul school were but apparent. Though it was a late example, some of the typically Moghul traits were preserved by the artists of Garhgaon. For example, the three-quarter profile, which is an inheritance from Persian painting for the Moghul artists, was continued in Assam till as late as 1791, though the Delhi artists had taken to the pure Indian profiles for portraits by the time of Jahangir. Secondly, contemporary artists of Patna and Koch Bihar by their very contact with Europeans of the East India Company could not but be influenced in their techniques by the latter. But Garhgaon school was saved from such undesirable European influences. Assam being an independent country was not till then penetrated largely by Europeans and thus was able to maintain the purity of style and developed a language of expression all its own.

"Portraiture is a prominent feature in much of the art of Asia but nowhere was it more highly developed than in the painting of the Moghuls."[1] The school of Garhgaon came very close to Moghul school in portraiture and surpassed in naturalism and grace those produced by the sister schools of Hindusthan. "Many

*Coomaraswamy, A.K, All the numbers of the plates etc. are from the Catalogue of the Indian Collections in the Museum of Fine Arts. Boston, Part VI, Moghul Painting,

1. Brown, P. Indian Painting under the Moghuls, Ch. VII, p. 142,

new and happy features appear in the secular branch of painting mainly due to influences of Mughal painting. The happiest of them are perhaps perspective and portraiture."[1] The Hastividyarnava furnishes portraits of the author Sukumar Barkath, the painters Dilbar and Dosay, and the royal patrons, Siva Singha and Amvika Devi along with the nobility. Of them the portraits of the royal patrons are most life-like and "those have all the qualities of the Delhi miniature portraits on ivory of kings, queens and noble men of the Mughal court, and yet the portrait of the dignified Ahom king and the beautiful Ahom queen with her hair done in a loose knot and wearing an embroidered scarf of golden Muga silk is quite a little gem . . . ."[2]

The demand for portraiture in both Garhgaon and Delhi was equally great. "All conditions were favourable for the development of this art, as the atmosphere of the time was a purely personal one and every individual was eager for some form of immortality, historical or pictorial. It was an age of materialism and portraiture seemed to be one of the means of satisfying an obvious craving for the realities of life, for there is nothing illusionary in a likeness—it is a definite and concrete proof of a person's existence."[3] But the volume of portraits was much restricted in Assam. Slightly different conditions prevailed in the Ahom court circles. The strictly monarchic, highly autocratic and contemptuous attitude born of an intense sense of superiority of the Ahom monarch banned all forms of luxury and privileges to the nobility to maintain the gulf of difference as vast as possible. The same spirit was reflected in his title, Swargadeo, which was a Brahmanic translation of the Tai, "Chao-God Pha-Heaven," i.e., divine beings (Tungkhungiya Buranji). This was perhaps the reason why we do not find any portraits of people other than the kings and their consorts. Lesser queens, maids and pages were also illustrated but they remained unnamed in the manuscripts. But this rare privilege was granted to the painters and authors who were instrumental in the production of the manuscript. Like Jahangir who was certainly the most frequently painted member of his dynasty, Siva Singha too had many portraits of himself and his queen painted showing them in various situations of life. Usually important male figures were done in profile while the three quarter profile was restricted for the queens' portraits as a rule. But in the case of a portrait of Pramathesvari Devi, she has been shown in strict profile, her long and well chiselled face standing out against the cool gray back-ground framed by the cinque-foil arch of the window (Sankhachuda Vadha, ms.).

But there was one fundamental difference between the nature of the two schools. "Moghul painting was essentially a masculine art, confining itself almost

1. Neog, M., The Art of Painting in Assam, pp. 10, 11.
2. Chatterji, S.K., The Place of Assam in the History and Civilization of India, p. 56.
3. Brown, P., Indian Painting under the Moghul, p. 144.

entirely to the lives of men and paying no heed to the doings of the fair sex. The social and domestic customs of the people of course were largely responsible for the omission, as the women of the country lived almost entirely behind the veil" This however was not the case with Assam. As Assam had never come under Islamic rule and its varied influences, Assamese women had never learnt to shun public places and be confined to the "zenana" only. Thus we find paintings of women in all likely places and all walks of life, where women are to be expected. From the great Maharani to the lowly Ligiri (maid) and the Nachani (dancer), all are portrayed in a life-like and candid manner. Those are real portraits for which the woman must have sat before the admiring eyes of the Khanikar who took pains to bring about an exact likeness of his model. That those are authentic portraits can be asserted since all the portraits of a particular person (whether male or female) are photographically alike, though not stereotyped and hackneyed in the manner of dressing and poses.

Secondly, the picture of Siva Singha and Amvika in court is unique in the treasury of mediaeval Indian miniatures. Since the Muslim days no queen has been shown to be sitting in court in public. Nowhere else we find the chief queen or Patesvari sitting on the throne except in the Bhagavata Book VI from Garhgaon. That royal ladies went out in processions carried in open litters or Dolas can be seen from the reverse of the same folio.

Gradually, since the Shahjehan period the strict profile became more popular specially for individual portraits whereas the other angle of the face was used mainly for group and crowded compositions. Similar was the case in Assam also. The king is generally in profile though the ladies are invariably depicted in the three quarter profile. Even the bust was shown in profile with the shoulders at an angle to denote foreshortening. Thus they became "decorative production." The head was poised differently according to the mood of the composition and the figure beneath the drapery was well suggested as we find from the portrait of Amvika Devi. The artist of Garhgaon like his Moghul counterpart "puts into the drawing of the hands a certain distinghishing quality, in some a nervous sensitive feeling, in other suppleness or muscular strength using one or the other as an aid to express the character of the sitter.[1] Siva Singha usually carries a bow in his posed portraits in the contemporary fashion while his lighter mood is expressed by putting a red rose held in his fingers.

As regards backgrounds of Garhgaon portraits, they were always simple—restricted to a monochrome ash or coal gray. This plainness is rather confounding

Brown, P., Indian Painting under the Moghuls, p. 160,

but "the simplicity of the background contrasting with the highly apparelled figure is evidently the artist's underlying idea,[1] to make the portrait stand out.

Speaking of the lines in Moghul portraits Percy Brown says, "Fine as hair, as clear and dignified as it is possible for human hands and eyes to make it, the line of the features in these miniatures is a remarkable piece of execution.[2] We can say exactly the same about Garhgaon miniatures "It was sureness of touch that characterised those sketches."[3]

Above All, being an aristocratic court art Garhgaon painting like the Moghul was a "faithful chronicler of the pomp, pegeantry and personalities of the court. Realism was its keynote."[4] This was a great point of similarity and both excelled in depicting contemporary fashion, music and dance performance, fights of animals, grandees of the court, public functions and important events of the court. Some of the important examples from Garhgaon are as follows :

(1) Contemporary fashion.

(2) Music and Dance parties

(3) Animal fights : Hastividyarnava manuscript.

(4) Important events – a Homage paid by Jayantia and Kachari Rajas : Sankhachuda Vadha.

(5) The English travellers to Rangpur—Hastividyarnava.

The Deccani school had also some points of similarity with the sister school of Garhgaon. In both the cases three quarter profile was more common than the strict profile (Hastividyarnava's portraits of eight kings and of females). The faces were never strongly outlined in Garhgaon as in Deccani portraits The body relegated to the background as being less important in the Deccani style but the Garhgaon artists paid little more care while finishing a portrait but some similarity in the treatment of figures in groups is discernible between the two schools. The scene of a nobleman riding an elephant in procession from the Hastividyarnava is strikingly similar to the miniature showing Abdulla Kutub Shah (mid 17th century) in a similar position (Sir Akbar Hydari collection, Prince of Wales Museum of Western India, Bombay). The large group of retainers and men accompanying the diginitary are in both the cases is treated as a 'massive of superimposed figures'.[5]

1. Brown, P., Indian Painting under the Moghuls, p. 161.
2. Ibid., p. 160.
3. Ibid., p. 143.
4. Iyer K. Bharatha, Indian Art, p. 76.
5. Kramrish, S. The Art of Painting in the Deccan.

The greatest contribution of the Garhgaon had been portraiture but the treatment of landscape was equally important. "Landscapes with green undulating plains and blue hills,[1] dominate and even become cliche. Though uncaptioned, the landscape immediately reminds one of the wide expanse of green meadows and grasslands around Garhgaon in the present Sibsagar District and the distant ranges of hills in the background are the Naga hills that bound the district. The natural beauty of Assam with its diversified landseape offered the Garhgaon artists to master the art of landscape painting as the Pahari painters did in the beautiful Kangra valley. "One thing marks off these 18th century paintings of Assam—there are beautiful landscapes mostly green and undulating plains with flowering trees, and hills and rivers. It is a wonder how the beauty of nature as spread over the face of the earth could captivate these artists in Assam in a way it never did artists in any other parts of India."[2]

Book Covers

The art of painting book covers was not popular in Assam. This was restricted mainly to Goalpara District, that too on the north bank of the Brahmaputra. A few are found in this district of Kamrup also. But those are generally carved on wood and not painted.

The practice of illustrating book covers was prevalent and was the only mode of miniature painting in Koch Bihar during the 16th and 17th centuries. Goalpara being conteguous with that former princely state, the art had filtered into that part of Assam. And the practice of illustrating only the book covers is a legacy of Bengal to Koch Bihar which had more intimate connections with Bengal since it was included within the Subah of Bengal since the days of Lakshmi Narayana and Man Singh.

The only book cover that has any stylistic affinity with Garhgaon painting is that of the Bhatti Kavyam.[3] It is unfinished and figures occupy the two ends of book cover. In the right half is the solitary figure of a sitting male figure with his hands in an expressive attitude. His blue complexion and the crown on his head suggests him as Rama. In the other half we have quite a little dramatic scene. A kingly make figure kneels with folded hands before a standing female, who wears a look of contempt in her eyes and motions with her left hand to clear off. This group evidently represents Ravana trying to entice Sita in her captivity and being refused in turn. An expression of defeat and at the same time longing

1. M. Neog, The Art of Painting in Assam, p. 10.
2. Chatterji, S.K., The Place of Assam in the History of Civilisation of India, p. 57.
3. Gauhati University Library : Manuscript Section.

is writ large on the face of Ravana while Sita is the spirited woman and the chaste wife, the Sati, idealised in all ages of Hindu civilization. The figure of Sita is unfinished and only in outlines. Angularity vanishes completely but the profile remains for all the figures. The mudras also play an important part. The colours are laid in plain uniform washes and no shading exists even in the finished figures. Absence of any background details succeeds in focussing our attention on the three figures that successfully tell this episode from the Ramayana.

Two similar book covers of an unidentified Vaisnava manuscript are also in the style described above. But they are finished and the figures stand out against a monochrome vermillion background and bounded by a creeper design. One is scene of Rama's coronation while the other is the Tambula-seva scene from the life of Krisna. With the minimum number of figures viz., the four brothers, Sita and Hanuman the story is deftly told. The suggestion of coronation is made by one brother holding a parasol above Rama's head, Hanuman doing obeisance to the lord and Sita demurely standing in Anjali mudra There is again a touch of early Jaina miniatures in the figures. They are restless and Rama stands in an unusual pose in between the Dvibhanga and Tribhanga. The figures pulsate with energy and are restless and passionate as are in blazing vermilion red, blue, green and red colours. The faces are all in profile ; there is no suggestion of angularity anywhere. From every other point they look like the creation of any of the Rajasthani schools. But their squatish figures and high sloping foreheads make them very close to Bundi or Nathadwara miniatures. They resemble in general composition an 18th century Bengal book cover from the Bharat Kala Bhawan, Banaras. The scene too is identical in each case though the costume types differ.

The other panel shows the Tambula seva scene, which consists only of Radha and Krisna and this scheme has been repeated thrice on the same surface. Other details remain the same as the "coronation" scene. Krisna is depicted as the Murali Manohara or 'plying-on-the-flute' aspect and stands in a highly stylised Tribhanga pose. Radha faces him and offers him a prepared betel leaf with one hand and fans him with the one she holds in her other. The most striking point is the well trimmed pointed beard of Krisna and this is quite a unique feature. Like Krisna figures from Bengal book covers, his hair-style also consists of a combined "chuda" and "veni". The calculated pose of Radha and the jutting out hip of Krisna remind us of the similar way of depiction in the Satriya school. And for a region like Goalpara with adjoining boundaries of Assam, Koch Bihar and Bengal proper it is quite possible to give birth to an art style with elements borrowed from the three regions.

The Syamarahasya manuscript has an equally interesting book cover.[1]

1. Shyamarahasya Ms. No. 1339, Gauhati University Library. Author : Purananda Paramhansa.

Here the resemblance with the Koch Bihar school is greater and this similarity is striking with that of a book cover from Koch Bihar of which the subject matter is also the same. Though badly damaged the artist successfully recreated in the original the fury of the battle field when goddess Kali vanquished the Asuras in the company of her associates. The figures are full of action and are perfect examples of the female form. The treatment of the female figures are full of naturalism and are candid. No shading exists but the treatment of volume of flesh and the roundness of the breasts and thighs are all brought out simply with lines. Only the feet of Kali have been preserved and they show what a great masterpiece the entire figure might have been, light of foot, slender and gracefully poise. The recumbent body of Siva on whom Kali had stepped accidentally is also a superb study of the youthful male nude. The peace and repose of a Yogi's soul is reflected in the perfectly motionless body of Siva and the well proportioned limbs represent the inner steadiness attained through Yoga. There is westernism of modelling in all the figures specially in that of Siva.

The book covers containing a manuscript titled Ashtamangala is full of Krisna Lila scenes on all the four sides (1802 A.D.). This is a unique set of pictures and combines many ancient and contemporary traits. The background is monochrome red and various episodes from Krisna's youth are depicted, each in a separate group unconnected from the other. But they are not separated by many borders as such. There is an attempt at individualising the faces of the human figures. There is so much of outside, specially Pahari, influence in these that one finds hard to believe they are from the remote corner of eastern India. The copyist's name Ganga Prasad Guha is typical Bengali but we are yet uncertain if he had painted the pictures too. Human figures have a striking resemblance with those of the Bilaspur school from Bharat Kala Bhavan, Banaras. The human figures in both cases are heroic in stature and have large cylindrical limbs with no suggestion of muscles and curves of the body. The Gopis are tall and slim and not petit as in Assamese miniatures. Their costume of Sari, Choli and Lahanga is also unusual for Assam, and their hair hang loose at the back.

The Dana-Lila scene offers drama and fine human studies. The bodies are well modelled but the fingers though long and sensitive have no nails depicted. Fish shaped eyes and linear modelling at the neck are interesting. The tree's crown is kidney shaped and leaves have been picked out in yellow against a green background. Large white dot design on the skirt of the prostrating Gopi is a pre-Moghul motif from Rajasthan.

In the Dadhi Bhat or "picnic" scene grouping is shown by means of two parallel rows of picnickers placed one above the other to denote distance. There is diversification of perspective, the Gopas in eye level view while the leaves which they eat out from are in bird's eye view. The sitting cow is a fine example of animal study and reminds one of southern Nandi figures. This was a very popular subject for Assamese Vaishnava painters beginning from the Nowgong Bhagavata (1539 A.D.). The leaf green complexion of Krisna traditionally known as the 'Durvadala-syama' or grass green is a point to note. Though common in Pala and eastern Indian painting it was not seen since the days of Ajanta. Rajput painters never used it, but it had been used in the Kashmir school of painting Ragini Dhanasri. One of the Gopas has a chocolate complexion. Though not very common in Indian miniatures the Mrigavati Charit (16th century A.D.) from the Bharat Kala Bhavan, Banaras, has examples of this type of complexion The pink complexion of another Gopa has parallels in the Gita Govinda from the N.C Mehta Collection

Architecture has been summarily treated as in Koch Bihar school in the scene of Sandipani's school where Krisna studied. The pair of striped shorts of a youth reminds one of the similar studies from Pahari examples.

The Rasamandala though has a defect perspective is quite forceful. Around the central figures of Radha and Krisna under a Kadamba tree are arranged the members of the "ringdance" in a way which reminds of a similar arrangement in the Nowgong Bhagavata. The viewer has to turn the picture many times to get the proper view of each pair of dancers. And when seen as a whole it gives the impression of a number of dolls lying on their backs and arranged in a circle. In spite of this archaism, the figures and profiles are very individualistic and their knees slightly bent in the process of the dance.

The two conversing male figures and that of the Vasudeva stooping beside sleepping Yasoda's bed are fine examples of male figure and portrait respectively.

Continuations of many old traditions and motifs are discernible in the miniatures from Goalpara District. The Laksmi Charita (C. 18th century) manuscript has a number of pen and ink drawings of unconnected subjects. Shading and modelling however have no scope. Two radiating lotuses represent an older Indian art tradition and are ultimately deprived from western Indian painting. Another unidentified book cover from Dhubri in Goalpara District too betrays this trait specially in the male profile. Paintings from Bharmal Ki Chattri at Ambar have similar figures, specially the tiger. The round shield carried by the male figure too is an ancient idiom.

The female figures show more of the continuance of the old idioms. The noses are big and aquiline. The eyes are lozange shaped and the collirium-line extends further than the outline of the eye, and eyebrows are highly arched.

Frontality is maintained in the torso though the faces are in profile. The 'odhni' (wimpole) leaves the chest bare, neither does it cover the heavy bun of hair. Half blown lotuses (Nila Kamala) held in the hands by the females is also an ancient concept. The unfinished female figure has pom-poms attached to the broad bracelets or Gamkharus are also worth recording as a traditional Indian motif.

A book cover from Nalbari shows a grand ceremonial barge rowed by a number of persons and carrying a dignitary. Intensely crude, this composition, however, does not claim its association with miniature painting in any way. It represents pure folk art having vitality and economy in expression. It is surprising how in this specimen we find miniature painting turning for inspiration to folk art. The figures of rowers with carelessly treated bodies but intense profiles with pig-tails and shaven or closely cropped hair resemble similar figures from folk mural painting of Mithila[1] This can only be explained by the long standing contact that existed between Kamarupa and Mithila from the earliest times. The book covers from Dhubri mentioned above deserve special mention for they represent the continuation of older motifs. These book covers do not antedate the 18th century and are painted in the primary colours. But they are calligraphic in treatment in spite of being painted. A close similarity exists between these and Orissan palm-leaf etchings. The illustrations include the incarnations of Visnu, viz. Matsya, Kurma, Varaha, Narasimha, Vamana, Parasurama, Rama, Valarama, Buddha and Kalki. The first four Avataras are in conventional synchratic form. The episode of the three steps of Vamana has been ingeneously depicted by supplying him with an extra leg which is lifted high for there was no place for him to place it since he had by taking two steps occupied both heaven and earth. Buddha sits under an architectural niche and Kalki rides high brandishing his sword. The priests sacrificing at an altar of fire bear the closest resemblance to Orissan figures. The intense eyes, arched eyebrows, pointed beards and the peculiar way of the moustache, all speak of the same tradition.

The existence and practice of a school akin to that of Garhgaon but inferior in technique and scope is offered by the two copies of the Bhagavata Book X in the Kamarupa Anusandhana Samiti, Gauhati. They are dated 1765 A.D. and 1804 A.D., the latter coming from the Dakhin Pat Satra of Majuli in Sibsagar District. Though the older manuscript is a little cruder in execution but otherwise they are identical in composition, colour scheme, treatment of nature and delineation of the human figure. This similarity is specially noticed when compared to the

1. Archer, W. C, Maithil Painting, Marg Vol.

Dharmapurana and Hastividyarnava manuscripts where lives of village folk have been depicted. And Krisna and the Gopis are here like rural youths and maids as in Pahari painting. The background is monochrome green though red has been used in the scene of Godhuli-Bela from the Majuli Bhagavat. Similarity of approach with the Garhgaon school is noticeable in the treatment of the background, and the costume, ornaments and coiffeur of the Gopis. Even the spiked gold-band for the top-knotted coiffeur is also common to both. The hair of Krisna and Valarama is also done like those of the Brahmins in the Hastividyarnava manuscript. The greatest degree of similarity exists in the treatment of the anatomy and the delineation of the eyes. The human figures are characterised by realism and seem to throb with the inner breath or Prana. The eyes are equally serene and expressive, forceful and rounded and the lips heavy and sensuous. Sensuousness and joi-de-vivre are the keynote of both the styles—for the one the pleasures of sophisticated court life and for the other of love making and romance in a pastoral setting In these paintings, the Gopi-Krisna theme has received an earthy treatment and yearning of lovers here is worldly and amorous.

Human figures in these folios are quite different from the general Satriya style that is followed for illustrating Bhagavata texts. These do not have the angularity and stiffness of later Gujarati painting to which the Satriya style resembles a great deal. These are rather "Ajantesque" and like later Ellora painting a gap between the classical and mediaeval pictorial traditions of India. In this they are really similar to the paintings of women on the 12th century book cover from the Jnan Bhandar of Jaisalmer.[1] The drawing is flowing and angularity is encountered in the sweeping curves, even the noses and the chins are well curved. Here too the figures, specially the female ones, have beautiful ovaloid faces, large eyes, well arched eyebrows, thick lips and well rounded breasts are more in line of Ajanta, Ellora, and the Pala paintings of Bengal. But the feet have the same careless treatment of the Satriya school.

Atmosphere is recreated with the simplest devices. By changing the background colour into carmine the effect of the Godhuli Bela is attained while the cool breeze is suggested by showing the peacock feathers tilted a little to the back. The folds of drapery are depicted by thicker lines. No modelling is attempted by shading, but by a cluster of lines in case of drapery around the curves of the body and with semicircular lines at the humps of cattles. The figures sometimes intrude into the margins on the script area which is an inheritance from the Garhgaon school. Otherwise not so expressive as the examples

1. Motichandra, Jaina Miniature Paintings from Western India, Figs. 191, 192.

are, a generous use of mudras has sought to compensate it as we see in the scene of Yasoda assuring the complaining Gopis. In spite of their diminutive size the treatment of hair is surprisingly fine in the human figures. Strands of loose hair that are being blown in the breeze are finely executed. In both the manuscripts the illustrations are bounded in a rectangular panel, sometimes with a wide triffoil-arch top.

Minor Arts

6

WOOD WORK

Wood was the most popular medium of architectural constructions as well as for other creative endeavours in the Ahom period. The easy availability of a variety of tropical and alpine varieties of timber from the sprawling forests in the plains and mountains of Assam, Nagaland and Arunachal was responsible for the wide use of wood. Being subject to frequent earthquakes it was found to build more safely in wood in Assam than with vulnerable materials like masonry and stone. Yet as in the previous epochs so also in the Ahom period ponderous temples and other examples of civil architecture were built in stone and bricks. Next to wood, bamboo was the common medium of construction either independently or in conjunction with wood. The large variety of bamboos and their tenacity and elasticity also made bamboo popular. Wood and bamboo were also used to fashion a variety of boats for civil, military and mercantile purposes. Modes of conveyances like carts, Dolas or litters and sedan chairs of various grades and designs were also made with wood and their poles usually with bamboos. Apart from the Buranjis of the period Mughal and foreign chronicles also testify to the high standard reached by workers in wood in Ahom Assam. Even if the Buranjis be branded as reflecting too much of national pride, Mughal chronicles like the Fatiyah-i-Ibriah or Tarikh-e-Asham of Shihabuddin Talish, a follower of Mir Jumla, remove any such suspicions. Talish had left a faithful description of the magnificent wooden palace of Garhgaon which he had personally seen. "There is not another city like this in the world. It is a collection of a large number of big villages. Around the palace is a wide road. The Divankhana or the Cholong Ghar of the king is 120 cubits by 30 cubits. It has 66 pillars of wood. They have a circumference of four cubits and though so huge, are really attractive. These pillars are wonderfully decorated with wood work beyond description. In the whole of the world there is no palace as beautiful and decorative as this. The outer walls of the edifice have unparalleled wood carvings and the inner walls are hung with huge brass mirrors. They dazzled the eyes of the beholder as they reflect the sun's rays. 12,000 carpenters worked for a year to finish it. It is really a wonderful land.[1] In the coronation ceremony three special pavillions were constructed of Singri wood known as Singri Ghar, Pat Ghar and Holong Ghar where the different ceremonies of the Abhiseka took place. The wooden Kareng or palace of Garhgaon was abandoned when in 1752 A.D. the new masonry palace was built by king Rajeswar Singha.

In a riverine tract like Assam with the Brahmaputra flowing as the main artery of communication and joined by a network of tributaries in the plains boats were the commonest and quickest mode of conveyance. The large number of royal highway or Raj-Alis of the Ahom period however were only a secondary link between the different parts of the kingdom. Boat building was both a royal as well as private enterprise. Places like Pandu, Gauhati, Kaliabar, Bisnath, Dikhon-mukh, Rangur, Garhgaon and Sadiya were centres of boat building, being established on the banks of important rivers like the Brahmaputra and the Dikhou. There were likewise some important river ports and harbours at Lata Sil in Gauhati, Sakbari in Rangpur,[2] Barnaosali at Garhgaon and others.[3] These harbours of riverine navy were known as Nao Sali. These were always kept full of navy boats ready for action. During Mir Jumla's invasion of Garhgaon, the Assamese burnt 12,000 boats at Barnaosali as a matter of scroched—earth policy against the Mughal army. Again in the 19th century Capt. Wales on occupying Assam acquired 20,000 boats from the Ahoms.

The various boats had names and were meant for special purposes like cargo boats, pleasure boats, passenger boats, fishing boats, scout boats and navy boats. Gun-boats were generally known as Hiloi Chara Nao. Boats of the rich people and the ceremonial barges of the royalty and of the temples and Vaisnava Satras were beautifully painted and their prows were fashioned as Makaras and other mythical animals. Boats with animal headed prows were the Magarlaga Naos. Such a boat is illustrated in the (1790 A.D.) Sahapari Upakhyan manuscript from Rangmahal in north Gauhati. The Mar-nao was an ingenious shape designed for maximum loading capacity. For this two boats were joined lengthwise with a broad platform on them. These sometimes had a shed on the top for the passenger while the rest of the platform was reserved for goods and animals. These were mainly plied between ferry points or Parghats. The design of the Mar-naos made them safe as well as gave maximum utility. Other boats were the Barnao, Chara-nao, Pansoi, Kapikol, Hayakali,

1. Pavie, T. (tr.) Tarikh-Asham.
2. Handiqui, B.C. Purani Asamar Shilpa, p. 62.
3. Ibid.

Sihu, Jap-nao and Chilapati.[1] Specially designed boats were used for the annual regattas or Naokhels patronised by the court and by the Satras and temples.

Next to that of the boats was the great variety of Dolas specified for use by the different strata of the officialdom and society by decrees of the highly aristocratic and beaurocratic Ahom court, e.g. Litters[2] of various kinds :

Dola—

Kekora dòla—

Dhekarlaga dola—

Parhi dola—

Dhekar laga Changi

Parhi Changi

Khatola

The Kekora Dola and Parhi Dola are similar in shape. But the pole over the Kekora Dola is rounded. The hoods of these Dolas have upturned ends and curved inwards. In the holes of the hood are inserted the pointed sticks on the pole. The hood is covered with red or white cloth, embroidered with gold thread. Little hangings shaped like banana-flowers Kaldilia made from red, green and yellow threads were hung from the pole of the Dola. A tassel made of 12 coloured silk threads was also attached for the passenger to hold on to. The seat is of cotton filled cushion spread with an embroidered Talsa The centre of the pole of a Kekora Dola is greatly curved while that of the Parhi Dola is slightly so. But that of the Charia or Athubhanga Dola is completely straight. The Dolas of the above two types are also fixed with a couple of mirrors.

The Arwan was a symbol of Ahom royal authority and was carried along with the Chattra or parasol. It was circular in shape and is woven from fine bamboo strips and sticks. It was encased in a white cloth cover tied at the right. It was decorated with gold and silver thread embroidery. The long pole which served as the handle was decorated with silver and gold sheets. The parasol is of white silk with tassels in gold and silver threads. The pole is decorated with gold sheet and set with jewels above the grip. The finial is in the shape of a small gold Kalasa.

These litters were chiefly made of bamboo and wood and were variously painted. The designs were carved and then painted with appropriate colours Of the designs the most popular were the Lotus, Scrolls, Magars (Makaras) and winged lions (Pakhi-laga Simha) of Ahom derivation. Gadadhar Simha employed

1. Handiqui, B.C. Purani, Asamar Shilpa, p. 63.
2. Gogoi, L., Ahom Jati Aru Sanskriti p. 179.

Muslim craftsmen for decorating the Dolas and Simhasanas with sheets of metal and paints.[1]

In architecture too wood played an important part ; in the royal edifices like Pat-Ghar, Singri Ghar and Holong-Ghar[2] most of the decorations were carved in wood which was painted. Though little remains of these specimens, yet the bigger Satras have preserved much of earlier wood work. The figures were mostly from the Puranas and epics and each figure was separately framed under a cusped arch as in Assamese miniatures of the Satriya school. The carvings were mostly done on the brackets (chati), poles and pillars, doors and windows and on the wooden portions of the Bat chara (gatehouse) or the litch-gate of the important institutions. As in Japanese domestic architecture also these gate-houses were an important member of the entire house plan. Here important personages were received and welcomed before entry into the house of the Satra. The Kirtan-ghar of the Barpeta Sattra has some of the finest wood carvings existing to this day. They of course belong to a later period but show the continuity of the art of wood carving till the last century. The entire wall surface is carved with high-reliefs showing scenes from the Puranas. The Gossain Ghar or the private chapel in the bouse of Sri H.M. Majumdar of Rampur village, Kamrup (17 miles west of Gauhati), also has beautiful carvings on the door. These as well as the carved torana and the large carved icons of Visnu, Laksmi, Garuda, Jaya and Vijay were also carved at the beginning of the present century by the father of Sri Majumdar. He was a painter too and illustrated a ms. of the Bhagavata in 1878 A.D.

In furniture making the Assamese followed a unique technique. They carved out of blocks of wood smaller pieces of furniture, chests, boxes, manuscript boxes, lamp stands and similar other accessories of daily life. These too were brightly painted The great variety of bamboos were also utilised for the purpose of furniture making. The Bhatuka Banh is so thick that a small bucket can easily be cut out of a joint of this variety of bamboo. From thinner variety of bamboos various cylindrical containers were made and painted in traditional designs. These were also closed by a tight-fitting cap made of another piece of the same material. Of these the Kharika Chunga (tooth-pick container) and letter-cases were important. Letters and decrees were rolled and inserted into these cylinders of bamboo. The aristocracy and the royalty often used metal immitations of bamboo cylinders. Green bamboo cylinders were used for baking the Chunga-Pitha pie. For this green-bamboo cylinders were cut into convenient ½ cubit lengths, were filled in with rice, sugar, water and spices and flavourings. Then these were put into ovens for baking. When the pie was ready the cylinders were split open. The greenness

1. Handiqui, B.C. Puranl, Asamar Shilpa, p. 63.
2. Ibid., p. 63.

of the cylinder prevented it from being burnt during the process of baking. Many of the tribal people use thick bamboo cylinders for cooking rice also. But these cylinders can be used only once.

For wood carving the commonest wood were Ajara, Gamar, Sai, etc. Items of furniture were usually the following :

Bar pira (a flat wooden plank with little raised support).

Tamuli pira (a variety of the above).

Dukharia pira (a variety of the above).

Salpira (a raised seat)

Boxes and chests

Pera (a chest)

Barpera (large size chest)

Chorpera (a variety of chest)

Batanipera (small handy boxes) etc.[1]

Another allied art was that of the pith-industry. Pith is the core of the jute plant of which Assam is an important producer. Pith was used mainly for toys, decorations and temporary icons. At present the industry is concentrated in the Goalpara district, specially in the princely seat of Gauripur. During the Ahom period the 'guild of pith workers' was known as the Kurhila Katia Khel. The pith objects are extremely fragile and are brightly painted. Masks for dances and worship were made of which the masks of Kali are quite numerous. Larger icons showed Kartika sitting on the peacock and the cylindrical images of Jagannatha.

"Simhasanas or thrones were used by the kings. These were usually 7 tiered and the four corners of each tier were decorated by winged Ahom lions or Gaja-Simha motifs. The sides of the thrones were carved and painted in the traditional manner. In the Satras also Simhasanas were kept to hold the Bhagavata Book X used for veneration instead of an icon. The royal throne became all the more elaborate along with other material aspects of culture during the Tungkhungiya period." Then it was 7 tiered, painted and varnished with lac. The stages were covered with gold sheets and embellished with rubies (Dalima Bakhar) and emeralds (Panna). The lions in the corners were covered with silver sheets but their necks were fitted with gold strips which too were jewelled. For the manes of the lions long silver threads were attached in clumps. The legs of the lions had gold rings and round gold Mehrapi ornaments. On the topmost or the 7th tier there were

1. Gogoi, L., Ahom Jati Aru Sanskriti. p. 179.

four poles instead of lions. These poles were also covered with silver sheets and were set with jewels in bands at a distance of 2 Angulis from each other. The tops of poles had a golden Kalasa each. The roof atop the poles is of fine white silk decorated with gold thread embroidery (Karchip or Karchobi). The middle of the right hand poles are fixed with silver bands to hold a silver pole on which are fixed three golden plates topped by a Kalasa. Here are fixed the Dhvaja and Pataka of the royal line On the steps of the throne are placed Hengdans (swords) with golden handles set with ruby and emeralds. Similarly decorated golden muskets were also laid in a like manner."[1] The king was fanned by Yak-tail and peacock tail fly whisks with golden handles set with jewels from Rudra Simha's portrait.

Simpler forms of this throne are seen in the Bhagavata Book X dated 1539 A.D. from the Bali Satra, Nowgong and the final folio of the Bhagavata Book VI from the D.H.A.S., Gauhati ; Simhasanas for the Satras were also designed like royal thrones. The four legs of it were carved as Gaja-Kachchhapa motifs while the rest followed the usual pattern as in the case of the one from the Barpeta Satra. But it has a wooden top instead of canopies. The dome of the small pavilion is melon shaped (fluted) topped by a lotus bud. Smaller replicas of it are arranged at the corners of it.[2]

Since wood was of many varieties in Assam and were put to multifarious uses they were chosen for each particular purpose. Thus for architecture, Sal, Singri and Koir were regarded as first grade wood.[3] These were used for making the framework of wooden buildings while Ikara, a variety of reeds, was used for filling up the wall space. Ikara was regardrd as good for the inner walls since it lasted long in dry places and was able to take and retain the plaster of mud on it.

In the Brahmaputra valley most valuable timber were available from Nowgong and Sibsagar. The best varieties from Nowgong were the following :[4]

(a) Sonaru (cassia fistula)

(b) Ajhar (lagerstrocemia reginae)

(c) Titasapa (michelia champaca)

(d) Gunserai (cinnamomum glanduliferum)

(e) Gomari (gumelina arborea)

Other varieties of wood used were

1. Gogoi, L., Ahom Jati Aru Sanskriti, pp. 89-91.
2. Pathak, G., Barpeta Satras Itihasa, Cover design.
3. Rajkhowa, B., Historical Sketches of Assam, p. 10, Dibrugarh, 1917.
4. Allen B.C., Assam District Gazetteer., Vol. VI., p. 139, Nowgong.

(f) Sal (shorea robusta)

(g) Sum (artocarpus chaplasha)

(h) Poma (cedreta toona)

(i) Nahor (mesua ferrea) and

(j) Koroi (albizzia procena).[1]

In Sibsagar area the Uriam (bischoffia javanica) or the guava, Amari (amoora spletabilis, Parali (Stercospermum chelonoides) and Khokan (duabanga soneratioides) were some of the most prized varieties of wood.[2] The second grade wood was Simalu (bombax malabaricum), Hollock (terminalia bicolorata), Hollong (dipterocar pus bondii), Hingori or Singri (castanopsis rufescenes) and Hilika (terminalia citrina) or Silikha.[3]

Nowgong was a centre of boat building for which Sonaru, Ajhar, Titasapa, and Gunserai wood were used. These boats were in the shape of dug-out canoes which were floated down the Kapili, the Jamuna and Barpani rivers to Chaparmukh. Merchants intending to buy boats thus flocked at Chaparmukh from Goalpara, and Gauhati.[4] In Kamrup and Goalpara, however, the Gameri was used for boat building. A Kamrupi folk song describing Krisna posing as a boatman to Radha emphasises the qualities of his boat since it is made of Gameri wood,

"Bhāga nahai chinga nahai
Gamerire sar
Hasti-ghora par karon
Radhar Kiman bhar ?"
(It is not broken it is not torn
It is made of pure Gameri (wood)
I ferry across horses and elephants
How weighty is Radha) ?

There was a separate department of the king for collecting good quality wood from the forests under the officer Kath-Barua.[5]

1. Allen B.C., Assam District Gazetteer, Vol. VI, p. 139.
2. Ibid., Vol. VII, p. 154, Sibsagar, 1906.
3. Ibid.
4. Ibid., Vol. VI, p. 139, Nowgong.
5. Sadar Amin, H.K. Barua : Assam Buranji, p. 122. Gauhati, 1962, 2nd Edn.

7

IVORY, BAMBOO AND WICKER WORK

In a mountainous country with large forest areas like Assam industries dependent upon forest products had naturally developed to great perfection. There was a great variety in wood also which were used in architecture, sculpture and for objects of daily use. But they have already been separately dealt with in the previous chapter. Of the forest products the most expensive and attractive was ivory. Often the rhino's horn was also as much valued as the ivory. Bamboos of great variety and sizes grow in Assam. Those too were used for house building and many uses in the daily life and ritual uses. Mats and screens were made in a myriad ways from the bamboos and an assortment of wickers, rushes and canes. The bark of the 'agaru' tree or the Aquilaria Agallocha was processed for making fine manuscript folios known as Sanchi-pat or 'preserving-folios'. Sanchi was derived from the Sanskrit Samchaya or 'preserving', as the folios preserved knowledge for the posterity. The Sanchi pat was not only good as a manuscript folio but an excellent carrier for miniature paintings with which the manuscripts of mediaeval Assam were embellished. Some of them even today carry paintings of the early 16th century like the Bhagavata Book X (1539 A.D.) of the Bali Satra, Nowgong.

I. Ivory

The antiquity of the Assamese ivory industry goes back to the days of the Mahabharata, according to Dr. V.S. Agrawala. "According to the Sabha Parva Bhagadatta brought to the court of Yudhisthira some presents including fleet horses, utensils of jade (asmasaramaya bhanda) and swords with hilts of white ivory (suddhadantatsarun asin, Sabha, 43.14).[1] The same had been said by Dr. Moti Chandra. "Ivory handles of the swords probably show that the ivory carvers' art was highly developed in Assam at least two thousand years back.[2] The

1. Agrawala. V.S., Presidential Address, All India Oriental Conference, 22nd Session, Gauhati (Assam), p. 3, 1965.
2. Das, D., Asamar Hati-datar Shilpa ; Asam Bani, Jan. 6, 1961.

Harsacharita of Banabhatta also records the splendid presents sent by Bhaskaravarman, the king of Assam to Harsa of Kanauj. "The last item refers to round ear-rings made of the long tusks of sea-elephants (jala-hastin). This seems to refer to walrus ivory which had been a favourite item of trade in antiquity, being in great demand from the Chinese to the Roman world and also known in the mediaeval times as 'sir-mahi' used for making handles of daggers and a variety of purposes. The head-bones of such large long-tusked aquatic animals were turned on the lathe for making round beads which were bored and stringed as necklaces possessing the charming translucent shine of pearls. The ear-rings sent as presents were beautified with pendants of such pearly beads (muktaphala-dama-danture) [1]

During the long history of the Ahoms ivory objects were exported from Assam and were also sent to neighbouring lands and presents to rulers by the Ahom monarchs. King Jayadhwaj Singha's (1954-63 A.D.) presents to the Mughal Emperor included mats, combs and back-scratchers made of ivory.[2] Kamaleswar Singha (1795-1811 A.D.) of the same dynasty also sent to the king of Bhutan boxes, bed steads and other objects made of ivory.[3] During the last phase of Ahom rule ivory objects worth Rs. 6500/- were annually exported from Assam at the check post of Hadira-chowki.[4]

Apart from hilts and handles of weapons and legs of furniture, ivory was used for making various kinds of boxes, containers, cylinders (chunga) for keeping letters and scrolls, back-scratchers, fans, combs and pins for the coiffure, shuttles and combs for the loom, pieces of ornaments, icons, dices and men for chess and other board-games. Small stools or Piras, Sarais or dish-on-stand, mats and even manuscript folios were made from ivory.

The Auniati Satra has a fine mat (Dhari or Pati) made of thin ivory strips cut to simulate cane. In the Hajo temple there are fine ivory replicas of elephants. The Barpeta Satra is fortunate enough in having an ivory-hilted knife made during the days of Sri Madhavadeva (16th century). The Prince of Wales Museum, Bombay, has an excellent ivory panel, evidently part of some box belonging to the early 18th century, though it is labelled as a Deccani product of the 17th century. It shows a prince and a lady in embrace standing face to face and framed by a shape derived from the Mihrabi design. The outer frame is rectangular and four rosettes

1. Agrawala, V.S., Presidential Address, All India Oriental Conference, 22nd Session, Gauhati, pp. 6-7, 1965.
2. Handiqui, Purani Asamar Shilpa, p. 59.
3. Ibid.
4. Ibid., p. 60.

occupy the interjunction of the rounded edges of the inner frame and the rectangular edges of the outer. The figures though not minutely carved for details are boldly conceived. The direct manner of presentation and the simplicity of composition along with a plain background make this piece unmistakably Assamese. The prince is clad in a long full sleeved 'Jama' reaching up to the ankles, a 'patka' and a 'Moglai-tupi' or the Chajjedar-pagri of the period. A shawl drapes his chest and falls at the back. The lady is clad in a native Assamese Riha-Mekhela suit and a choker of large beads decks her slender neck. The brushed back hair terminating into a looped coiffure is exactly in the manner shown in queen Ambika Devi's portrait in the Hastividyarnava manuscript. It is identical with the Siamese Klau Phom type of hair style. The lady also carries a curved sword on her shoulder. Does the sword indicate that she is a Ligiri or palace maid ? Can this pair represent the young prince Siva Singha and Phuleswari, the Ligiri, of whom he was enamoured before they became king and queen after the death of the former's father king Rudra Singha ? The treatment of the body in almost a single plain, the tasselled ends of the scarves and the pounced design all remind one of the terracotta plaques from Ghanashyam's House at Jaysagar, which also belongs to the period of Rudra Singha. Bahadur Gaonburha was a famous ivory carver during the last phase of Ahom rule.[1]

The museum of the Indian Institute of Art in Industry, Calcutta, has a fine ivory loom-comb. It is used for combing and separating the threads arranged in the loom. The long comb has for its handle a fret-work design of the Gaja-simha. The elephant is realistically treated but the crouching lion almost the size of the elephant, is the Ahom-lion so commonly met with in Assamese art. The details are picked out in a crimson paint while the entire comb is left with its original ivory colour.

Technique of treating ivory : Ivory tusks are straightened in the following manner. A thick coating of clay is applied to the tusks and then they are slowly heated. Thus they get soft and are pliable and hence are easily straightened. After that the tusks are left to cool and the clay coating removed. From these tusks thin strips are extracted for making ivory mats or Dharis. These thin strips are similar to the cane strips with which normal mats are woven. The technique of weaving ivory mats is the same as that of cane mats.[2] For making other objects the tusks are cut into required shapes and sizes after being straightened in the above manner.

1. Das, D., Asamar Hatidatar Silpa ; Asam Bani, 6.1.1961.
2. Handiqui. B.C., Purani Asamar Silpa, p. 59.

During the Ahom rule ivory carving was a an important industry and was practised by a group of Khanikars. Writing in the 19th century (1807—14 A.D.) Hamilton had indicated royal patronage of this art. "The king has, in his house, some men who make very fine mats, fans and head scratchers of ivory, all Chinese art."[1] But gradually the industry declined at such a speed that by the time the 'Statistical Account of Assam' by W.W. Hunter 1879 A.D.) and the Census of 1891 were produced it was almost an extinct art in the Assam Valley. In 1891 only three workers in Kamrup and one in Sibsagar were recorded. In 1900 there was only one Muslim ivory worker in Jorhat named Fiznur.[2] "Once an important art in the days of the Ahom rajas, ivory carving has, since Assam came under British rule gradually declined."[3] This was the case with most of the native arts in Assam though the establishment of British rule in other parts of India did not have so acute an effect on the native industries. "The gradual dying out of ivory carving in Assam since the cessation of the rule of Ahom rajahs is attributed to the consequent removal of the incentives due to direct royal patronage, assuming regular occupation and a stated salary or recompense to the individual corners. Moreover, the main sources of supply of ivory have been cut off by the strict enforcement of Elephant Preservation Act, as now only the tusks of dead elephants found in the jungles are available, while in former days a plentiful supply of ivory was secured from the elephant herds kept by the rajahs, as well as from the tusks of wild elephants slaughtered by hunters."[4] The socio-economic set up of Assamese life was also responsible for acceleration of the process of decline. Being primarily agriculturists the Assamese took the earliest opportunity to shift to agrarian life. The following observations by Donald clearly bring out the point. "Here the Assamese character asserted itself. Under the rajas the work was not altogether an optional one. There was a compulsory element. Care was taken to see that each man was kept busy at his trade, while at the same time the means of livelihood was certain. With the disappearence, however, of the rajas their influences ceased. The carvers, who had land and capital, settled down principally to a life of agriculture, a life involving little labour on their part yet ensuring a comfortable living. Not pressed by want, or compelled by force, to earn his livelihood, the ivory carver took no steps to push his industry or to create a demand. An occasional order for an article in ivory would be executed generally at a profit so considerable that the worker could afford to lay aside his tools for

1. Hamilton, B. An Account of Assam, p. 63.
2. Donald, J., Ivory Carving in Assam ; Journal of Indian Art and Industry, Vol. IX, No. 75. p. 57, 1901. July.
3. Ibid.
4. Kunz, G.F., Ivory and the Elephant in Art in Archaeology and in Science, p. 117. New York, MCMXVI.

some time before undertaking another commission. What was the result of this ? What was spasmodic in the past became despised by the child ; he saw in it merely a secondary means of livelihood demanding long and much perseverance, with no immedidte prospect of prosperity. . . ."[1] It has now reached the point of extinction, not so much because there is no demand, but rather because the workers, from want of energy or material, have so hidden their talents that but few know of their existence."[2] But historical factors are equally responsible for this sad state of affair. The last days of Ahom rule witnessed the decline of economic life and the breaking of the aristocratic families and the general impoverishment of the land-drawn Moamaria rebellion, the Burmese invasions and the final occupation of Assam by the British. All these factors conspired for the complete economic collapse of Assam from which she has not yet been able to recover. Under all these conditions no art or industry can flourish or continue. Assam is still famous for its one-horned rhinoceros. Its horn had an equally great demand. It was also exported and had a local market.[3] But it was prized for its medicinal and pseudo-magical properties. Rhinoceros hide was also used for making shields and armours.[4] Buffalo horn was also worked upon to produce combs,, Pepa (horns), hilts and handles for knives and toys and men for games. Workers in other forest product like hides and skins, feathers and bones were also grouped under Khels with their respective Baruas. Among these were the Pakhi-maria Barua (Superintendent of feathers), Hati-Barua (Superintendent incharge of elephants) and Nomalar Barua (Superintendent incharge of furs).[5]

II. Mats and spreads

These were the Dharis and Patis for the various occasions made from different materials.

Some were plaited and others woven on the loom. These are of three broad varieties, viz. Kath, dhari and pati.[6] The Kath is woven in a wooden frame and the work is not confined to any particular caste. Better varieties of Kath are made from Kuhila plant (aeschynomene aspera) and the cheaper variety from murtha (marantha dichotoma) and hoga! (typhanagustifolia) plants. Majuli in Sibsagar is another centre for Kath making.[7] The Maduri plant was also used for making mats. The Dhari is made of split bamboos by the Mikir, Lalung and Kachari

1. Donald, J., Ivory Carving in Assam. Journal of Indian Art and Industry, vol. IX. No. 75, p. 57, 1901 July.
2. Ibid. p. 58
3. Handiqui, B.C., Purani Asamar Shilpa. p. 60.
4. Ibid.
5. Handiqui, B.C., Purani Asamar Shilpa, p. 61.
6. Allen, B.C., Assam District Gazetteer, Vol. VI, Nowgong, p. 149, 1905, Calcutta.
7. Ibid, Assam District Gazetteer Vol. VIII, p. 164, Sibsagar.

tribes.[1] The superior variety is the Chok Dhari while the inferior is called Naga Dhari.[2] In Sibsagar mats are made from strips of Jati-bamboo also.[3] The Pati is the superior form of mat and is made from the Patiodoia plant (clinogyne dichotoma). The trade is entirely in the hands of the 'Patias' who are a section of the Kewat caste.[4] In Nowgong the chief centres of production were Raha, Baropujia and Kathiatoli. The outer seath of the Tonga plant is also made into patis in Darrang.[5] In Sibsagar a section of the Ahoms as Kewats make Pati and are grouped as the Patiyas. Here the Patiyas are looked down upon by the people. Sibsagar patis are cool and of a light blue colour due to being boiled in a solution of potash.[6] Chief centres of pati making were Bakata in Sibsagar subdivision, Salmara and Hazari in Jorhat and Ahatguri in Golaghat [7]

Goalpara had special varieties of mats known as Kathia and Hara. The Kathia was made from Moj grass and was woven in the loom like cloth while the Hara was from reeds.[8] Kamrup produced a variety of mats made from different materials like bamboo (at Gauhati, Palasbari, Bajali), 'nal' or phragmites roxburghii, cane (calamus sp.), mutha or cyperus rotundus (at Chamaria, Chaygaon, Hajo and Patidarang) and Sola or aeschomyne aspera. "Mats made by the first four materials are plaited by hand, but if mutha or Sola is employed strips of reed are placed in wooden frames and the mat is woven almost as though it were a cloth."[9]

III. Japi (Jhapi)

"The jhapi is the national hat of the Assamese and is made in every district of the valley, but the hats of Nowgong are noted for the decoration and the excellence of the finish."[10] The Japi was of many grades and for many occasions to be used by different sections of the people, and on diverse occasions. The difference in the Japi was indicative of rank and social status for men as well as women. "It was the Ahoms, however, who probably, introduced into Assam the large broad-brimmed hat or jhapi which is an adaptation of the Shan head covering."[11] The japi, however, has its counterparts in Burma, Thailand, Cambodia,

1. Allen, B.C., Assam District Gazetteer Vol. VI, Nowgong, p. 149.
2. Assam District Gazetteer, Vol. V, Darrang, p. 160.
3. Allen, B.C. Assam District Gazetteer Vol. VII, Sibsagar, p. 164, 1906.
4. Allen, B.C., Assam District Gazetteer Vol. VI, Nowgong, p. 149.
5. Allen, B.C., Assam District Gazetteer Vol. V, Darrang, p. 160.
6. Allen, B.C., Assam District Gazetteer, Vol. VII, p. 164.
7. Ibid, Vol. VII, p. 164.
8. Ibid, Assam District Gazetteer, Vol. III, Goalpara, p. 89, 1905.
9. Assam District Gazetteer, Vol. IV., pp. 161-62, Kamrup.
10. Allen, B C., Assam District Gazetteer Vol. VI, p. 150, Nowgong, Ch V.
11. Anderson, J.D., Encyclopaedia of Religion and Ethics, Edinburgh, 1908. Ahoms by Hastings, J., Vol. I p. 235, New York.

Indonesia, China and Japan. In the west it is seen up to Bengal, specially Bangladesh where it is known as the Toka or Mathal. In the Bilaspur region of Madhya Pradesh a kind of Japi is used known as the Khumri. Similar broad-brimmed hats are also to be seen in Tibet, Mongolia and among the Turkish races of Central Asia.

The jhapi is made of bamboo and the leaves of the "takau" palm (livistonia jenkinsiana). The general principle is invariably the same. The head is inserted into a circular and a conical erection about five inches high, which rises from a broad flat brim, but with regard to the breadth of the brim considerable latitude is allowed The largest varieties of Jhapi are about four feet in diameter and are generally held over a lady or a priest to protect them from the sun. The hats that are actually worn, are usually two feet in diameter. The foundation consists of strips of bamboo arranged horizontally and vertically at intervals of about two inches. On this is laid a small neat mesh-work of tiny bamboo slips, which support the 'takau' leaves which form the actual protection against sun and rain. Similar mesh-work on the top keeps the leaves in position, and the whole is decorated with strips of red and blue cloth, silver braid and little balls of thread. These ornamental hats are known as Sorudoia jhapis, and are generally worn by women, and more specially by Muhammadans and by the members of the lower Hindu castes such as Nadiyals and Brittial Baniyas. The ordinary jhapi for common use is known as 'dhoriah, and the cheapest form of hat worn by plough men to protect them from the sun and rain as 'halwah' (i.e., ploughman). The best jhapis are made at Kandali, Uriagaon, Jagi and Kathiatoli.[1] Sibsagar, with a concentration of Ahom population was also famous for its jhapis. There the japi makers were known as the 'japihajia's and many villages settled by them were similarly known as 'japihajia-gaon' or simply as 'japihajia'. Raidong[2] was a famous centre for making women's japis. These and other japis in Upper Assam were made by Chutias and Ahoms both were known under the common professional name 'Japihajia'. Dopdar, Lahing, Mahimelia and Ghiladhari were other important centres for japi making.[3] In this area the ordinary japi was known as the 'Khorua japi.

The japi was not only a mark of distinction for the officers and courtiers but also for their wives. But the wives had some more privileges and were shown more courtesy in the royal household than that was due to their respective husbands.[4]

1. Allen, B.C., Assam District Gazetteer, Vol. VI, Ch. V, p. 150. Nowgong.
2. Allen. B.C., Assam District Gazetteer, Vol. VII, V. p. 164. Sibsagar, 1906.
3. Ibid.
4. Sadar Amin, H K Barua, Assam Buranji, p. 109.

Wives of the Dangarias were allowed to wear the 'Sarudoia Sia japi' when they entered the royal city. They could use it for protection from rain or sun. The same concession was allowed to the wives of the Bar-barua, Barphukan, Chararphukan and other Phukans. The ladies were respectively designated as the Baruani and the Phukanani. But they had to enter the inner city on foot. These special japis or the 'Sarudoia Sia japi' were covered with Banat (i.e. Banat) cloth and was embroidered with multi-coloured threads and decorated with gold work and bunches of coral beads to simulate plants and boughs. But the difference in status was maintained by specification of colours or the cloth or of the embroidery threads.[1] Wives of inferior officers were to fix a single Champaka (Sapa) flower on the hat and those still lower in rank were allowed only artificial Champaka flowers made of silver to be fixed on their hats.

The royal priest or the Parbatia Gossain had the rare privilege of being protected from sun or rain with a large Pani-japi held over his head by attendants. The Pani-japi was decorated with gold work and gems.[2]

A rough type of japi was also made in Goalpara from split bamboo and leaves of the Sal and Nahar trees.[3]

IV. Baskets and containers

Baskets and containers of various shapes were made for different uses. Baskets were commonly known as the 'Pasi'.[4] Large bamboo bins for storing grains were called 'Dul' or 'Dhuli'.[5] 'Jopa'[6] was a special basket for keeping clothes. Petera was similar to the Jopa but while the former was made of split bamboo the latter was of cane.[7] These baskets were often laquered and decorated with paintings on the laquered surface. Other varieties of fine baskets were the Pera and the Khang.[8] The most popular colours for these were red and yellow.

Bamboo poles were mainly used for carrying loads and were known as 'Bahangi' and the baskets that were slung from the pole as 'Tola'.[9] The better quality of these slingpoles which were used for sending wedding gifts were the

1. Ibid, p. 110.
2. Ibid, p. 111.
3. Allen, B.C. Assam District Gazeetter Vol. III, Goalpara, p. 89, 1905.
4. Ibid.
5. Ibid.
6. Ibid.
7. Ibid.
8. Handiqui, B.C., Purani Asamar Shilpa, p. 64.
9. Allen, B.C. Asamar Shilpa, Gazetteer, A.D.G., Darrang, p. 160.

'Dabeli Bhar'.[1] Apart from these Kula (winnowing fan) and Salani (seive) were also made of very fine strip bamboo for cleaning rice..[2]

Bamboo had a very wide range of uses for architecture, boat building and for making weapons of war. Those have already been discussed in their respective chapters and sections.

Another important material available from trees was Sanchi-pat or bark of the agaru tree (aqrilaria agallocha). The Sanchi-pat was primarily used for miniature painting and it has already been described. An elaborate process was undergone for treating raw agaru barks and finally they were ready to be used as manuscript folios or for book-illustration. Its effectiveness as a carrier prompted some artisans to make high grade hand-fans (Bichani) out of Sanchi-pat strips which were beautifully painted with appropriate scenes evoking erotic or amorous sentiments.

One such fine piece of Bichani in the collection of the manuscript section of the Gauhati University Library, is from Nowgong. The style of its painting indicates that the fan was painted in the 16th-17th period in the Satriya style of miniature painting. The fan was formerly in the collection of Sri Mukidev Goswami of Nowgong.

It is a circular fan consisting of fifteen blades of Sanchi-pat, each blade being 22 6 cms. × 7.2 cms. The blades are painted with Krisna-Lila scenes on both sides and are fastened to a handle consisting of two wooden plaques. When folded the wooden plaques also act as covers of the blades while the lower ends of these which are slender act as the actual handle. Each face of the fan is divided into three concentric circular bands containing only a section of the whole painting which is visible only when the fan is fully opened.

Obverse of the fan : This side has in the outermost rim representations of the various gods, Munis and mythical beings. The figures are painted in full colour against the deep carmine background of the blades. They include the deities and their respective 'Vahanas' or vehicles. There is very little of angularity in the figures and all sharp angles are avoided. The paintings on the fan were evidently never finished since the figures are only painted silhouttes devoid of details like, the eyes, mouths, and details of dress and ornaments. Whatever the position of the body might be the face is invariably in profile and the figures are outlined in black. Though the figures of deities have an iconic stiffness, their 'Vahanas'

1. Ibid, p. 160.
2. Allen, B.C. Assam., District Gazetteer, Vol. VII, p. 164.

like the ram, deer, hare, 'Hamsa' and 'Garuda' etc., are full of life and are realistically treated. On the fifteen blades twelve gods like Vayu, Surya, Brahma, Visnu, Karttikeya, Genesa, Indra and Siva have been depicted.

The middle panel is an ornamental border of floral design known in Assam as 'Lata'. It is a very fine specimen of the 'Lata' or creeper design which was often used to decorate the borders of illustrated manuscripts. The 'Lata' is in black as are the buds against the yellow background of the band. But the large flowers of the 'Lata' are composed of red circles superimposed by four yellow petals. The middle penal is bordered on two sides with narrow black bands filled in with yellow dots. All the details and outlines of the 'Lata' are picked out in thin black lines.

The innermost penal is like a spectrum with red, yellow and green arches merging into one another.

Reverse of the fan : The outermost panel shows Mithunas on the blades, engaged in erotic embraces, some of the poses being very passionate in nature. Here also the figures are not finished like those on the obverse of panel. The male figure is surely Krisna since the complexion is a deep indigo, dhoti of yellow colour and hair done in a Chuda or top-knot. Radha is shown in native Assamese dress of coloured Mekhela, Riha and Chelleng of varied colours. The breasts are often shown bare and in profile view. In one section Radha is shown sitting on the thigh of sedant Krisna, who undoes her coiffeure. In other scenes they are either conversing or are in embraces of each other.

The central panel here is a meander of green or a yellow background. Flowers and buds in red and burnt-sianna are clinging to the Lata and are being pecked at by a number of birds The central panel here is also the same as the one on the obverse.

Colours used on the fan are opaque and consist of red, yellow, blue, green and mixed colours like pink and brown.

8

METAL WARE AND JEWELLERY

The metal ware industry of Assam was flourishing under Ahom rule. But some new elements were introduced by them in the shapes and designs of the utensils and jewellery. These were different from the standard Indian shapes and had parallels in the neighbouring countries of Tibet, Burma, Siam and even in distant Indonesia. The main difference was that each plate or bowl had a little stand at the bottom, ranging from about a couple of inches to about a foot in height. Thus these new vessels had the look of chalices and goblets rather than bowls and dishes. These shapes were introduced by the Tais and such vessels had a general prefix "Ban" before the actual name of the vessel, e.g. Ban-bati, (Bowl with stand), Ban-thal (Dish with stand), etc. The earliest example of the dish-on-stand in India is the wheel turned terracotta piece from Cemetery R 37 at Harappa.[1] Here as in Assam the plate has raised brims and the stand has a wide bottom. The flower vase shaped tumbler from the same hoard also has a parallel in the Ahom tumbler though the latter have a more slender stand. The general Assamese term Ban has an equivalent in Thai as Pan or a bowl A large sized Pan is known as 'Toke' (pronounced Tou) in Thai which too has an Assamese equivalent in Tou,—a large brass basin for washing rice and other edibles before cooking. Some of the dishes-on-stand had hemispherical lids with a long tapering handle. These were known as Sarai or a receptacle and the name is derived from the Sanskrit Saravam or a bowl. The shape of a Sarai is exactly like a miniature Stupa, complete with its 'Hti' finial. Some of the elaborate Sarais had circular discs attached to the finial and they represent the Chattravali of a stupa finial. The number of such discs range from 3 or 5 or 7 according to the size of the vessel. The shapes of the Sarai clearly shows that it is derived from the stupa-shaped metal reliqueries of the Buddhist period of Indian culture. The earliest example is a bronze relic casket from Manikipal.[2] The wall paintings from the Central Asian shrine of Bezeklik

1. Wheeler, M., The Indus Civilization, p. 77, Second ed. 1960, Figs. 1 and 2.
2. Fergusson, J., History of Indian and Eastern Architecture, p 94. A.S.I.R., Vol. II, p. 167, Pl. 65. Relic casket with 5 Chatras from Burj-i-Yak-dereh tope, east of Kabul.

(shrine III) show a devotee holding before the Buddha on his out-stretched hand "an imposing censer."[1] It is very much like the later day Batas and Sarais of Assam and even the etched designs showing full-blown lotus petals are also common to both. This censer also has little round baubles hanging around the main member of the vessel. The only difference being that the Bezeklik vessel has a large platter for its base as in Tibetan ritual vessels, while the Assamese ones have a plain lotus petal bases. Such vessels have been found from Ceylon and Eastern India also In Ceylon the Sarai is known as the Patra while the lidless Bata as the Bulathwattiya. Both the Bata and the Bulathwattiya are used for offering 'pan' or betel. Best examples of the Bulathwattiya have been found from Ruvanaveli and Tiriyay belonging to a period ranging from the 6th to the 8th ct. A.D.[2] But these examples carved out of single blocks of stones served as flower alters in ancient Ceylon. Here too the lotus dominated the design and shape of the vessels since the lotus form is popular in the Buddhist art of Ceylon according to D.T. Devendra. 'Lotus stalks, intertwining with leaves most realistically sculptured, end in an open flower which is the "table-top" of the flower.[3] Colombo Museum has some very interesting examples of these from Anuradhapura belong to a period between the 8th and the 9th centuries A.D., Bata like forms have also been found in Eastern Indian sculptures of the Pala-Sena period. Four actual examples in copper were found by R.D. Banerji from Naihati, in Burdwan district, Western Bengal. He identifies them as being stands for Pani-sankha or water-filled conches used in in pujas. But it does not seem probable since the Pani-Sankha has a round bottom and wont stay on a platter like object. To this day the Pani-sankha is in use but it has a ring-like frame on stand where in the Pani-sankha fits properly and does not topple. Thus it is clear that the above vessels were used for offering eatables to the deities and not for holding the Pani-sankha. "The four stands are very simple in design. They consist of a round base and lathe turned or plain round shafts."[4] These belong to the 11th year of the reign of Vallalasena as the accompanying copper plate grant would suggest The Bata and the Sarai are similar in shape, except that the shaft is more elaborate and consists of an "amalaka" in the centre flanked by two discs on either side. The top and the bottom of the shaft and in full-blown lotuses with flared mouths. The members

1. Andrews, F.H.. Wall Paintings from Ancient Shrines in Central Asia, p. 70 Text Volume, Pl. XVIII, No. BEZ, iii, S.U Oxford University Press, London, 1948, Plate Volume.
2. Devendra, D.T., Classical Sinhalese Sculpture (300 B.C. to A.D. 1000), p. 40, Pl. 119. Alec Tiranti, London, 1958.
3. Devendra, D.T., Classical Sinhalese Sculpture (300 B.C. to A.D. 1000), p 40.
4. Banerji, R.D., Eastern Indian School of Mediaeval Sculpture, Metal Objects, Ch. VII, p. 143. Pl. LXXIV. Archaeological Survey of India, New Imperial Series, Vol. XLVII, Delhi, 1933.

of the shaft are however all detachable and a rod passes through the holes in the centres of the members. They are held together by a screw system.

Other important shapes in metal were are the Bati or Ban-Bati, i.e., smaller bowls for curries, the Jara and the Bhog-jara, i.e., ewers and jugs, and the Gacha and the Chaki, i.e. lamp stands and lamps respectively.

The Ban-bati is of Ahom derivation as the name suggests. These resemble in shape the 'Tibetan butterlamps lit in the monasteries.[1] Here too the lotus flower and the trumpet-like base is present. But the Ban-Bati has more the look of a chalice with its hemispherical bowl standing upon a simple cylindrical stand with a disc-like base. The only decorations are the concentric circles incised on the the disc of the base. The brim outside is also decorated with a couple of incised lines running around. What Tucci says about the symbolism of the shapes of the Tibetan butter lamps, tea-cup and censers also apply to these vessels from Assam. He says, "The shape is that of a chalice, either hemispherical or slightly flared out as though to symbolise a blossoming flower resting upon a high stand which incor porates the symbolism the bumpa. The latter is the vase that holds the water of immortality, a form of ritual and decoration that has travelled from Mesopotamia to India and to many other parts of Asia."[2] In a like manner the shape had entered Assam. Vessels very similar in shape to the Ban-Bati have been found at Amlash in Iran belonging to the period 9th to 8th centuries B.C. Both are in silver but they have a handle each like in our modern tea-cups. These are in private collections in Tehran and in New York.[3]

The Bhogjaras and Jaras are of east metal, mainly of bronze, gold and silver with stout bodies which are deeplo incised. In this respect tge Assamese wares are more like the Tibetan tea pots and water vessels af Arunachal region (N.E.F.A.) known as the Khoding, According to Tucci such vessels do not have the lightness of Chinese and Persian wares.[4] Like the Tibetan wares the Assamese wares also have bulging bodies and stout necks The Bhogjaras have intricate spouts ending in 'makara' and animal heads. They have the same beauty as the Tibetan tea pots have in their handles. The length of the spout is sometimes like the scaly bodies of serpents and other aquatic animals In Tibet the Makara shape is married to the Chine:e dragon and in the same manner the Vyala form is married to the Chinese dragon in Assam. Lamp stans or Gachas are all cast in

1. Jisl, L, Tibetan Art, p. 166. Spring Books, London.
2. Tucci, G., Tibet : Land of Snow, Art, p. 121. Oxford and Ibh Publishing Co., Calcutta, 1967.
3. Ghrishman, R., Persia, From the Orissa to Alexander The Great, The Art of Mankind Series, 1964.
4. Tucci, G., Tibet : Land of Snow, Art, p. 121, Calcutta, 1967.

bronze and usually have a single deeply chiselled figure carrying the actual lamp. These figures are placed on elaborate and bold lotus pedestals. Rampant Ahom lions, elephants and Garudas are the usual figures carrying the lamp. The central figure, the lamp-base and the base of the figure were separately carved in the cire-perdue technique and then soldered together. The lamp was either built in the stand with one or multiple mouths or a shallow depression served to hold the separate Chaki or lamp. Two exquisite examples of the 17th century from Prof. S.K. Saraswati's collection, Calcutta, serve to illustrate the popular types of lamp stands. The one with Garuda has a high lotus base on which sits a kneeling Garuda with outstretched wings and hands folded in Anjali pose. A cylindrical member stands from the head of Garuda on which a perforated lotus base for holding the Chaki. The Garuda figure has a flowing uttariya and the front pleat of the dhoti dangling in front. The crown and kundalas are typical of the Ahom metal images. Feathers of the wings are stylistically and conventionally treated. Garuda is completely human except for the beak-like nose suggesting his bird character. The other lamp-stand shows a rampant Ahom-lion among boughs emerging from a pot carried by deeply cut lotus base. This design is reminiscent of a carving on the Um-nyakneh bridge between Jarain and Syndai in the Khasi-Jaintiya Hills. The lamp base is soldered between the curled up tail of the lion, its ears and manes. The lamps mentioned above were found in north Bengal where they had found their way through to export. Assamese brass and bell metal goods were in great demand in the adjoining areas of Bengal till the 19th century as we find from the accounts of Sir B. Hamilton.[1] Similar Garuda and Lion lamps are seen in the Assam State Museum, Gauhati, Bharat Kala Bhawan, Banaras and in the personal collection of the Maharaja of Banaras. The Assam State Museum also had some bird shaped Sanotas (betel nut slices) and votive bells of exquisite design. King Krishna Chandra of Kachar was converted to Hinduism in 1790 and the Hiranyagarbha ceremony was performed to proclaim him born of a cow, a deity. But the effigy of the cow was made of copper and not of gold as is usual for such ceremonies.[2]

Technique : In Assam metal ware are made both from brass (Pital) and Bell-metal (Kanh). While the former is beaten from thin sheets of brass the latter is cast in moulds. The sheet metal is worked by the Marias (the beaters) who are a Muslim community, but who have eschewed their orthodox customs like circumcission and the Namaz and freely take wine. The brass sheets are cut and beaten to shape over the anvil known as Belmuri Chutuli.[3] Other implements of

1. Hamilton, B., An Account of Assam, p. 60.
2. Gait, E.A., History of Assam, p. 309.
3. Allen, B.C., Assam District Gazetteer, Darrang,, Ch. V, p. 158.

work are the hammers, pincers, chisels of various sizes. Goat skin bellows attached to a hole in the floor of the workers' hut complete the simple furnace. "When it is desired to join two sheets of brass together, nicks are cut in one edge, into which the other edge is filled, and the two are then beaten flat. A rough paste is made of 'pan', a substance which consists of three parts of sheet brass and one part of solder, and borax is then smeard over the joint. The metal is heated, the pan melts, and the union is complete."[1]

Objects : A good account of the traditional metal ware of Assam is found in Gait's account in the Journal of Indian Art, Vol. VII, No. 54, April, 1896.[2] The list of articles given below is after Gait.

Brass

1. *Berha* : It is a tripod consisting of a ring about a foot in diameter, supported on three hollow legs, the interior of which is filled in with pieces of broken brass which produces a jingling sound. The tripod stands about 14" high and is used for supporting flat dishes out of which the upper class Assamese eat their meal.

2. *Chaki* : A lamp and sometimes a lamp and a stand combined. In a combined one the top is a cup-shaped hollow for serving as a lamp which holds the oil and the wick.

3. *Chariya* : It is a wash-hand basin and is also used as a common bowl for keeping sundry things. It is also made of bell metal. In Surma valley it is known as Tagar.

4. *Don* : It is a measure holding five seers of rice or other grains.

5. *Ghagari* : It is a decanter-shaped vessel with an ornamental mouth shaped like an open eight petalled lotus. It is for carrying and storing water.

6. *Ghati* : It is a common pot for holding liquids as is similar to the Lota of north India.

7. *Gacha* : It is a lamp stand sometimes with a built-in lamp bowl on the top.

8. *Kalas or Kalsi* : These like the Ghagari are for holding water but are provided with rims for keeping upright. The top is either plain or flower shaped. These are made also of bell metal and copper, the latter being used for keeping water for religious purposes. In Surma valley also they are known as Kalsi and and in Mainpur as Tukna.

1. Ibid.
2. Gait, E.A., The Manufacture of Brass and Copper Wares in Assam, Journal of Indian Art and Industry, Vol. VII, No. 54, April, 1896, p. 3.

9. *Karia* : A milking pot.

10. *Kharahi* : It is a sieve for rinsing rice and is also used in Surma valley as the Jhanjari.

11. *Khundana* : It is a handy pestle and morter, shaped like a thimble and is used by old folks for pounding pan and tamol or betel nut.

12. *Lota* : A small vessel for holding water and also for drinking. It is also known as the Lota in Surma valley and the Khujai in Manipur. Also made in bell metal.

13. *Sarai* : It is a round tray with a stand used by Hindus for offering food and edibles as religious offering and is also made of copper.

14. *Seta* : "It is a large spoon with a handle, thin towards the bowls and thick towards the opposite extremity and is used for distributing rice and curry." Gait seems to have confused the spelling. In Assamese it is actually pronounced as Heta and is written with the aspirant "h" and not the sibilant "s" although in Assamese normally the sibilant is changed into the aspirant in pronunciation. In the Surma valley it is known as the Hata.

15. *Tema* : It is a small round box for keeping arecanut and is the same as the Dibi of the Surma valley. It is also made of bell-metal. Those for royal use were of gold set with jewels. Indian Museum, Calcutta, has some exquisite specimens of Tema and Temi.

16. *Temi* : Made both in brass and bell-metal, it is smaller in size than the Tema. and is used for keeping lime to be eaten with pan. It is known as the Chunati in Surma valley.

17. *Thali or Jhaka* : A large boiling vessel. Thali is derived from Sanskrit 'Sthali' or a cooking vessel and the actually pronounced as Jhaka in Assamese.

18. *Tou* : It is a basin-shaped vessel for boiling paddy, cooking large quantity of food and also used for keeping water and other things. Its affinity with a vessel of the same name from Thailand has already been mentioned. In the Surma valley the name is Tasla.

Bell metal

19. *Banbati* : It is a cup joined to a circular rim at the bottom for holding curry. (In Thai it is known as Pan.)

20. *Banthal* : A concave shaped round dish joined to a circular rim at the bottom for holding rice.

21. *Barkah* : A gong of bell-metal or Kah and hence the name.

22. *Bati* : Made both in bell-metal and copper, it is a round bottomed cup for holding curry. In Surma valley it is known as Bati and as Tengkol in Manipur.

23. *Bata* : It is a flat circular basin with raised edge and is generally ornamented. The upper basin is joined to a circular rim at the bottom and is used for betel-nut.

24. *Dog-dogi* : It is similar to a Lota.

25. *Kahi* : It is circular Thal with a raised rim and is used for keeping rice. The name is derived from Kanh or bell-metal of which the objects are made. In Manipur it is known as the Pukam and as Thal in the Surma valley.

26. *Maipong* : This vessel is similar to the Banthal but has a cover in addition.

27. *Pandhoa* : It is a flat basin with an ornamental raised rim and is also used for keeping rice.

28. *Pikdan* : It is spittoon but as the name suggests it might have been introduced from Hindustan. In Manipur it is known as the Kwasen.

29. *Tal* : These are brass cymbals used in religious orchestra of Assam and are known as Kartal in the Surma valley and as Kardan in Manipur. The tal is also known as the Bhor-tal or Bhot-tal, i.e., Tibetan or Bhutanese cymbals. These vary in sizes from about six inches to eighteen inches in diameter and give a deep sonorous note when struck together. Exactly similar cymbals are used in Tibetan Lamaistic worship and hence the name, both the Tibetans and the Bhutanese being designated by the generic name Bhota in Assam. These people still have contacts with Assam due to their annual visits to the temple of Hayagriva Madhava in Kamrup district. Over and above, the annual winter fairs held on the Bhutan frontiers or Duars of Assam are also places of economic as well as of cultural exchanges between the two countries.

30. *Modhara* : These are narrow necked water vessel used by the Khasis and the Jayantias. The Modhara is placed in conical baskets of bamboo which are slung from the forehead of women with straps. The Khasis and Jaintias, however, imported these vessels from Sylhet.

Centres of production : During the Ahom period this industry was mainly concentrated near the capital and also in Kamrup district. But other centres also flourished. Since the Khasis did not produce any wares themselves they imported articles from Habiganj and Panchakhanda in Sylhet. Nijpat Jaintiapur became a trade centre for such imported articles.[1] The centres in Assam continued to flourish as before and were recorded district-wise during the early British rule.

Centres in Sibsagar :[2] Namdang, Dopdar, Salmara, Titabar, Kakajan mauza and Chariali in Jorhat subdivision. Kacharihat in Golaghat sub-division. The Moria craftsmen of Sibsagar and Jorhat also migrated to Mangaldai and Silghat respectively.[3]

Centres in Lakhimpur : The centres are inhabited by Morias only.[4] There are Japaragaon, Tekelasising, Japihajia, Ghorbund and Jarwa. The usual articles are Hata (vessels for boiling rice) and Daos or native choppers.[5] The workers are engaged in the industry only when they are of agricultural activities.

Centres in Darrang : "The number of braziers is, however, very small, and of workers in bell-metal smaller still."[6] The chief centres are Chutia tehsil, Becheria, Modopi, Bihuguri, Mangaldoi and Patharughat.[7]

Centres in Nowgong[8] : Here centres are many though the products are not as remarkable as those of Kamrup and Sibsagar. The centres are Kuwaritol, Raha, Jagial, Samaguri, Moriagaon in Sarbhagia mauza, Sutargaon in Khatoalgaon mauza and Kahargaon in the Raha tehsil.

Centres in Kamrup :[9] Kamrup excels in its metal-wares. The brass industry is concentrated in Hajo and Gauhati while that of bell-matal at Sartheibari. Iron wares and implements like plough shares, Daos, knives and sickles are also produced at different places. Shantipur, a suburb of Gauhati and situated just at the foot of the Kamakhya hill, has a settlement of bell metal workers.

Weapons of War : Being a "war-like people" the Assamese had developed many engines of warfare and had also excelled in the use and manufacture of guns and canons of a varied nature Guns and muskets were known as Hiloi and canons and Top or Bar-top,—the prefix 'Bar' meaning great. The sword was the Khanda and the shield the Baru. Arrowheads were varied, i.e., plain, barbed etc. Manucci describes a peculiar weapon of torture used by the Ahoms against the straglers of the Moghul army who had accompanied Mir Jumla during his invasion

1. Gait, E.A., The Manufacture of Brass and Copper Wares in Assam, Journal of Indian Art and Industry, Vol. VII, No. 54, p. 1 : April, 1896.
2. Allen, BC., Assam District Gazetteer, 1906 Vol. VII, p. 162.
3. Ibid, p. 1.
4. Allen, B.C., Assam District Gazetteer, Vol. VIII, Ch. VI. p. 207.
5. Ibid, p. 208.
6. Allen, B.C., Assam District Gazetteer, Darrang, Ch. V, p. 159.
7. Ibid.
8. Allen, B.C. Assam District Gazetteer, Nowgong, Vol. VI, p. 148.
9. Allen, B.C. Assam District Gazetteer, Kamrup, Vol. IV, p. 161.

of Assam. "To as many as they caught they inserted in the anus an iron like a Turkish padlock, which once in, could never be withdrawn ; its shape was thus. It shut up as it went in, and once inside it opened out, leaving the handle projecting. The poor things returned to the army lamenting, and died in a desperate state."[1]

The French traveller Tavernier refers to a tradition that Pegu in Burma had learnt the use of guns and gun powder at an early period directly from Assam. When Mir Jumla attacked Assam he received a huge number of guns and canons as booty which have been preserved in the Mughal records.[2] The records of Travernier clearly mention the use of fire arms in Assam. "On tient que c'est ce meme peuple qui a trouve anciennement l'invention de la poudre et du canon, laquelle, a passe d' Asem au Pegu du Pegu a la Chine, ce qui est cause qude d'ordinaire on l'attribue aux Chinois."[3] In China, says Maclagan that, petroleum from the Western Provinces was used for a Greek Fire as a combustible material. "Assam also, it may be observed, is a petroleum country."[4] Hence in Assam natural petroleum as well as Khar or gun-powder might have been used as combustible materials But Ahom records do not mention the use of petroleum for the purpose.

The guns and canons were of a great variety and were often artistically cast having mouths shaped like the Makara, the tiger and the elephant. The more important ones were highly polished and damascened or inlaid with gold wire. Gold inlay work was known in Assamese as 'son-khatowa'. Some good specimens of Ahom Bar-tops can be seen on the bank of the Sibsagar tank in front of the Sibsagar court.

Types of canons and their names: "Guns (Hiloi) and canons (Top and Bar-top) of many descriptions were made in mediaeval Assam.... Even the inimical Mughals were full of praise for the Assamese guns and canons in their chronicles like the Fatiyah-i-Ibriah and the Baharistan-i-Ghaibi. Sahabuddin Talish mentions the famous Basadari Hilois (guns) which were finely enamelled and decorated. Under king Gadadhar Singha a Muslim gunsmith of North Gauhati, named Gercta cast the famous Ripunjaya canon in 1703 A.D.[5] During the temporary success of Mir Jumla, the Mughals captured in Assam about 8,000 guns and canons of various shapes and sizes. The Bar-Hiloi was a large

1. Manucci, N., Storia Do Mogor or Mogul India (1653-1708 A.D.). Indian Texts series. Translated with Introduction and Notes by William Irvine. London, 1907, p. 99.
2. Maclagan, R., On Early Asiatic Fire Weapons, Journal of the Asiatic Society of Bengal 1876, Pt. I, p. 62.
3. Voyages de J. B. Travernier, II, p. 427.
4. Maclagan, R., Ibid.
5. Handiqui, B.C., Purani Asamar Shilpa, p. 25.

canon which used canon balls 3 maunds in weight. Other kinds were Ramsangi, Kamayana, Jhumur, Mitha-holeng and Tubuki. Some of the canons were decorated with damascened work and brass relief work, designs of gods and goddesses."[1]

The Muslim inhabitants of Garhgaon, the Ahom capital had informed Mir Jumla of the huge dump of guns and canons in the Padu Pukhuri tank which the Raja and the Phukans had thrown in it. The finest Ramchangis and Zamburaks were collected from there by Farhad Khan and Mir Sayyid Muhammad of the Mughal army."[2] According to Irvine the Ramchangi is a light field piece. Hodivala opines that Ramchangi (Ramsangi in Assamese pronunciation) is derived from Persian 'Ramjani'[3] or a 'pleasure-girl' who dances at command. Its recoil when fired, resembling a dance in the mind of a love-lorn gunner was responsible for this unusual nomenclature. Describing the war-boats of the Assamese, Manucci says (trilhoens) and petrechos of bronze, of which the muzzles whence the ball issues were fashioned into shapes of animals—tigers, lions, dogs, elephants and crocodiles."[4] Such was the admiration of the Mughals for Assamese gunsmiths that Mir Jumla ordered that the Assamese experts in gun making were to be sent to Dacca, the provincial Mughal capital to be employed by the Mughal army.[5] The warboats filled with artillery were given the general term Hiloi-chara-Nao. Famous Assamese canons were often captured by the Mughals while the reverse was also happening. Two historic canons with inscriptions were found by Simson in the Dikhou river.[6] The larger of the two was made of brass. The older of the two has a Sanskrit inscription in Assamese script. It runs as follows :

> "Saumaresvara Sri Sri Sa . . .
>
> tra . . . svarganarayanasya Sake 1560".[7]

It is dated 1560 saka or 1638 A.D. when the Ahom king Susenpha (Pratap Singha) or Buddhisvarganarayana was ruling. The name of the king Satra-savarganarayana, might have been another name of Susenpha. It cannot be Satrajit, the Hindu Jamindar of Dacca who accompanied the Mughal invading army under the

1. Das Gupta, R., Metalware of Assam, Art in Industry, Vol. VIII, No. 2, pp. 12-13, 1966, Calcutta.
2. Sarkar, J. N., Life of Mir Jumla, p. 247, Calcutta, 1951.
3. Ibid., p. 248.
4. Manucci, N., Storia Do Mogor, Vol. II, London, 1907, p. 100.
5. Sarkar, J. N., Ibid, p. 249.
6. Bandopadhyaya, R. D , Two Inscribed Guns from Assam, 1909, p. 465. Journal of the Asiatic Society of Bengal.
7. Ibid., p. 466.

command of Sayyad Hakim and Abu Bakr. The two titles Saumaresvara and Svarganarayana were exclusively used by the Ahom monarchs.

The other gun which is of brass is bigger and has two inscriptions in Assamese script and Sanskrit language and in Persian. The Sanskrit inscription is in incorrect spelling and is dated 1604 Saka (1682 A. D.). It is deeply incised and runs as follows :

Sri Sri Suragganarayana deva saumaresvara Gadadhar simhena Ya—

Vanam jitva Gurakahatyam idam astram praptam sake 1604.

The Persian inscription on this gun is in a bad state of preservation. The English rendering of it by R. D. Banerji is as follows. "The just king Shah Alam Bahadur . . . Year 1124."[1] The era used is the official Mughal era Hejira and it comes to 1716 A.D. Thus the king mentioned is none but the eldest son of Aurangzeb.

The guns and canons were of great variety regarding size and potency. Apart from Hiloi and Bartop other fire arms and artillery weapons were Patharkalai, Kamayana, Jamur, Kesai, Towa, Gathia-jumur, Pahlangi, Khoka, Hath-hiloi, Ramsangi, Tubuki, Mitha-holong, Hathi-muria, and Bagh mura.[2] Of these the Ramsangi has already been discussed above. Kamayana seems to be a Sanskritised form of the Persian Kaman, i.e., a missile. The Hath-hiloi as the name suggested was either a gun or a small field piece which could be held in the hands, or may be it was one cubit long. The last two in the list are named after the heads of the elephant and the tiger, shapes in which their muzzles were designed.

Swords and sabres also had varied names and shapes like the Taroal, Hengdan, Mit-da, Kapi-da, Mesi-da, Nakoi-da, Nara-da, etc. The Taroal was the local form of the Talwar or sword of Hindusthan while the Hengdan had a special place among the Ahom royal and upper classes. The Hengdan was a ceremonial sword which was held only by the king and his courtiers.[3] In about 1846 A.D. when the European tea-planters occupied the palace of Garhgaon found among many objects a fine sword with a silver hilt and its scabbard was made of gold and ivory.[4] The "da" was the native chopper which was heavy and curved with a wooden hilt. It was an all-purpose weapon and was also used for cutting fire

1. Bandopadhyaya, R. D., Two Inscribed Guns from Assam, Journal of the Asiatic Society of Bengal, 1909, p. 465,
2. Gogoi, L., Ahom Jati Aru Asamiya Sanskriti, p. 179, Sibsagar, 1961.
3. Ibid.
4. Foster, J.M., Note on Garhgaon, Journal of the Asiatic Sociaty of Bengal, 1872, No. 1, Pt. I, p. 40.

wood, slicing vegetables and meat or even for cutting bamboo and chopping straw for housebuilding. The "da" of the Nagas and of the Nara tribe were famous and were often used in war. In the Buranjis the sabre and shield were commonly termed as Khanda and Baru respectively. Spears and javelines were known as Jathi or staff, evidently derived from the Sanskrit Yasti. Those used by the Nagas were often decorated at two places of the pole with tufts of human hair dyed crimson. These not only added to the beauty of the weapons but also aided them in their flight when hurled.

Gold and silver were not much used for making utensils and every day wares. "Although it would not be correct to say that the gold and silver 'wares' of Assam comprised exclusively articles of dress, that is jewellery, yet the number of gold and silver products which are not jewellery is so small as to be quite insignificant. . . . Whatever may be the case Assam has very little to offer but jewellery. . . . The Assamese who is very luxurious, keeps his betel nut in a silver box called 'tema' and has a plate (bata) or bowl (bati) of silver, but few or none of these things show any artistic design . . . ."[1] The above observations of Henniker only state the situation when the artistic and economic life of Assam had completely broken down due to the Burmese wars and plunders. Even with the establishment of the British rule the Assamese craftsmen did not react favourably. They receded from the forefront and their places were taken by immigrant workers from Bengal and Hindustan as far as the towns were concerned. But true and native Assamese forms and designs were continued by the Assamese craftsmen in the rural areas.

Gold washing : Gold was obtained in Assam mainly by gold washing technique. During the rule of Rajeswar Singha (1751-1769 A.D.) Upper Assam thus produced 2,500 ozs. of gold dust for the royal treasury.[2] The Ahom king Sukrangpha (1259-1335 A.D.) organised on a grand scale the guilds of Sonwal and Rupwal who washed gold and silver dust from the sands of the rivers like Subarasiri, Dikrong, Lohit, Disoi, Jaglo etc. Gold washing was practised more in the north bank of the Brahmaputra while in lower Assam Dhing, Chatia, Ghatguri and other places sent the annual requisite of gold dust to the court at Garhgaon. The Paiks or the individual gold washers worked under a Kheldar Barua or a superintendent of the guilds. The Ahom kings engaged a large number of Chutiyas and Kacharis since they had better knowledge of the technique of production. Every year the Paiks worked from the months of Kartika to Vaisakha and returned home for agriculture in the month of Jaistha. Each man had to produce 2½ tolas

1. Henniker, F.C., The Gold and Silver Wares of Assam, Shillong, 1905, p. 1.
2. Allen, B.C., Assam District Gazetteer, Lakhimpur, Vol. VIII, Ch. VI, p. 198.

of gold and if he produced anything more he kept it."[1]

A detailed account of the process of gold washing is given in the Assam District Gazetteer for Lakhimpur district. "The gold washers selected a gravely shore opposite to a falling bank, where the current flowed fast round a corner. The stream was diverted over the selected spot till the surface sand had been washed away and the gravelley strata exposed, and was then turned back into its former channel. The auriferous sand was thrown on to a bamboo strainer placed over a wooden trough, and water was poured over it, the trough being tilted to a slight angle, so that the water and lighter substances ran off, while the gold and the heavier matter remained at the bottom. When a sufficient quantity of this matter had been collected, it was placed in another vessel and quick-silver added to attract the grains of gold. The mixture of quick silver and gold was then put in a shell and placed on a fire. The shell was converted into lime, the quick silver evaporated and the gold was left lying in the lime. The lime and gold were then thrown into a vessel full of water, when the precious metal at once sank to the bottom."[2]

Silver was collected in a different manner. "Silver or Rup was extracted out of Rupmati from the slopes of the Garo-Khasi hills by the Rupwal Khel. The Chalapthar of Sibsagar derives its name from the straining of Rupmati to get silver."[3] Rupmati was the name given to the silver in one form mixed with earth and other minerals.

Jewellery

The Buranjis and the illustrated manuscripts of the Ahom period throw light on the great variety of ornaments and jewellery of the period. Of all the Buranjis, the Assam Buranji compiled by Sir Harakanta Barua Sadar Amin is most prolific regarding the information. The ornaments can be subdivided according to their use, i.e., for the neck, waist, or fingers etc. They were either plain, enamelled (Minakara) or jewelled (Bakharpata or Bakharmani). Finger rings were known by general terms as Anguthi, necklaces as Biri, beads as Mani, ear-ornaments as Keru and bangles and bracelets as Kharu. The Tripura Buranji compiled during the days of King Rudra Singha gives an exhaustive list of Assamese jewellery of the period.[4]

1. Das Gupta, R., Metal-ware of Assam, Art in Industry, Vol. VIII, No. 2, 1966, pp. 10-11, Calcutta.
2. Allen, B.C., Assam District Gazetteer, Vol. VIII, Lakhimpur, Ch. VI, pp. 198-99.
3. Das Gupta, Ibid.
4. Bhuyan, S.K., Tripura Buranji (ed.) p. 15, IInd Edition 1962.

Anguthi

Siripata	
Senepata	
Jethinejia	—lizard tail shaped
Bakharami	—set with jewels
Maranejia	—peacock tail shaped
Hirakhatoa	—set with diamonds
Barabiphulia	—shaped like the Barbi flower
Uka-anguthi	—plain finger ring
Padumkali	—shaped like a lotus bud

The names of the rings depended more on the shape and characteristics of their bezels.

Mani (Beads)

Silikha	—shaped like the Haritaki or terminalia citrilina fruit
Parachakua	—shaped like pigeon's eyes
Poalmani	—beads of coral
Phutimani	—beads like melons
Sonar mani	—beads of gold
Mukuta Mani	—beads of pearls
Nayanamani	—beads with eyes

The beads were often strung together to form a string and these were known as the Biri with the type prefixed in the name, e.g., Silikhabiri or a necklace formed of Silika shaped beads. Sometimes a necklace was also known by the shape of its locket.

Biri and Hara (necklaces)

Jon-biri	—necklace with a crescent shaped pendant (Jon—moon; biri-necklace)
Dholbiri	—necklace with a drum shaped pendant (dhol—long cylindrical drum)
Madali biri	—Similar to above, Madali is an amulet case
Gejera	
Bana	
Dugdugi	
Panchsari	—a necklace with five strings of beads
Satsari	—a necklace with seven strings of beads
Nasari	—a necklace with nine strings of beads
Chandrahara	—a necklace
Kanthahara	—a necklace

Keru (ear-ornaments)

Jangphai Keru	—cylindrical ear plug of amber (Jangphai—amber)
Long Keru	—Clove shaped gold ear plug set with rubies (Long—Lavanga—Clove)
Barailaga Keru	—decorated ear plug
Dighal Keru	—long ear plug (Dighal—long)
Nejepata	—tail shaped ear-rings
Thuria	—These were either of gold or silver and were plain or set with jewels
Karnabala	—ear-rings shaped like the bala or bangles, i.e., large hooped ear ornaments
Latkan	—Long dangling ear ornaments
Lokapar	—An ear ornament specially popular among Ahom circles
Kanria	—A special kind of ear ornament

Miscellaneous ornaments

Gamkharu	—There were special wristlets of silver or gold and were either plain or jewelled
Kankana	—heavy bangles
Kalka	—paisly shaped ornament for the turban.
Keyura	—an ornament of the upper arm
Kardhani	—jewelled girdles
Kankali	—girdles
Junur	—a jingling ornament for the waist
Nakhachandrika	—a finger ring with a small mirror as the bezel for checking up toilet
Ujhanti	—A jingling ornament for the calves of the legs. Similar to the ancient Bhringipada ornament of Siva Nataraja and infant Krsna.[1]

The above description of the state of the jewellers' art during the Ahom period is complimented by early British writing after the annexation of Assam. During the early 19th century and down to our century Jorhat, Sibsagar Barpeta, and Goalpara have remained major centres of Assamese jewellery, the former for the enamelled and the latter for plain or filigree work. Writing after Darrah, Henniker says the following about the quality of Assamese jewellery, "Assam jewellery is by no means without merit. It incurs the stock reproach of being 'unfinished'; It is no doubt rather crude, the precious stones used are not very precious or very well cut. But it is quaint and characteristic. The gold used is of a high degree of purity."[2] Speaking about the individuality of designs in Assam he further

1. Gogoi, L., Ahom Jati Aru Asamiya Sanskriti, p. 178.
2. Henniker, F.C,, The Gold and Silver Wares of Assam, p, 1, 1905, Shillong.

says that, "many of the bracelets and necklaces, etc., are distinctly pleasing even to the critical eye and would attract notice in the midst of quite a grand collection of Indian wares."[1]

Enamelling : The name of Jorhat is linked with that of enamelled jewellery. "Jorhat in the Sibsagar district is the place centre for the manufacture of purely Assamese jewellery and the particular speciality of Jorhat workmen is their enamelling."[2] The state of this art and industry during the last decade of the 19th century is recorded by Darrah writing in 1896. "Enamelling is done mainly at Jorhat in the Sibsagar district. The artificers are Sunars, and possess a fair amount of skill. As, however, they work almost entirely for the native trade, the articles produced lack the finish to be seen in ornaments manufactured for European customers. There are many sunars in Jorhat, who work in nothing but gold. These do not enamel, but those who enamel also work in gold . . . . The enamel is usually of three kinds, a dark blue, dark green and white. But red and yellow are also sometimes used."[3]

Implements : The Assam enamellers' tools are few. They mainly cansist of the Hola, Ghar and Khan.[4]

(a) *Hòla* : A small instrument like a knitting needle, flattened at one end, used for putting the enamel into the interstices of the ornament to be operated on. (Hola-Sala-Salaka in Sanskrit).

(b) *Ghar* : A half cylinder of baked clay about 3 or 4 inches long closed at one end and perforated with holes. The ornament is heated under this in the fire to fix the enamel.

(c) *Khan*—A file made in the following way : A stone called jaran (like a heavy sandstone in appearance) is obtained from the neighbourhood of Gauhati. It is usually brought to Jorhat by Telis or oil merchants and sells at 4 annas to 8 annas a seer. This is pounded to a powder, and then a piece of lac is heated and pressed into the powder, some of which adheres. The lac is heated again and takes up more powder and so on till the whole has become a close compound of lac and jaran powder. The mass so formed is pressed on the end of a piece of bamboo, and made roughly into a square column. This forms a very fine grained file for smoothing the surface of the gold."[5]

1. Henniker, F.C., The Gold and Silver Wares of Assam, p. 1.
2. Ibid, p. 2. Shillong, 1905.
3. Darrah, Notes on Some Industries of Assam, Shillong, 1896.
4. Ibid. p. 3.
5. Henniker, F.C., Ibid, p. 3.

Enamelling technique : "The finished ornament usually shows narrow threads of gold arranged in fanciful patterns in the body of the enamel. These are formed by wire, and are laid on before the enamel. When the wires have all been put on, and the pattern which is to appear through the enamel formed upon the ornaments in the process of completion, some powdered enamel of the desired colour is mixed with water in a shell (Khamuk) and the coarse paste so formed applied by means of the hola to the space between the gold wires. These having been filled up, the ornament is fixed by a hole purposely left in it to the top of a nail, standing up out of a flat piece of iron (halpatta), such as is used for binding boxes. The 'ghor' is then placed in the 'aphuri' (furnace) in a clear space which has been made for it in the charcoal, and the ornament carefully put inside. The whole is then covered with red charcoal and the 'bhati' (bellows) applied. Very shortly the ghor and its contents are red hot, the enamel melts and forms a solid mass in the place it had just previously occupied in a form of paste. When cool, the ornament is boiled in a solution of lime-juice and water. It is then carefully examined to see if there are any spaces left without enamel where enamel ought to be. If, there are, more enamel is added, and the heating and boiling gone over again. The process of applying and melting the enamel is known as 'bharandia'. When it is finally perceived that no enamel is wanting, the workman takes up the Khan, and files the ornament until the surface of the enamel corresponds exactly with the upper edge of the gold wires. The latter then look as if they had been inlaid. While being filed the article is kept wet. It is then boiled again in the solution mentioned above and when cool brushed with a small bundle of hog's bristles called Pachrangi and filed again. This is repeated two or three times until the object presents a perfectly smooth, albeit unpolished surface. To put a polish on the enamel some care is needed. The ornament is put again under the 'ghor' in the middle of the fire, and red charcoal piled up around. The 'bhati' is not used but a hand punkha or fan instead. When the article is red, and it is seen that the enamel is again in a state of fusion, the ornament is taken out of the fire, and cooled with the aid of a blow pipe (nalichunga). It is then boiled once more in the acid solution and the enamel is found to be smooth and polished. The last process employed puts a reddish colour on the gold. Into a small earthen ware vessel a little water is poured and the sides of the vessel rubbed with sulphur. Next, quantities of salt, sulphate of copper and the leaves of a tree called 'thekera tenga' (Ixora acuminata), and put into the water and the solution boiled. Then a string of thread is tied to the now almost finished article, and is dipped into the boiling liquid and kept there for a minute or two. When taken out the ornament is rubbed with a cloth and the enamelling process is complete."[1]

1. Henniker, F.C., The Gold and Silverware of Assam, p. 4.

Enamelled jewellery of Jorhat

1. *Gejera* : This is a boat shaped shell of gold suspended from a 'dhar' or necklace of gold and coral (Poyal) beads. Only one side of the gejera is enamelled the back being engraved gold. The inside is filled with lac.

2. *Thuria* : These are ear plugs for women about 1½" long and are cylindrical in shape. One extremity of each expands into a kind of flower, often ornamented with stones. The sides of the cylinder only are enamelled.

3. *Keru* : The Keru is very similar to the Thuria but is smaller in size.

4. *Biri* : It is a casket shaped locket, attached usually to a necklace. Often a row of these form a semi-circle. One side is enamelled, the other side either plain or set with false rubies. These are used both by men and women. But those used by men were smaller in size.

5. *Dugdugi* : A heart-shaped pendant for a necklace, very graceful in form, and usually tastefully decorated with an elaborate gold wire pattern set in the enamel. One side only (that which rests on the bosom) is enamelled, the other being usually set with stones.

The Jorhat jewellers also make a bitter infusion from the plant known as tengesi tenga. Boiling in this infusion gives better colour to gold and makes it appear purer. "The material used for enamelling is believed to be a preparation of silicates." The jeweller also does not necessarily use wire to form the pattern, as a partition between the spaces to be filled with enamel can be made of fine strips of gold. The above techniques were in vogue in Jorhat even at the time when Henniker was writing.

Filigree ornaments : This type of ornaments are made at Jorhat and Barpeta. The main types have been grouped by Henniker in the following manner, e.g., Thuria (earrings), Hara (necklace), Sitipati (tiara) and Kharu (bracelets) [1]

1. *Thuria* : This type is a hollow cylinder narrowed at the middle (diameter ½" and length about 2"). The cylinder is filled with a composition of sand and lac. The Thuria is pushed through a hole in the lobe of the ear. At the end visible in front of the wearer is a rosette or star with 12 points, large and small alternating. Each petal is set with a Dalima bakhan or ruby.

2. *Hara* : These are of many patterns, each with a different name.

(a) *Gajamati* (or elephant pearl). Hara is set on six gold wire cables (fine drawn wire). It has three pendants, each set with rubies and one central

1. Henniker, F.C., The Gold and Silverware of Assam, pp. 5-7.

emerald below. The gold clasps attaching the pendants to the cables are set with rubies. A little rosette at either end serves as a guard to keep necklace in place.

(b) *8-stringed necklace* of gold and coral beads. For the pendants there is a crescent shaped locket or Bana. The Bana is set with rubies and enamelled black between the stones with a fringe of small gold beads. The reverse of the pendant is enamelled dark green and is more artistic than the front face. (This type of necklaces were commonly made of 5, 7, or 9 strings and known as Panch sari, Sat sari and Nasari haras).

(c) A more elaborate variety of the above type was made of larger beads of of coral and gold strung on a silk tassel. There were, in addition, more strings of smaller gold beads.

(d) *Cipat mani* : It was a five stringed beaded necklace without pendants. The string consisted of alternating gold beads and large gold buttons set with rubies.

(e) *Mani* : Though Mani stands for beads, a four-stringed necklace was also so named. There are four strings of beads which alternate at the back of the neck. On each side of the neck there are 15 filigree beads alternating with solid gold beads. In front there are 20 solid beads, the centre one set with rubies strung on four threads of silk. The five beads are on separate strings.

(f) *Rewa Bangali Biri* is the most artistic of all Jorhat pieces of jewellery. It is a gold chain slung with nine filigree caskets shaped like drums. Though Biri is the name for the casket-pendant here the entire complex is so termed (The term Bangali here indicates a foreign origin of the design since Bangal in Assamese means alien). The Biri is fastened by the simple hook and eye device and the work is very handsome.

(g) *Galpata* : (It is a flat choker of artistic design and very popular in Kamrup). It consists of fifteen segments, each dovetailed into the other but not rigidly. Each segment is in the form of a St. Andrew's cross-set with rubies on the face—and handsomely enamelled in green and blue on the back. There are two rows of small gold beads on each side of the flat band. In Kamrup, however, thin cylindrical coral beads are used in place of the gold beads on two sides.

3. *Sitipati* : It is a sort of tiara for the ladies and derives its name from 'Siti' or the parting of the hair where it is worn. In shape it resembles the Galpata

necklace and has 29 segments. At the centre of the band is an upright 1½″ long and it rests at the parting of the hair. Beneath is a crescent shaped pendant about an inch wide. Each segment carries as a minor pendant two small rubies set in gold. The segments are strung between two rows of gold beads The whole is kept in position by a string passing over the head and fastening at the back.

4. *Kharus* are of great variety as the name applies to wrist ornaments in general.

(a) *Bakharami kharu* : These are made in two halves, uniting with two pins, one pin being hinge and the other being the fastening. Embossed gold Kharus are set with rows of rubies in vertical and horizontal tows. The upper and lower borders of the Kharu are fluted and the inside is smooth. This barrel shaped bracelet is about 3″ in length.

(b) *Bala* : These are heavy bangles of gold set with uncut rubies.

(c) *Gam-Kharu* : The Gam-Kharu is longer in shape and is worn by men.

Barpeta in Kamrup district is an important centre of filigree jewellery in Assam. Enamelling and setting of jewels are not done here. "The finest of their work is filigree, which distinguishes the Barpeta wares, just as enamel and set stones mark the Jorhati productions."[1]

Filigree work is known as 'Rewa' in Assam and mainly work is done in gold wire. The goldsmiths themselves produced the wires they needed by an ingenious method.

"Gold wire is fined and drawn out by means of an iron plate perforated with holes of various degrees of fineness through which the wire is successively passed. The end of the wire is pointed with a hammer on the anvil till it will pass through the next finer hole for perhaps half an inch. This is sufficient to grip with the pincers, and the well-known ductility of the metal permits it to be dragged through and so fined and elongated. (The wire work of Indian workmen is celebrated, indeed it has never been surpassed but no particularly fine specimen of this kind of work is produced in Assam so far as is known). . . ." Filigree work is usually done by successive welding of one minute globule of gold on to the preceding one. For this the blow pipe is used and a kind of joining material, which is an alloy of copper and gold called 'pain'. "Borax (vernacular sohaga derived from the 'tincal' of commerce largely imported from Tibet) is applied to 'flux' the gold and the two edges soon fuse and unite under the oxygen flame.

1. Henniker, F.C., The Gold and Silverware of Assam,,p. 8.

Precious stones are not usually mounted in filigree work but many ornaments consist of links and pendants of which some are filigree and others stones The stones are apparently rubies (dalima bakhar) and emeralds (pana)..''[1] But some of the red stones are also garnets.[2] The rubies are said to come from Burma.[3]

Stone setting : "The Assamese technique of setting stones is similar to those followed in the Tamil lands and Ceylon. The peculiarity of this technique had already been pointed out by Comaraswamy. First, the place intended for setting stones is scooped or depressed a little and fixed by means of resins, so that the top of the stone is on the same level as the gold surface. A similar technique was followed by Mughal jewellers specially for setting stones to articles of use other than jewellery. The technique in Persian is known as mutussa."[4]

Although the plain tribes, specially the royal and aristocratic circles of these were influenced by the Assamese modes the Khasis had some special designs and motifs for their jewellery which though not very fine were remarkable for their boldness of design and large size. "The wares of Jorhat, the Khasi Hills and Manipur are much more interesting, because they are distinctly national and possess special features, not shared by Bengal and other Indian provinces."[5] The most typical of Khasi jewellery are as follows. [6]

Men's jewellery

(a) *Usrong* : It is a pendant of gold worn by men.

Women's jewellery

(a) *Lakartiang* : It is like the Usrong of men.

(b) *Lal Shuniad* : A silver ornament in the shape of a cap worn by women.

(c) *Shiashfar* : A kind of ear-ornament for women.

But the Khasis imported most of their jewellery made by Bengali craftsmen from adjoining Karimganj and Sylhet as they did in the case of textiles produced by the Assamese from Kamrup. Except in the field of music the Khasis are one of the most unartistic people in India The above jewellery is used by the Siems or tribal chiefs and the women when they perform the famous ceremonial dance of

1. Henniker, F.C., The Gold and Silverware of Assam, p. 5.
2. Census Report, Part I, page 165, para 218. 1901.
3. Henniker, F.C., Ibid.
4. Das Gupta, R., Mediaeval Assamese Jewellery, Art in Industry, Vol. VIII, No. 4, 1968. Calcutta.
5. Henniker, F.C., Ibid., p. 12.
6. Ibid, Appendix ; vi.

Nongkrem. The chiefs wore necklaces of gold and coral beads of enormous size on state occasions. The plain silver coronet of women dancers at the Nongkrem dance is also interesting. These were "peaked at the back and a tassel at the end of a long rope"[1] hung at the back. All the members were of silver. Men also used wide silver belts and crossed chains joined at the chest like the ancient Indian Channavira, so frequently met with in the Yaksha and Yakshi status of the Sunga period. The coral for beads were imported and the large gold beads were hollow but filled in with lac.

Goldsmiths and their castes : In Assam everybody is primarily an agriculturist. His caste vocation is secondary to his agrarian pursuits. Though the Ahom kings upheld caste yet people of one caste often chose the vocation of the other. Goldsmiths in general were known as Sonaris or workers in gold. "Jorhat goldsmiths are commonly either Brittial or Sonar by caste."[2] Many villages in Assam, where the Sonars settled in groups still bear the name Sonari.

"Raja Rudra Singha (1696-1714 A.D.) of Assam imported goldsmiths from Benares to teach the Assamese how to manufacture better sorts of gold and silver ornaments. It appears the Raja selected certain Kalitas to learn and to do the work, hence Sonaris formerly were Kalitas only. The business proving lucrative and there being no check to any people taking to any trade or profession during the last days of Ahom Rajas, people of other castes, such as Keots and Koches learned the work and became Sonaris The Haris (Brittial Banias) applied themselves earnestly to the trade, as, besides their original work of seavergers, they had no art or trade to fall back upon for their maintenance By this means some of them became so rich that they were made Hazarikas and Saikias (head of a 'thousand' and a 'hundred' respectively of their own community). We have, therefore, in the community Sonaris (goldsmiths) who are Kalitas, Keots, Koches, Domes and Brittial Banias."[3] The above account was gathered by Henniker from the late Rai Madhab Chandra Bardalai Bahadur of Assam. Since the Hari-Brittials were originally scavengers by caste and profession they were branded on the forehead with the sign of a broom by royal orders. Thus the upper caste persons could easily recognise them and shun any physical contact with the Haris.[4]

1. Henniker, F.C., The Gold and Silverware of Assam, p. 11.
2. Ibid., p. 5.
3. Ibid.
4. Rai Barooah Bahadur, Goonabhiram : Assam Buranji, Calcutta, 1900. p. 239.

9

TEXTILES AND COSTUMES

The field of artistic activity in which Assam excelled during Ahom rule was the art of textile weaving. Apart from cotton textiles and a small quantity of woollens, Assam produced three kinds of silks, viz., Muga, Pat and Endi or Eri. Assam textiles were in great demand in the adjoining countries of Tibet, Bhutan, Sikkim, Burma and Bengal. The sophisticated Mughals also prized Assamese silk textiles which were either sent as gifts to the Mughal court or were exported for sale in Hindustan. Assamese textiles were known for the fine quality, brightness of colour and durability. On the other hand cotton goods were known for the bright colours, durability and the bold loom-embroidery designs, the motifs of which though taken from nature were given abstract and geometrical shapes. Printed textiles or resist-dyed textiles were not in vogue but very little of 'tie-dye' textiles were produced. Though in general Assamese cotton textiles resembled Shan and Indonesian products yet the Batik was unknown. Another special feature about Assamese textile weaving was that it was not confined to any particular community or artisan group. Textile weaving was a woman's work and was produced in every home. Though orthodox Hindus, no stigma was attached to weaving and rearing of silk worms by members of all castes. The Brahmins did not rear silk-worm though their women too practised weaving. Writing in the early 19th century before Assam was annexed by the British, Hamilton has given an accurate account of the state of weaving in Assam. This industry was directly patronised by the state, so much so that queens established weaving schools in the palace to teach the art to the daughters of the nobles and the grandees. Widows and other female members of the household of executed prisoners were also employed by the state for spinning and weaving as a means of subsistence. The neo-Vaisnava movement of Sri Sankaradeva was also equally ponent a force for the development in the art of weaving, specially of figured cloth. Though textile weaving dwindled like all other arts with the fall of the Ahom rule, it never became extinct as many other branches of Assamese art. It is still a living art and as much in demand as it had been in the mediaeval period.

Historical perspective

The fame of Assamese textiles has been recorded even in the Harsacharita of Banabhatta (7th ct. A.D.). The presents sent by King Bhaskaravarman of Assam to Harsa of Kanauj included a variety of fine textiles. The most important variety of textile was in the shape of the white silk parasol known as the Abhoga[1] which was also a gift from Assam. It, however, was the family heirloom of the king of Assam or Kamarupa. An important item of presents typical of ancient Kamarupa textile industry were the linen cloths (Kshauma) that were bright like the rays of the autumn moon, and that were capable of undergoing washing treatment (saucha-kshama). The exact nature of these fabrics has not been made clear by previous commentators, although Bana has indicated sufficient hints for the purpose. This seems to have reference to a special kind of scarfs that were rolled up (Kundalikrita), not folded in the ordinary way, and hence required to be specially packed in round or cylindrical baskets of wicker-work (vetra-karanda) tastefully coloured on the outside. Bana referred to them as bhangura uttariya in a list of textiles specially being made on the occasion of Rajyasri's marriage, which were so called because of the series of gadrooned folds along their length, this precluded folding and necessitated a different kind of packing.[2]

In the beginning of Ahom rule also the kings were taking interest in the progress of the textile art. King Sutupha or Suteopha (1268-1364 A.D.) engaged a thousand Chutias and Kacharis to rear worms for silks like Pat, Muga and Mejankari.[3] The Ahom introduced into Assam silks like Muga and Pat. During the early years of Koch rule textile industry had received state patronage in western Assam and Baranagar was a great centre.[4] But the Ahoms of eastern Assam were extremely proud of their own textiles. When King Naranarayana of the Kochas sent the Ahom king Sukhampha or Khoraraja presents including fine pieces of flowered silk saris of Barnagar, the Bargohain replying on behalf of the Ahom king told the Koch envoys to take back the saris for in Assam such dresses were used by the prostitutes only.[5] But there were other items of textiles among the gifts like Gomcheng silk, Chit or Chintz and Ghagari and other dress materials.[6]

During the lifetime of Sri Sankaradeva tapestry weaving developed under his direct supervision. At the request of the Koch King's brother Chilarai

1. Cowell, E.B. and Thomas, F.N., The Harsacharita of Bana, 1961. p. 212 ff.
2. Agrawala, V.S., Presidential Address, All India Oriental Conference, 22nd session, Gauhati, 1965, p. 3.
3. Handiqui, B.C., Purani Assamar Silpa, p. 50.
4. Bhuyan, S.K., Buranjir Vani, P. 125, Gauhati, 1951.
5. Ahmad, A., Koch Biharer Itihasa, Cooch Behar, 1936, p. 104.
6. Ibid, p. 105.

Sri Sankaradeva took up the project of tapestry weaving for which he engaged the weavers of Tantikuchi or Barpeta. Their leader was Gopal, the master weaver.[1] The tapestry was 120 cubits long and 60 cubits[2] broad and it took about a year to finish the weaving.[3] Since the scroll depicted Krisna Lila scenes it was known as the Vrindavani Vastra or the Vrindavali Vastra The designs were woven with a large variety of coloured threads like red, white, black, yellow, green, etc. Of the colours some were evidently of mixed colours or 'misravarna' like Kach-nila, Gaura-syama etc. The above colours are still popular in Assamese loom embroidery work. The scenes depicted included those from Krisna's birth in the prison of Kamsa, to the vanquishing of Kamsa by Krisna. Each scene had its caption below it and these letters too were loom embroidered.[4] The tapestry was presented to Ghilarai, the brother of the Koch king with due ceremony only a little before the expiry of Sri Sankara Deva [5] While the saint was at Patbausi he used to go every day for inspecting the progress of the tepestry being woven at the 'Karkhana' of Kenduguri at Tanti Kuchi[6] (Barpeta). The master weaver Gopal later on became a disciple of Sri Sankara Deva through Madhava Deva and was given the name Mathuradas.[7] Eventually the Vrindavani Vastra was lost though the last place of resort for the Vastra was the Madhupur Satra in Cooch Behar.[8]

The days of Pratap Simha or Susengpha (1603-41 A.D.) witnessed an era of State patronage for the textile industry. Momai Tamuli, who was the Barbarua made a rule that every woman in Assam was to spin two or three bundles of yarn for weaving. Each morning the Gaonburha or the village headman was to inspect the working of the previous night at every household.[9] This boosted the overall production of textiles in the kingdom. Women who failed to produce the specified quantity of yarn were severely punished, even physically. Pratap Singha also settled many weavers at Sualkuchi from many places on the south bank of the Brahmaputra.[10] Even today Sualkuchi on the opposite bank of Gauhati is the greatest centre for weaving. Every household had to send the king about 250 grammes of silk yarn per year.[11]

1. Neog. M., Sri Sri Sankara Deva, p. 137.
2. Das, Arjun, Vrindavani Vastra Journal of the Assam Sahitya Sabha, Vol. XIV, No. 1, 1877 Saka, p. 20.
3. Neog, M., Ibid, p. 144.
4. Neog, M., Ibid.
5. Ibid., p. 136.
6. Ibid. pp. 136-37.
7. Ibid, p. 137.
8. Das, A., Ibid.
9. Bhuyan, S.K., Buranjir Vani. p. 126.
10. Handiqui, B.C., Purani Asamar Silpa, p. 54.
11. Bhuyan, S.K., Ibid., p. 127.

Next we hear about Assamese textiles from the Tarikhe-Asham or Fatiyah-i-Ibriah (1662 A.D.). It is said that the people were very skilful in weaving embroidered silk.[1]

Though the Assamese were proud of their national culture including that of costumes yet during the days of King Rudra Singha (1969-1714 A.D.) many changes were brought about. At first when he wished to introduee the Mughal style court dress consisting of Pag (turban), Jama (frock-coats) and Izar (pajamas or pantaloons) and Poijar (shoes) the nobles resisted his attempts. On one occasion, the grandees returned their presents consisting of the new suits of dresses expressing their disapproval of wearing foreign dresses.[2] Rudra Singha had established two posts of the Khaond and the Vairagi who were to travel all over India and inform the king of new ideas prevalent in the main land.[3] The Vairagi was to roam about India in the guise of a mendicant and collect all sorts of informations for the king.[4] Thus in the teeth of great opposition King Rudra Singha was successful in introducing new court dresses for males and females. The new dress for the courtiers consisted of the Churia (dhoti), Chola (shirt), Paguri (turban), Jama (frock-coat), Buku chola (tunic) and other dress items of various cloths like Tobta (tafta or tafetta ?), Jijira and Karchipi (karchobi). Fachau was the Ahom style turban used by the true Ahoms and also Baswal and Tangali as cummer-bands.[5] For women the court dress was specified as the Riha and the Mekhela. The Tripura Buranji, an Assamese chronicle of the days of Rudra Singha however gives in great details the textiles that were produced in Assam in that period. Those were sent as gifts to the king of Tripura for diplomatic reasons.

Textiles in the Tripura Buranji

Details of textile goods in this chronicle show that under the patronage of the Tungkhungiya kings not only a large variety of fabrics were produced but foreign textiles were imported mainly from China, Tibet and Bhutan and Mughal India. The Tripura Buranji chronicle also mentions some of the varieties of fine cloth produced in the period.[6]

Textiles in the Tripura Buranji :

1. Sonwali Sira
2. Ruper Jalardia Patar Patuka-Silk Patka with silver tassels.

1. Rajkhowa, B., Historical Sketches of Assam, Saka 1877, p. 1.
2. Bhuyan, S.K., Buranjir Vani, p. 126.
3. Sadar Amin, H.K., Barua, Assam Buranji, p. 64.
4. Ibid, pp. 64-65.
5. Ibid, p. 65.
6. Bhuyan, S.K., (ed.) Tripura Buranji, p. 15.

3. Kimkhap-Kinkob.
4. Nara Kapor —Cloth produced by the Nara people.
5. Raghunarani —plain and butadar or spotted.
6. Makhmal —Velvet.
7. Kirmiji —Bhutanese woollen cloth.
8. Tao Kapor —Plain cloth kept in rolls.
9. Rupawali Chelleng —Fine chadar of silver colour or of silver thread.
10. Chikan Athua —Fine mosquito nets.
11. Kala Phulam Barkapor —A heavy cotton winter shawl of black colour and floral designs.
12. Ranga Phulam Barkapor —Do. Of red colour.
13. Sonwali Orni —Golden coloured Odhni or wimpole.
14. Nara Kapor Guti bulua —Dyed Nara cloth with dotted designs.
15. Sahan Tao —Unidentified variety of cloth.
16. Khasa Tao —Manipuri cloth
17. Gujrati Tas Kapor —Gujarati cloth.
18. Badami Kapor —Unidentified variety of cloth.
19. Chit —Chintz or printed cotton cloth.
20. Atlanch —Atlas.
21. Dhekeri Bhuni —Dhotis produced in Lower Assam.
22. Efalia Barkapor —a large shawl
23. Khania Barkapor —} Shawls vinter
24. Bar phulam Barkapor —}
25. Majha Bhuni —A special kind of Dhoti.
26. Chal Kapor —cloth made from hemp like fibre (as a shawl).
27. Chikan Malmal – fine muslin
28. Elas —a special cloth for making Izar
29. Dhakeri Dhara —cloth from Lower Assam for making Izar.
30. Agphulam Barkapor —decorated shawls.
31. Katipa —a variety of cloth.
32. Bapta i.e. Wafta, a kind of piece goods for making dresses.

Atlas was the name for Indian satin and Banat was a woollen cloth. The Barkapor was a large coarsely woven heavy cloth and was worn double as a wrapper in winter. The size varied from $15' \times 2\frac{1}{4}'$ to $27' \times 4\frac{1}{2}'$[1]. Other important textiles were Dinga-Kheh and Dwarka. The Dinga Kheh was a silk of either Chinese or Manipuri origin. The Dwarka cloth however was imported from Bhutan though traditionally it was connected to Dwarka in Gujarat.[2] Other names in textiles found in the Buranjis and charita-puthis or biographies of Saints are Sagarjuli,[3] Mejankari,[4] Gomcheng,[5] Chaton.[6]

But the most important act of state patronage to the art of weaving was yet to come. Queen Sarvesvari, the third wife of King Siva Singha established a school in the palace for girls to be taught the arts of weaving and music.[7] It was a remarkable act on the part of a queen of the early 18th century to think in terms of the education of women and also of the economic upliftment of the realm.

During the last days of Ahom rule also the textile trade was flourishing. Of all the exports to Bengal and the rest of India Muga cloth and yarn and Athua or 'mossaries' (mosquito nets) were the most important. Hamilton's account also mentions the 'mossaries' in the following manner. "Mossaries are a piece of 30 cubits long, $1\frac{1}{2}$ to 2 cubits wide and are intended for curtains. They are of very thin fabric and are flowered.[8] These were exported from the frontier posts at Hadira Chowki and Phulbari Chowki in Goalpara.[9]

Of tribal textiles mention may be made of the Mako of the Nagas, Jim or a light warm cloth of the hill tribes like the Miris, Abors and Daflas, Nara Kapor of the Naras of Shan extraction and the Laisem of the Manipuris.[10]

Though Assam produced cotton goods yet the specialization was in the varieties of silk, viz., Muga, Eri and Pat.

SILK WEAVING

Muga : The Muga worm is generally fed on the Sum tree (machilas odoratissima). Five different broods are distinguished by vernacular names, but in the Darrang district the only broods commonly reared are the Katia in October-

1. Bhuyan, S.K., (ed.) Tungkhungiya Buranji, Appendix III.
2. Ibid.
3. Handiqui, B.C., Purani Assamar Silpa, p. 55.
4. Ibid, p. 50.
5. Gogoi, L., Ahom Jati Aru Asamiya Sanskriti, p. 177
6. Ibid.
7. Bhuyan, S.K., Buranjir Vani, p. 127.
8. Hamilton, B., An Account of Assam, p. 61.
9. Ibid, p. 46.
10. Handiqui, B.C., Purani Asamar Silpa, p. 56.

November, the Jarua in December-February, and the Jethua in the spring. The complete cycle of the insect lasts from 54 to 81 days, the bulk of which is occupied by the life of the worm. When the moths hatch out the females are at once attached to straws which are visited by the males who are allowed to remain at liberty. Each female produces about 250 eggs, which are placed in a dark place, and when the worms appear they are at once transferred to the Sum tree. A band of straw or plantain leaves is fastened round the trunk to prevent them from descending and during the night they take shelter under the leaves. Constant vigilance is, however, required to keep off crows, kites, owls, large bats and other pests which prey upon the worms and hail and heavy rain not unfrequently do damages. When fully grown the worm is about 5 inches long and is nearly as thick as the forefinger. In colour it is green with a brown and yellow stripe extending down each side, while red moles with bright gold bases are dotted about the surface of the body. When the worms are ready to spin they descend the tree and then are removed to the house. The silk is reeled from the cocoon, 250 of them yielding one oz. of thread."[1]

Some important centres of Muga weaving had been Mangaldai in Darrang, and in Sibsagar district, villages on both sides of the Jhanji river and also in the Naharani Mauza of Golaghat subdivision. Muga is most popularly reared by all castes except the Brahmin caste.[2] Predominantly Kachari localities like Dimarua, Beltola, Panbari, Rani, Barduar, Chaygaon, Pantan, Upper Barbhag and Patidarrang[3] in Kamrup district are the chief centres of Muga production.

Eri : "The Eri worm (attacus ricini) derives its name from the eri or castor oil plant (ricinus communis) on which it is usually fed. Patches of the plant are to be seen in the gardens of most villagers and the worm is proportionately common. From five to six broods are usually reared in the year, those which spin their cocoons in November, February, and May yielding most silk. As with the Muga moth the females when they emerge, are tied to pieces of reed and are visited by the males who are left at liberty. The eggs are hatched in the house and take from a week to 15 days to mature. As soon as the worms appear they are placed on a tray which is suspended in a place of safety and fed on the leaves of the castor oil plant. When fully grown they are about 3½ inches long and of a dirty white or green colour. After the final moulting, the worms are transferred from the tray to forked twigs suspended across a piece of reed and when they are ready to spin, are placed on a bundle of dried plantain leaves or withered branches which is hung from the roof of the hut. The matrix of the cocoon is very gummy, and the silk which is of a dirty white colour, has to be spun not reeled off. Before this

1. Allen, B.C., Assam District Gazetteer, Darrang, Vol. pp. 153-54.
2. Allen, B.C., Assam District Gazetteer, Sibsagar, Vol. VII, pp. 158-60.
3. Allen, B.C., Assam District Gazetteer Kamrup p. 158.

is done the cocoons are softened by boiling them in water and a solution of alkali. Empty cocoons yield about three quarters of their weight in thread."[1]

Eri silk is produced mostly in Lower Assam,[2] and is not so popular in Upper Assam. In Darrang district the chief centres are to the north of Mangaldai inhabited by the Kacharis. Kalaigaon is a silk market. Chief products of the area are Barkapor (20′×5′), Mekhelas and cloth for making coats and cholas.[3] In Kamrup Eri silk worm is not reared by caste Hindus like the Brahmins, Ganaks and Kalitas. It is the monopoly of the Garos, Kacharis and Mikirs. Eri and Muga are the chief silks produced in this area. Chief centres of production are Barduar, Chaygaon (Champaknagar), Pantan, Tamulpur, Barama and Palasbari.[4] No other silk except Eri is developed in Goalpara where Barkapor and Gilap are produced out of it. Rangjuli, Salmara and the Eastern Duar areas are the chief centres.[5]

Pat : Pat is the most expensive and the finest of silks and comes first in the list of Assam silks, the other two being Muga and Eri in descending grades. It is shiny, white and strong. Each successive washing makes it shinier, but the shine is subdued and pearly in appearance. Pat silk is produced from two types of worms, viz. Bar Polu (Bombyx Textor) and Soru Polu (Bombyx Croesi). The Bar Polu is the univoltive type while the Soru Polu is multivoltive. Both types, however, are reared indoors and are fed on the leaves of the mulberry (morus indica) or the Panchapa.[6]

"The eggs of the Bar Polu take ten months to hatch, the worms usually making their appearance about the beginning of January. The life of the worm lasts forty days, and the cocoons take six days to spin. The cocoons are of a bright yellow colour, but the silk when boiled in potash water, becomes perfectly white. From twelve to fifteen thousand cocoons are required to yield one pound of thread .... The thread obtained from the Soru Polu is not so valuable as that of the bombyx textor, but as the worm yields four broods in the year it finds greater favour with the cultivators."[7]

This cloth is expensive as none but the Jugis undertake rearing the impure worms. Shortage of mulberry trees in Assam is another reason for the smaller volume of production. Large number of worms die even before they

1. Allen, B.C , Assam District Gazetteer, Darrang, p. 155.
2. Allen, B.C , Assam District Gazetteer, Sibsagar, Vol. VIII, p. 160.
3. Allen, B.C , Assam District Gazetteer, Darrang, p. 155.
4. Allen, B.C , Assam District Gazetteer, Kamrup, p. 158.
5. Allen, B.C., Assam District Gazetteer, Goalpara, p 84.
6. Allen, B.C., Assam District Gazetteer, pp. 152-53.
7. Allen, B.C., Assam District Gazetteer, Darrang, Ch. V, p. 153.

spin.[1] Though in Assam weaving and silk rearing is not a taboo for caste Hindus either, only Pat silk is reared by the Jugi caste. The Jugis are looked down upon by the rest of the Hindus as the former follow the Nath-Sahajiya sect which is derived from decadant Tantrika Buddhism. According to a native Assamese tradition the Jugis fled to Assam when Buddhism was being persecuted in Bengal by King Ballala Sena[2], who reorganised and reestablished Hinduism in Bengal. Important centres of production are Becheria and Bihuguri near Tezpur and Sipajhar and Pa'hrughat near Mangaldoi.[3] Pat is also produced at Marabazar, and Salaguri near Namtidol in Sibsagar.[4]

COTTON WEAVING

Cotton weaving is comparatively lesser in volume compared to the silks. Cotton, however, is popular in Bhati or Lower Assam and Dhekeri, i.e. Goalpara, Cooch Behar and other adjoining areas inhabited by Koches and their allied tribes. The Kacharis, Garos and Miris also produce fine cotton cloth. These tribal cloths are known for their durability, heaviness, bright colours and exquisite loom embroidery. Though normally Assam silks are not dyed, the cotton goods are gaily coloured. Even caste Hindu women in Lower Assam wear coloured cotton Mekhelas, the most popular being green, red, yellow and vermilion. Cotton is grown in the hills and are dyed with the vegetable dyes from the hills.[5]

Main articles of cotton are the Gamochas or napkins which are used for bathing as for using as an ordinary turban, chellengs or women's chadar to be used over the Mekhela, or the Sarong and other dress materials for common use. Darrang produces the Barkapor or the Chadar Khania and the Paridia Kapor or fine shawls with borders.[6] Goalpara specialises in the Patani or the Sarong which is tied at the breast and thus leaves the shoulders bare, Pachara or smaller shawls and the Gilap or Barkapor.[7] The Patani in other areas is known as the Methani and has the appearance of an off-the-shoulder evening dress of modern western women. Kachari women of Goalpara also use a similar dress of a striped material known as the 'Dokhona'[8] which is sometimes accompanied by a Chadar for the breasts and shoulders.

The Loom : In Assam women used the throw-shuttle loom in the plains and the throw-shuttle loin loom in the hills. The looms in the plains were fitted with an arrow bench for the weaver or Sipini (Silpini—the female artist) and the

1. Allen, B.C., Assam District Gazetteer Darrang, Ch. V, p. 153.
2. Handiqui, B.C.. Purani Asamar Silpa, p. 52.
3. Allen, B.C., Assam District Gazetteer, Darrang, Ch. V, p. 152.
4. Allen, B.C., Assam District Gazetteer, Sibsagar, Vol. VII, p. 158.
5. Allen, B C., Assam District Gazetteer, Darrang, Vol. V, Ch. V, pp. 156-57.
6. Allen, B.C., Assam District Gazetteer, Darrang, Ch. V, p. 152.
7. Allen, B.C., Assam District Gazetteer, Goalpara, Vol. III, p. 85.
8. Pakyntein, E.H., Census of India, 1961 : Titaguri (Jonagaon) Assam, 1965, Vol. III, Pt. VI, p. 9.

pitloom was not used. Articles produced on the loin-loom were narrower and long strips were stitched lengthwise to form a whole piece of cloth.

Throw shuttle loom (Tat)

"The loom consists of four, stout posts which are driven into the ground so as to make a rectangle about 5'.10" × 2'.6" and are joined together at the top by cross beams."[1] "These are composed of warp and cloth beams, healds and reed etc. A hand-shuttle is thrown through the shed (the opening of the warp threads) by a slight and quick wrist movement of the hand from one side of the cloth and caught by the other hand on the opposite side of the cloth. As soon as the shuttle is out of the shed, the weft thread is beaten to the fell of the cloth with the reed fitted in the sley hung for to and fro motion. The warp beam is placed at a bit higher level than the cloth beam to avoid reed marks and thereby to effect good cover of the cloth."[2] The different parts of the loom are made of wood and bamboo and the old looms were ornamented by carving the different sections into animal or floral shapes and were lavishly painted. "In the loom, an arrangement is made with the help of two solid wooden bars fixed horizontally on both sides of it to keep the warp. There is also an arrangement whereby a whole group of warps can be lifted, so that the weft can be made to pass through the open spaces between the lifted warps and the dormant ones. As soon as the lifted warps are released, the space closes up as they fall back and the weft falls automatically into the weaving process.[3]

The device that performs this function is known as the 'heddle'. There are two heddles in the loom. One heddle is passed under every alternate warp. The remaining warps are tied to the second heddle. By alternately lifting each heddle, the warps are lifted while weaving. The weft is passed through the gap by means or a wooden bobbin. It is securely lined against the woven material with the help of a comb. The design in the cloth is given by laying in differently coloured wefts and warps."[4]

Throw shuttle loin loom

This type is very common in the hill areas of the country. The warp of manageable length and breadth usually of about 6 yards × 18 inches is prepared in a circular form and woven with bamboo-tube shuttle. One end of the circular warp (6 2 3 yards) is fastened to the wall of a house and the other end is attached to the waist of the weaver, mostly female, with a cotton or leather belt.

1. Allen, B.C., Assam District Gazetteer, Darrang, Vol. V, Ch V, p. 156.
2. Medhi, D.N., Handloom Weaving and Designing, p. 3.
3. Pakyntein, E.H., Census of India, 1961, Vol. III, Assam, Part VI, Village Survey Monographs 1. Titaguri (Jonagaon) 1965, p. 23.
4. Ibid, p. 23.

No reed is used for heating up the weft. In the warp various colour schemes are adopted. Moreover extra weft figurings, lappet, swivel and various figures of animals and natural views are very decoratively produced by land.[1] Extra weft figuring is known as Ba'tola in Assamese and is popular among the tribals and non-tribals alike.

Motifs and designs

Motifs and designs are known as Phul (floral pattern or flower) or Phuljali (flower and creeper). Primarily raised from the body of the textile the designs are all rendered in terms of cross-stitch or double cross-stitch much like the Bulgarian motifs. The designs are taken from Nature, are geometrical or abstract and a combination of both.

Typical designs—

Kalka	—Paisley design
Juria Kalka	—Double paisley
Bawari	—A kind of flower
Tinipatia	—clover design (Three petalled flower)
Tengesipatia	—like the Tengesi leaves. A kind of clover design
Panchpatia	—five leaved rosette
Satpatia	—Seven leaved rosette
Kesh Bachha	—Like the Uzbeg Raduga design
Mara	—Peacock motif
Gach	—Tree motif
Champa	—Champaka flower motif
Chakali	—rosettes
Chanphul	—rosettes
Gunaphutuki	—Dots of gold or silver thread
Pukhuriparia	—pond or tank design
Jutia Kalka	—Joined paisley design
Para	—Pigeon motif
Juria Para	—Double pigeon motif
Machh	—Fish
Pakhila	—Butterfly motif
Leheri	—a traditional motif
Pankata	—like the betel leaf (or heart shaped)
Bakul	—Like the Bakula flower

The larger flower motifs with petals showing are the Malati, the Champa (Champaka), and Kathi chamkara. Similarly tree and plant motifs are of the following variety, viz. Padum Gach (lotus plant), Kadam Gaoh (Kadamba tree), Panch Kadam Gach (Kadamba tree with five large Kadamba flowers), Sat Kadam Gach (Kadamba tree with seven large Kadamba flowers). Larger motifs are composed by assimilating a few smaller or part motifs into one whole. Running motifs are called the Lata (creeper). The latter are named according to the Kathi, e.g., Panch Kathir Lata, Sat Kathir Lata, Na' Kathir Lata But the Kalka

1. Medhi, D N., Handloom Weaving and Designing, p. 2.

is the most versatile of all motifs and is suitable for larger and narrower areas. Its size is varied according to the exigencies of available space. Larger surfaces are available in the Gosain Dhaka Kapor or the scarf for the icon. The interior of the larger Kalkas are filled in with plant motifs mainly the Dhekia or the fern. A row of minute Kalkas form the narrow border of the male scarf. The Juria Kalka motif is formed by placing two Kalkas face to face or side by side. The Kalka suits best the corners of the shawls known as the Barkapor and the Eri Kapor or Endi scarf. The ancient Gomcheng and Kingkhap silk dresses like the Riha and the Mekhela were also lavishly decorated with Kalkas of various sizes and shapes, and the cushion for the bride. The Malati and the Champa motifs are usually of gold thread and Anchu. The Maraphul is either single (Gaigutiya), double (Juria) and tailed (Nejal Mara). The Machphul is more popular in the Miri tribal textiles and is either single or double. The Diamond motif in red, yellow, or green on a black surface is typical of tribal textiles. Another abstract motif showing a walking bird is seen in Kachari textiles. The Pahar Bilai design in Kachari scarves is a combination of geometrical rosettes and a wide band of plane surface in a different colour. The colours are extremely bright in this design. The Tara phul (star-flower) is formed by rotating a square around a centre and filling in the corners thus formed with small Butis. The Taraphul is similar to the Russian motif Snijinka (small snow-flake) which being derived from the snow flake is also geometrical in shape.

The Gachphul and a combination of Gachphul and bird motifs in red and black on a cream or white ground is popular among the Miris. This again is similar to the Ukrainian waist cloth where too red and black are the usual colours. The borders of the Muga Riha are of the Simha pinjara type as seen in Gupta architecture. The Anchala of this Riha consists of a number of bands of triangles, rosettes and meanders of the Greek type. Formerly, the motifs were preserved either on pieces of cloth or on banana leaves.

Assamese and other textiles

Usually comparison is made between the Patola and Bandha textiles of Gujarat and Orissa with the Ikat textiles of Indonesia. But we fail to realise the much greater similarity between Indonesian textiles and those of Assam. Similarities exist also between some of the dress items and textiles of Assam on the one hand and Siam, Laos, Cambodia as well as far off Uzbegistan and Ukraine in the U.S.S.R. on the other.

The basic dress of Assamese females is the Mekhela or the stitched Sarong as in Sumatra, specially from Minangkabau region. In the rest of Indonesia the Sarong is only one piece of cloth wrapped round the waist as among the women of Manipur, Nagaland and among the hill tribes of Assam. But the dress of a plains tribes of Assam, known as the Boros or Kacharis (Dimasa, Koch etc.), as well as their textiles are almost identical with those of women from Bali. This affinity between the Balinese and the Kacharis is to be noticed in the dances, facial features and many other domestic details. Hindu and Muslim women from the plains of Assam used a breast band called Riha (Riah in Tripura) normally in place of the blouse. It is identical with the Pahoum of the Thai and the Slendang of Indonesian women respectively. Kachari women sometimes wear a turban-like head dress which again is like the Tjarik Langah or perforated turbans of Bali women.

Assamese folk textile is of heavy, multi-coloured cotton on which woven designs (rosettes and patterns from nature) in contrasting colours stand up as in Indonesian shawls, etc. The Batik of course has no parallel in Assam. All forms however takes a geometrical shape when turned into a design for the handloom. Thus these motifs appear similar to counterparts in Norwegian, Mexican and Latin American Indian embroidery and weaving.

The designs on the Bihu Gamochas or New Year Scarves are again similar to Ukrenian designs both in design and colour. In both cases the cloth is white and the designs are in red. In Assam as in the rest of India red symbolises amour and passion. The Bihu Gamochas are actually tokens of love given by young women to their lovers and husbands. But gradually these scarves came to be presented to other male members of the family like fathers-in-law, brothers and sons as tokens of love and affection. In Ukraine the scarves are long with designs at the ends and are used as offering to icons. The scarves are draped from the back and the ends hang in front and this manner is also identical with the Tibetan Buddhist custom of offering Khatas to icons in Buddhist Viharas or domestic shrines. The Gamocha is also offered to distinguished guests as a gesture of honour as the diaphaneaus Khata is offered in the regions influenced by Tibetan culture.

The end of the Riha normally has a band of multi-coloured parallel stripes. The stripes are of yellow, green, white colour. This design known as the Kech Bachha Riha is also similar to the Atlas design of Uzbegistan textiles. But while the colours of the Atlas run into one another the Kech Bachha colours are strictly and sharply demarcated as in the Uzbeg Bekasam design.

Assamese printed textiles

Printed textiles are not common to Assam. Some simpler form of Bandhani or tie-dye was practised in a restricted scale.

But the presence of a unique printed cotton cloth at the Bharat Kala Bhawan poses a new problem. The piece is printed all over with a running black print design showing a temple among tropical landscape. The border of this kerchief-like piece shows the repeated pattern of pointed niches housing some icon.

The centre figure is of a temple complex reached by a long flight of steps. Then again there is a descent to a chamber housing a huge Yonipitha, the emblem of Sakti at the Kamakhya temple at Gauhati. The double eliptical Sikharas also house two idols evidently of Laksmi and Visnu. Horizontal ribs emanating from the Sikharas recall the Sikharas of the famous Kamakhya temple and of the temples of Kamrup group. The Yoni chamber has a detached pavilion to its right where priests are performing Homa, and the entire arrangement is identical with the plain of the Kamakhya temple complex. A tall torana stands at the top end of the long flight of stairs as on the Kamakhya hill. The hill and rocky surface has been suggested by the regular rows of rectangular blocks through which the steps go up. The twin-Sikhara temple might represent the famous Visnu temples of Janardana at Gauhati or the Madhava temple of Hajo a few miles away. Just a little away stands another temple atop a stylised rocky surface. Through its open door can be seen a Sivalinga under the beautifully proportioned dome of Kamarupa style to which mention has already been made in the chapter on architecture.

The surrounding landscape and fauna faithfully represent the swampy landscape around the Kamakhya Hill and Kamrup district in general. Long clumps of grass, large fruit bearing trees as well as the beautifully shaped Nageswara (Nahar) tree, all typical of Assam, complete the picture. Among birds kingfishers and herons which actually frequent the marshes of Kamrup have only been depicted. Lotus filled pools have swimming ducks. At the bottom of the main hill-shrine sits a hermit in meditation on a spotted deer skin. Another sits outside the minor temple which too stands on a hillock. Strangely enough an Indian spade (Kudal or Kor) for digging lies near second temple. But there is something definitely Chinese about the large trees with their much twisted bodies and large leaves and flowers. But the Nageswar trees by the main temple is Indian, more like the stylized trees that we start meeting from the days of early Malwa paintings. Plants of the arum (Kachu or Man Kachu) family with very broad leaves also add a touch of local colour to the landscape. On the whole though oft-repeated the design is pleasing and in spite of the large number of figures does not appear unbalanced or over-crowded. Rather, one seems to visualise the tropical verdure of Assam surcharged with shapes and colours of the flora and sounds from the fauna.

Colours are restricted to black, yellow, pink, blue and a dull green.

Costumes : Costume type was extremely varied in Assam since it was a frontier land where many races and tribes met and mingled. Apart from the Hindus and the tribals, in Assam, the Ahoms and other Shan tribes brought new modes of dressing. The Buranjis themselves contain many direct and indirect reference to costume types used by the different communities. Illustrated manuscripts of the period and the relief sculptures from Jaysagar temples are eloquent testimonies to the great variety and richness of mediaeval Assamese costumes. In spite of the diversity in culture, the Ahom ways and manners including modes of dressing came to be prominent due to association with the rulers. But the Ahoms who were proud and aristocratic by nature reserved many concessions and privileges to their own circles. Many items of dress and ornaments were not allowed to non-Ahoms in spite of their prosperity or high ranks.

Male costume : Initially the Ahoms in Assam wore black Churias (dhoti) or lungis and black Nara-chola. The Nara chola was short but full-sleeved and their heads were shaven.[1] In another Buranji the dress during Sukapha's days is described as consisting over and above the Churia, of the Baswal, Tangali and the Gamocha with red flowered borders.[2] The Baswal was a waist cloth reaching about the knees and was worn over the Churia like an apron. It thus resembles the waist cloth of Malayan men of today.[3] The Tangali was a waist band tied over the Baswal. The Gamocha is a narrow fine cotton scarf which was tied as a turban and the ends stood up like feathers. All these items of dress have been depicted faithfully in the Phung Chin manuscript (1478 A.D.) mentioned earlier. Gradually Muga became the commoner fabric prized by Ahoms of all classes. "The dress of an Ahom noble man used to consist of a turban of silk, or a cap called jema, a short coat, mirjai, made of Assamese mugha or pat silk reaching to the waist, a long coat, also of silk, worn over the mirjai reaching down to the ankles, and a Churia or silken waist cloth.[4] But the term jema has been misinterpreted here. Jema is the Assamese form of Persian Jama or shirt, which was used by the Mughals for men's tunic or frock coat. Jama was introduced by King Rudra Singha in Assam.[5] The Ahom style turban was known as the Fa-Chau which along with other items of Ahom dress, was disliked by Kachari (Barahi) and Chutia people at the beginning.[6] The natives of Assam like the Kacharis, Marans and others dressed in Churias striped red or black when the Ahoms entered Assam.[7] When Suhungnung, the Dhingiya Raja became friendly with the local semi-independent chiefs known as the Baro-Bhuyans (1505 A.D.) he adopted some items of the latter's dress, like the Baswal, Tangali, and Hachati[8] (small sack of ornamental cloth for keeping Pan and betel nuts which were hung from the waist band). There were minor difference in the designs of the Baswal and Tangali of

1. Bhuyan, S.K., Assam Buranji, p. 10.
2. Sadar Amin, H.K. Barua, Assam Buranji, p. 14.
3. Bhuyan, S.K., Tungkhungiya Buranji, Appendix III.
4. Anderson, J.D., Ahoms ; Encyclopaedia of Religion and Ethics, ed. by James Hastings, Vol. I, p. 235, 1908, Edinburgh and New York.
5. Bhuyan, S.K., Tungkhungiya Buranji, p. 30.
6. Handiqui, B.C., Purani Asamar Silpa, p. 55.
7. Bhuyan, S.K., Satsari Asam Buranji, p. 7.
8. Gogoi, L., Ahom Jati Aru Asamiya Sanskriti, p. 55.

the native tribes. Thus gradually there evolved a common Assamese costume, at least for formal occasions and for the court.

New trends and influences from Hindustan started entering Assam from the days of King Susengpha or Pratap Singha (1611-49 A.D.). He appointed Vairagis or wandering mendicants to inform him of all developments in cultural and political spheres in India and countries adjoining Assam.[1] Thus he learnt of the contemporary trends in dressing in the Mughal circles many of which were adopted by the king himself. He adopted royal costumes of seven countries, viz. Burma, China, Mungkong (Upper Burma), Bengal, Delhi and Assam etc. These costumes consisted of dresses and ornaments in great detail. But these could be worn only on special occasions like marriages, the Bihus and religious festivals. These were brought out only when the three Dangarias, the six Charar Phukans, the twelve Rajkhowas unanimously agreed to their use on a particular occasion [2] The costume for the court consisted of dresses and a large variety of jewellery. The Churia was of fine Pat or Mejankari silk and the Chola also was Pat. Over the Chola was a gold worked Jama, which in its turn was topped by another Jama of Karchipi (Karchobi) and decorated with floral motifs. The Pag was also of white Pat silk with bands of Siri for decoration. The Poijar or shoes were made of deer skin soles and the top was of Bonat cloth decorated with gold work. The dresses were in charge of attendants called Chola Dhara (shirt-holder) who were under the Chola Dhara Phukan.[3] The king's dress for excursions consisted of one suit comprising of a Churia of Pat silk with gold borders and with floral decorations on the body, a Pag and an Enga Chola (Angiya) of Karchobi work, a Chelleng and a Thuria Kapor along with the usual ornaments and jewellery.[4] King Chakradhwaj Singha (1648-63 A.D.) returned the Siropa sent to him by the Mughal emperor Aurangzeb since it was deviced to extract subordination from the Assam king.[5] Till the days of king Gadadhar Singha the father of Rudra Singha the Fa-Chau was the official head dress for the Ahoms. In Folio No. 129 (Obv.) of the Samkhachuda Vadha manuscript Gadhadhar Singha is shown wearing the Fa-Chau in court.[6] The full court dress of the pre-Rudra Singha days was known as the Kunmin-Kunkha and the king distributed this suit to the grandees when he ascended the Singri Ghar as a part of coronation rituals.[7] But with the coming of Rudra Singha to the throne (1696-1714 A.D.) the Mughal court dress was officially

1. Sadar Amin, H.K. Barua, Asam Buranji, p. 39.
2. Gogoi, L., Ahom Jati Aru Asamiya Sanskriti, pp. 91-92.
3. Ibid. p. 93.
4. Ibid., p. 94.
5. Sadar Amin, H.K. Barua, Ibid., p. 48.
6. Das Gupta, R., Manuscript Painting In Mediaeval Eastern India, Vol. I, p. 576.
7. Sadar Amin, H.K. Barua, Ibid., p. 45.

adopted by the Ahom court. The full ensemble consisted of Pag, Jama, Izar for men and Riha and Mekhela for women as already described.[1] Since then the dress continued in the court circles though initially there was much opposition by the grandees to the introduction of foreign costumes.

The court dress for the three Dangarias was the same as prescribed by Rudra Singha but their marks of distinction were the Sarudoia Pani Japi and the Tupi Japi hats which were decorated with gold and silver work and tassels. The Bar baruas and Bar Phukans had to wear Churia of Pat, Baswal, Tangali, short sleeved Cholas of flowered (Buta) material. Their Japis were the Bar Japi, Tupi Japi and Sarudoia Pani Japi. The Charar Phukans and the Rajkhowas were to dress alike in Churias of Mejankari silk, Chellengs with gold embroidery and plain Pags.[2]

Examples of commoners' clothes are to be found in detail in the book-illustrations of Vaisnava texts produced between 1539 A.D. and 1714 A.D. But many of the illustrations being Puranic in content the illustrations of dresses sometimes tend to be conventional. Children went about bare bodied except for the Kachani[3] or a very short loin cloth and only on special occasions they are given the Pichaura[4] or an Uttariya (scarf) which hung on the chest after coming from behind the neck. Silk dhotis were also worn by grown-ups and were known as Pat Bhuni. Dhotis were often secured with belts or Bertis. People of higher ranks dressed in Bhunis, Pichauras and Pags. The dhotis were sometimes coloured but very rarely patterned. In the Nowgong Bhagavata X (1539 A.D.) the patterned dhoti is shown with scroll work and arabesques in crimson and these resemble the Rameng Chapta Dhuti of Manipuri male dancers. Kings are in various kinds of tunics and coats and they faithfully depict the dresses mentioned in the Buranjis described above. Most of the materials used are either candy-striped or are flowered and in arabesque designs. But the most faithful and realistic depiction of costumes and textiles are found in the illustrated manuscripts like the Samkhachuda Vadha, Hastividyarnava, Dharmapurana and the Bhagavata Book VI, all belonging to the Siva Singha period (1714-44 A.D.). In the Hastividyarnava manuscript (1734 A.D.) folio 37 Obv. the Buragohain is shown wearing the Japi atop the formal Pag, since the former was an emblem of authority and rank.[5] "Male dancers were as much popular in Assam as female dancers. The dancers wore a long flowing Jama with tight full sleeves and lapels overlapping on the chest and fastened at the right. It was also known as the Ghagra. The dress was white, often wrought with gold thread and reached down to the ankles. A Tangali was also fastened at the waist and a Paguri

1. Sadar Amin, H.K. Barua, Asam Buranji, p. 65.
2. Ibid., pp. 96-97.
3. Das Gupta, R., Manuscript Painting In Mediaeval Eastern India, Part I. p. 583.
4. Ibid, p. 584.
5. Das Gupta, R., Ibid, Vol. I, p. 618.

decorated the head. The Uttariya left the chest bare (Bhagavata Book VI). The orchestra consisted of the Gayan or the male chorus and the Bayan or musicians playing on the Pakhwaj and the Tala or large brass cymbals."[1] Other variations of the Jama were Choga, Chapkan, Hatisuria Chola etc. which penetrated gradually the upper circles and even the Satras.[2] The Sutradhara who conducted the Bhaona or religious opera was also dressed in a Ghagra which also enabled him to dance and the flowing gown lent grace to his foot-movement. Soldiers wore a shorter and tighter variation of the court dress of inferior material.[3] Acrobats, wrestlers, and also soldiers wore striped shorts known as the Thenga.[4] The Kula type cap was sometimes worn by servants and soldiers. Perhaps they were of Nepalese origin. Surprisingly enough not much representation of tribal costume is seen in the paintings except in depiction of Miris, Bhots etc., in the Dharma Purana manuscripts.

Female costumes : In spite of the minor differences the basic costume of women of Assam had been the Sarong or the Mekhela in this period also. The Mekhela when tied at the breasts was known as the Methani and it could also be worn at the waist along with a Riha or a breast band. Sometimes a Chelleng or Chadar was draped over the Riha-Mekhela for added decency and modesty, as a result of Hindu influences. In contrast to modern Assamese preference for white or very light coloured Mekhelas the mediaeval dresses were gaudily coloured, flowered and heavily embroidered in cotton, silk and Guna or gold thread.

The Mekhela is a cylindrical sack-like garment and is stitched lengthwise to form the sack. It is tucked at the waist with a few broad pleats hanging in front. But earlier the Mekhela was not stitched,[5] and was wrapped round the waist and then pleated at the front. The stitched Mekhela is similar in form to the Sarong of Sumatran women and to the Lungi of Burmese women. The unstitched variety was similar to the dress of women of Kerala, Ceylon, Thailand, Cambodia, Laos, the Shans and Indonesia (except Sumatra). Mekhela is derived from the Sanskrit term Mekhala which is a girdle for the waist. Since the Mekhela was tucked at the waist it was associated with the girdle.

"Ahom females dress in a similar manner to Assamese women wearing either silk (varying in texture) or cotton, according to the circumstances of the wearer. All the silk is spun and woven in Assamese home steads. . . . A specially large and gaily decorated hat being reserved for the bride on her wedding

1. Das Gupta, R., Manuscript in Painting Mediaeval Eastern India, p. 620.
2. Gogoi, L., Ahom Jati Aru Asamiya Sanskriti, p. 56.
3. Das Gupta, R., Ibid.
4. Ibid, Vol. I, p. 637.
5. Barua, B.K., Asamar Loka Sanskriti, p. 151.

day."[1] The Phung Chin manuscript depicts the early Ahom female dress authentically. "The lower garment is the striped Lungi reaching down to the ankles and sometimes trailing behind on the ground. A short jacket which covers the breasts leaving the shoulders bare is worn. A waist length of plain material is worn atop the jacket. A narrow piece of cloth or the Riha is worn above the coat. It passes across the chest covering the left breast and partially exposing the other.[2] The Riha is similar to the Riah of Tripura, the slendang of Bali and the narrow folded scarf worn by Thai women. Dancers in the above manuscript are shown with a long Dupatta-like scarf thrown across the chest with its two ends hanging behind the back.[3] On the whole the dress is simple verging on stern uniformity. The full sleeved jacket was not popular among the non-Ahom women who ordinarily wore the Methani with or without a Riha or Chelleng. Thus to bring about uniformity in the court costume for the ladies King Rudra Singha specified the Riha-Mekhela[4] ensemble and the ladies were to wear specific Japis[5] indicative of their and their husbands' ranks. From the days of Rudra Singha Riha became popular among all sections of women of Assam. The Riha was given as gifts on all marriages to the brides by Rudra Singha. He also engaged Muslim women to produce embroidered Rihas and those decorated with tassels of Guna and Barai or beads. The Riha-Mekhela ensemble, specially the Riha, was introduced into Assam by the Ahoms[6] and it is associated with other Tai races of Thailand and Indo-China.

The Ahom queens sat in the court with the king and the three wives of Siva Singha ruled successively during the Chattrabhanga Yoga of the king. Hence the queens too needed formal dresses for the court. When the queen officiated as the ruler of the country she wore Mekhelas of Pat, Gomcheng or one coloured Satin which were embroidered with gold thread.[7] The embroidered Riha was made of Gaj cloth.[8] She also wore a long sleeved blouse (Maiki Chola or female's shirt) of Pat decorated with Karchobi embroidery. Some days she could wear Mekhela of Pat and a Ghuri or transparent scarf tucked around the waist in flounces and pleats like the Manipuri Rasa dancers. The Ghuri was also decorated with Karchobi work.

The Methanis was represented in the painting of a Kirata or Indo-Mongo-

1. Anderson, J.D., Ahom ; Dress, Encyclopaedia of Religion and Ethics, Vol. 1, Edinburgh and New York, 1908. p. 235.
2. Das Gupta, R., Manuscript Painting In Mediaeval Eastern India, Vol. I, p. 578.
3. Ibid., p. 579.
4. Sadar Amin, H.K. Barua, Asam Buranji, p. 65.
5. Ibid, pp. 109-110.
6. Barua, B.K., Asamar Loka Sanskriti p. 150.
7. Gogoi, L., Ahom Jati Aru Asamiya Sanskriti, p. 93.
8. Ibid, p. 93.

loid tribal woman in the Nowgong Bhagavata (1539 A.D.). It is also similar to the manner of dressing of Khampti women of Assam. "The principal garment is a piece of dark coloured cloth, the mode of wearing which . . . reminds one of at least one representation of it in the Ajanta paintings."[1] The famous painting of the sitting woman in the Samkhapala Jataka from Ajanta reminds one of the Methani clad beauties of rural Assam.

The above manuscript shows a variety of dresses as used by 16th century women of Assam. The dress of goddess Yogamaya is typical of the period. "Like the costume of Yogamaya the usual costume of Assamese women of the early 16th century consisted of three pieces of garments over and above the tight fitting blouse. . . . A striped Patuka dangles at the front being tucked at the waist. A long narrow Dupatta comes from behind the neck and the two ends are crossed at the waist and hang in front leaving the chest bare."[2] The chief item of dress was the Mekhela over which a thin Chadar or Chelleng was draped and it was often coloured and patterned. "The way it was draped resembled the style of Odhnis in Rajasthani and early Malwa paintings. One end was tucked at the waist, the sheet covered the hips, came again to the front, and after covering the breasts, the remaining portion dangled at the back from the left shoulder. The left breast was visible. Over this Chadar was tucked the Patuka or an ornamental piece of cloth at the front. Above all an Uttariya was used. The festive dress of the Gopis has been described as Neta Khontajali and Neta Sari, which is a garment of Neta or fine silk. The Sari mentioned in the above manuscript is not the usual Sari but it has been used in Assam to mean a fine Chelleng as the same term was used in Rajasthan to mean an Odhni which was draped over the skirt or Lahnga. The Sari was synonimous with the Odhni or Wimple (Boston Museum Catalogue, Vol. Rajasthani Painting by A.K. Coomaraswamy). Khontajali has been described as the silk Sari worn like a Ghuri.[3] Ghuri is the name for the short skirt like costume worn over the main voluminous skirt of the Manipuri Rasa Dances. It is usually of a very fine, often transparent material and is about a cubit in breadth and comes in a long sheet. It is fixed at the waist in folds and pleats atop the main skirt to resemble a Tutu or the very short skirt of European ballet dancers. The Ghuri is also worn by Assamese classical dancers of the Satriya school and is also worn in the same way by the Natis or Devadasis of Dubi and Hajo in Kamrup District.[4] The Ghuri was thus a festive dress of mediaeval Assamese women and it was only a top skirt worn over the Mekhela. Though sometimes called the Sari, the Ghuri was not a Sari in the true sense of the term. The Chellengs of the ladies depicted in the Nowgong Bhagavata (1539 A.D.) appear

1. Ghurye, G.S., Indian Costumes.
2. Das Gupta, R., Manuscript Painting In Mediaeval Eastern India, Vol. I, p. 593.
3. Sankaradeva, Srimadbhagavata, Book X, Part I, ed. by Datta-barua. M.N., Nalbari, 1956. p. 38.
4. Das Gupta, R., Ibid.

printed with scroll work, foliated forms and arabesque designs commonly known as Jangla work in India. But the printing of textiles was not very common in mediaeval Assam. Their blouses were sleeveless and round necked and were known as Kanchuli. Similar blouses are still popular in rural Assam.

Assamese women neither veiled themselves nor any head covering was used. Only the Dasis or Ligiris in the Siva Singha period are painted as using a part of the Chelleng to cover the head. But goddess Kamakhya in the Tirtha Kaumudi manuscript (1688 A.D.) from Darrang is shown with a bizarre head dress. It is unusual for Assam and resembles that of high born Tibetan ladies. "On her head she has the five pointed crown of gold. From the two sides emerge two hornlike members studded with white jewels. A long and voluminous veil of green material is attached to the horns and it forms a sort of Prabhavali for the goddess."[1]

Radha and the Gopis in the Gita-Govinda manuscript from the days of Rudra Singha show a type of female costume more akin to those of the Bodo or Kachari women who belong to the plains tribal group. Their costume consists of a lower garment or Dokhona and a Chadar or shawl. Unmarried and young women generally prefer dresses in all shades of yellow.[2] Their dresses are remarkable for bold stripes and fine embroidery and there are prominent tassels at the fringes. All these traits are seen in the above paintings. "Over and above the skirt and the sleevless blouse, two chadars are used. One passes to the front from behind the neck and is crossed on the chest thus making a V-shaped opening on the chest through which the blouse is seen. Another one is tied around the waist and sometimes covers the head.[3]

In the manuscripts of the Siva Singha period realistic depiction of dresses is noticed. The dresses closely resemble the descriptions in the Buranjis. The Patuka was commonly used and the Chelleng was either tucked at the waist and draped around the body or was placed on the chest in the manner of Punjabi women using their Dupatta. The second style is however not in vogue in Assam at present, though it still continues in Manipur. Though no head covering was normally used, the Japi was reserved for special and formal occasions. But in one painting a princess is shown wearing a Mughal style Taj or cap with a plume, while she is flying pigeons on the terrace (Fol 139, Hastividyarnava manuscript). A fine and representative portrait of queen Ambika Devi (Fol. 163, Hastividyarnava) has been appreciated by Dr. Suniti Kumar Chatterji in the following lines," . . . the beautiful Ahom queen with her hair done in a loose knot and wearing an embroidered scarf of the golden Muga silk is quite a gem. . . ."[4]

1. Das Gupta, R., Manuscript Painting In Mediaeval Eastern India, Vol. I, p. 603.
2. Pakyntein, E.H., Census of India, 1961, Vol. III, Assam Part VI. Titaguri (Jonagaon). p. 9, 1965.
3. Das Gupta, R., Manuscript Painting In Mediaeval Eastern India, Vol. I, p. 605.
4. Chatterji, S.K., The Place of Assam in the Civilization of India.

BIBLIOGRAPHY

A

Allamah Shah Syed Mukibul Haque—The Advent of Muslims in Assam—Assam Tribune, Magazine Section 27.3.60.

Ahmed, Khan Chowdhury Amanatullah—Koch Bihar Itihas (B).

Assam District Gazetteer

Goalpara, Kamrup, Nowgong, Dorrang, Sibsagar, Lakhimpur,

Ashraf, M.—Later Mughal Art, Marg Vol. XI, No. 4, 1958.

Archer, W.G.—Maithil Painting. Marg, Vol. I.

Andrews. J D.—Ahoms, Encyclopaedia of Religion and Ethics, Edinburg, 1908.

Andrews, F.H.—Wall Paintings from Ancient Shrines in Central Asia, Oxford University Press, London, 1948.

Agrawala, V.S.,—Presidential Address, All India Oriental Conference, 1965, Gauhati.

B

Bagchi, P.C.—India and China.

Barua, G.C.—Ahom Buranji.

Beal, S.—Buddhist Records of the Western World.

Beal, S.—Life of Hiun Tsiang.

Bhuyan S.K. (ed) Tungkhungiya Buranji (A).

-do-(ed)—Asamar Padya Buranji. (A).

-do- Annals of the Delhi Badsahate,

Bhuyan S.K.—Ahomar Din. (A).

-do-(ed)—Jaintia Buranji. 1964. (A).

-do- Administrative System of the Ahoms : Aspects of the Heritage of Assam, Indian History Congress, 22nd session, Gauhati, 1959.

-do-(ed)—Studies in the Literature of Assam, 1936. (A).

-do-(ed)—Tripura Buranji, 1962. (A).

-do- Buranjir Vani, Gauhati, 1951. (A).

Barua, B.K.(ed)—Ankiya Nat. (A).

Barua, K.L.—Early History of Kamarupa.

Barua, B.K.—Sankara Deva, Vaishnava Saint of Assam. 1960 Gauhati.

Barua (Sadar Amin), Hara Kanta—Assam (A).

Barua, B.K.—Asamer Loka Sanskriti. (A).

Bloch, T.—Archaeological Survey of India Annual Report, 1902-03.

Barooah—Bahadur-Rani Gunabhiram Assam Buranji. 1900 (A).

Brown, P.—Indian Painting, Calcutta, 1960.

-do- Indian Painting Under the Moghals.

Bhattacharya, 'B K—Pronouncing Anglo-Assamese Dictionary.

Bhattacharya, B .K.—Kya Gauhati Kabhi Bharat-Rome Vyapar Ka Kendra Tha. Dharmayuga, 17.8.1969 (H).

Banerji, R.D.—Eastern Indian School of Medeoerd India, Archaeological Survey of India, New Imperial Series, Vol. XIVII, Delhi, 1933.

Bandopadhyaya, R.D.—Two Insesibed Guns from Assam, J.A.S.B. 1909.

Bareh, D.H.—The History and Culture of the Khasi People. Shillong 1967.

C

Chowdhury, P.D. & Das, P.C.—Ancient Treasures of Assam Through The Assam State Museum, Gauhati, 1959.

Coomaraswamy A.K.—Indian Drawings.

Cushning,—Shah Grammer, Rangoon, 1871.

Cowells, E.D. & Thomas I.N.,—The Harshacharita of Bana. 1961.

Chowdhry, P.C.—The History of Civilization of The people of Assam, Gauhati, 1966.

Coomaraswamy, A.K.—Catalogue of Collections In the Museum of Fine Arts Boston, Part VI.

Census Report—Part I, p. 65, Paro 218, 1901.

Chatterji, S.K.—The Place of Assam in The History and Civilization of India.

Chaterji, B.R.—India and Java, Greater India Society Bulletin, No. 5, Calcutta, 1933.

D

Das Gupta, R.—An Architectural Survey of the Kamakhya Temple, Gauhati, 1960.

-do- Nepalese Miniatures, Varanasi, 1968.

-do- —Eastern Indian Manuscript Painting, Bombay, 1972.

Dhaki, M.A.—The Vyala Figures on the Mediaeval Temples of India, Varanasi, 1966.

Dikshit, K.N.—A Note on An Ahom stone Pillar Inscription, Archaeological Survey of India, Annual Report, 1924-25.

Das, D.—Asamar Hati Datar Silpa, Asam Vani, 6.1.1961. (A).

Domald, J. Ivory Carving in Assam, Journal of Indian Art and Industry, Vol. IX, No. 75, July, 1901.

Derendra, D.T.—Classical Sinhalese Sculpture 300B.C. To A.D. 1000). London 1958).

Darrah—Notes on Some Industries of Assam. Shillong 1896.

Das, A.—Vrindavani Vastra-Journal of the Assam Sanebya Sabha Vol, XIV, No. 1, 1879 Saka, (A).

Dutta-Baduah—H.N., Srimadbhagavata (Sankaradeva). Nalbau, 1956 (A).

-do- Prachin Kamrupiya Kayastha Samaja. Itivritta. (A).

Diwakar, R.R. Bihar Through the Ages. Orient-Longmans.

E

Elwin, V.—A Philosophy for N.E F.A. Shillong, 1960.

-do- The Art of the North East Frontier of India. Shillong. 1959.

F

Fergusson, J.—History of Indian and Eastern Architecture.

Foster, J.M.—Note an Garhgaon, Journal of the Aslatic Society of Bengal, No. 1, 1872.

G

Gait, E.A.,—A History of Assam.

Gogoi, L ,—Buranjiye Pavasha Nagar. (A).

Ghosh, D. & Mitra, P.—Itihaser Khaspur, Amrita, Baisakh, 1371, B.E.

Gait, E A.,—Manufacture of Pottery in Assam, Journal of Indian Art, Vol. VI, No. 54, Jan. 1896.

Gray, B.—The Development of Painting in India in the 16th century, Marg, Vol. VI, No. 3, 1953.

Gogoi, L.—Ahom Lipir Puthi, Purvakash, July, 1960 (A).

Goswami, H.A—Descriptive Cotalogue of Assamese Manuscripts.

Gogoi, L.—Ahom Jati Aru Asamiya Sanskriti, Sibsagar, 1961, (A)

Ghurye, G.S.—Indian Costumes.

Goswami, C.—Aniruddhadwar Charita. (A).

Gurdoa, P.R.T.—The Khasis.

Grishman, H.—Persia—from the origins to Alexander the Great. 1964,

Gait, E.A.—The Manufacture of Brass and Copper Wares in Assam, Jl. of Indian Art and Industries, Vol. VI No. 54, April 1896.

H

Hastings, J.—Encyclopaedia of Religion and Ethics. Vol. I. Edinburg and New York, 1908.

Handique, B C.—Sibsagar Guide.

-do- (ed) —Changrang Phukanar Buranji. Pt. I Joysagar, 1959 (A).

Hannay, Journal of Asiatic Society 1851.

Handique, B.C.—Purani Asamar Shilpa.

Hamilton, F.—An Account of Assam.

Hutton, Journal of the Asiatic Society of Bengal, 1926.

Henniker, F.C.—Gold and Silver Wares of Assam. Shillong. 1905.

I

Iyar, K. Bharatha—Indian Art.

J

Jisl, L.—Tibetan Art. Spring Books. London.

K

Kramrisch, S.—On Indian Art, Characteristics of Court Art.

-do- A Survey of Painting in the Deccan.

Khandoloval, K.J.—Pahari Miniature Painting.

Kunz, G.J.—Ivory and the Elephant in Art in Archaeology and in Science. New York, MCMXVI.

M

Majumdar—Parichaya.

Majumdar, R.C.—History of Bengal, Vol. I. Dacca, 1948.

Mc. Cosh, John—On the various lines of Overland Communication between India and China, Proceedings of the Royal Geographical Society, London. Vol. V, 1860-61.

Mc. Cosh, John—Topography of Assam.

Motichandra—Jaina Miniature Paintings from Western India.

Maclogan, R.—On Early Asiatic Fire Weapons. Journal of the Asiatic Society of Bengali, Pt. 1976.

Medhi, D.N;—Handloom Weaving and Designing. Gauhati.

Manucci, N—Storia Do Mogos. Introduction and Notes by William Irwine, London, 1907.

N

Neog, M (ed)—Usha Parinaya by Pitambar Dwija. (A).

-do- —The Vaishnava Renaissance in Assam; Aspects of the Heritage of Assam, Indian History Congress Sourena, Gauhati, 1959.

-do- —The Art of Painting In Assam, Madras.

-do- (ed) —Lava-Kushar Yuddha. (A).

-do- —Pavitra Assam. (A).

-do- —Sri Sri Sankaradeva (A).

P

Pelliot—Bulletin dul' Ecole Francaise d' Extreme Orient, 1904·

Peal, S E.—Note on the Old Burmese Route Over the Patkai Via Nongyang, Journal of the Asiatic Society of Bengal, Vol. II, Pt. II.

Pavic, T (tr.)—Tarik-i-Asham. (F).

Pathak, G—Barpeta Satrar Itihasa (A).

Pyanktien, E.H.—Census of India, 1961-Titaguri (Gonagaon) Assam, Vol III, 1965.

Pemleerton, R.B.—Report on Bhooton : Reprint, Indian Studies, Past and Present, Calcutta, 1961.

R

Rowland, B.—The Art and Architecture of India : Buddhist, Hindu and Jaina.

Rajkhowa, B.—Historical Sketches of Assam, Dilemgarh. 1917.

Railhrishnadasa—Bharat Ki Chitrakala (H).

S

Sarma, S.K.—Neo-Vaishnavite Movement and the Satra Institution of Assam, Gauhati, 1966.

Sankalia, H.D.—Kamrup Ki Ghati men Pragaiti-hasik Avasesa (2). Dharmayug 26.4.1970 (H).

Sarkar, J.N.—Life of Mirjumla, Calcutta, 1951.

T

Tucci, G.—The Sea and Land travels of a Buddhist Sadhu in the sixteenth century, Indian Historical Quaterly, Vol. VII.

Thakur, Daityari—Sankardeva-Madhavadeva Charita. (A).

Thapa, R.J. Nepalese Art, Catalogue of Art Objects Exhibited in Paris, 1966.

Thaw Ka—The Early Art of Burma, Perspective of Burma, An Atlantic Monthly Supplement.

Tucci.G.—Tibet, Land of Snow, Oxford and I.B.H. Publishing Co. Calcutta, 1967.

V

Vidyalankar., J.—Bharat Bhumi Aur Uske Nivasi (H).

Vidyavinod, P.N.—Kamarupa Sasanavali, Rangpur, 1938. (B).

W

Whiteley, J.L.—The periphes of the Erythrean Sea. Thesis for Ph.D. at the London University, 1940

Wilkinson, J.V.S.—Indian Painting—Indian Art, Faber and Faber.

Wheclev, M.—The Indian Civilization, 2nd ed. 1960.

INDEX

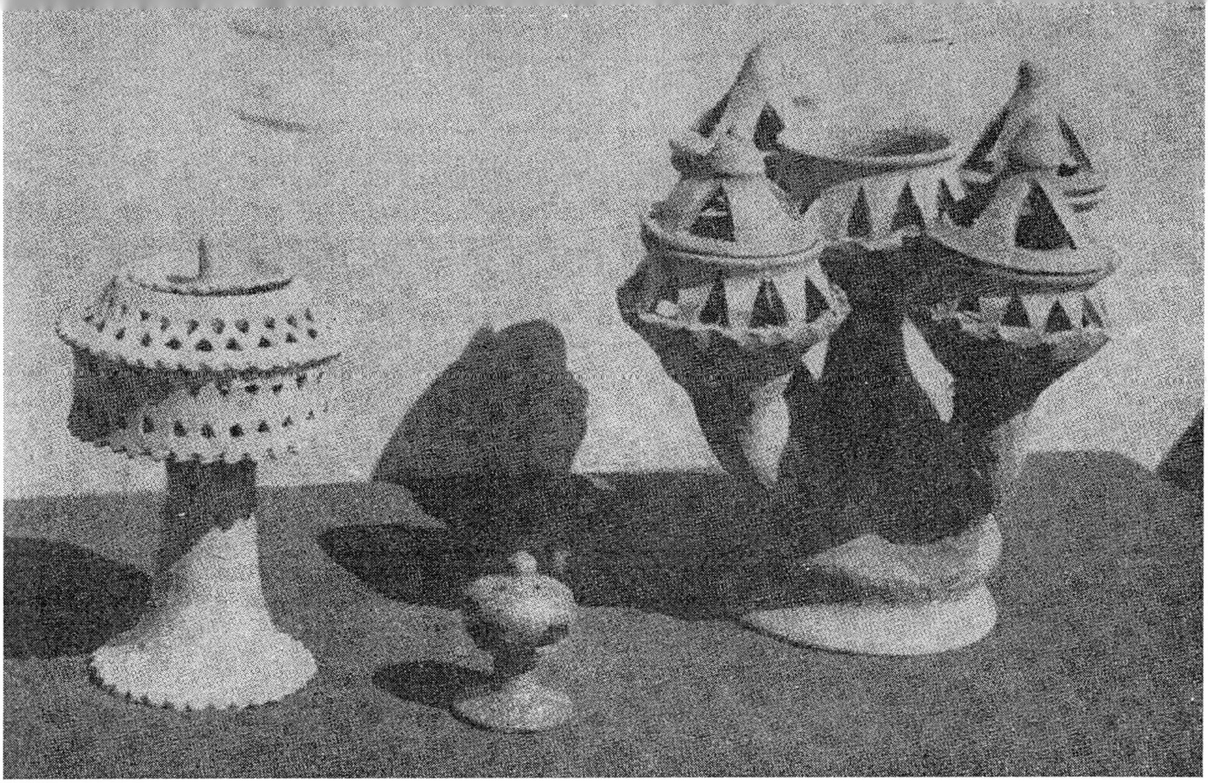

perforated pottery, kamrup

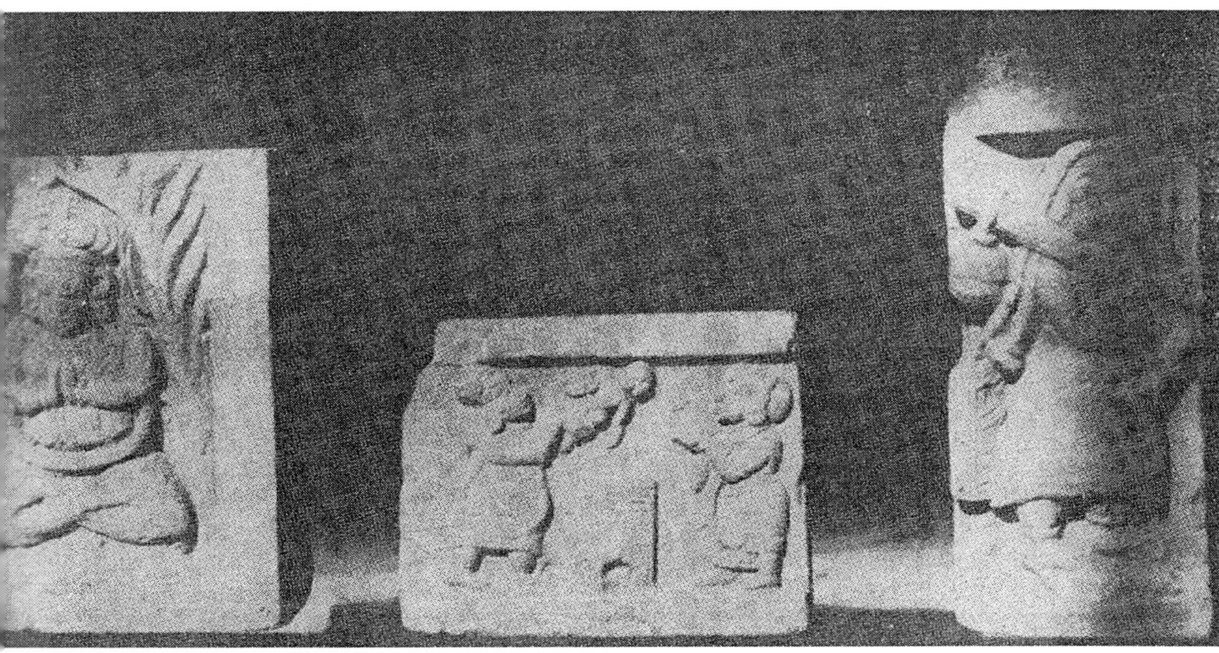

Terracotta Plaques, Gauhati

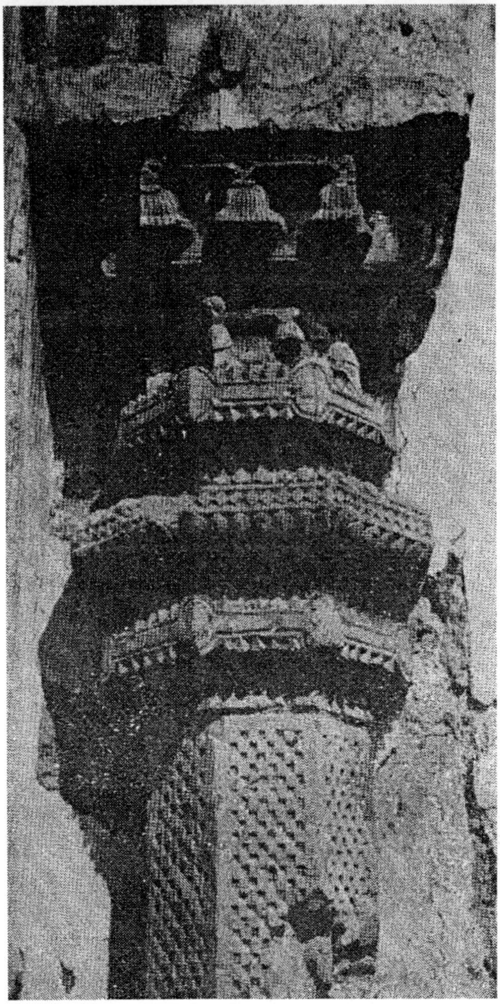

Terracotta Pillar, Nal Math, Gauhati.

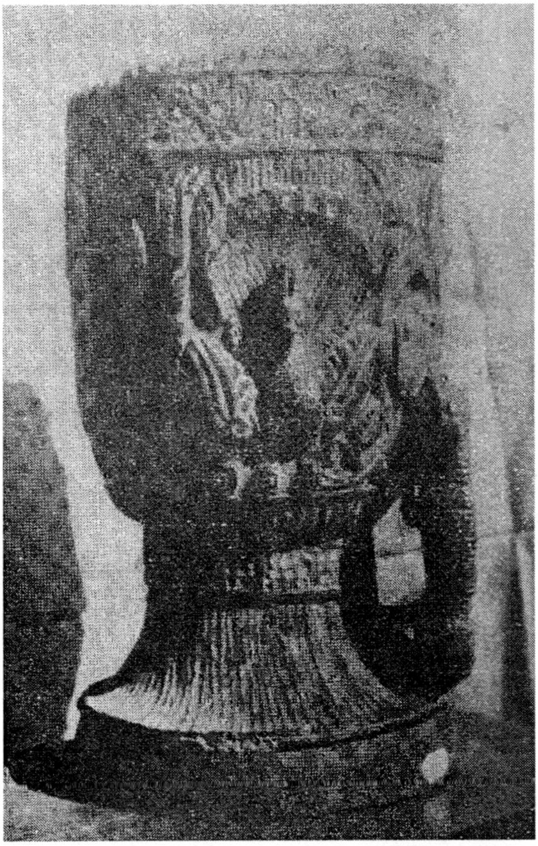

Carved Wooden morter.
Late Ahom Period, Gauhati,

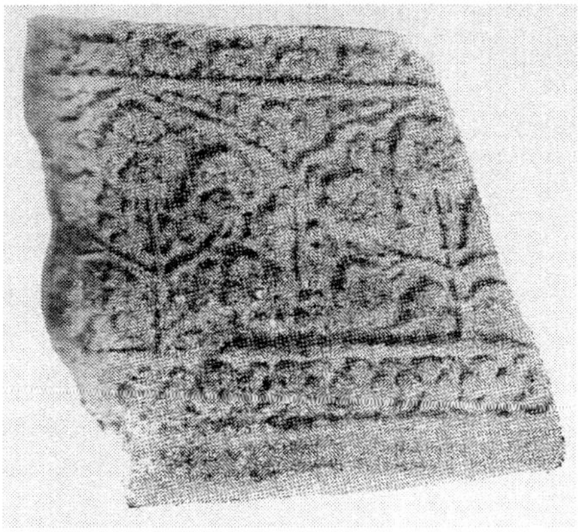

Terracotta tile with arabesare motifs, Gauhati

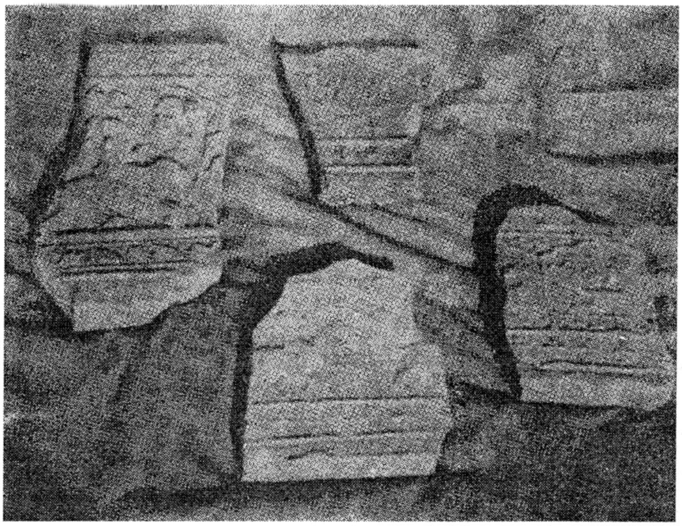

Terracotta tiles, Gauhati

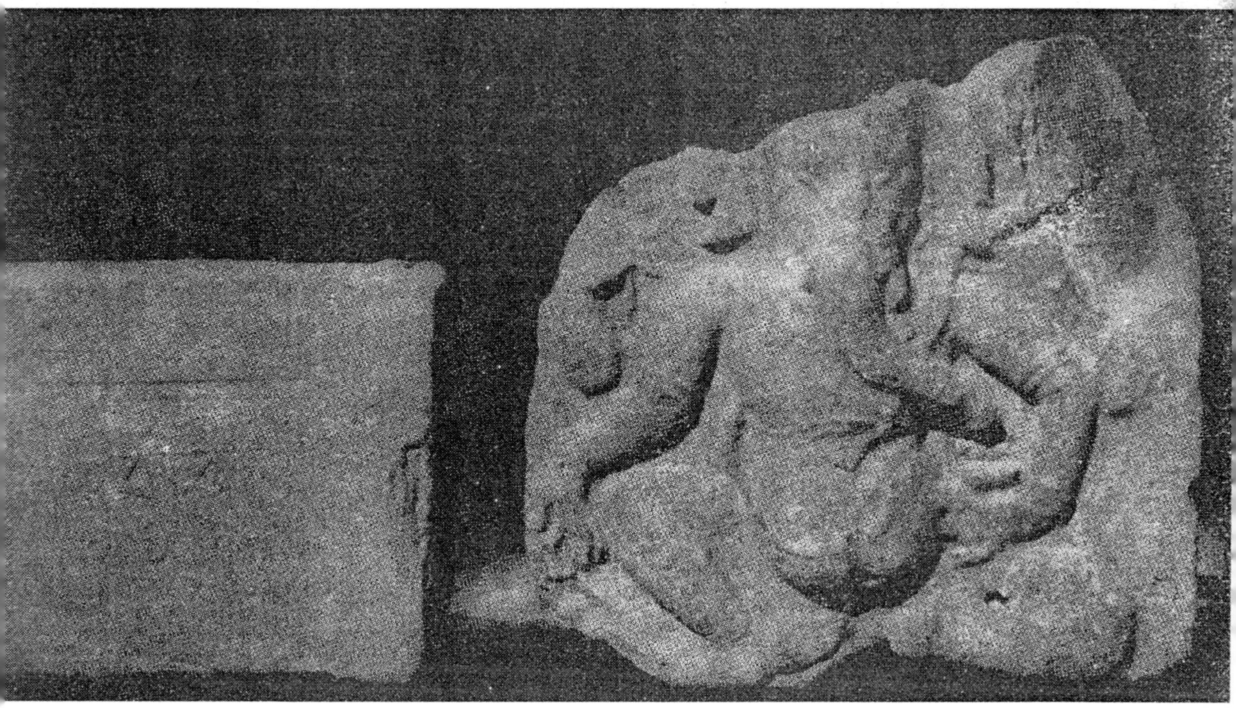

Terracotta Plaques, Kamrup

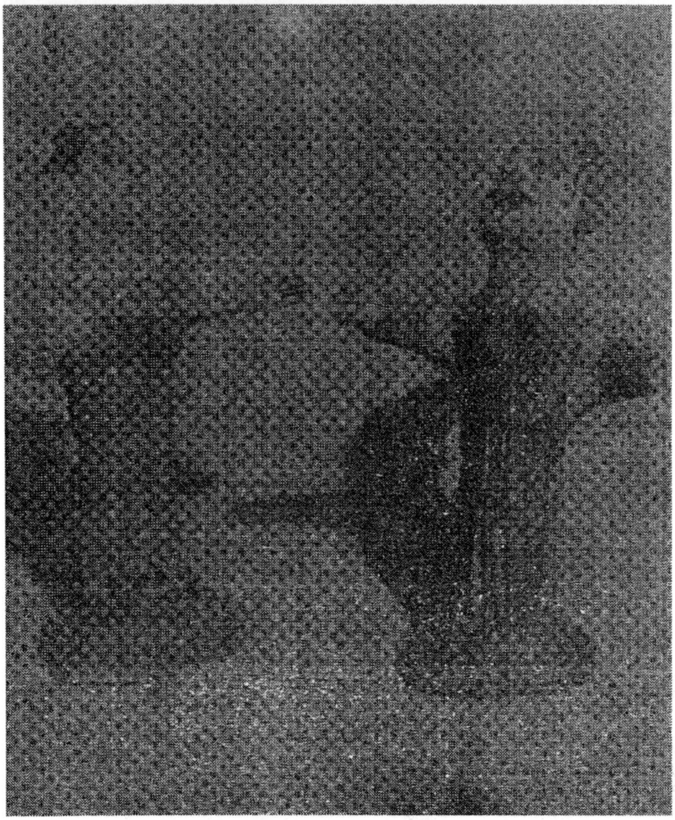

Terracotta dolls, Gauhati

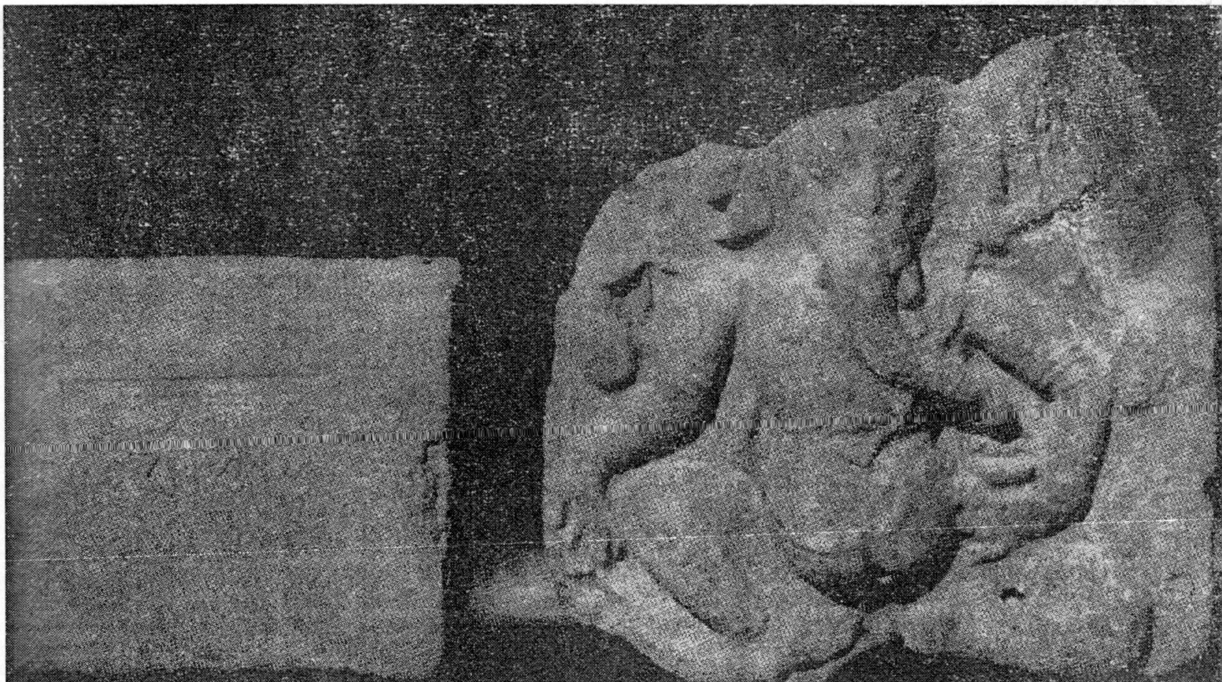

Terracotta Plaques, Gauhati.

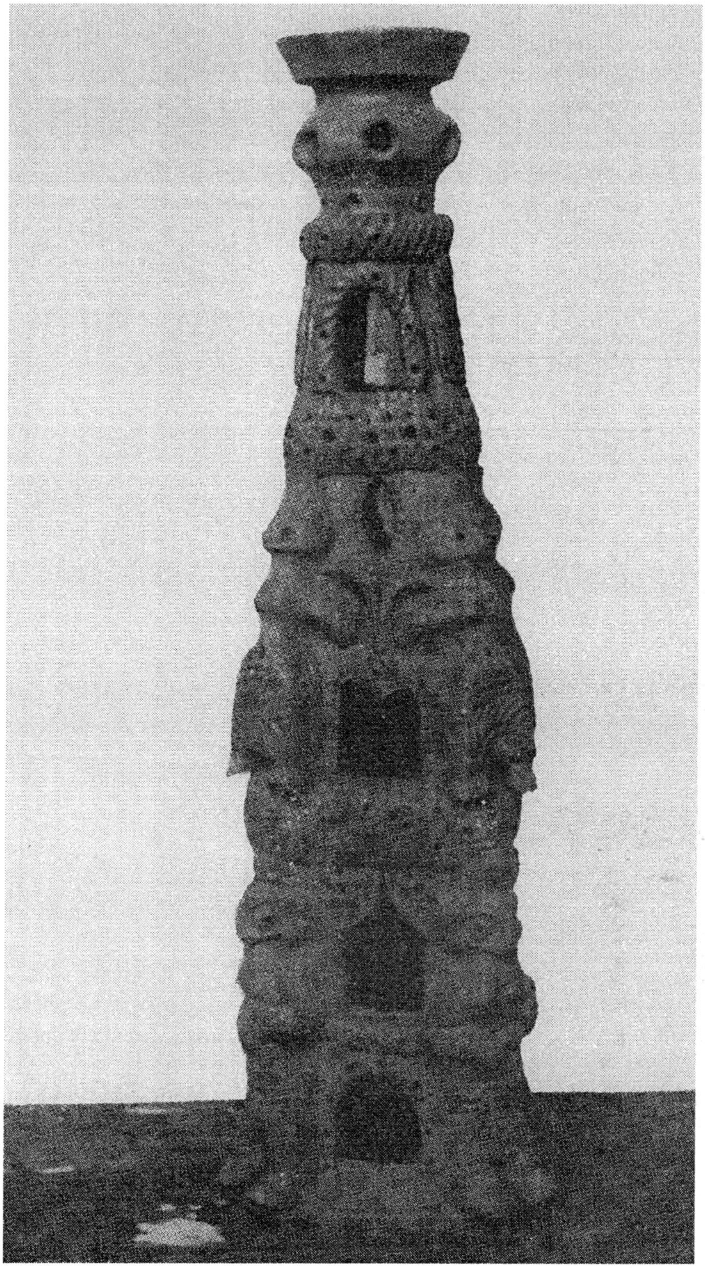

Terracotta lamp Stand, Gauhati.

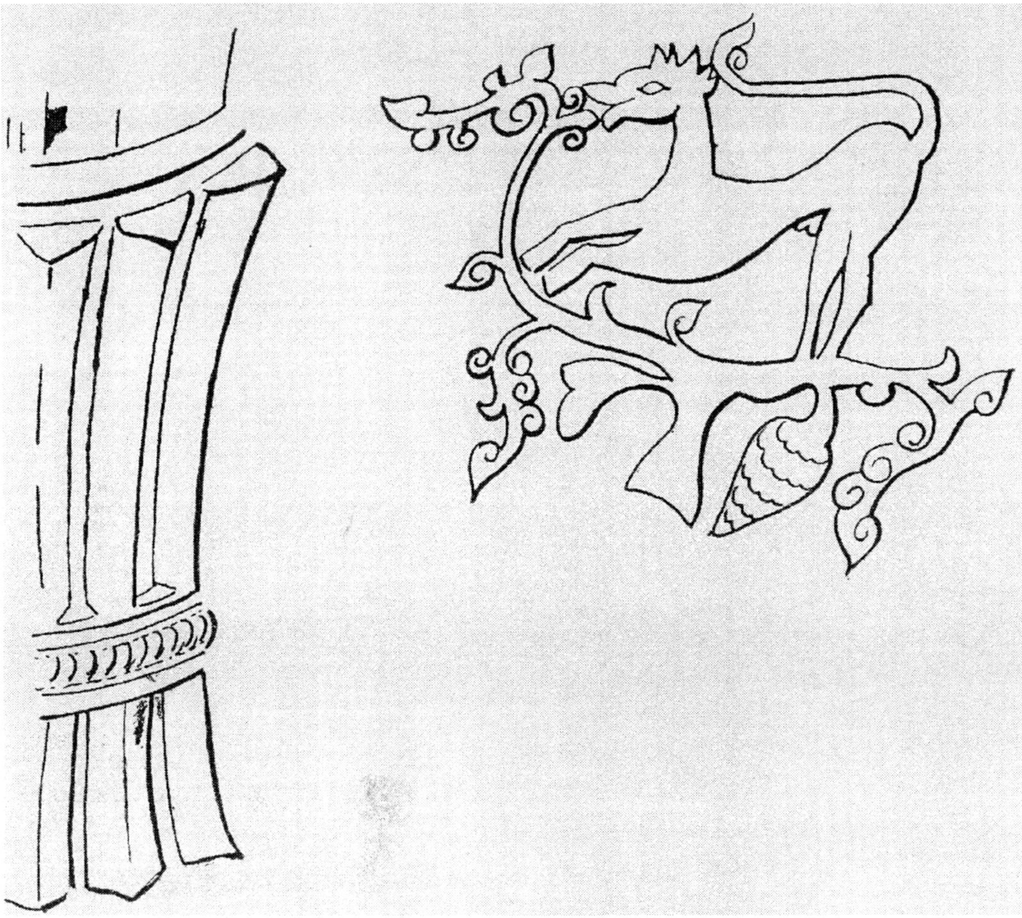

(I) The Lion carved on the km-myakanch bridge K & J hills
(ii) Rail of Moulding corner Pillars.

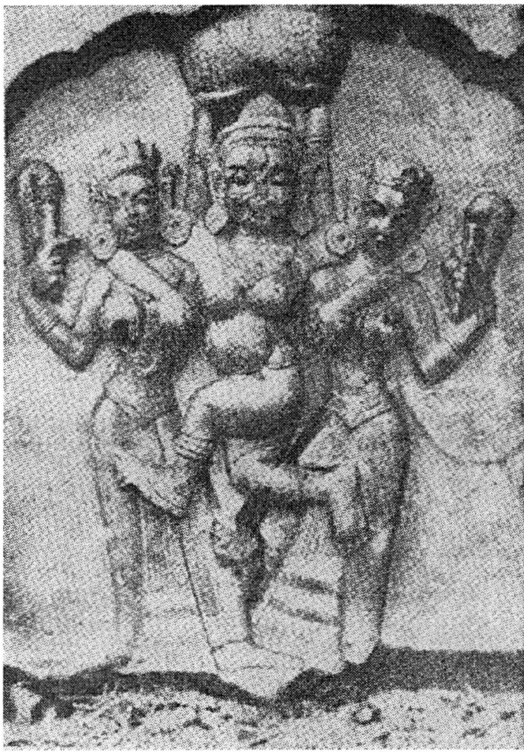

Naginis, Gossanimari Kamatapur.

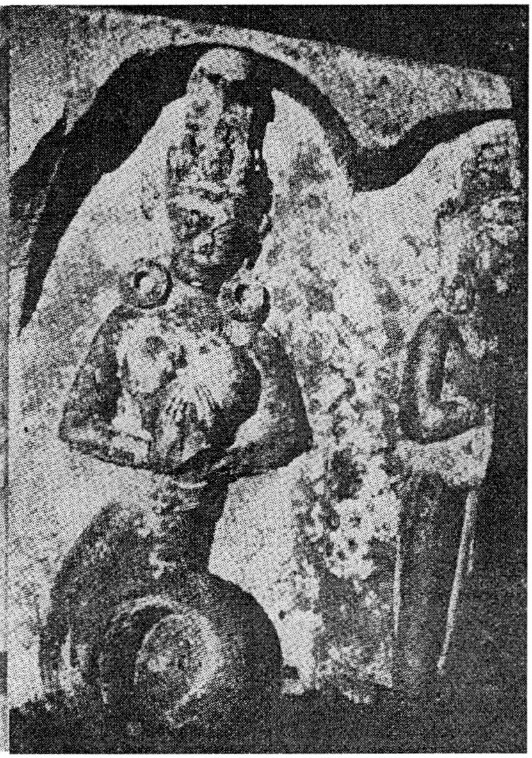

Gopis & Krishna, Gossanimari

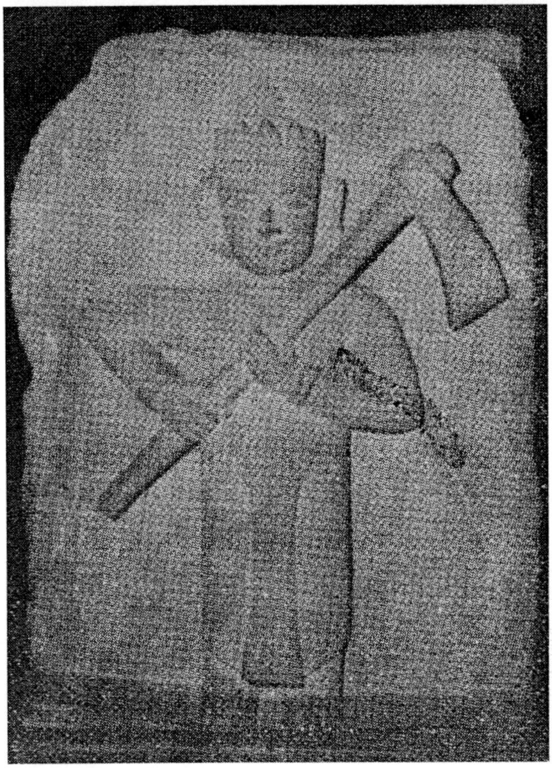

Parhsurama,
Grey sand stone, Tezpur.

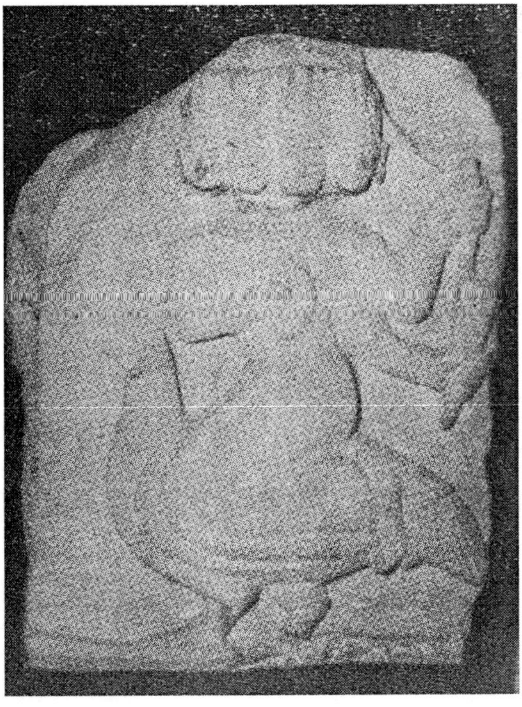

Brahma, Grey sand stone, Tezpur

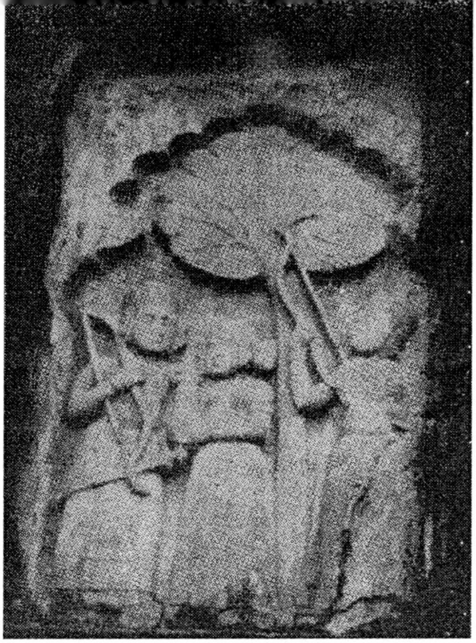

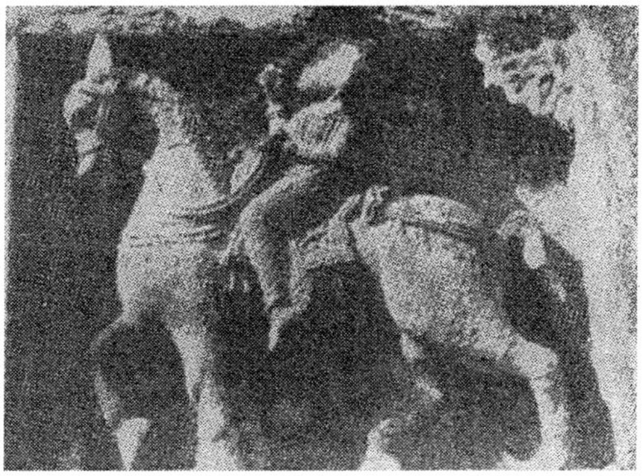

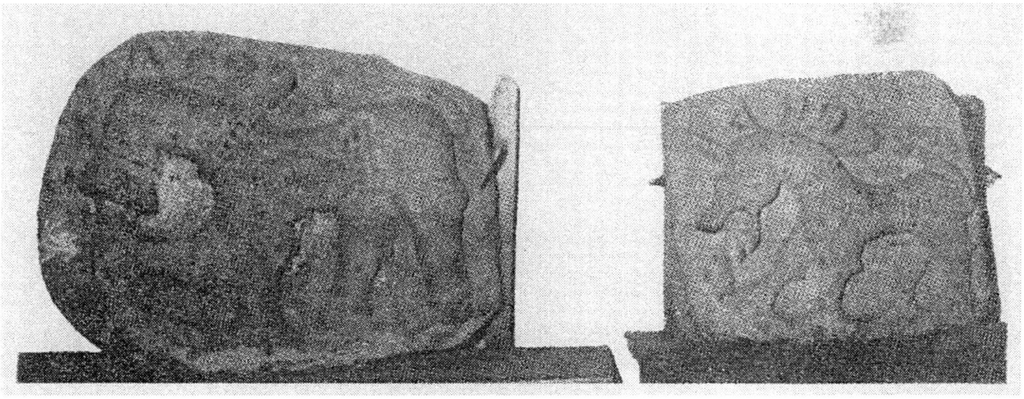

A. Rama, Sita and Lakshman-Stone relief , Sibsagar.
B. Sukleswar Temple, Gauhati, Stone relief.
C. Lions, Grey sand stone, Maibong.

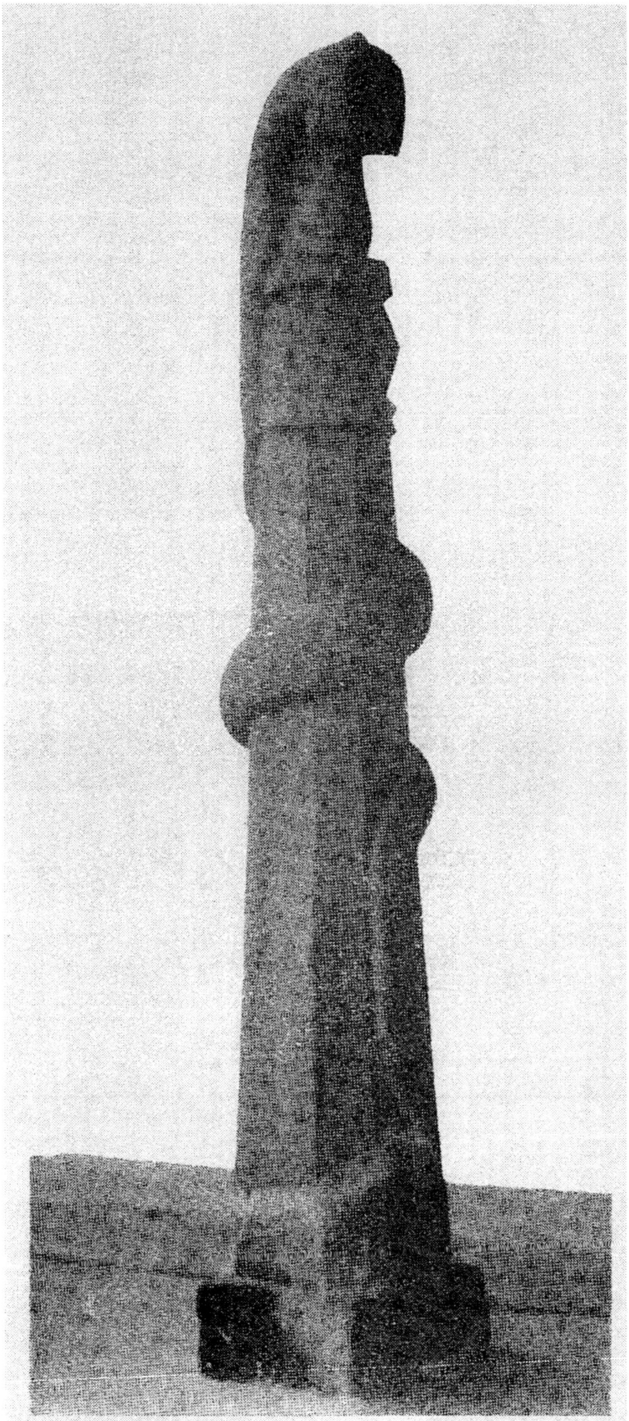

Snake Boundery Pillal, Sadina
Grey sand stone.

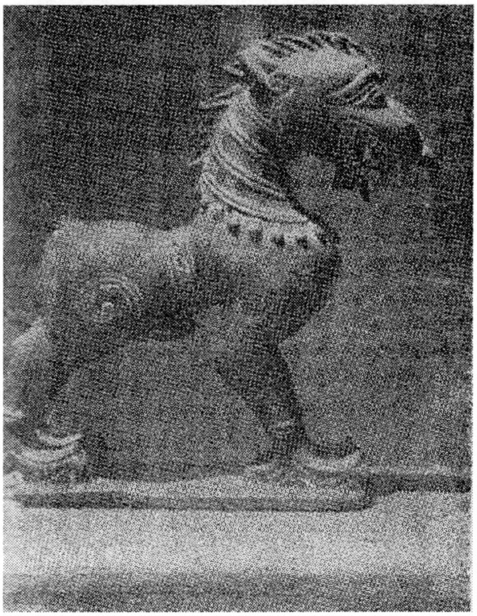

Brass Lion, Sibsagar.

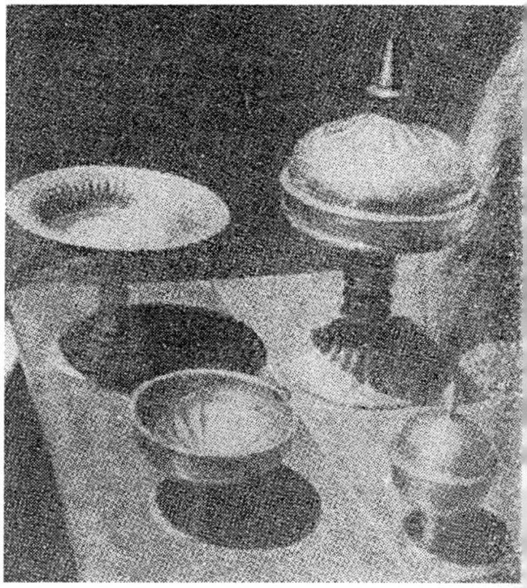

Brass and Bronze utensils of the Ahom Age. Utensils of the Native design.

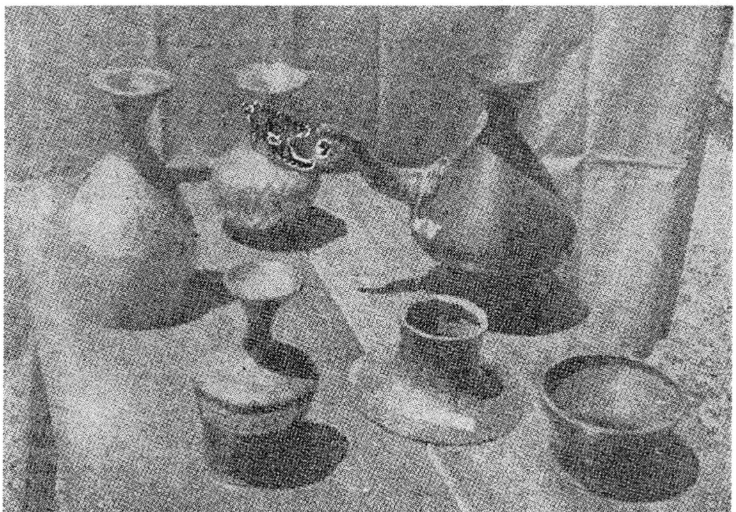

Metalware of the Ahom Age. Utensils with the Islamic influences.

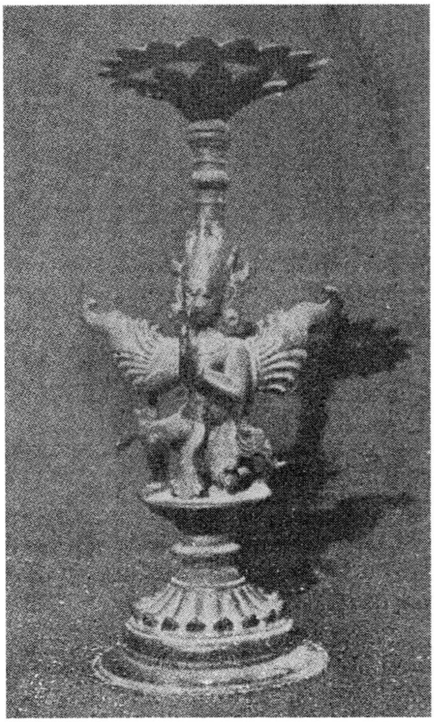

Durga from Tinsukia, Bronze.

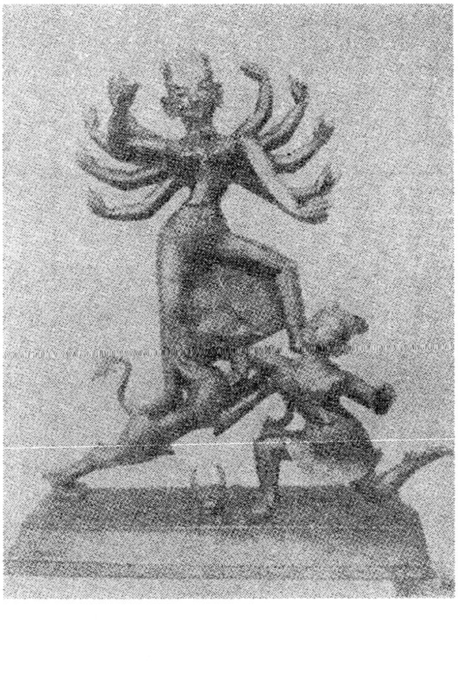

Bronze Lamp stand, Assam

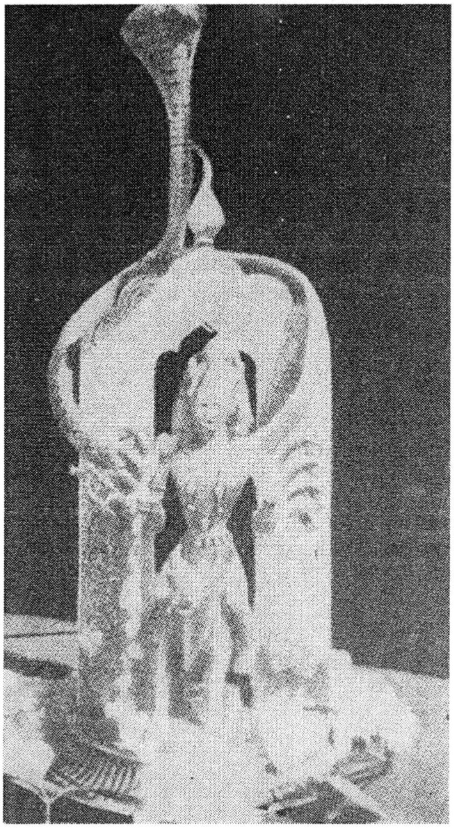

Icon of Shiva. Umanande Temple, Gauhati.

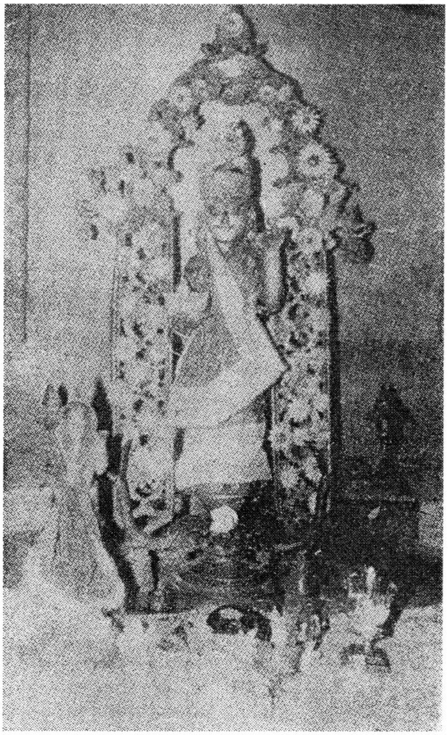

Icon of Devi

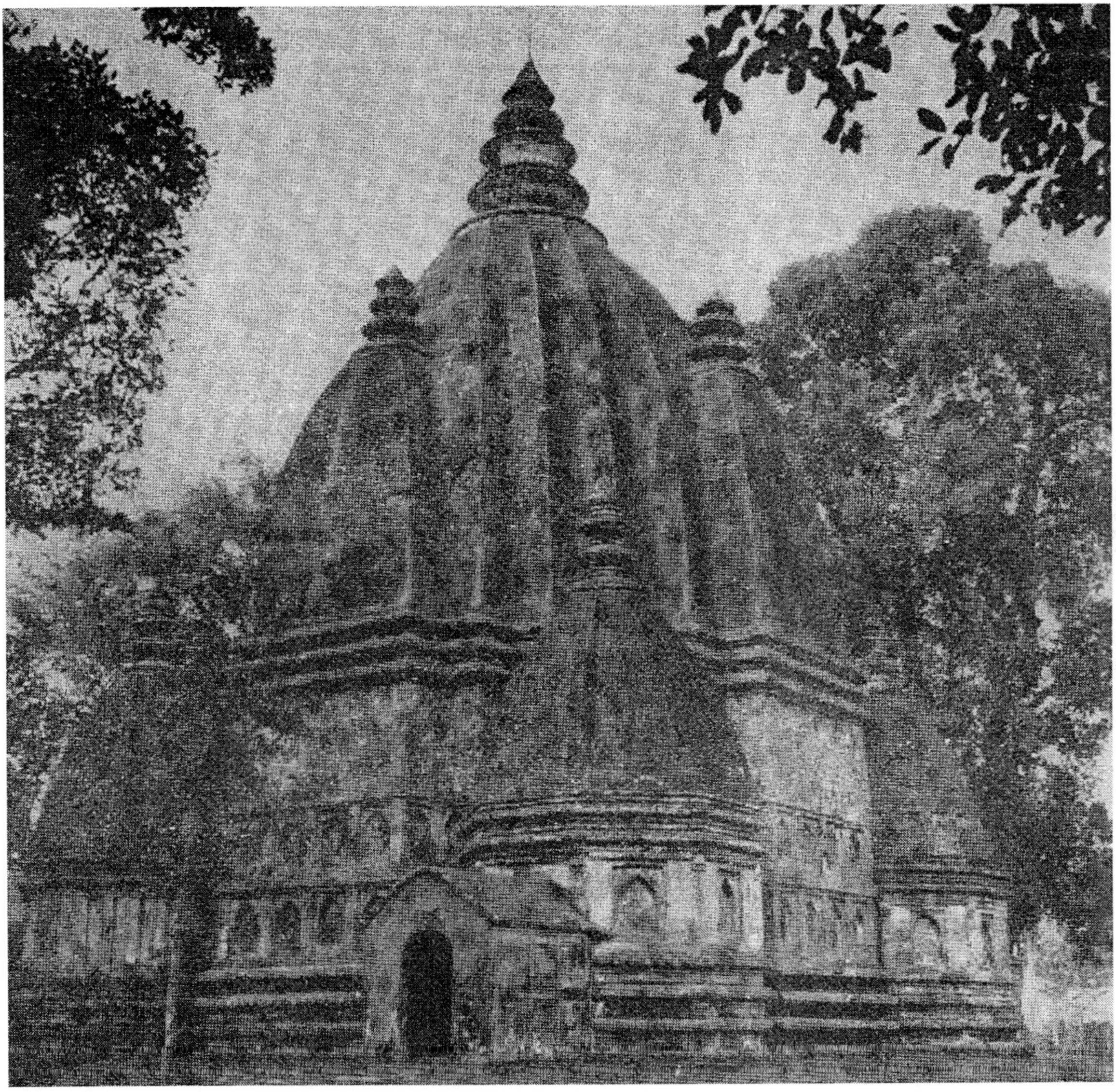

General view of Temple, from West.
Nigriting, Dt. Sibsagar, Assam

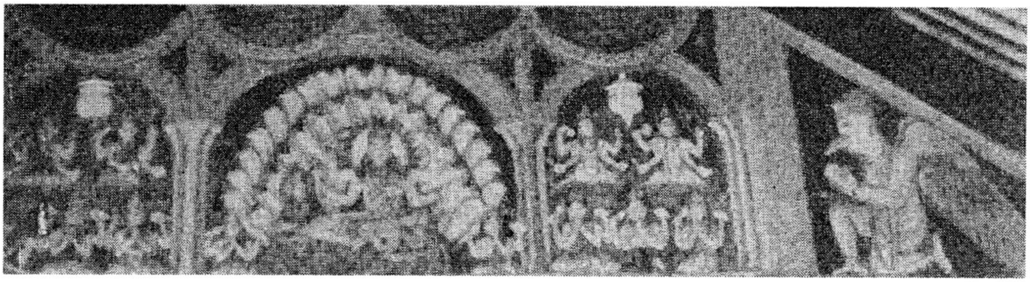

Wood carving on Wails, Barpeta.

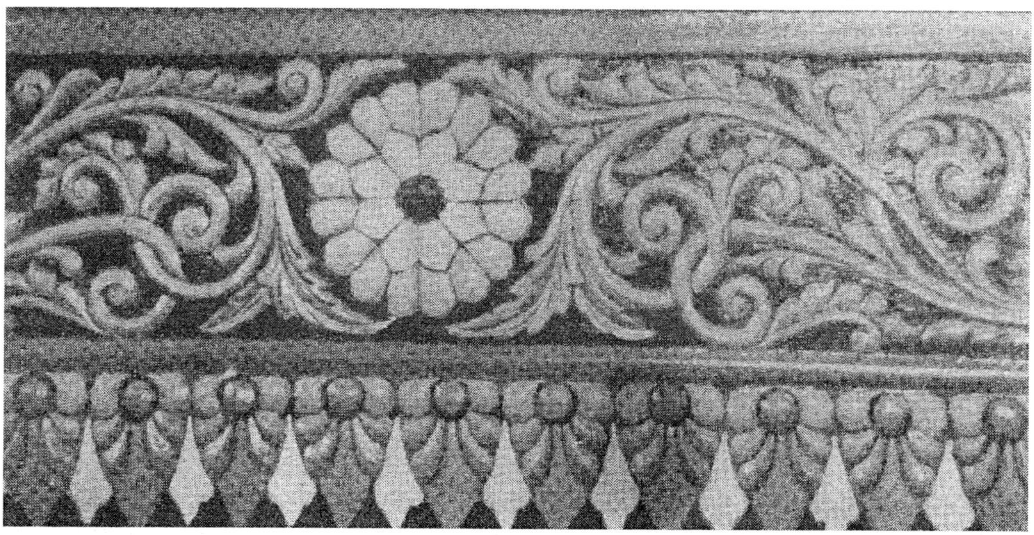

Details of Simhasana Carving-painted wood work, Gauhati

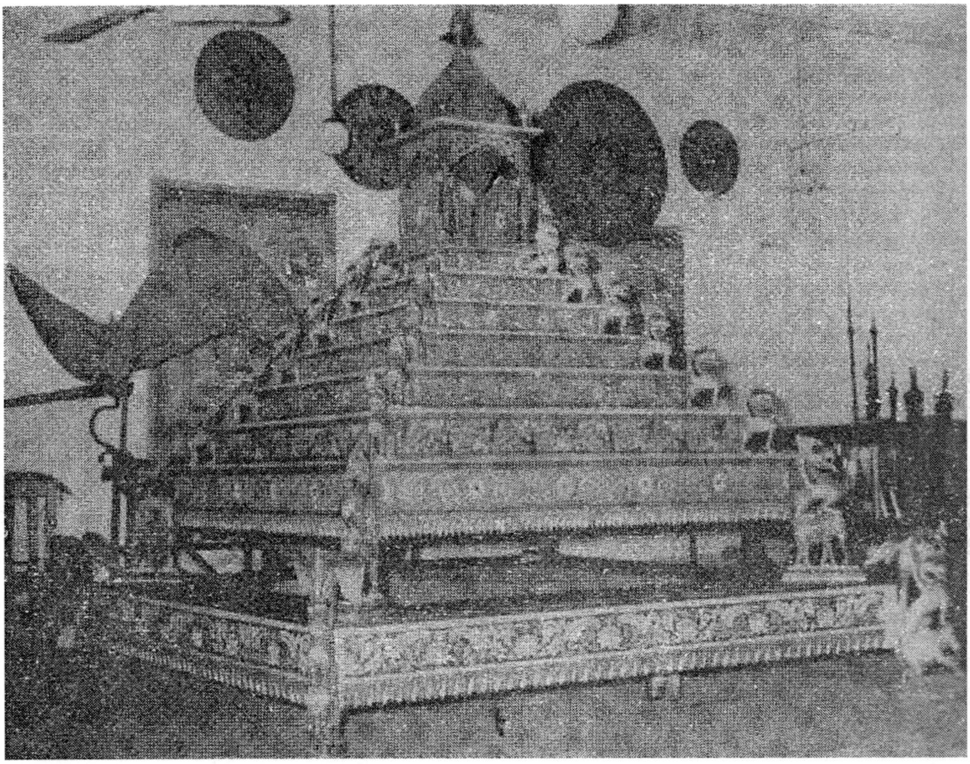

Simhassna for a Namghar. Painted wood work, Barpeta.

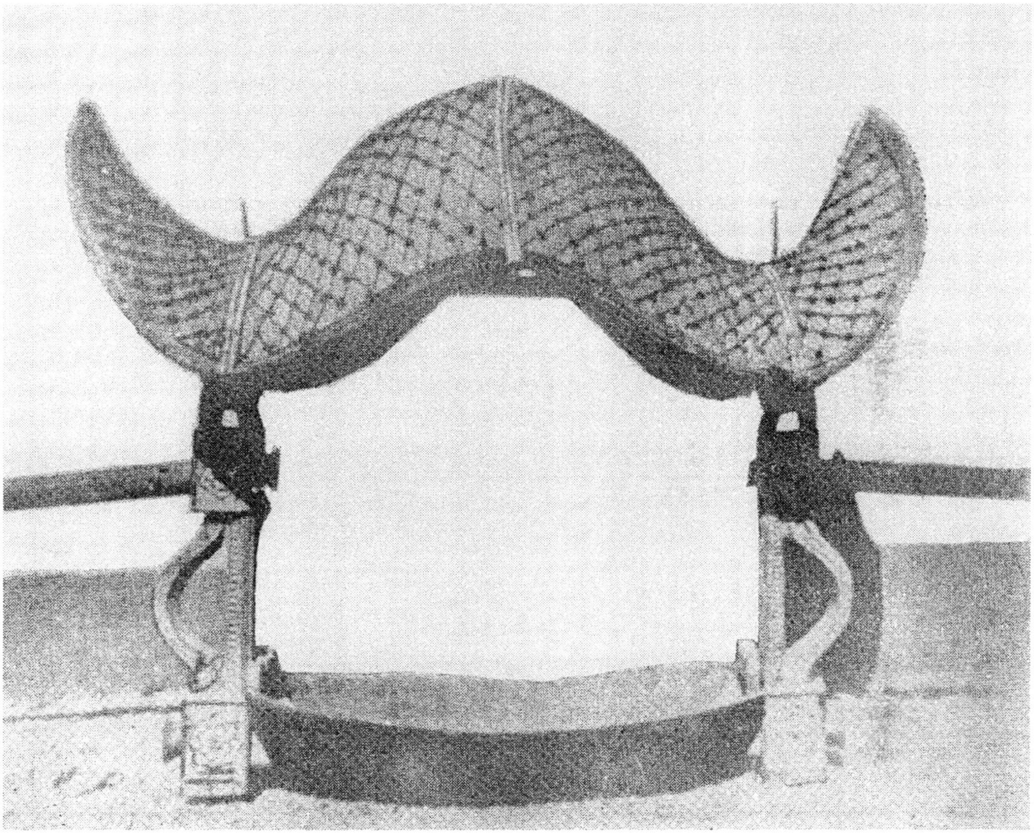

Dola or Litter (Ahom Period) Wood and Metal.

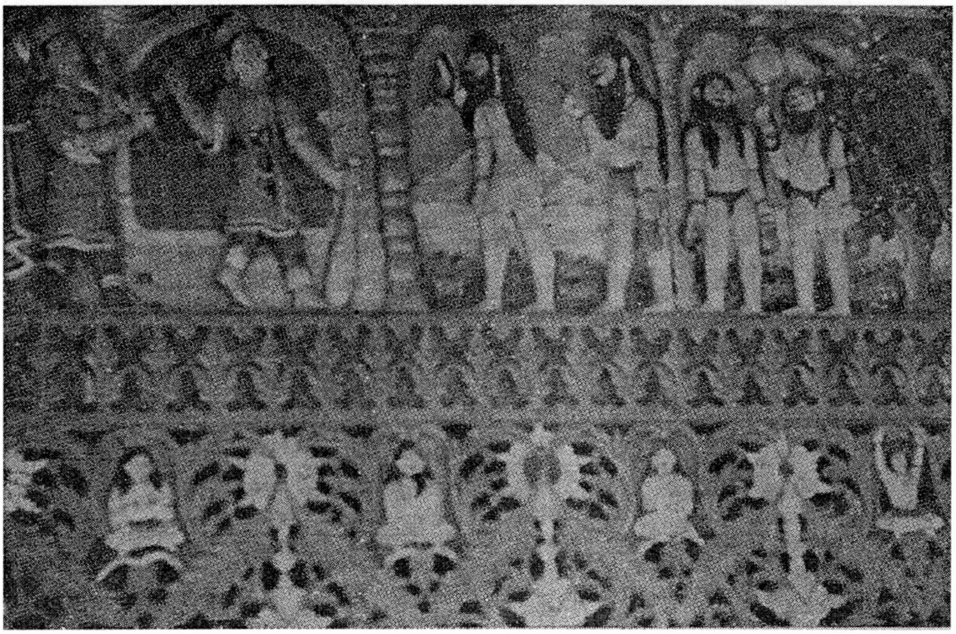

Wood Carving on Walls, Barprta.

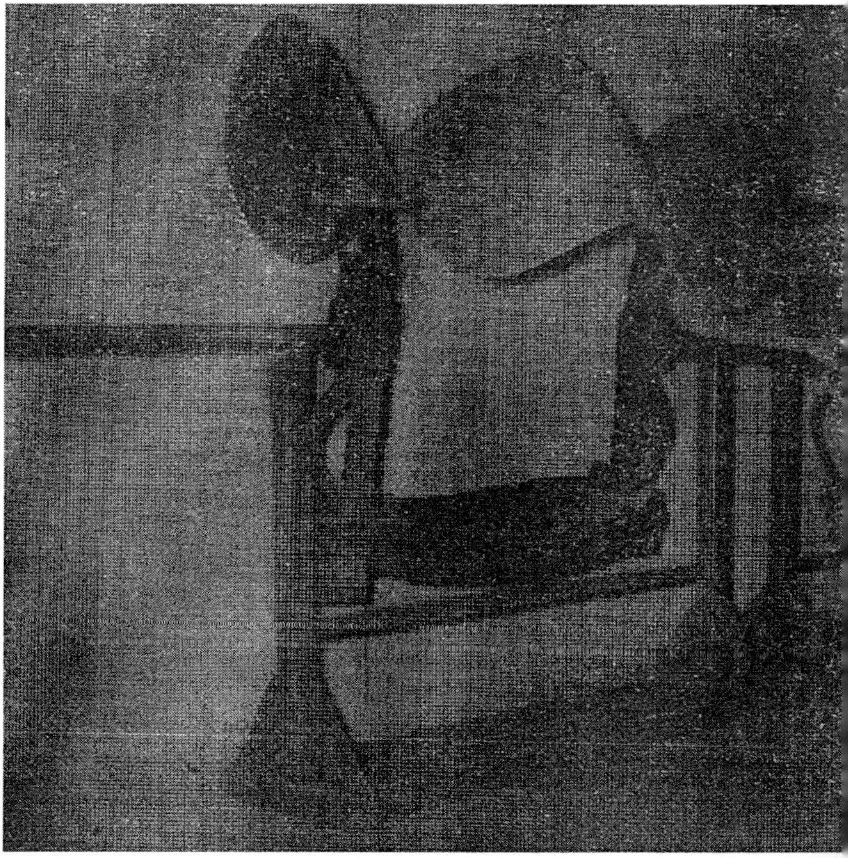

Dola or litter with seen-shade. Wood, Metal & Bamboo Work.

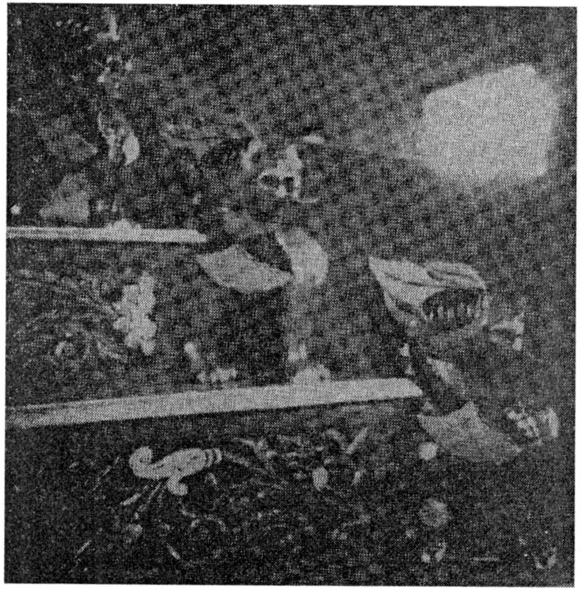

Upper stage of the Wooden Simhasana, Gauhati.

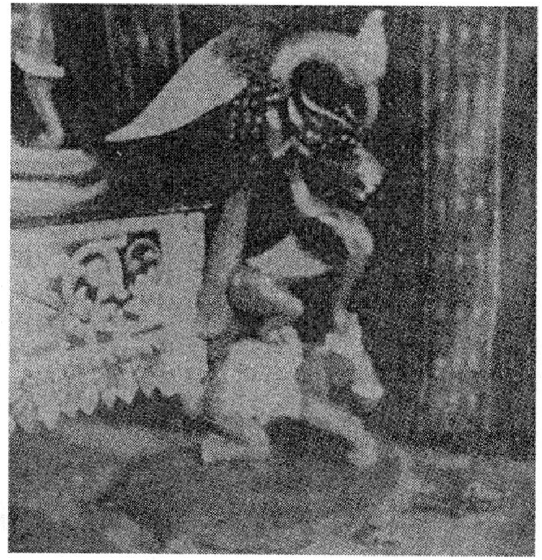

Lowest stage of Wooden Simhasana, Gauhati.

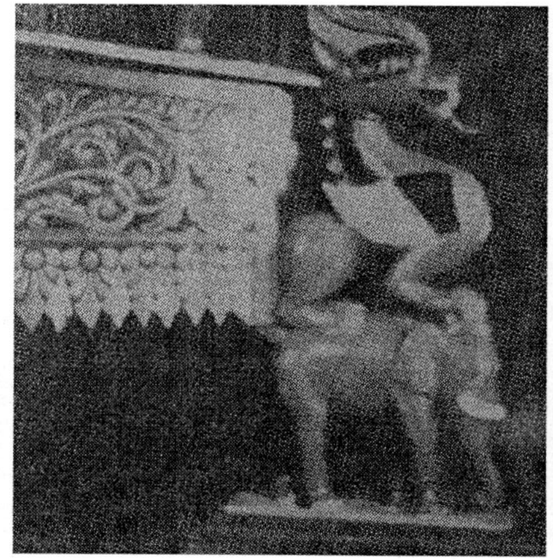

Second stage of Wooden, Simhasana, Gauhati.

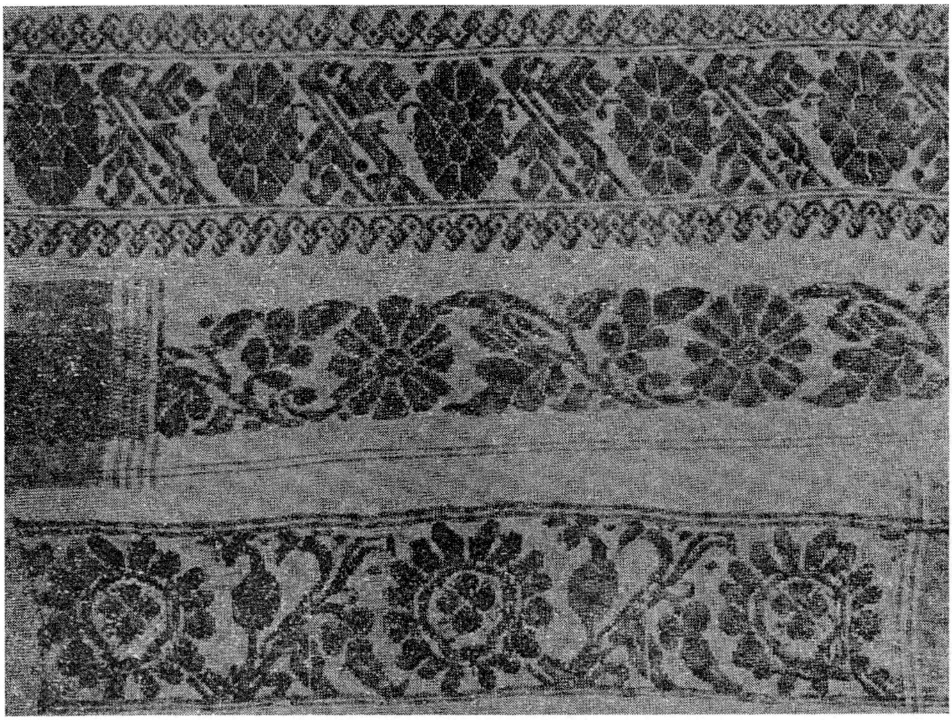

Border design from Phulam Gamochas.

Kachari Costume, Goalpara.

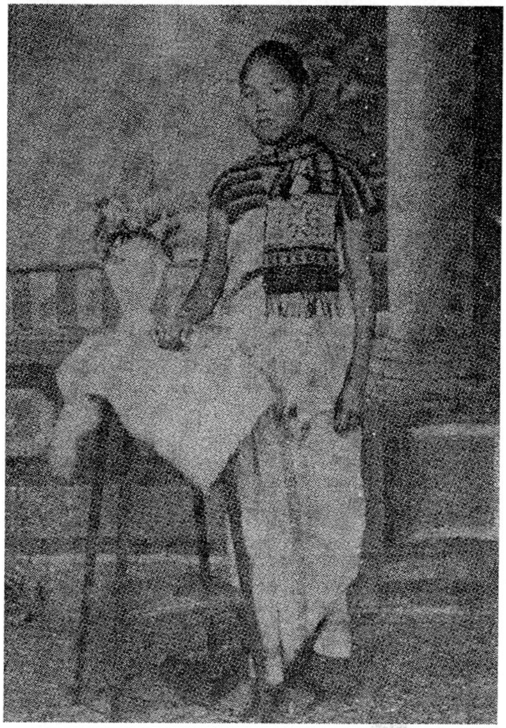

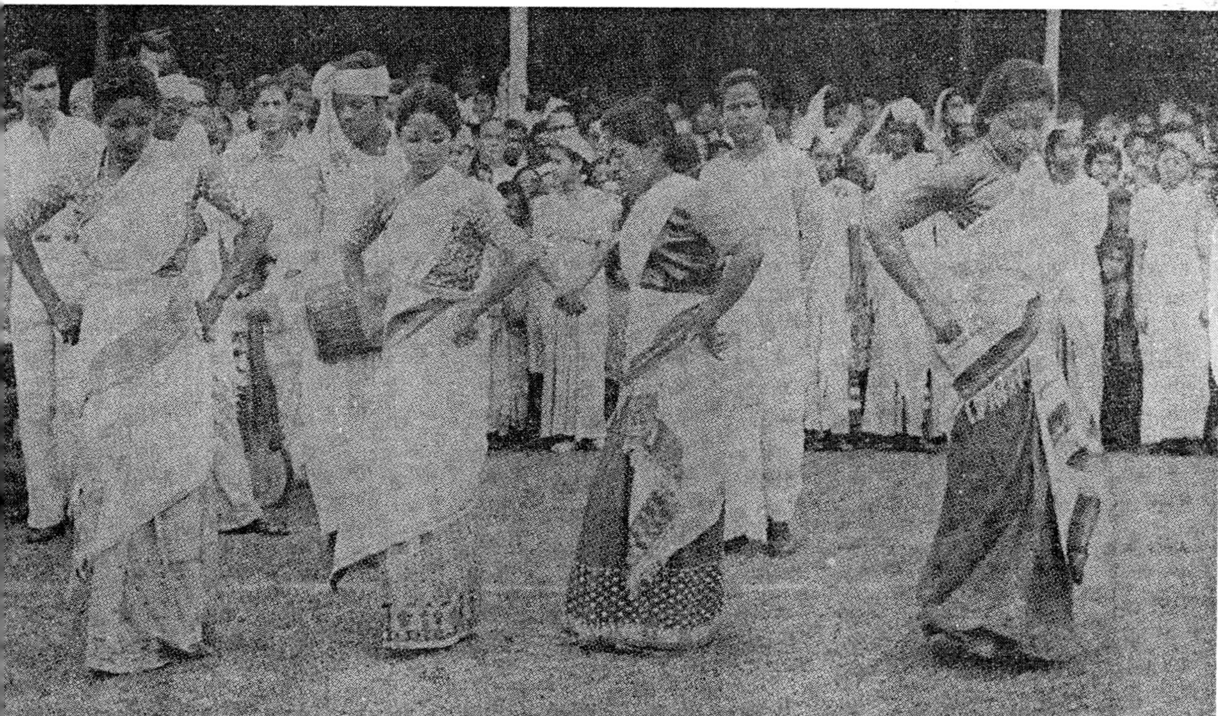

Bihu Dance in Traditional Dress.

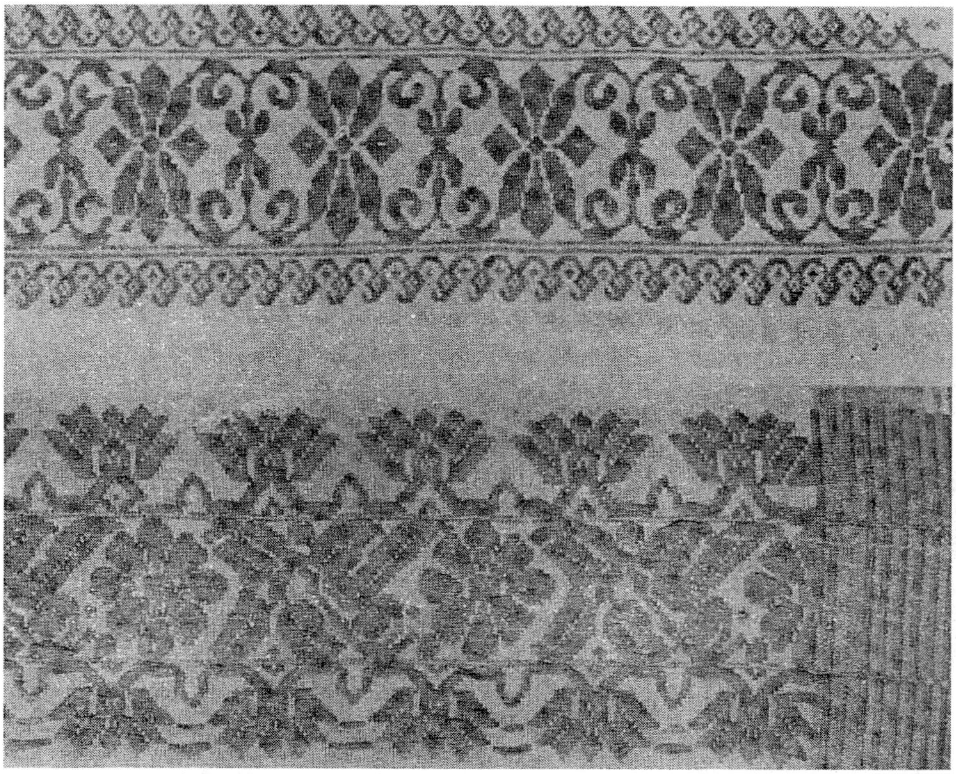

Border design from Phulam Gamochas.

Drawings form the Sankha chada Vadha mas.

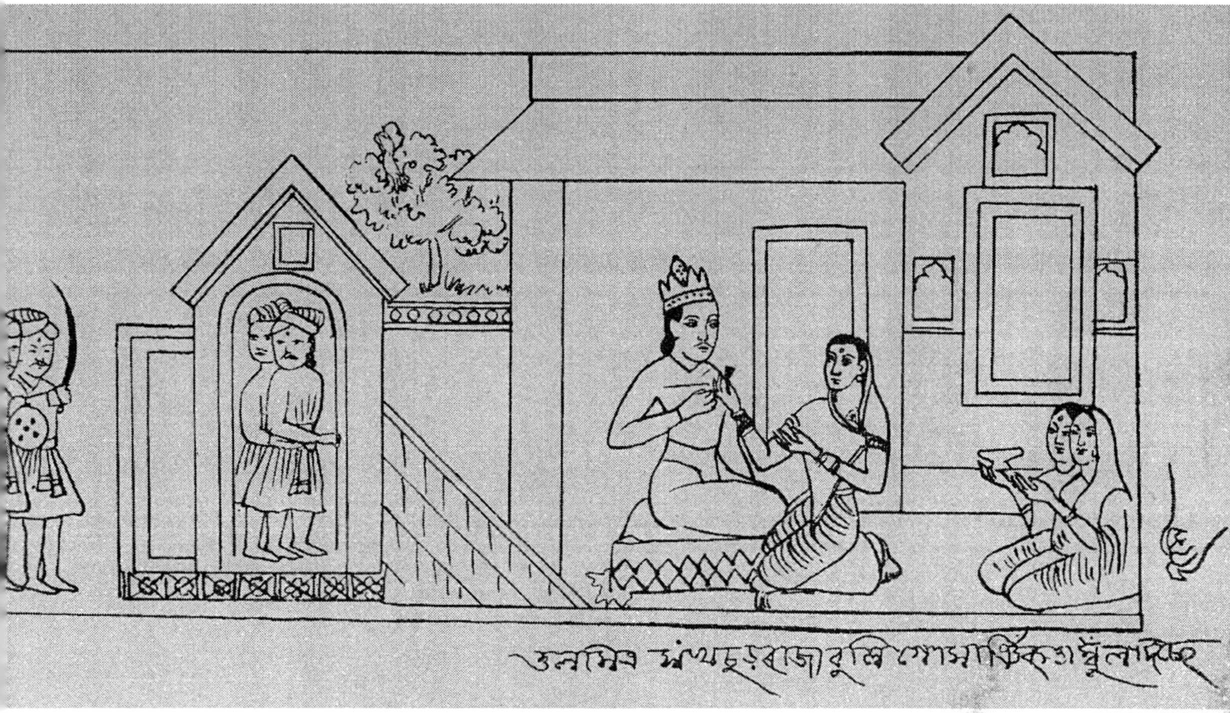

Ticha offers pan to Krishna.

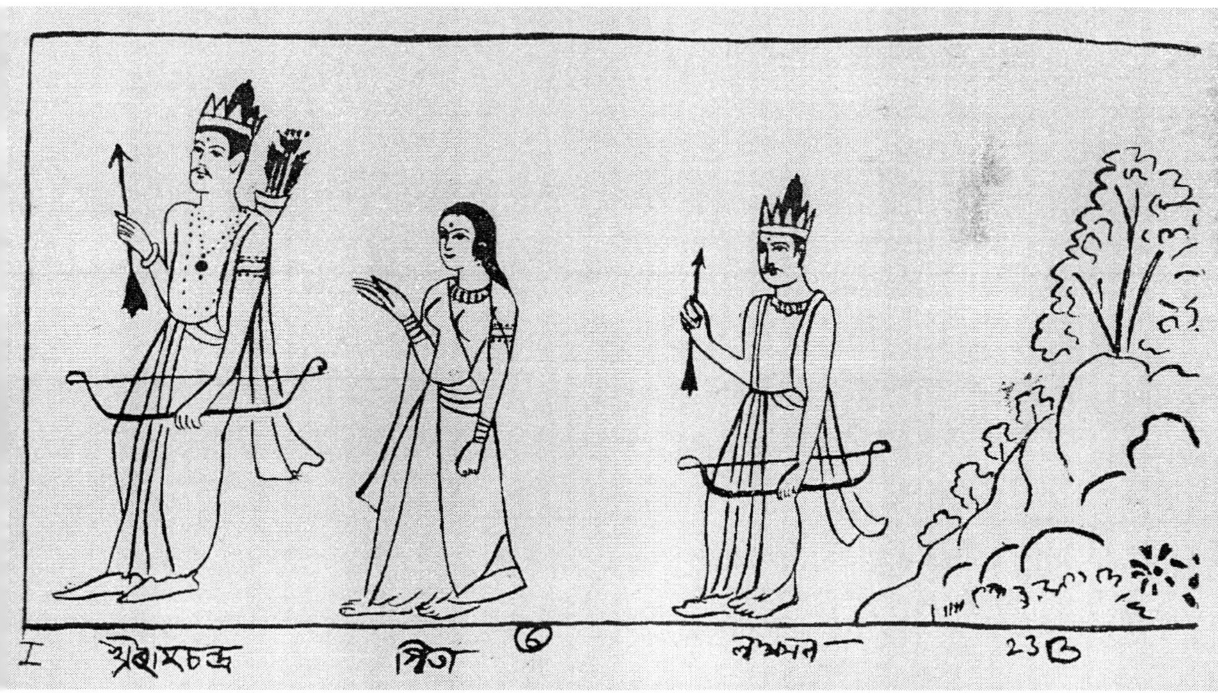

Rama, Sita & Lakshmana.

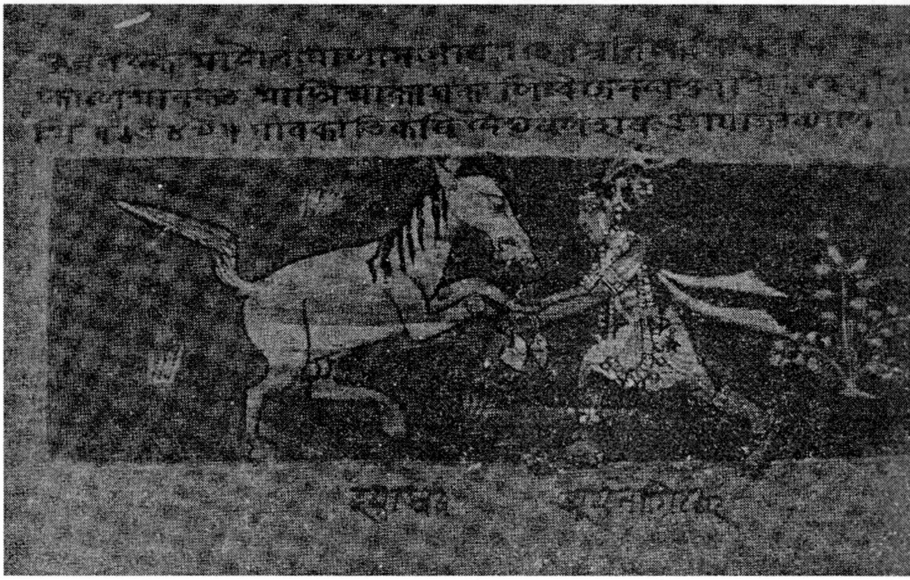

Bhagavata Book X
Ahom Style, Gauhati

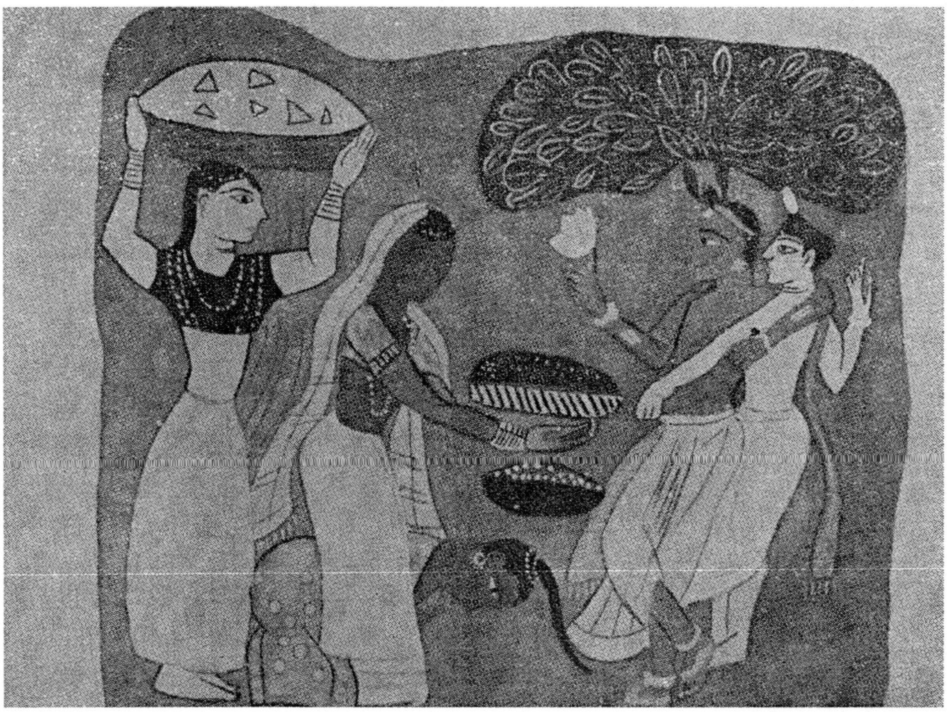

Danalila. Book
Cover, Goalpara.

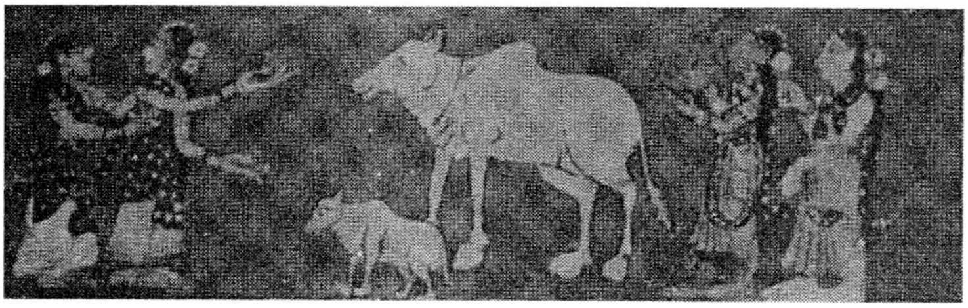

Bhagavata Book X.

Book Cover Assam

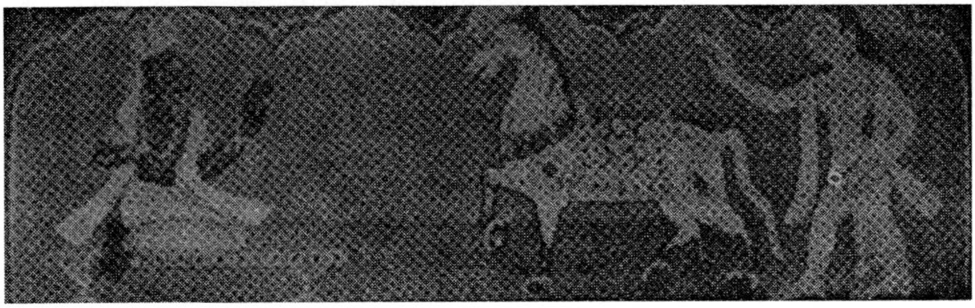

Lava Kusha Yuddha Manuscript.

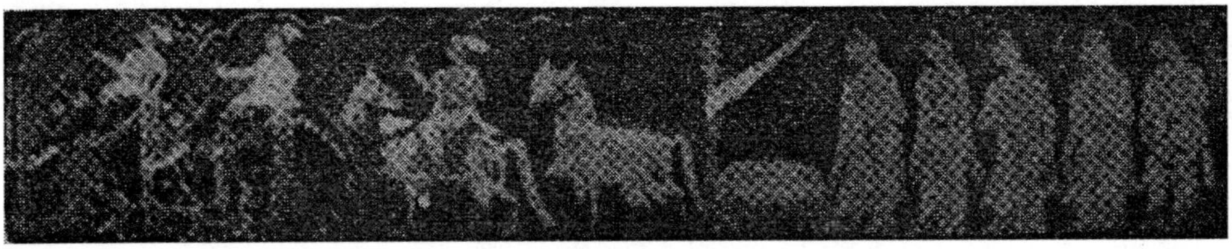

Lava Kusha Yuddha Manuscript, 17th Century

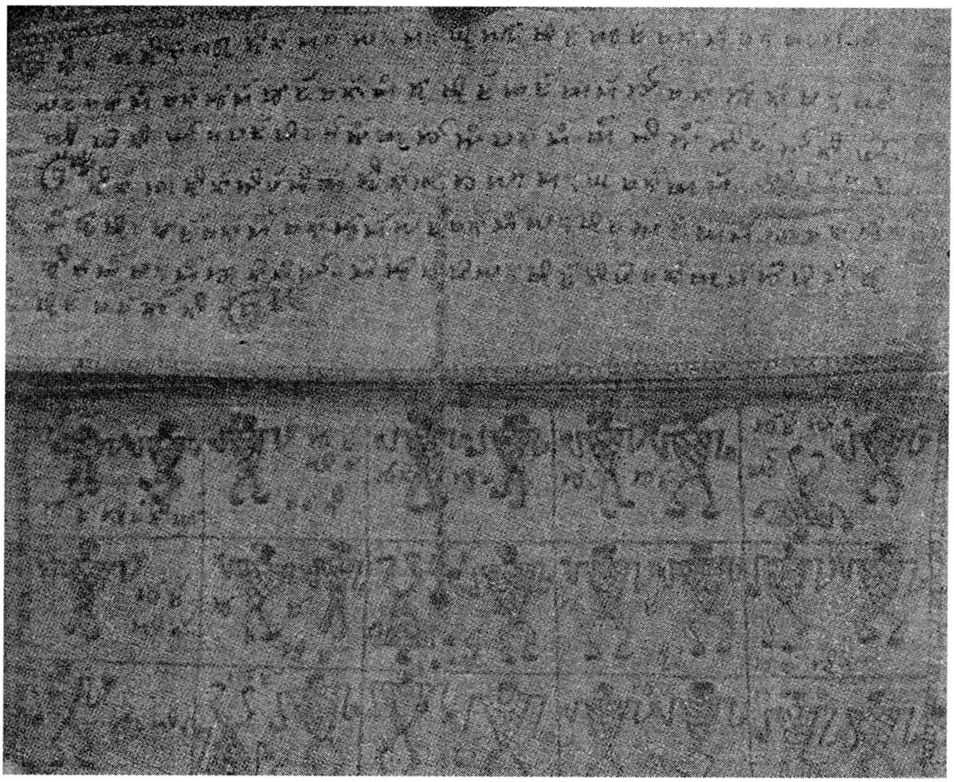

A hom Mss. on Natch Making, Sibsagar

Bhagavata Book Vl. Details of Golophone Page. Date 1659 Gauhati.

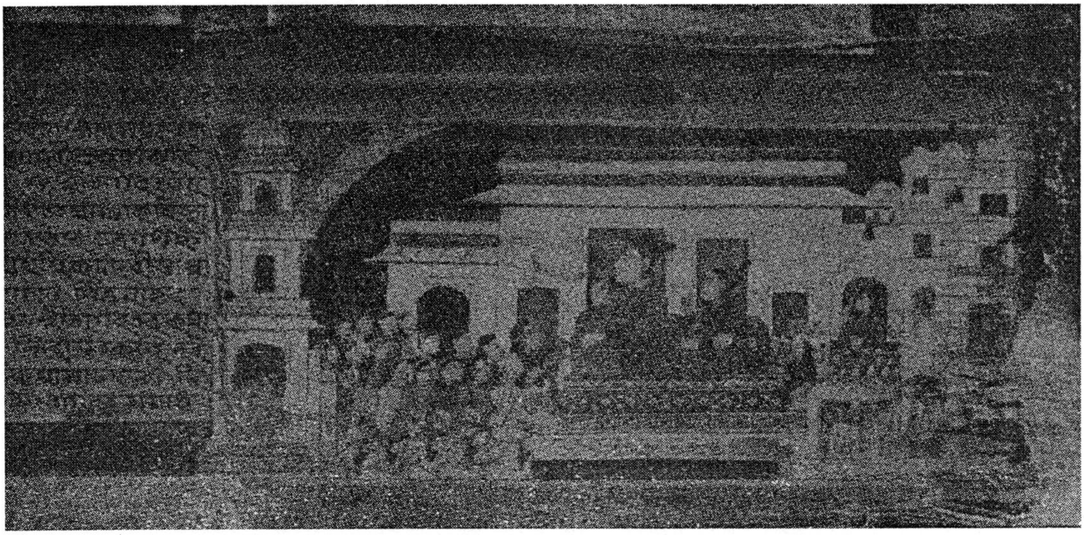

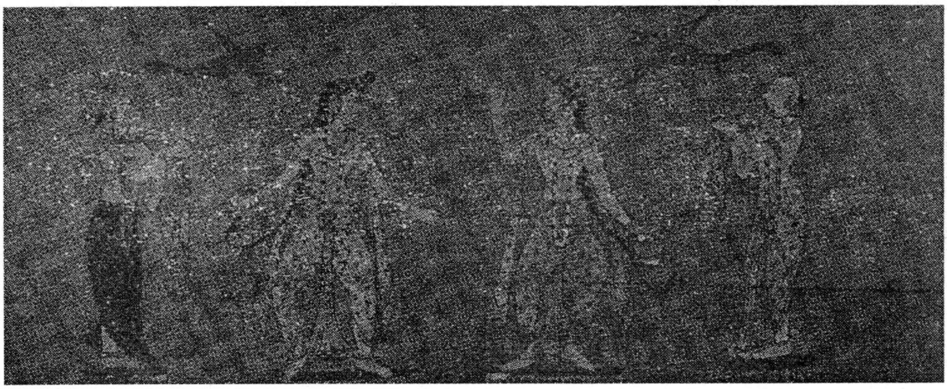

Krishna & Brahma, Painted Book Cover.

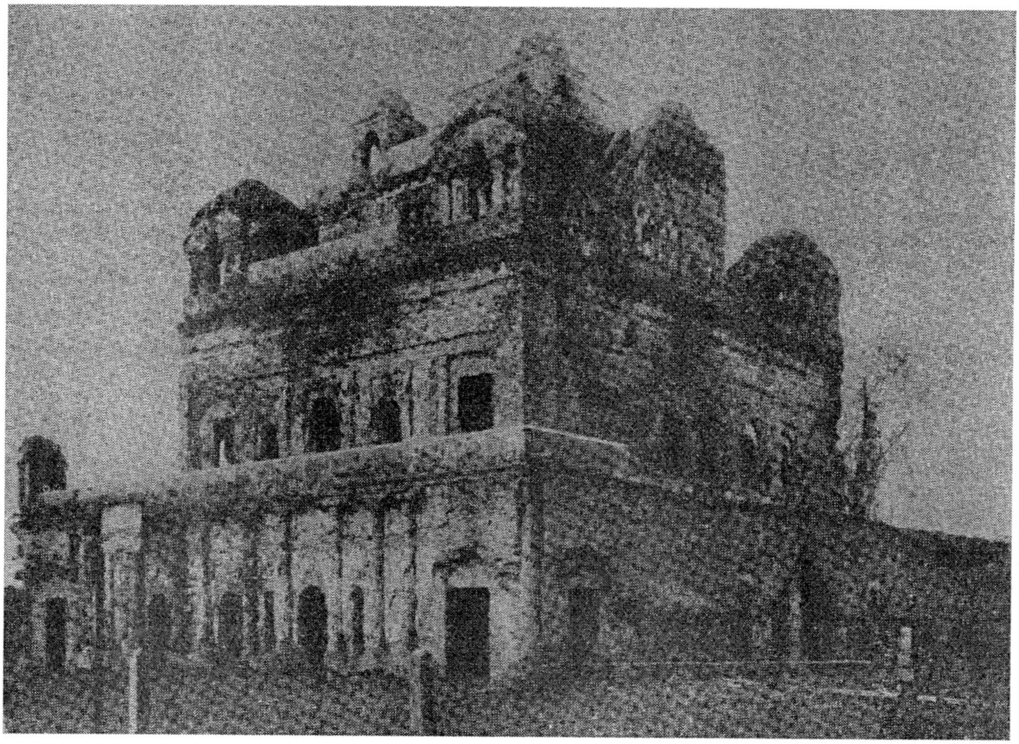

Gorhgaon Palace. from South Sibsagar.

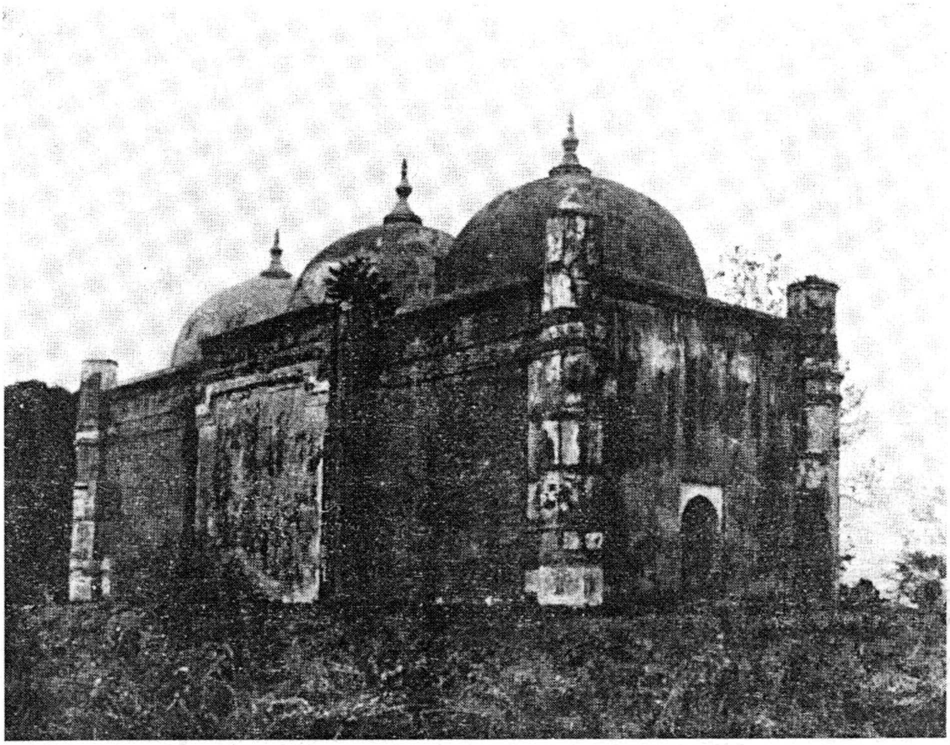

Mosque from South West Goalpara.

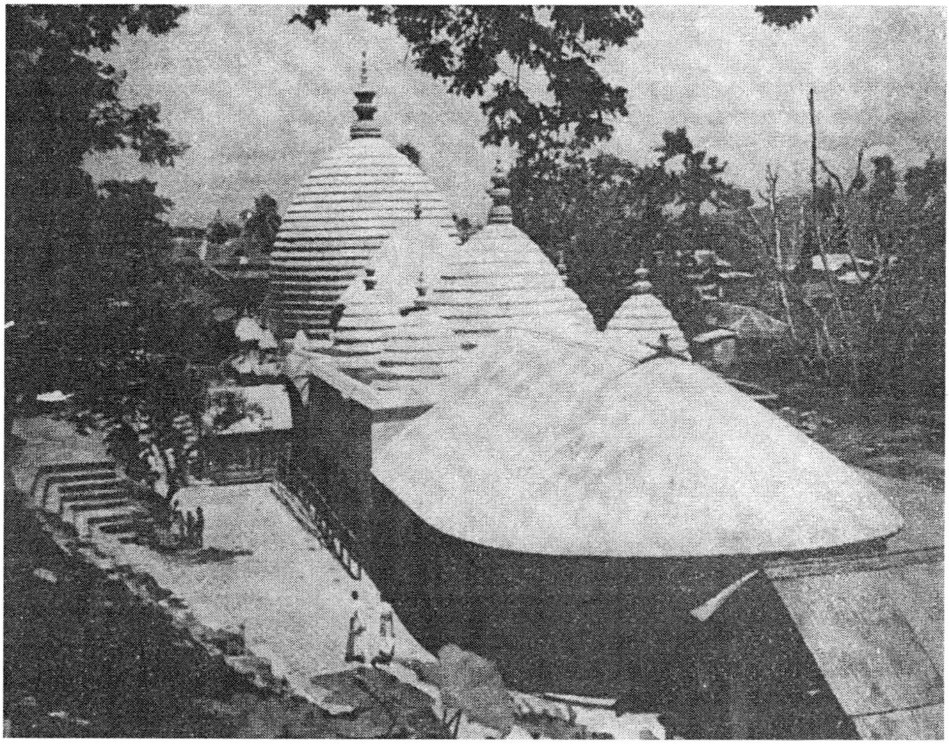

General View of Kamakhya Temple

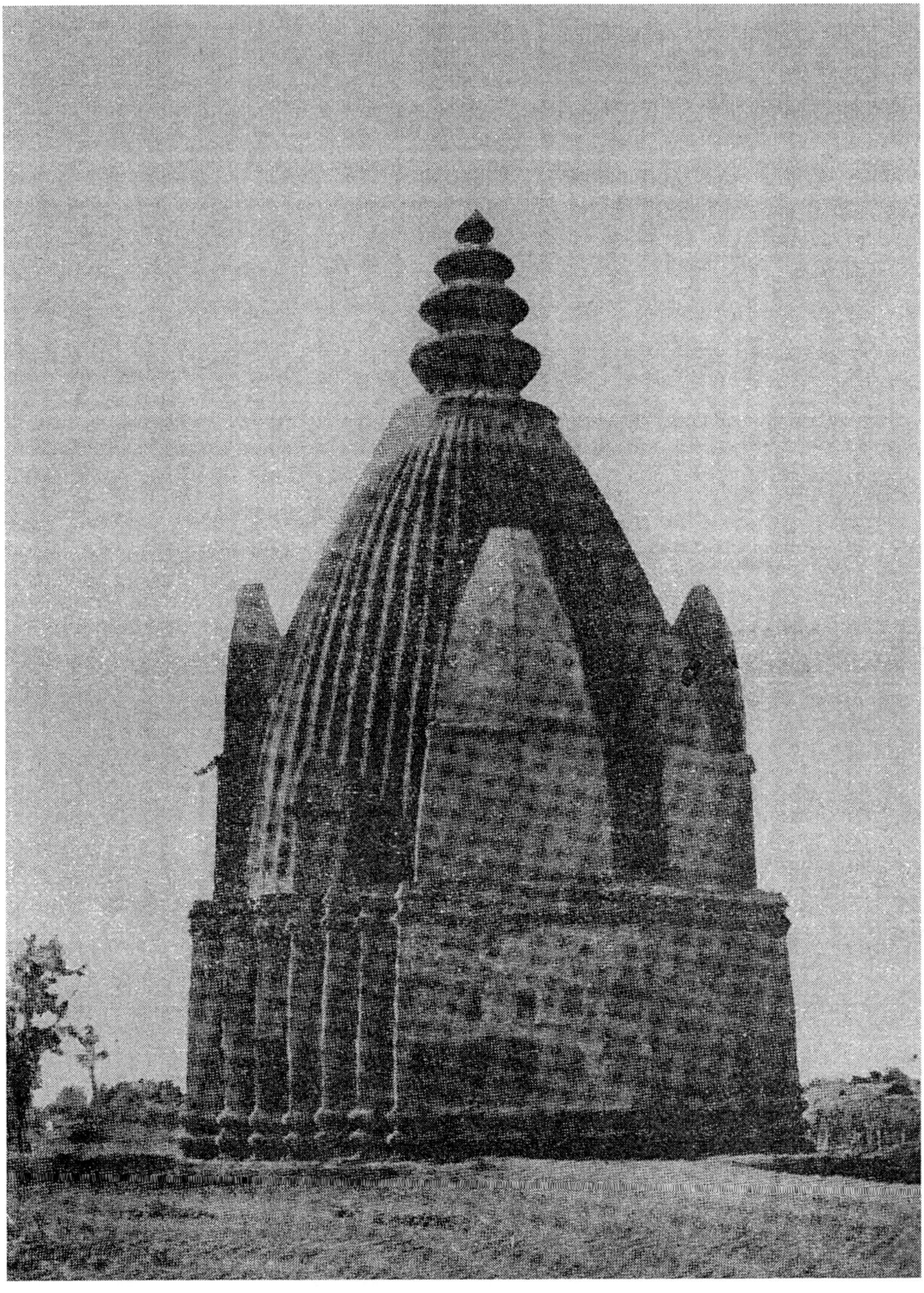

General view of Sivdol Temple, Sibsagar.

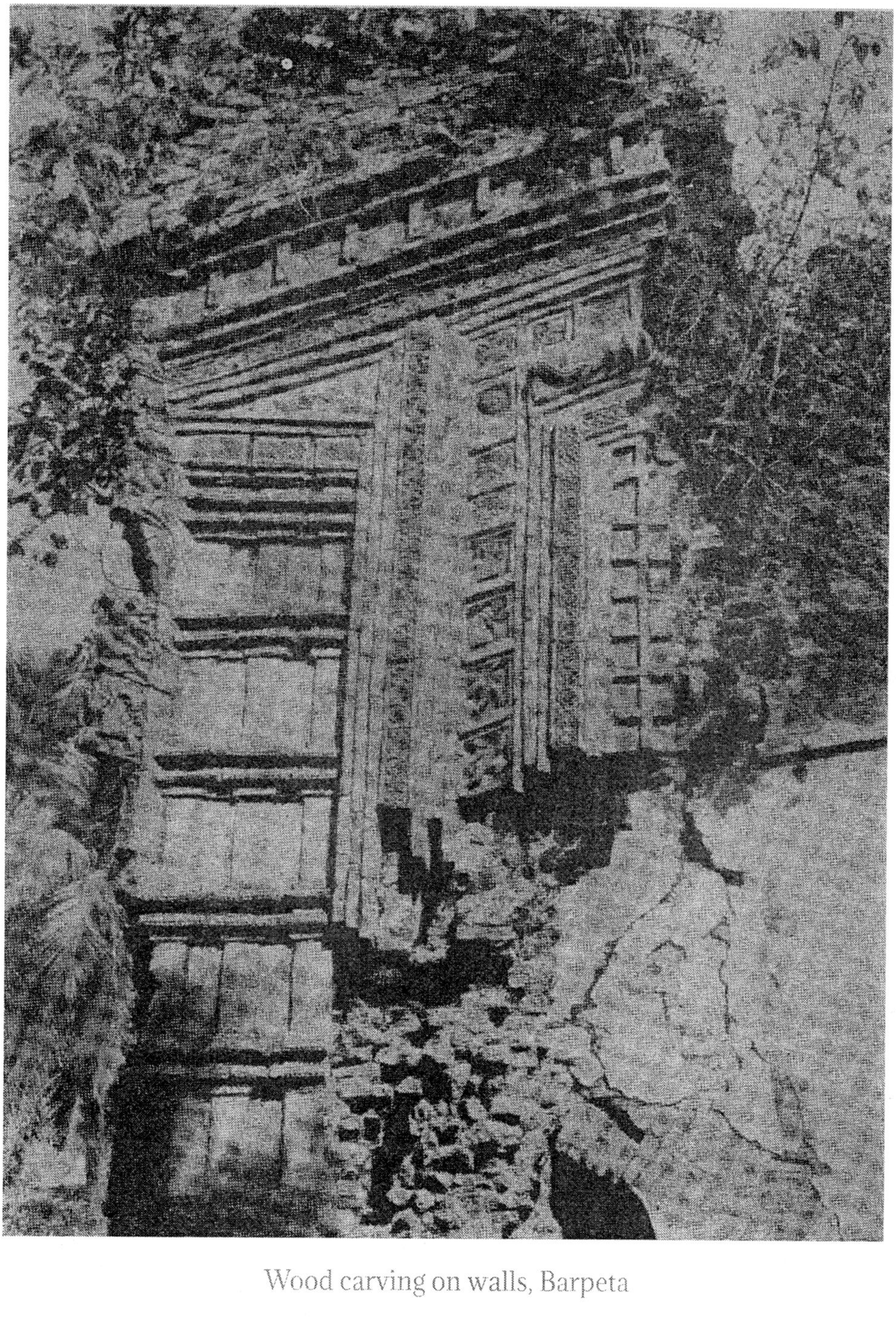

Wood carving on walls, Barpeta

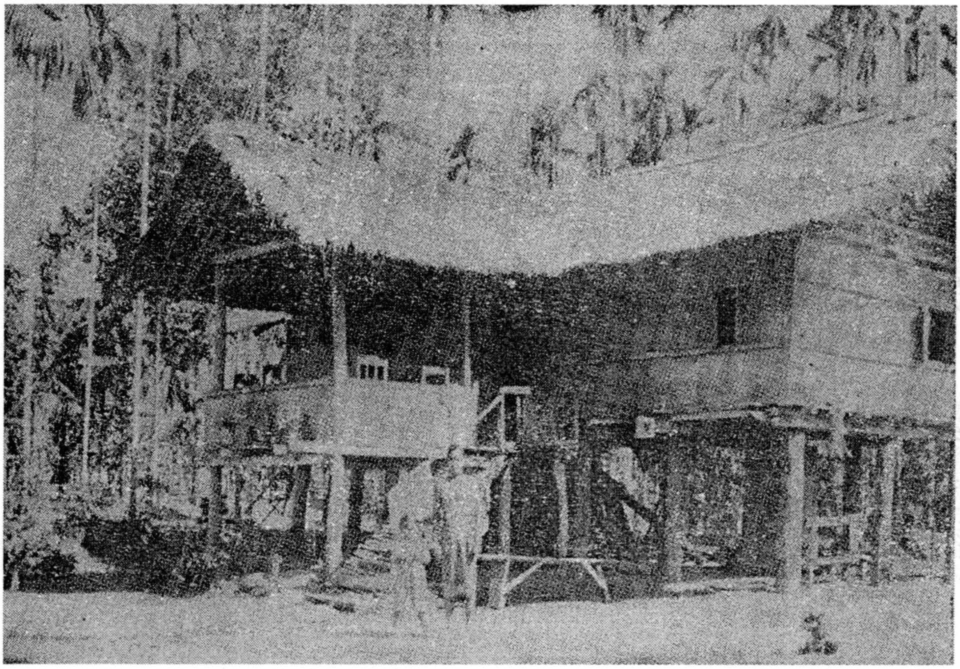

A Typical Assemese house. Note the elevation.

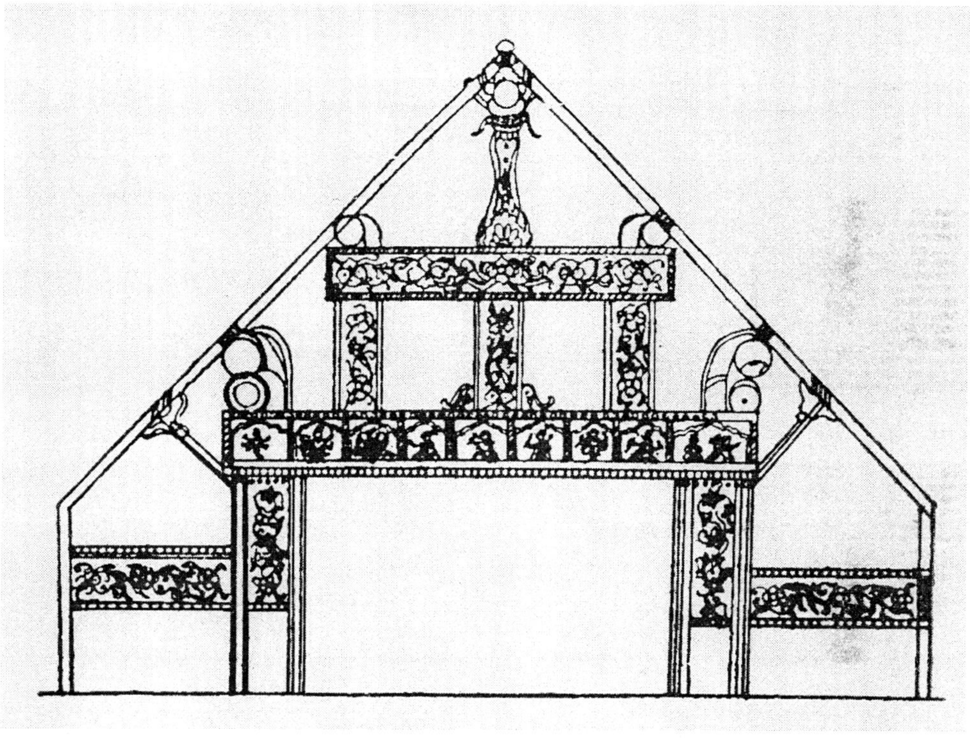

TIMBER ROOF FRAME OF KIRTAN GHAR< KAMALABARI SATRA
Wooden architecture Kamalabari, Sibsagar.

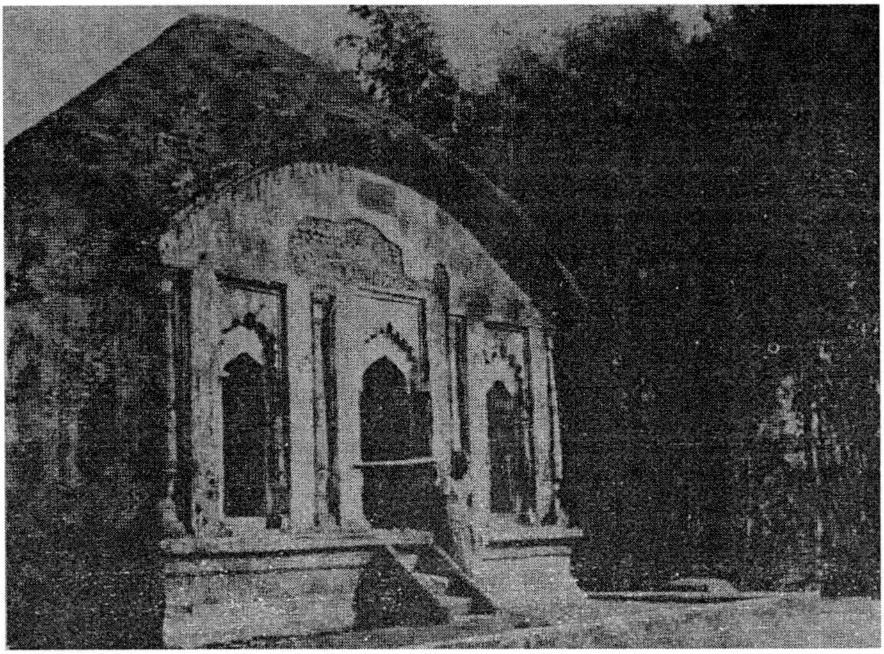

Ramachadi Temple, Khaspur.

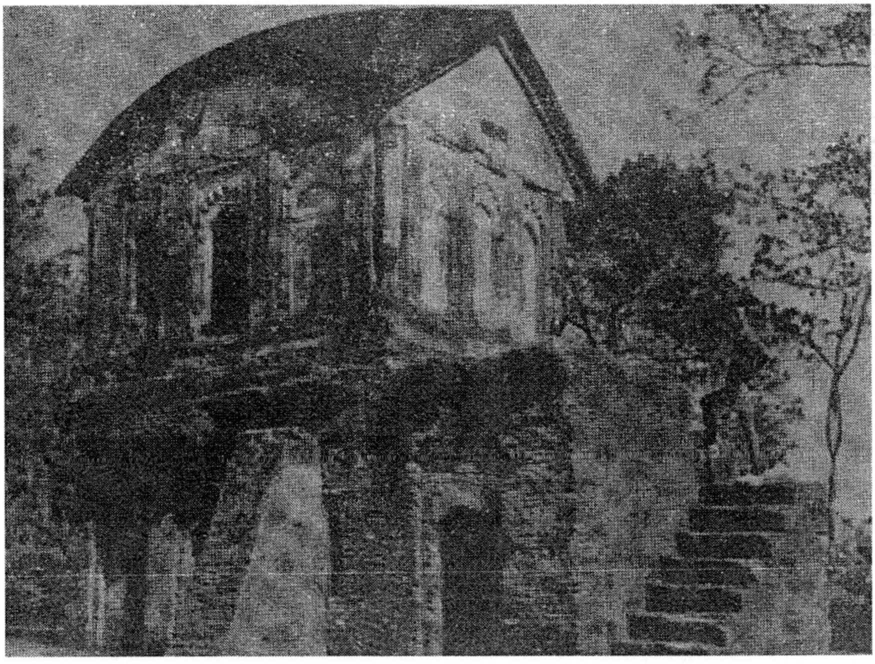

Baraduari (Close View), Khaspur.

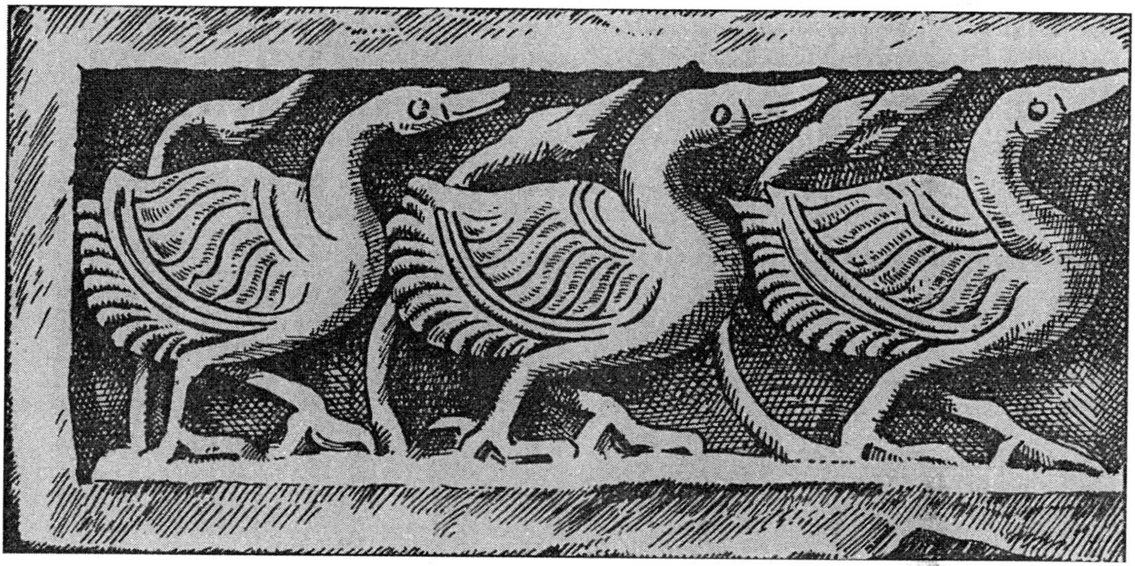

Terracotta Panel, Coachar.

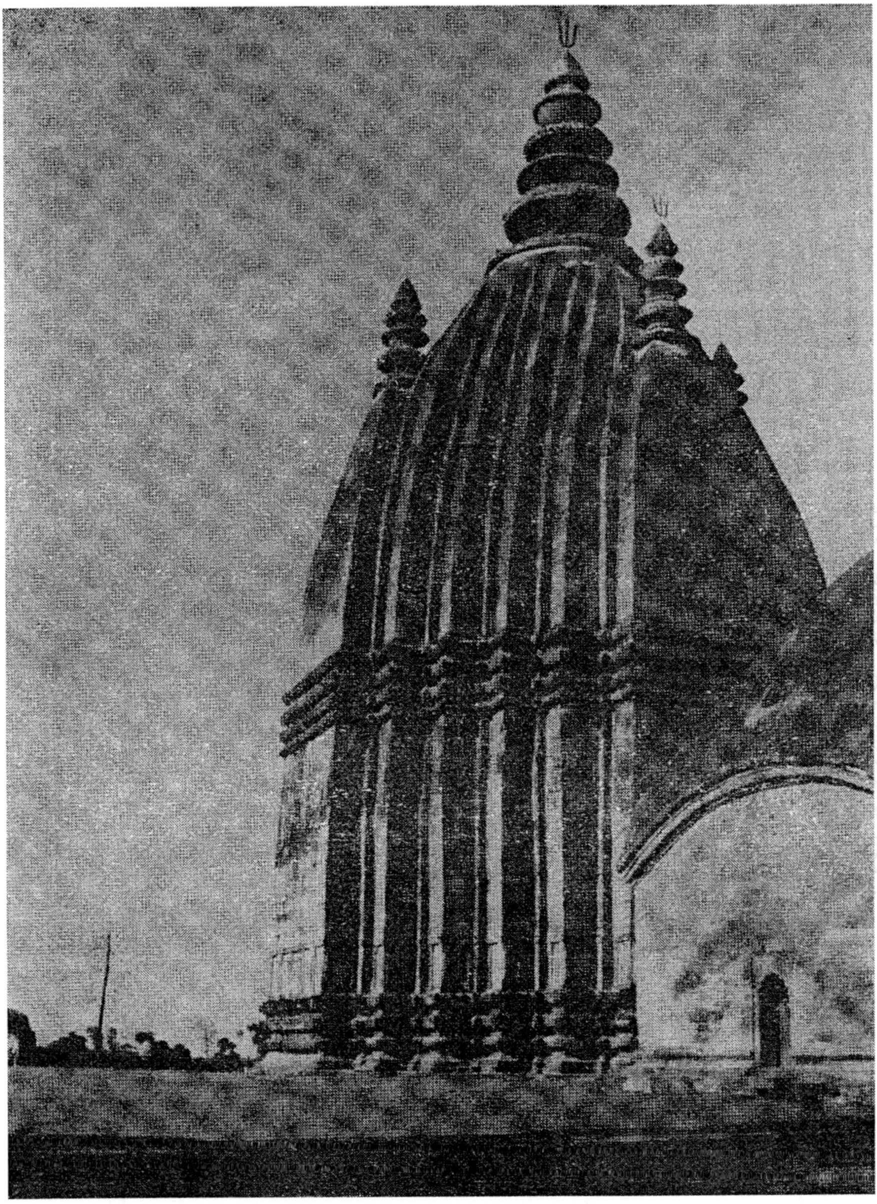

General View of Sibdole Temple, Sibsagar.

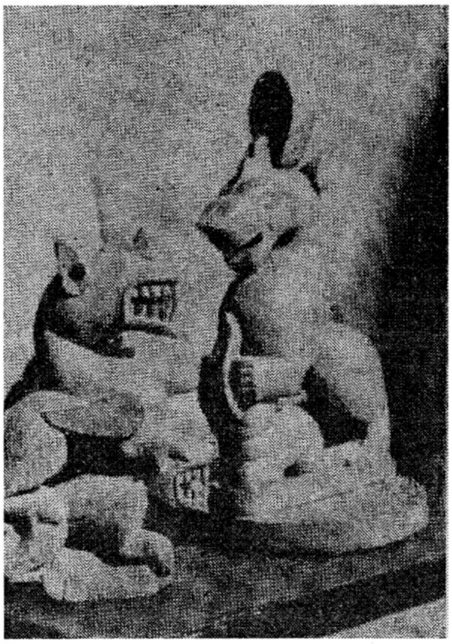

Gaja Simhas in Wood
Gauhati.

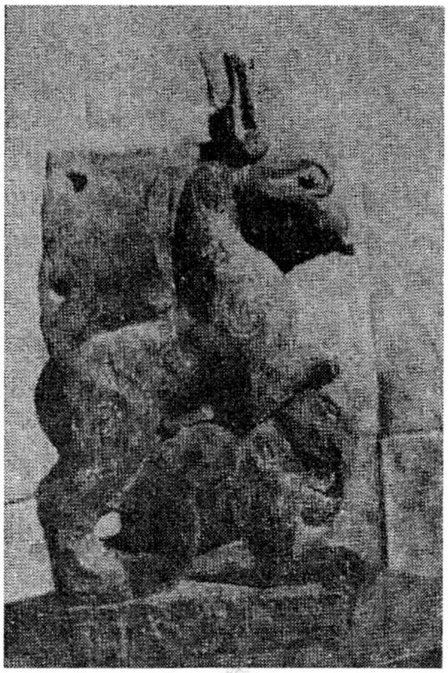

Gaja Simha in wood, Gauhati.

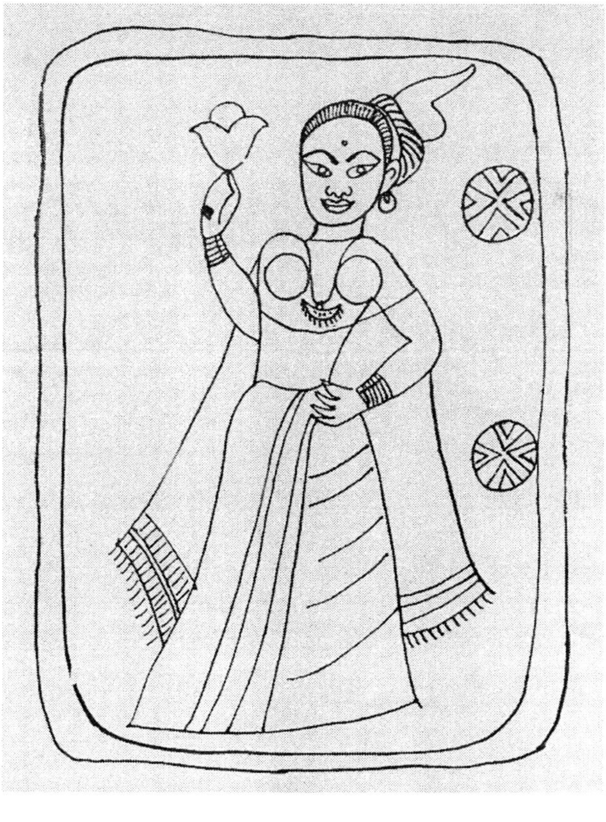

Painting Ahom Style, Book X, Gauhati.

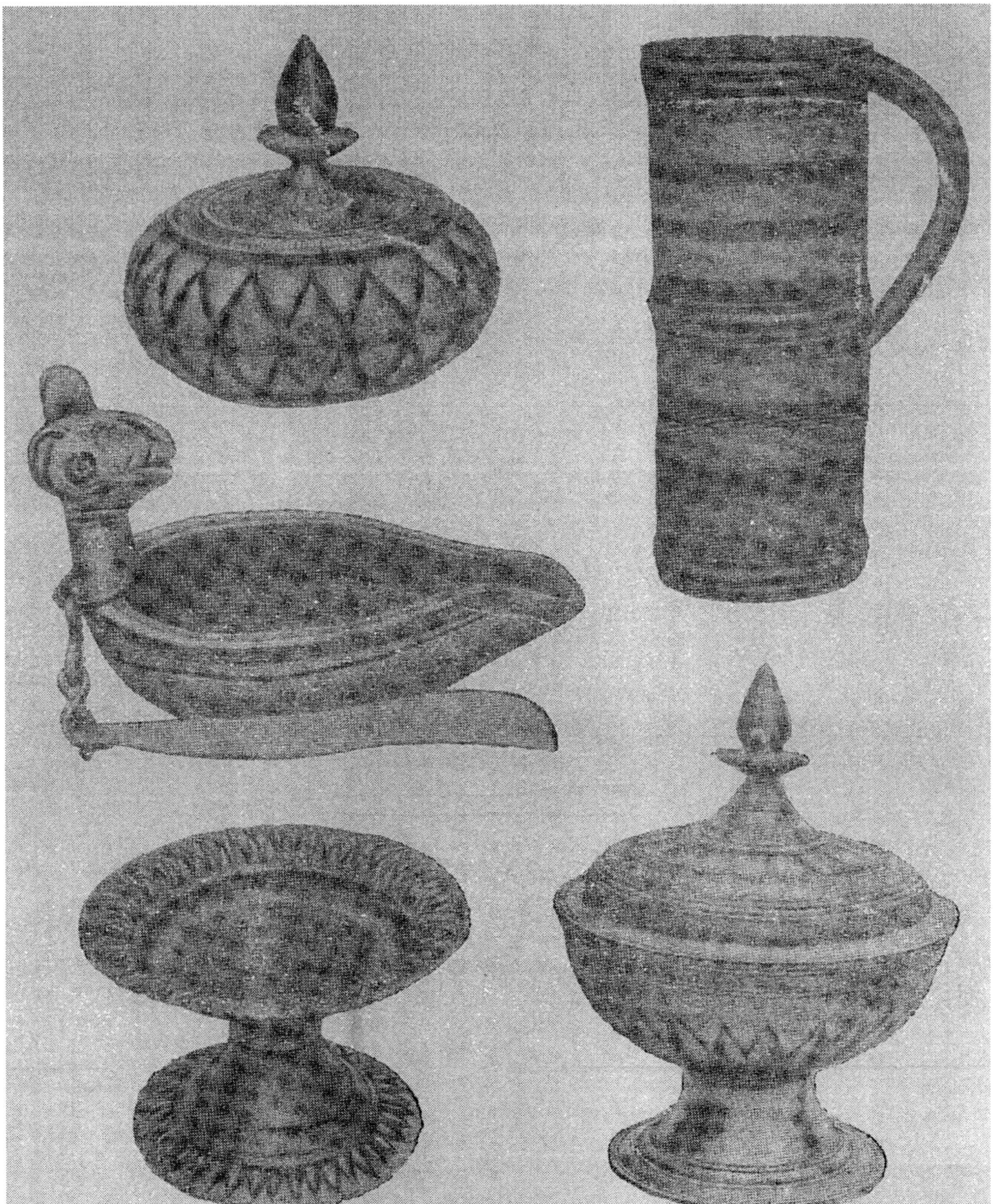

(a) Jemi or a bellmetal box for containing lime to be eaten with pan.
(b) Karia or a milking pot.
(c) Cuaki or a Lamp.
(d) Banbati or recptacle for holding curry, made of bellmetal.
(e) Bata or a vessel made of bellmetal for keeping pan & betlenub.

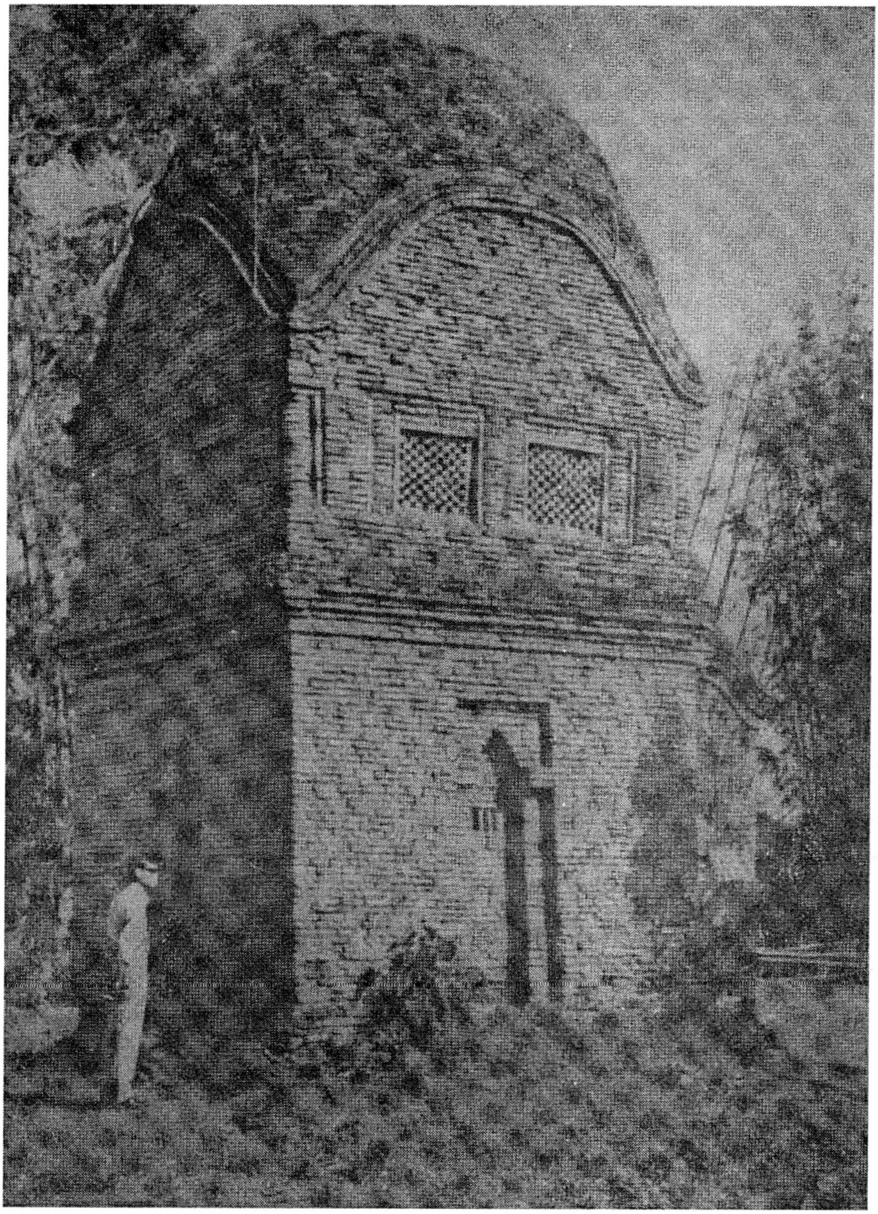

General view of Vishnu Temple, Manipur.

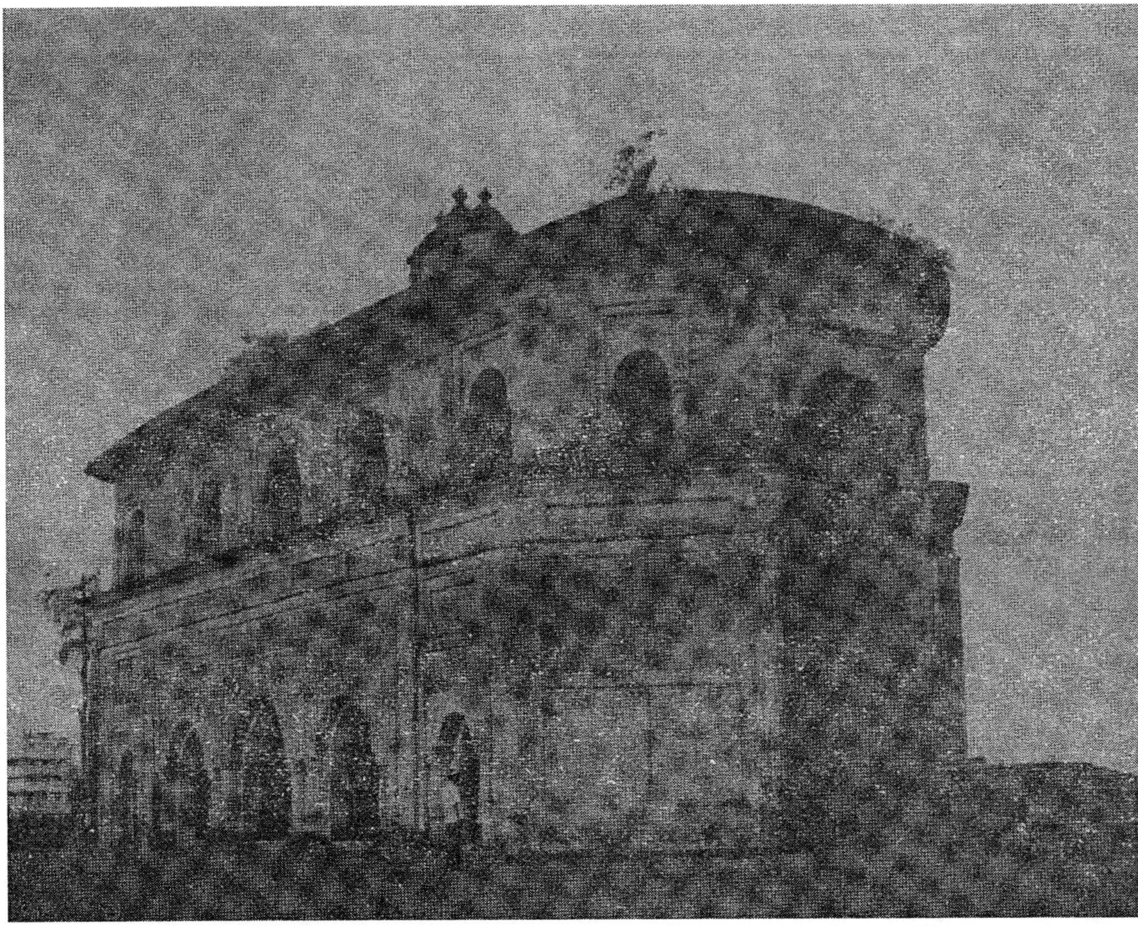

General view of the Ranghar Pavalion, Sibsagar.

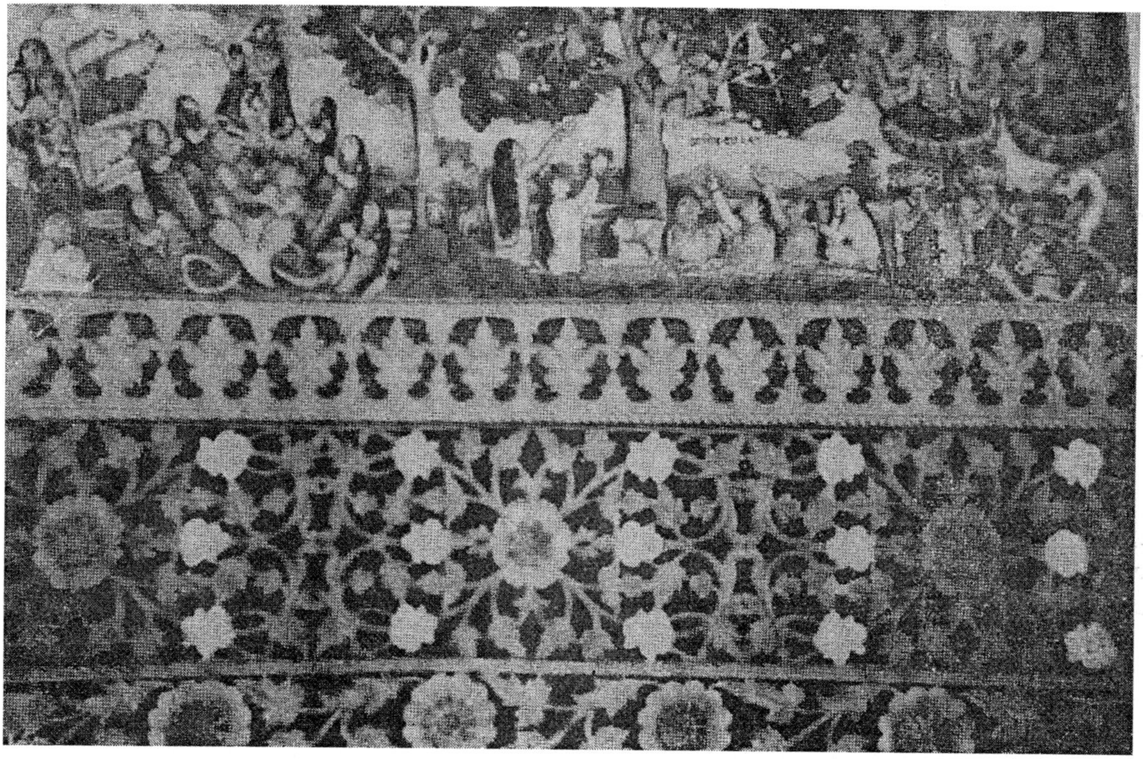

Wood Carving on Walls, Barpeta.

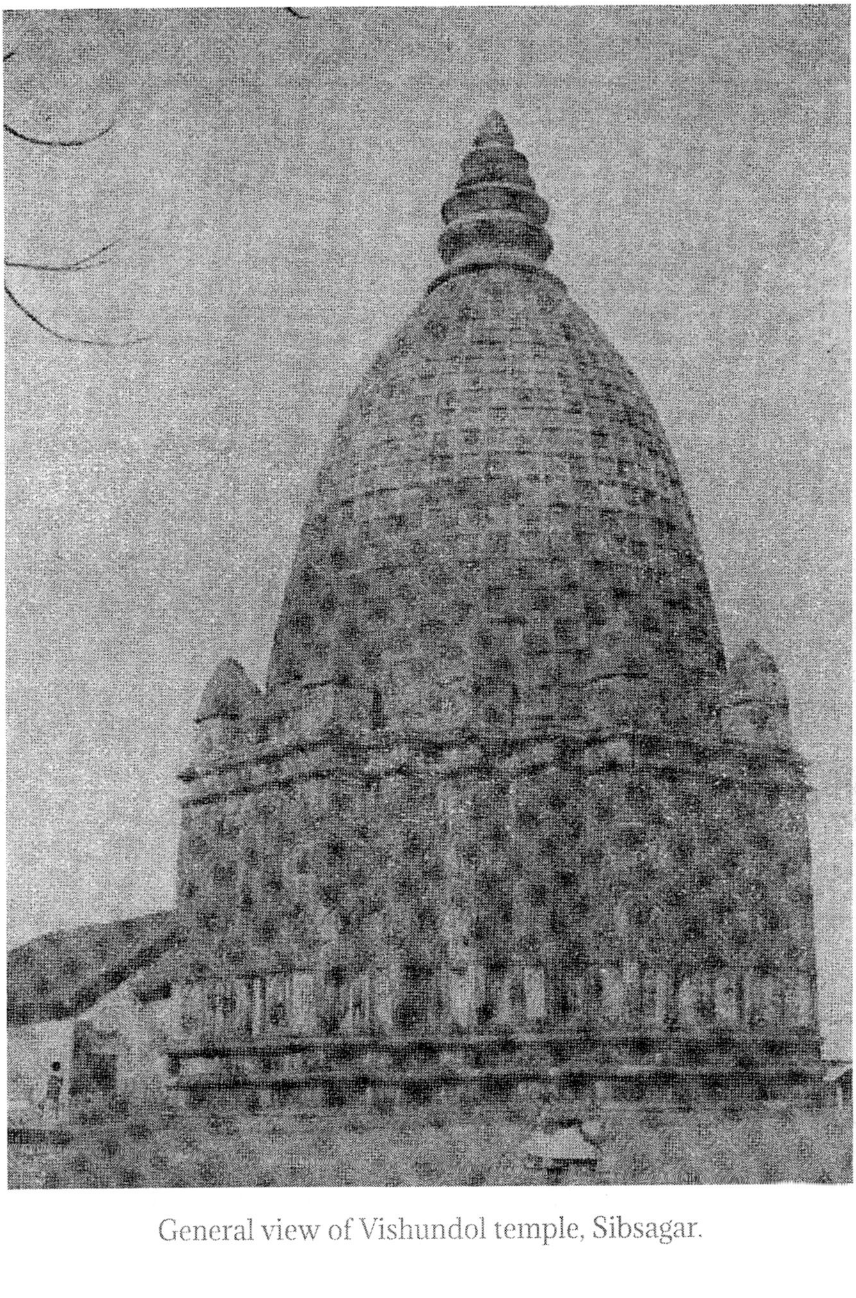

General view of Vishundol temple, Sibsagar.

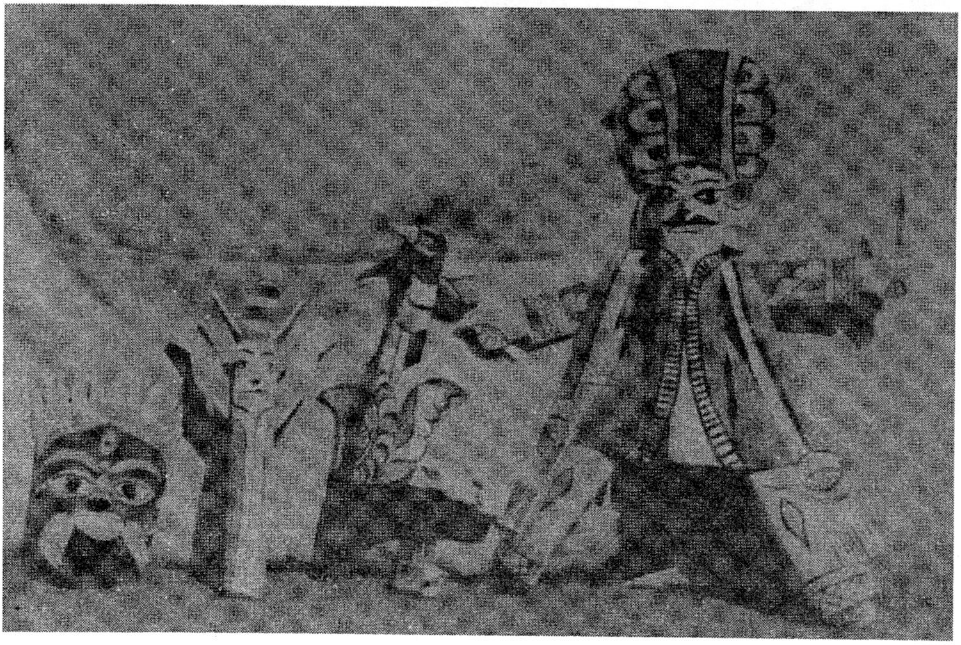

Icon paintings of Manasa

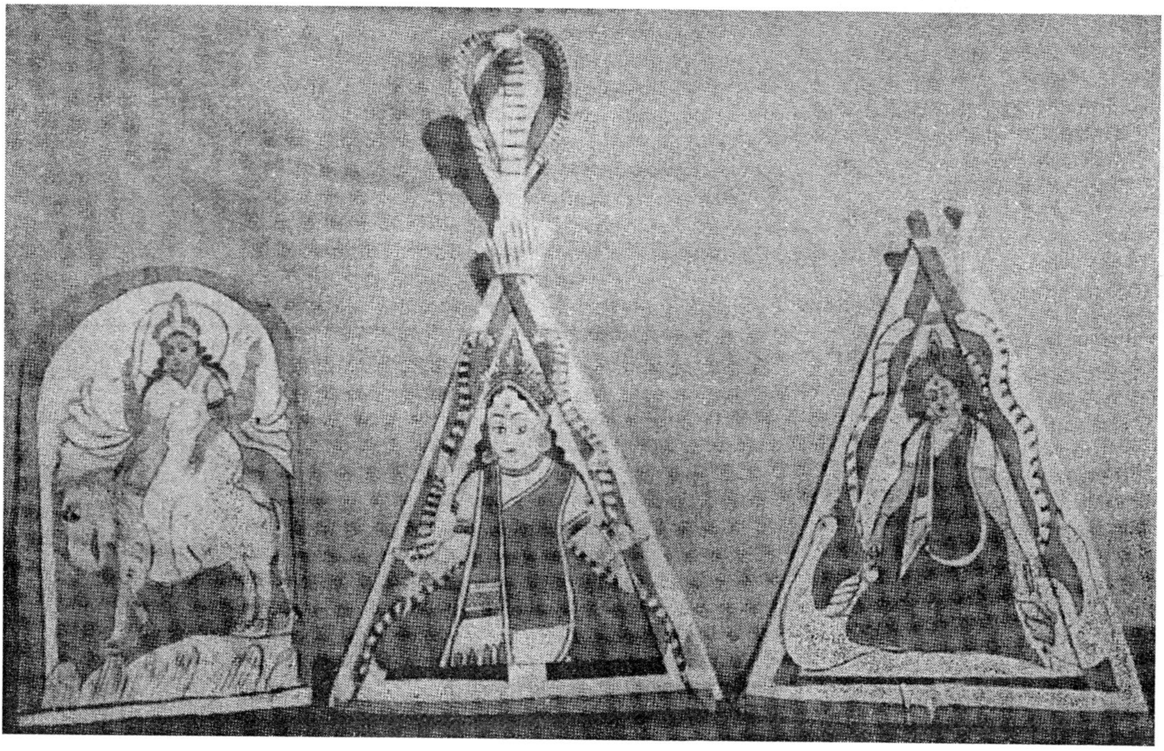

Pith mask & icons, Gauripur.

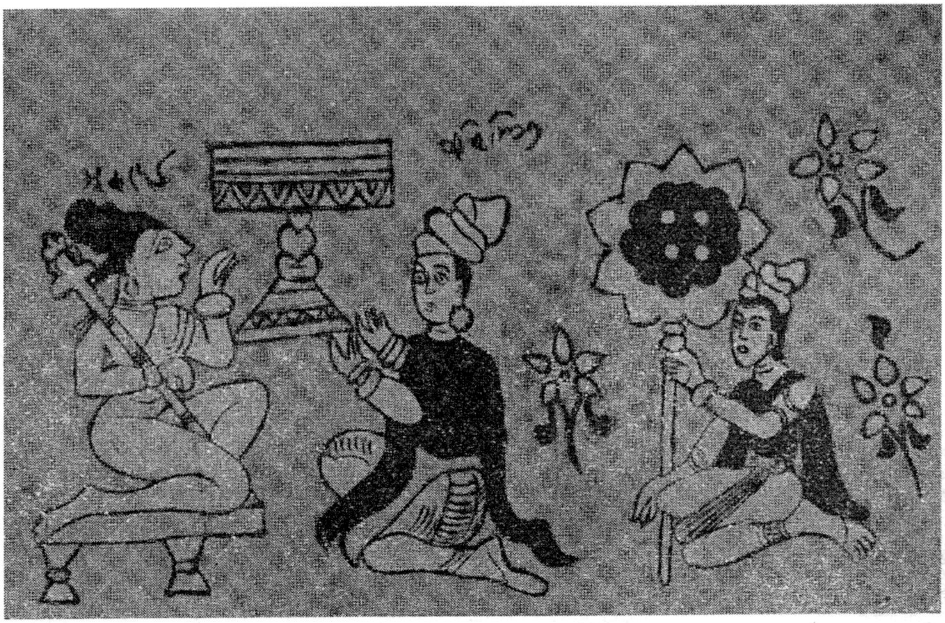

Bhagavata Book X. A hom Style, Gauhati.

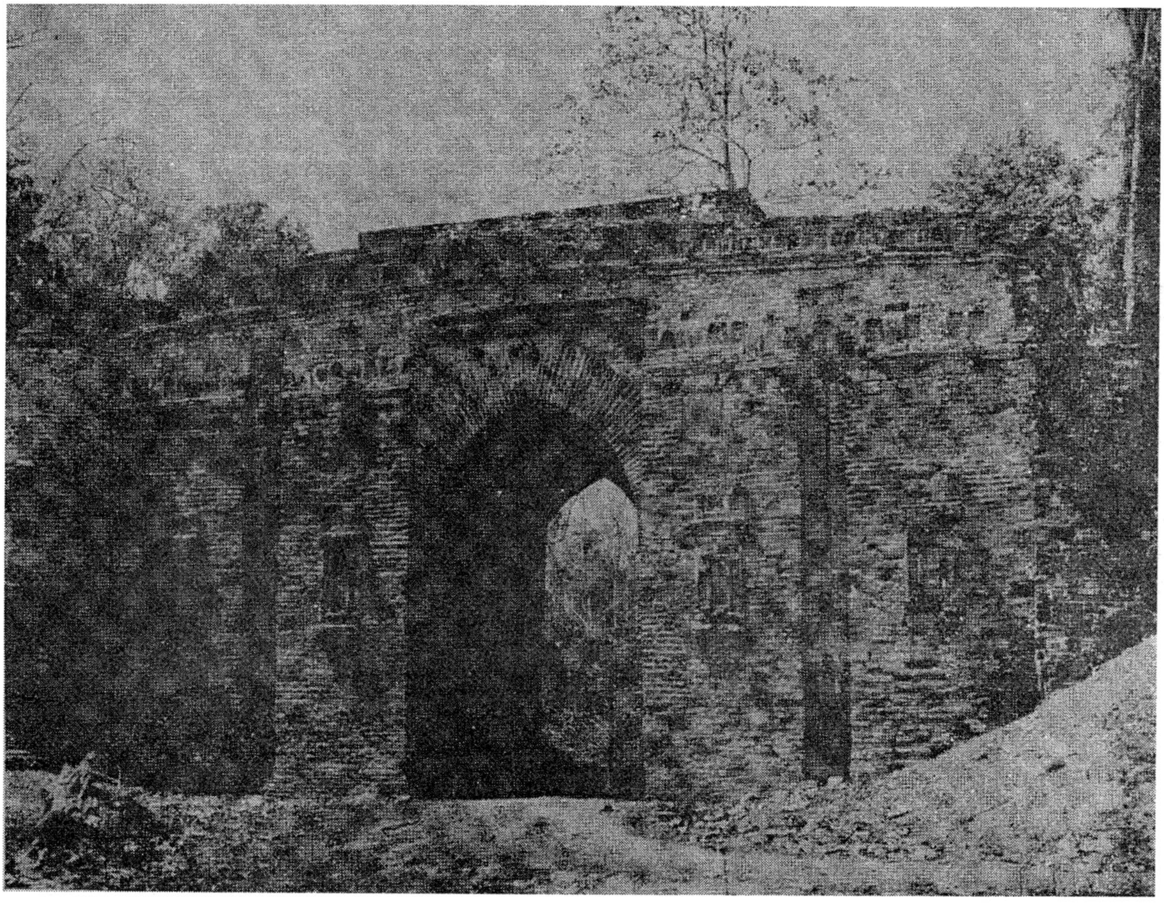

Gateway from outside, Naga Hills.

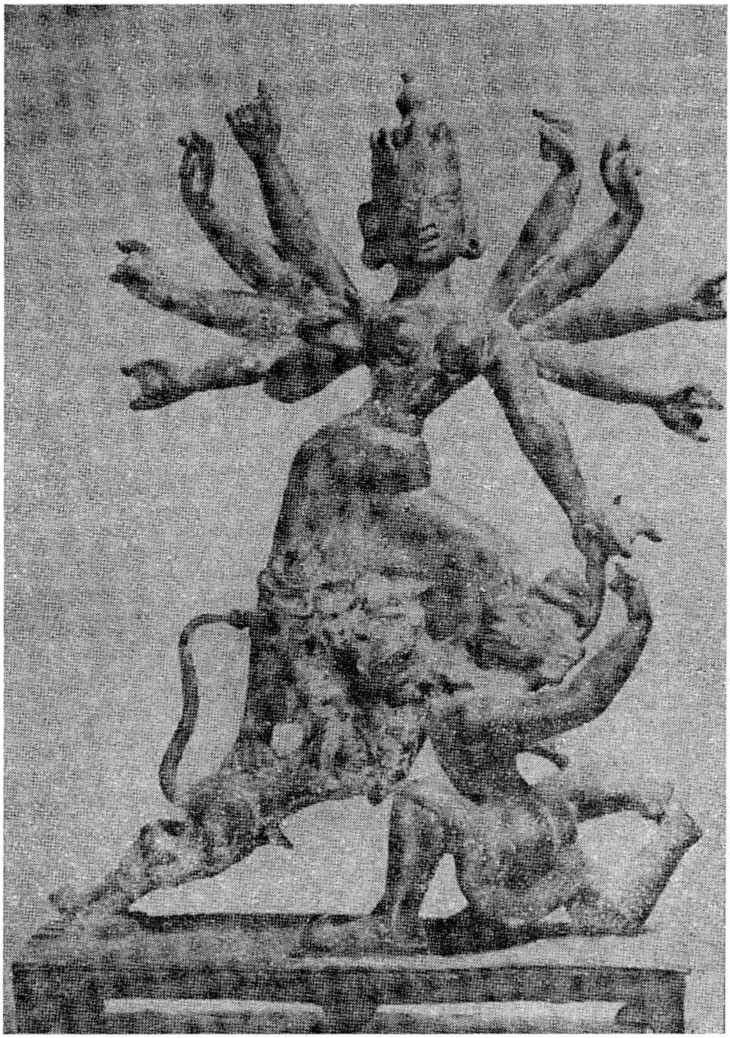

Mahisavramardini Bronze